DI

Women and War in Lebanon

Women and War in Lebanon

Edited by Lamia Rustum Shehadeh

University Press of Florida
Gainesville · Tallahassee · Tampa · Boca Raton
Pensacola · Orlando · Miami · Jacksonville

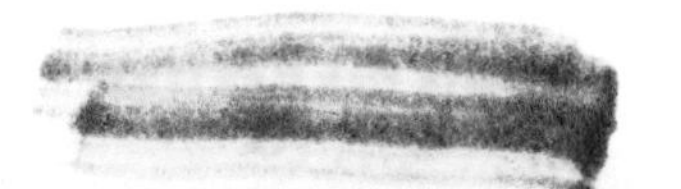

Copyright 1999 by the Board of Regents of the State of Florida
Printed in the United States of America on acid-free paper 4
All rights reserved

04 03 02 01 00 99 6 5 4 3 2 1

Library of Congress Cataloging-in-Publication Data
Women and war in Lebanon / edited by Lamia Rustum Shehadeh.
p. cm.
Includes bibliographical references and index.
ISBN 0-8130-1707-6 (cloth: alk. paper)
1. Women—Lebanon—Beirut—Social conditions. 2. Women—Lebanon—Beirut—Psychology. 3. Women in public life—Lebanon—Beirut. 4. Women soldiers—Lebanon—Beirut. 5. Lebanese literature (Arabic)—Women authors. 6. Lebanon—History—Civil War, 1975–1990. I. Shehadeh, Lamia Rustum, 1940–.
HQ1728.W63 1999
305.4'095692'5—dc21 99-17516

The University Press of Florida is the scholarly publishing agency for the State University System of Florida, comprising Florida A&M University, Florida Atlantic University, Florida International University, Florida State University, University of Central Florida, University of Florida, University of North Florida, University of South Florida, and University of West Florida.

University Press of Florida
15 Northwest 15th Street
Gainesville, FL 32611-2079
http://www.upf.com

Dedicated to my husband, Isam

There is in every true woman's heart a spark of heavenly fire,
which lies dormant in the broad daylight of prosperity, but which
kindles up and beams and blazes in the dark hour of adversity.

Washington Irving, "The Wife,"
Sketch Book of Geoffrey Crayon, Gent, 1819–1820

CONTENTS

TABLES

ABBREVIATIONS

AUB	American University of Beirut
AUH	American University Hospital
BDI	Beck Depression Index
COM	Comorbid.
DIS	*Diagnostic Interview Schedule*
DSM	*Diagnostic Statistical Manual*
ICD	*International Classification of Disease*
IDRAC	Institute for Development, Research and Applied Care
IJMES	*International Journal of Middle East Studies*
LF	Lebanese Forces
NCS	National Comorbidity Survey
NCSR	(Lebanese) National Council of Scientific Research
NIDA	National Institute on Drug Abuse
NIMH	National Institute of Mental Health
PLO	Palestine Liberation Organization
PRM	Palestine Resistance Movement
PSA	Pure Substance Abusers
PTSD	Post-Traumatic Stress Disorder
SCID	Structure Clinical Interview
UNESCO	United Nations Educational, Scientific, and Cultural Organization
UNIFIL	United Nations Interim Force in Lebanon
USJ	St. Joseph University
WEQ	War Events Questionnaire

PREFACE

Here were the end, had anything an end. . . .

The act, over and ended, falls and fades:
What was once seen, grows what is now described,
Then talked of, told about, a tinge the less
In every fresh transmission; till it melts,
Trickles in silent orange or wan grey

Across our memory. . . .

Robert Browning, *The Ring and the Book,* xii.

In early 1991, normal life returned to Lebanon. The internecine war had ended and Beirut, its capital city, was united once again. The Lebanese were still in a period of normalization. They had just discovered that movement from one sector of the city to another or from one district of Lebanon to another was truly possible. Their world was suddenly enlarged: All barriers and barricades, whether physical or psychological, had come tumbling down. It would be some time, however, before the Lebanese could move firmly and surely confident of each other and the future, but a start had been made. Part of the healing process seems to be a subconscious effort to block the preceding sixteen years of interminable nightmare from their memory. For, even during the war years, the Lebanese did their best to forget their unwelcome guest and lead a normal life described by the international press as the "dolce vita." Their motto seemed to be to go on living until one is killed: "It is as if everyone becomes the voyeur, the spectator of one's own impending death" (Kassab, 72). Dominique Eddé described Beirut as the city where children carry on about the senselessness of life. The unwelcome guest, the intruder, invaded every crevice of the city and the lives of all Lebanese: streets, apartments, balconies, market place, schools, hospitals, churches, mosques, synagogues, cinemas, theaters, university campuses . . . everything was profaned (ibid., 77).

Today, all one sees is the legacy of destruction and devastation the war has left in its wake whether on the animate or inanimate levels. Men, women and children from all over Lebanon visit the downtown area, which changed from being the throbbing heart of a prosperous Beirut, to the arena of the fiercest battles of the war, and take pictures of the grotesquely disfigured and mutilated buildings still standing, just like foreign tourists, mystified and awed by the destruction. This surrealistic dichotomy, being both player and spectator, is due to the imperative of survival: to continue, to go on, to heal, to reconstruct, one has to forget—painful memories are the first to disappear. The Lebanese, today, seldom, if at all, mention the shelling, kidnapping or killing, but they do reminisce about parties held in the shelters or jokes recounted, games improvised, and mentally reconstruct those days or moments fondly if not with nostalgia. But even though these painful experiences are deeply buried in the collective Lebanese subconscious, they have not failed to leave their indelible imprint on the thoughts, attitudes, and actions of the Lebanese. Yet, any attempt at understanding the present or future necessitates an understanding of the immediate, painful past. The purpose of this book is, therefore, to record part of this experience before it is completely forgotten and analyze its effects on the lives of women and the roles they played during this prolonged interval.

In fine, I would like to thank all the friends and colleagues who encouraged me to pursue this project, read parts of the manuscript, and gave invaluable advice. In particular, I would like to thank Salwa Ghali Najjar, Farid Khazen, Miriam Cooke, and Kari Karamé. I would also like to thank my secretary, the indefatigable Suzy Khatchadourian, without whose efficiency, capabilities, patience, and selflessness this manuscript would not have been completed. Last but not least, words fail to describe my thanks to my husband, Isam Shehadeh, without whose constant encouragement, reading and rereading of the manuscript, suggestions to add or delete, and patience and understanding of my moodiness and occasional seclusion to complete the project this book would have never seen the light.

I

Introduction

1

Introduction

The study and analysis of the impact of the Lebanese war on the lives of women and the roles they played during this protracted period of time is necessarily Janus-faced. It describes a double reality of strife and normalcy, which shaped the daily life of the Lebanese for sixteen years and left such deep scars that they may prove to be incurable. The war has indeed ended but its effects are still present, which may prevent one from conducting an objective study. But this accumulated experience simultaneously challenges prevalent scholarship on the subject of women and war and provides it with additional fertile material for further research at all levels. Lebanon, thus, provides a litmus test for recurrent questions that have been addressed to other similar cases pursued by different scholars in a variety of disciplines. What possibilities are created for the emancipation of women? What constraints or social strictures have been removed? How has armed conflict affected women's behavior in the domestic and public spheres? Have women taken a more active part in public life? If so, are they the initiators of social change or the beneficiaries of circumstances liberating them from their traditional roles as women? Do women, in times of crisis, seek a creative role and a cohesive worldview? Do they assume leadership and do they envision keeping it once the discord is at an end? Finally, with all the new pressures on women, do they suffer from depression or drug and alcohol abuse, areas previously dominated by males? How have women reacted to a war not of their making? Did they support the initiators of this madness in word and deed or did they follow the example of Athenian women in Aristophanes' *Lysistrata* and boycott men? Can this survey add anything to the ongoing controversy or dialogue regarding women's nature? In other words, are women pacifists by nature or is their pacifism the result of a socialization process imposed by patriarchy? Some observers have argued that while it is true that prolonged violent conflict encourages men and women to cast off old roles and develop a new and more egalitarian relationship, they revert to their traditional roles as soon as the conflict is brought to an end. It is these questions and more that the following chapters will attempt to answer.

It would seem that wars are indubitably periods of social change for women, but does this change initiate progress in women's lives or the roles they play, and if so, in what realms? Is it possible to assess such change? This book, then, is an investigation into the impact of the sixteen-year war on women in general and a survey of the various ways in which women have worked and contributed to the war or its peaceful settlement. A vast and interesting literature exists concerning women and war, brought on partly by the dynamic development of women's history in the latter part of the twentieth century egged on by the pressure of unceasing feminist demands. This book aims at finding a place for itself in this literature by exploring the impact of a war economy on the female labor force, the attitudes and values of the women who live alongside combatants and build a support structure for them by providing food, clothes, nursing and paramedical help, communication, and household management, including education and upbringing of children. This support structure is not limited to the physical domain, which includes actual military combat, but transcends it to the psychological and parapsychological realms. Thus, despite their abhorrence of war, women continue to support war efforts by joining the men in the battlefield and providing them with a state of mind that would facilitate the fighting and prolong its duration.

The war can be seen now, six years after its conclusion, as a completed whole and, as such, it seems to offer an interesting and fruitful subject for historical, sociological, or psychological treatment upon which tentative judgments could be made. Some of the current misconceptions may be corrected and a sounder factual basis offered for the use of scholars or writers interested in the field.

In an effort to answer questions regarding the impact of the sixteen-year war on women, I have provided an extensive introduction in the hope of contextualizing the war and creating some kind of order out of the chaos that insidiously invaded all crevices and corners of Lebanon. A brief history of Lebanon and the war was, therefore, necessary to introduce the reader to the complexities of Lebanon and the causes, direct and implicit, that led to the war and its conclusion. Since the subject of the book is the impact of the war on women, it also became necessary to give a brief description of the condition of Lebanese women before the war in an effort at contextualization and the emplacement of a measure against which to weigh the changes effected by the war.

The chapter on women in the public sphere became necessary due to the war's invasion of the home, politicizing thereby the daily lives of women and forcing them out into the public arena to meet new situations armed only with primitive skills, which they masterfully used to help their families and communities survive. The war, inadvertently, introduced new variables that had distinct effects on the labor market, women's work, education, the media, and the economy in general.

These were not the only imprints the war left on women. In an effort to fill the void created by the war and to make sense out of the madness that prevailed, women, in an attempt at catharsis, resorted to writing poetry and short stories and to painting. This is described at length and analyzed in the four chapters of part three.

But not all Lebanese women resorted to sublimation or the public sphere to create order out of chaos, an impossible task as shown by the Second Law of Thermodynamics. There were those who confronted the war by becoming actively involved either in politics and dissemination of ideology or actually carrying guns and joining the fighting themselves. These acts helped many control their fear and anxiety by giving them a sense of control over their lives. Such roles, imposed on women during the war, are described, rationalized, and analyzed in the three chapters of part four, while the fourth chapter is dedicated to a fascinating account of the journey of one female combatant from gunpowder to the consecration of herself to God.

"Profiles of Foreign Women in Lebanon" was intended to lend this account of the war an air of objectivity as well as to give a live testimony of the atrocities of the war and how women coped under such conditions. Interviews were conducted with six Western women who stayed in Lebanon and braved the war together with the Lebanese.

The war, in addition to its death toll, the acts of maiming, kidnapping, displacement, and exile, produced a variety of stressful life experiences that resulted in several somatic disorders as well as a wide range of psychiatric disorders, such as depression, anxiety, and poor interpersonal relations. The three chapters, under the rubric "Psychological Sequelae," describe at length the impact of the war on women's psyche in contradistinction to that of men. The studies cover, in addition to the somatic and psychiatric disorders, substance abuse, drug use and abuse of cannabis and alcohol.

Finally, the conclusion, based on the evidence provided by the different contributions, attempts to demonstrate how the war lifted all social strictures imposed on women in prewar Lebanon and emancipated them to broach all fields previously reserved for men including the carrying of arms. The conclusion also argues against the preconceived notion that women are pacifists by nature.

The formal historian of a very recent period, however conscientious, must labor under tremendous disadvantages. These concern materials still largely unassimilated or unpublished; one's own power of perspective, which is liable to distortion by the proximity of the objects discussed; and the subjectivity and tendency to prejudice in a field in which one participated emotionally and certainly with some partiality.

While I may not have consulted all possible sources on the subject due to their infinitely varied nature and the unavailability of others, what is available is certainly well worth documenting.

It is important to note at this point what will become evident later on. First, most chapters deal with Beirut rather than Lebanon as a whole. This is due to the fact that Beirut was and remains, certainly to a lesser degree today, the hub of Lebanon, housing all its sects, factions, and parties. The vast majority of intellectuals and scientists live and work in Beirut. Thus, most published studies center upon and emanate from Beirut but do reflect the general Lebanese map. Furthermore, the war centered mainly in and around Beirut. Except for the brief Israeli-instigated war of the mountains, the rest of the country remained relatively calm, especially the rural areas. The situation in the south was entirely different since it was the staging area of conflict between Palestinians and Israelis.

Second, women in Lebanon, before the war, were mostly regarded as inferior to men in all respects—prowess, capabilities, education, work opportunities, and dependability. Yet, they embodied the so called "family honor." Accordingly, they were to be protected and cared for, but excluded from decision-making positions. This explains why they enjoyed more safety than men, allowing them to enter the public sphere with less tribulation: All factions avoided targetting or attacking women (except for indiscriminate shelling and occasional sniping); this is also why they were never allowed positions of leadership in the militias, or any other venue for that matter.

2

The War in Lebanon

Terror, violence, conflict, carnage, chaos, cruelty, and mayhem are all evoked by the mere mention of Lebanon. For those who have known Lebanon in better times, the fact that Lebanon has come to be synonymous with bloodshed is a source of deep sadness. Lebanon, even in the worst times, can be a remarkably seductive place. In my judgment, no other Middle Eastern country, perhaps no country in the world, is as enthralling as Lebanon. Its social and political complexity, the keen skill of its citizens in dealing with (and manipulating) foreigners, and its lovely climate and splendid food combine to imbue those who have known it—in good times or bad—with a sense of emotional attachment that is hard to shake. Lebanon entices and ensnares even the wary. Though the encounter is often bitter sweet, it is long savored.

Augustus Richard Norton, *Amal and the Shiʿa.*

Historical Background

Lebanon is the smallest country in the Levant. It is 210 kilometers long and 30 to 90 kilometers wide. The fertile coastal strip on the eastern shores of the Mediterranean is 7 kilometers wide and around 10 kilometers in the northern plain of ʿAkkar. The largest cities lie on the coast: Tripoli, Beirut, Sidon, and Tyre. The territory is comprised mostly of the rugged mountain of the parallel ranges of the Lebanon and Anti-Lebanon. It is bounded on the north by the Eleutherus River (Nahr al-Kabir), on the east by the Anti-Lebanon, and on the south by a line across the highlands of Galilee. Between the two mountain ranges lies the Biqaa Valley.

The Lebanese often called their country "the Switzerland of the Middle East." The similarities were remarkable: In a small rugged terrain, which lacked natural resources but flourished in the sectors of banking, trade, and tourism, different religious and cultural groups learned to coexist peacefully. Both countries exercised freedom of expression and of the press and practiced a policy of neutrality in foreign affairs. However, whereas Switzerland was able to maintain its neutrality due to the political climate of its regional environment and its sizable military force, Lebanon, without a sustainable military force, had to contend with a resentful environment of authoritarian political systems starkly contrasting with its democratic parliamentarian system.

Hence, it can be safely said that until 1975, Lebanon was the only stable and developed democratic system in the Arab world. It held regular elections in an arena of diverse political parties and open competition, changed governments peacefully, and elected its presidents according to the specifications of the 1926 Constitution. Lebanon was also known for its freedom of expression and was thus an open forum for social, political, religious, and economic dialogue. This freedom also made it a natural haven for all dissident elements in the region, and contributed to its developing the best educational system, medical centers, and the most sophisticated mass media in the region. Thus, Albert Hourani in his *Political Society* describes Lebanon before 1975 as "a country which had achieved an almost miraculous balance between different communities and interests, and which was enjoying political stability and peace, comparative neutrality in the conflicts of the region, and a prosperity which seemed to be self-perpetuating."[1]

Furthermore, Lebanon is one of the very few countries in the world that can claim to be so intricately composed of minority groups. In addition to the confessional minorities of Christians, Druze, Jews, Shiʿa, and, in a sense, Sunnis—because they do represent a minority within Lebanon but not in the Arab world—a number of immigrant minorities reside in Lebanon as well. The Armenians arrived in Lebanon as fugitives from the massacres in Anatolia at the end of the nineteenth century and again in 1920–21 and from Alexandretta when Turkey annexed it in 1939. The French authorities granted the 175,000 refugees Lebanese citizenship in 1924. One hundred and fifty thousand Palestinians arrived as fugitives from Palestine following the 1948 Arab-Israeli war. Those of Lebanese origin were granted Lebanese citizenship. Later, more Palestinians entered Lebanon illegally, either for brighter prospects or as fugitives, after the 1967 Arab-Israeli war and the 1970–71 Palestinian defeat in Jordan. The estimated numbers today vary between 350,000 and 500,000. Syrian and Kurdish workers settled in slum areas around Beirut and other towns during the rapid expansion in the fifties and sixties.

Of the confessional minorities, sizable groups of Shiʿa have been living in what is now Lebanon since the seventh century. From the twelfth century on, they were reduced to the status of dissenters who congregated in two main areas of Lebanon: Jabal ʿAmil in southern Lebanon and the Hirmil and Baalbeck regions of the northern reaches of the Biqaa. Politically weak and economically backward, they took little part in the politics of the region. In 1920, when Jabal ʿAmil and the Biqaa were incorporated into Greater Lebanon, they comprised 17 percent of the population.[2] Since the 1960s, the homeland of the Shiʿite community in southern Lebanon was the battleground between the Palestinian guerrillas and Israeli army, both of whom consistently ignored the welfare of the peaceful Shiʿites who invariably suffered the heaviest casualties. Thus Amal began as a protest movement demanding reform. It was the creation of its charismatic religious leader Musa al-Sadr. Amal is the Arabic word for hope as well as the acronym for *Afwaj al-muqawamah al-lubnaniyyah* (Lebanese resistance battalions). Al-Sadr was an Iranian cleric of Lebanese origin who came to Tyre in the sixties as the religious leader of the Shiʿite community in southern Lebanon. By the early seventies, he had successfully entrenched himself as the most prominent political voice of his community. Ushering in a new era in the history of the Lebanese Shiʿite community, he declared to an audience of 7,000: "They say we are Matawila, but our name is not Matawila, our name is the rejectionists, the protesters, the dissenters, the rebels against all oppression, the obstructers in the face of all tyranny."[3] In a press conference held on July 6, 1975, Musa al-Sadr declared that Amal symbolized the sacrifice of those "who responded to the call of the wounded homeland."[4] In September 1978, the imam went on a fund-raising trip to the Arab world. He was last seen in Tripoli (Libya) and never heard of or from since. By the early eighties the Shiʿite community was going through a period of economic, political, and social renaissance.[5]

A second group of Shiʿites called Hizballah (The Party of God), modeled after the Iranian militia bearing the same name, gathered around the local clergy. The name is derived from a verse in the Qurʾan that promises triumph to those who join the "party of God." Hizballah emerged in 1982 in the wake of the Israeli invasion. Their first goal was the foundation of an Islamic republic in Lebanon after the model of Iran and the second, the eviction of Israel from southern Lebanon through repeated guerrilla activities.

The Maronites moved from the Syrian interior into Lebanon in the second half of the seventh century due to differences with the Jacobite sect and persecution at the hands of the Byzantine government. Led by Patriarch Yuhanna Marun (d. 707), they sought safety in the rugged terrain of Mount Lebanon. They were joined centuries later by the Mardites who were brought from the Amanus and Taurus Mountains by the Crusaders to protect the coastal towns from Muslim Arab attacks. In the twelfth century and under the influence of the Crusaders, Maronite relations with

Rome were initiated. It was not, however, until 1439 that partial union with the Vatican was achieved at the Council of Florence. Full union was to take place in 1736 at the Synod of Luwayzah.[6] Unlike other Christian sects, mainly Greek Orthodox, who lived along the coast and in cities, the Maronites were "warlike mountain peasants with strong ties to the land" and, therefore, relatively secure from external attacks. "Their attachment to Mount Lebanon, which they regarded as their homeland, their strong spirit of independence and their particularism were to blossom into a full territorial and ethnic nationalism."[7]

The Maronites also distinguished themselves in their strong attachment and loyalty to their church. A. Hourani says, "More even than other Syrian sects they were dominated by their clergy. The priests were national leaders, the centre around which turned the struggle of the community to survive and retain its identity; and the Maronite Patriarch, the only Patriarch residing in Lebanon itself, was a temporal as well as a spiritual power. . . ."[8] This explains the prominent roles that the church and, in particular, the patriarch played in Lebanon's political history from the nineteenth century to the present. It was the church that nurtured and preserved the ideology of a Maronite state that had, for centuries, been independent or autonomous and situated in Mount Lebanon.[9]

The Druze, a splinter sect of Islam, born in the eleventh century, originated in Egypt during the reign of the Fatimid caliph, al-Hakim (996–1021). When the caliph was assassinated, Mohammed al-Darazi, the founder of the Druze religion, took refuge in the Shouf area of Mount Lebanon, where other Muslim clans were converted to the new religion. Their participation in the wars against the Crusaders produced a warrior aristocracy from whom the Maanid dynasty was to emerge.[10]

The Sunnis of Lebanon, many of whom were prosperous merchants, inhabited the coastal towns of Tripoli, Beirut, and Sidon. They identified themselves with the general Sunni population of the Arab world and, in particular, Syria. They constituted the mainstay of the Ottoman government in the area and became, therefore, the dominant political class of the empire.

Lebanon's foreign relations have always been influenced by its twofold Christian-Arab identity. This Janus face of Lebanon helped in the promotion of an established neutral foreign policy: It carefully stayed out of inter-Arab conflicts and played a very passive and limited role in the Arab-Israeli conflict, while pursuing an open-door policy with the West. Lebanon's special character as defined by the National Pact was consecrated by the Arab states. Thus, at the founding conference of the Arab League in 1944–45, a special resolution was introduced pledging the members' unanimous "respect for the independence and sovereignty of Lebanon within its present frontiers." Furthermore, while the Arab governments agreed at their summit meeting of August 1967 at Khartoum to support Palestinian guerrilla action against Israel from Egypt, Syria, and Jordan, Lebanon was excluded. It was not, however, until 1969 that Lebanon, according to the Cairo Agreement, was to allow Palestinian guerrillas to launch their operations against Israel from Lebanese soil, and was thus slowly drawn into the web of the Arab-Israeli conflict.[11]

Thus, while for three decades Lebanon was looked upon as "an example of successful, peaceful and democratic coexistence, as one of the few viable cases of consociation outside Europe, in the following decade and a half it became the proverbial case of a country torn apart by bloody and internecine warfare."[12]

The events that took place in Lebanon were momentous, with palpable effects on global politics. In order to understand what happened over a period of sixteen years, it is essential to describe the arena in which the Lebanese and other surrogate wars took place.

Causes of the War

When war erupted in 1975 a host of explanations was advanced and a wide variety of theories propounded. With the war at an end and the development of the kaleidoscopic portrait of this period focused, it has become clear that there was never "a Lebanese conflict," but a complex variegation of conflicts. The Lebanese did not go to war to change their political system; they joined a war fought on their land by the Arab states, Israel, and the superpowers to defend certain policies and ideologies.[13] The war in Lebanon has been described as a communal war between Christians and Muslims, a continuation of the 1845, 1860, and 1958 clashes, a class war between the rich and the poor, a struggle for leadership, and a war over the identity of Lebanon, whether Mediterranean or Arab. Yet, it is noteworthy that Lebanon had managed to cope with these internal conflicts for a period of over thirty years since its independence in 1943, and for fifty-five years since its establishment as Greater Lebanon in 1920. Theodor Hanf, in his book *Coexistence*, says, "I am convinced that the Lebanese would have been able to solve their own problems without resorting to arms. There would have been the normal economic or political conflicts, but they would never have led to war. No, in the absence of the Palestinians this war would never have started. However, the domestic Lebanese problems created a climate favorable to the outbreak of war" (374). Of the twenty-six distinct confrontations, according to Hanf, there were six that involved only non-Lebanese parties, nine that involved Lebanese fighting foreign forces, three in which Lebanese fighters joined non-Lebanese, and only nine involving internecine conflagrations, and, of these, six were intracommunal rather than intercommunal. This leaves only three confrontations between the two major Lebanese blocs over a period of sixteen years.

Takieddine Solh, former prime minister, described the causes of the war as being internal due to the Christians' feeling of fear, the Muslims' feeling of inequality, and the exploitation of Lebanon's unique qualities of freedom, prosperity, and progress that helped turn Lebanon into an arena for others to fight in; and external, where the Palestinian factor was foremost. Thus, he describes them as "Aliens—worse: armed aliens who allow themselves certain liberties, and go beyond accepted limits—aliens who show no respect for the law must come into conflict with the inhabitants of the country. Of course the Palestinians are our brothers, but even among brothers such behaviour causes conflicts."[14]

The nature and history of Lebanese society made it extremely susceptible to external pressures. In the 1950s, the emergence of Nasserism and the subsequent unity of Egypt and Syria, the tripartite invasion of the Suez Canal and the Western offensive to contain Nasserism and the communist threat brought on the 1958 crisis in Lebanon. Similarly, in the late sixties and early seventies, the emergence of the Palestinian Resistance Movement and the armed presence of the Palestinians on Lebanese soil, the Israeli incursions into Lebanon to preempt Palestinian guerrilla attacks, and the Western offensive to bring about a peaceful settlement of the Arab-Israeli conflict converged to bring about the 1975–76 war in Lebanon.

During the sixties, Beirut was fertile ground for the breeding of different ideologies—Nasserism, Arab nationalism, Baathism (Syrian and Iraqi), Palestinian nationalism, communism, and so forth—providing a focus for disgruntled Lebanese and an arena in which other Arab states could settle their private disputes.

Of all the external actors in the Lebanese war of 1975–76, Syria played a major role that proved to be both intricate and controversial. The intricacy of Syria's role was exacerbated by her direct interests in Lebanon as well as the role the Baath regime wanted to play in regional and international affairs.[15] Syria's newfound political stability under Assad's Baath regime made it possible for her to pursue her economic, political, and security goals. Syria had never relinquished her claim over Lebanon, or, at least, the parts of Lebanon that were annexed in 1920. Furthermore, the open political society of Lebanon has always posed a threat to Syria's closed political system. In addition, both Syria and Israel could use Lebanon as a launching pad against the other. By 1973, Syria had replaced Cairo as the Lebanese Muslims' external guiding power and slowly but surely acquired virtually full hegemony over Lebanon's domestic and foreign policies.[16] This interest in Lebanon will become clearer in the course of the Lebanese war.

The second major external actor in the Lebanese war was Israel. Until 1969, the Lebanese-Israeli border was very peaceful. But as the Palestinian guerrilla action increased across these same borders, hardly a week passed without Israeli attacks against targets in Lebanon. The initial intention was to force the Lebanese government into taking action against the Palestinians, but, before long, Israel was attacking Palestinian targets in Lebanon by land, air, and sea with occasional commando forays.

The third major external actor on the Lebanese scene was the Palestine Liberation Organization (PLO). The first group of Palestinians to arrive in Lebanon was the 150,000 refugees who either fled or were evicted from their homes during the 1948 Arab-Israeli war. The first to leave their homes were businessmen, doctors, lawyers, and intellectuals who rallied to Lebanon because of its open society, freedom of expression, and its commercial and Western orientation. This group was immediately integrated with the local communities. The rest of the refugees were settled in fifteen different camps around the country. The main refugee camps were situated on the outskirts of the major cities of Tripoli, Beirut, Sidon, Tyre, and Baalbeck. Successive Lebanese governments refused to naturalize the refugees in compliance with the policy decreed by the Arab consensus and in fear of an overwhelming majority of Muslims, which would wreck the intricate balance between the different Lebanese communities. The second group of refugees arrived in Lebanon after the 1967 Arab-Israeli war, to be joined in 1970 by a third group evicted by King Hussein from Jordan. The majority of the latter group were seasoned fighters who had confronted the Jordanian army in a bloody war.

At the Arab summit meeting of October 1964, in retaliation for Israel's decision to divert the waters of the Jordan River (whose sources were in Lebanon with tributaries in Syria and Jordan) and to appease the Arab masses, two steps were taken: the formation of the Palestine Liberation Organization under the leadership of Ahmad Shuqairy and the establishment of a unified Arab military command comprising Egypt, Syria, Jordan, and Lebanon. Lebanon stipulated, however, that no Arab troops were to set foot in Lebanon unless requested to do so by the Lebanese government and no military training of Palestinians was to take place on its territory and no foreign military presence would be tolerated.

The PLO was immediately allowed to open offices in all the Arab capitals and started on a campaign of recruitment and organization of Palestinians from all over the Arab world. Al-Fateh (the Arabic acronym for Palestine National Liberation Movement, *harakat al-tahrir al-watani al-filistini,* read in reverse to mean "conquest") captured the imagination of the Arab and Palestinian masses when it issued its first communiqué on December 31, 1964, to describe its first operation within Israel. With the humiliating defeat of the Arabs in 1967, the PLO was catapulted to prominence and Yassir Arafat replaced Ahmad Shuqairy as head of the organization, which comprised the three major guerrilla factions: Fateh, the Popular Front for the Liberation of Palestine, and the Saiqa. Lebanon, with about 300,000 Palestinian inhabitants and a large base of popular support, was the natural place for Palestinian political activities. Between 1967 and 1969, the PLO had penetrated all the refugee camps and established its military force. The Palestinians organized themselves in the Arqub region in southern Lebanon at the foot of Mount Hermon. Fatehland, as it became known, was conveniently situated to launch its attacks against Israeli settlements in the north of Israel. Soon after, the Lebanese army deserted that part of Lebanon as it slowly grew to be the battleground of the Palestinians and Israelis.

The Lebanese did not realize how entwined Palestinian politics had become with their own until December 1968, when Israel attacked Beirut's international airport and destroyed thirteen civilian planes. This brought on the first political clash between the progressive left wing, which pressured the Lebanese government to become more involved with the Palestinian Resistance Movement (PRM), and the conservative right wing, which repudiated any Palestinian military presence. The Palestinian camps had slowly been transformed into strongholds of the guerrilla organizations and, by April 1969, armed clashes were flaring up between them and the Lebanese army, which was accused of trying to liquidate the resistance. In fact, in October 1969, fighting broke out in various parts of the country and eventually led to the signing of the Cairo Agreement on November 3, 1969. The signatories were General Emile Bustani, commander of the Lebanese army, and Yassir Arafat, chairman of the Palestine Resistance Movement (PRM). The agreement legitimized the presence of the Palestinians in the Arqub region, allowed Palestinian residents in Lebanon to join the PRM, guaranteed lines of supply from Syria, and gave the Palestinians autonomy within the camps as long as Lebanese sovereignty was respected. The PLO had become a state within a state. The Lebanese parliament ratified the agreement in complete ignorance of the full text, which both sides had agreed to keep secret. Thus, "in effect, the Cairo Agreement legitimized the armed Palestinian presence in Lebanon. It tried to reconcile and regulate this presence with Lebanese sovereignty, an exercise which turned out to resemble an attempt to square the circle."[17]

With the defeat, in 1970, of the resistance in Jordan, in what became known as "Black September," all its leaders, as well as the rank and file, left Jordan. The majority settled in Lebanon due to the greater freedom afforded them by the Cairo Agreement and the importance of Beirut as a media and information center. In contrast, those who settled in Syria were faced by a strong army that kept them under close surveillance and control. The number of Palestinians in Lebanon had risen to around 500,000 by the mid-seventies.

After the Cairo Agreement, no major clashes took place between the Lebanese army and the PRM until May 1973: On April 10, 1973, Israeli commandos raided Beirut and killed three prominent leaders of the resistance. This triggered renewed clashes with the Lebanese army. Once again the fighting was stopped by the signing of a new agreement, namely, the Melkart Agreement or Protocol, which was considered an appendix to the Cairo Agreement. The army had to lift its siege of the camps when Syria closed its borders with Lebanon, thereby completely cutting it off from the Arab hinterland so pivotal for its economy.

The Lebanese authorities, especially the Maronite leadership, resented and feared the growing power of the PRM, which was, simultaneously and recklessly, drawing Israeli reprisals onto Lebanon, while it continued to undermine the state and its institutions: The PLO militias frequently set up roadblocks and checked people and vehicles. They often molested, detained, or kidnapped Lebanese as well as foreigners under the pretext of opposing the revolution. One of those kidnapped was Bashir Gemayel (March 29, 1970).[18] These infractions were confirmed by their ally and defender, Kamal Junblat, the Druze leader and founder of the Progressive Socialist Party: "One must admit that the Palestinians themselves, by violating the Lebanese law and by carrying arms and functioning in a police role at the entrances to the capital, have facilitated the preparation and conception of the conspiracy. In certain cases Palestinian patrols used to arrest government employees and director generals to check their identification, and in other cases Lebanese and foreign residents were kidnapped and imprisoned for . . . weak reasons. . . . These violations, taken lightly at first, became unbearable. . . . Had there not been this degree of transgression or violation of law we would not have seen this level of outrage over the Palestinians in isolationist [Maronite] circles."[19]

Consequently, the Maronites, represented mainly by the Phalangist and National Liberal parties, recognizing the impotence of both the government and army, began arming themselves to check the Palestinian encroachments. This took place at a time when the PRM was acclaimed all over the Arab world, including Lebanon, as the savior and hope of the future Arab society. With this overwhelming support, the PRM succeeded in polarizing the Lebanese, undermining internal security and inviting foreign intervention.

The Palestinian ministate in Lebanon, referred to by the right wing as the "alternative or substitute homeland" (*al-watan al-badil*), had all the characteristics of a bona fide stature—control over people and territory, government bureaucracy, legislative and executive branches, army, communications network, flag, stamps, and head of state. During the 1970s and, to a greater extent, after 1975–76, it replaced the Lebanese government in the south, even establishing Palestinian courts; its army grew from 6,000 in the sixties to 20,000 fighters in the mid-seventies and was well stocked with heavy arms, artillery, and tanks. Palestinian power in Lebanon continued to grow until June 1982, when Israel invaded Lebanon to destroy it.[20] According to the U.S. official count, following the agreement negotiated by Philip Habib and accepted by the Israelis, 8,300 PLO fighters left Lebanon together with 3,600 Syrian troops and Palestine Liberation Army combatants.[21]

The external actors on the Lebanese battlefield were not alone. They were joined by disgruntled Lebanese factions. The Lebanese actors on the eve of the war could be divided into two major blocs, which became known as the Lebanese Front and the National Movement. The first comprised, mainly, the Phalangist and National Liberal parties, al-Tanzim (The organization), the Guardians of the Cedars, the Maronite Monastic Orders, and the National Bloc and was headed by former president Camille Chamoun. The second included six major parties (the Progressive Socialist Party, the Syrian Social Nationalist Party, the Baath Party, the Communist Party, the Organization of Communist Action, the Independent Nassirite Movement—Murabitun) and several minor ones, including the four Nassirite organizations, and was headed by Kamal Junblat.[22] While the Lebanese Front feared the growing power of the Palestinians and started arming themselves in case of future confrontation, the National Movement members were sympathetic with the Palestinian armed presence. Some even joined the ranks of the guerrillas in support of their revolutionary struggle hoping that the radical refugees would in turn help them effect the reforms they considered necessary in Lebanon. The PLO, in turn, and after its experience in Jordan, realizing its need for a large popular base in the host country, won their allegiance by generous financial contributions, armaments, and coercion.

By 1975 the Lebanese government had become paralyzed and the four different issues central to the Lebanese conflict were in place: the struggle over Lebanon's identity and the minority problem, the reform of the Lebanese political system, the Middle East conflict and its repercussions on Lebanon's security, and last but not least the threatened sovereignty of Lebanon.[23]

The Two-Year War (1975–76)

The war, which destroyed the Lebanese economy, fragmented the population, and disintegrated political institutions, erupted on April 13, 1975. According to police reports, on the morning of that fateful Sunday, while Pierre Gemayel, the head of the Phalangist Party, was attending the inauguration of a Greek Catholic church in the Beirut suburb of Ain al-Rimmaneh, two Phalangist bodyguards and two other members were killed by unknown gunmen, believed to be Palestinians, shooting from a car with covered license plates. On that same day, Palestinians from the various refugee camps around Beirut were attending a commando parade in another part of the city. As a group of them was returning by bus to Tell el-Zaatar camp in the afternoon, Christian gunmen, believed to be Phalangists, ambushed the bus in Ain al-Rimmaneh and killed its twenty-seven occupants in retaliation for the morning assassination of their comrades. Armed clashes between the Palestinian commandos and the Phalangist militia erupted, soon after, all over Beirut.[24] By September of the same year, the conflagration had spread further to ensure control of strategic points. This culminated in December, when each bloc tried to cleanse its territory from any hostile presence.

The Maronites held a meeting on January 13, 1976, in the presidential palace in Baabda and issued a statement describing the conflict in Lebanon as one between predominantly Lebanese Christians and the Palestinians who did not live up to the agreements they had signed with the Lebanese state. In April 1976, at the request of the president, Suleiman Franjieh, and his two allies, Pierre Gemayel and Camille Chamoun, Syria intervened to enforce the status quo. The army, unable to move, soon disintegrated with soldiers joining the warring factions according to their confessional loyalties.[25] On October 15, 1976, the Saudi government called for a six-member (Egypt, Syria, Saudi Arabia, Lebanon, Kuwait, and PLO) Arab summit, to be held in Riyadh the following day. The summit called for the enforcement of the Cairo Agreement (withdrawal of Palestinians to the camps) and the establishment of the 30,000-Arab Deterrent Force (ADF) under the command of the newly elected Lebanese President, Ilyas Sarkis. With the deployment of the ADF in Lebanon and the formation of a new cabinet by Prime Minister Selim el-Hoss, the two-year war came to an end.

While the Riyadh Summit may have ended the fighting, it did not resolve the four-faceted conflict: Syria's quest for hegemony, the Palestinian phenomenon, Israeli concerns, and the continuing domestic conflict—despite the reforms stipulated in the Constitutional Document that was passed in February 1976.

By the end of the 1975–76 war Beirut was partitioned into East (mainly Christian) and West (mainly Muslim and the PRM), symbolizing the schism and divisiveness that came to afflict Lebanese society for another fifteen years. During and immediately after the war, each of the two camps made efforts to consolidate its territory. Thus Beirut lost its unity as an urban center and communications between the two sectors became rather difficult, despite the five main crossing-points, as they were severely restricted by sniper fire. This, plus the government's slow and hesitant resumption of its power and sovereignty, led to the establishment of three "proto-states" in the different sectors: the Christian, the Druze, and the Palestinian.[26]

The 1978 War

Slowly, the alliance between Syria and the Lebanese Front started to weaken as the latter accused Syria of becoming more of a foreign occupier than a savior. Christian discontent culminated in a drawn-out battle between the two (February–July 1978), resulting in the establishment of the Christian 1,000-square-kilometer "liberated areas."[27] This was followed, in April 1979, by the formation of "Free Lebanon" in the small territory in southern Lebanon under the control of Major Saad Haddad consequent to the first Israeli invasion of the south in 1978, dubbed the "Litani Operation." On July 7, 1980, the Phalangist militia under the leadership of Bashir Gemayel attacked the militia of the National Liberal Party—in an effort to unify and consolidate the Christian front—dissolved it, and united all Christian militias (with the exception of Franjieh's militia) under the rubric of the Lebanese Forces.

The growing power and confidence of the Lebanese Front with greater Israeli support and the temporary weakness of the Syrian regime induced its leadership to extend its military and political presence to Zahlé in the

Biqaa Valley. This was interpreted by Syria as an attempt to change the status quo and to undermine its position in the Biqaa, which is most vital to its interests. The resultant conflagration of March 1981 was of ominous dimensions and the Lebanese Forces had to retreat.

The Israeli Invasion (1982)

By 1982 the Lebanese conflict was revealed to be truly regional and international in character: The war had greatly weakened the judicial, political, and administrative structure while the government's security forces maintained a limited presence. In contrast, two-thirds of the country was under Syrian hegemony; the PLO, the National Movement, and other Syrian allied forces held limited powers under the ADF umbrella; the Lebanese Front was in total control of the Christian enclave; UNIFIL (United Nations Interim Force in Lebanon) controlled parts of southern Lebanon subsequent to the 1978 Israeli "Litani Operation"; and Israel controlled the "safety zone" on its borders with Lebanon through the dissident Lebanese army officer Major Saad Haddad.

Israel, aware that its problem in the south of Lebanon could not be solved independently of the wider Lebanese crisis and that the reconstruction of the Lebanese state would be in its own interest, became convinced that a large-scale invasion of Lebanon was inevitable and initiated it on the sixth of June, 1982. Within one week the Israeli army was at the gates of Beirut. The blockade lasted for nine weeks, but, by the third week (July 3), the blockade had turned into a medieval siege seeking to starve the inhabitants of West Beirut into surrender: fresh water, electricity, and fuel were cut off, and garbage filled the streets, topped with intense shelling, often of cluster bombs, which came to be labeled "the napalm of Lebanon." Thursday, August 12, though few appreciated this at the time, marked the end of the war against Beirut. The Lebanese government formally requested that the Multi-National Force be deployed in Lebanon to oversee the evacuation of the PLO and Syrian forces from Beirut. The war seemed finally to be at an end.[28]

This, however, was not to be: In the late afternoon of September 14, 1982, Bashir Gemayel, former commander of the Lebanese Forces and President-elect, was assassinated together with some thirty of his associates by an awesome explosion while delivering his farewell address to the Lebanese Forces at their headquarters in Achrafieh. A week later, his brother Amin, who had a different conception of the war and the peace that followed, was elected president in his stead.

The Mountain War (1983)

During the following months normalization seemed remote as the struggle over Lebanon's character and future continued and the regional and international players remained as entrenched as ever. Bashir Gemayel had had a clear-cut strategy: to assume office and demand the evacuation of Syrian forces with the help of the Israeli army, who, in turn, would withdraw pending negotiations with the Lebanese government. But his brother, Amin, had a different approach altogether.

On May 17, 1983, Lebanon signed an agreement with Israel negotiated by the United States. The agreement stipulated the withdrawal of Israeli troops from Lebanon, the ending of the state of war between the two countries, and the cessation of all hostile activities against each other, as well as the abrogation of all laws and regulations contrary to the spirit of the agreement. Although the Lebanese Parliament ratified the agreement, the president never signed it. This made it possible for Syria, by the fall of 1983, to regain its hegemony and the influence it had lost in 1982. Israel, disappointed by these developments, withdrew its forces to the south of Lebanon. With this withdrawal, the entente, brought about by the Israeli invasion and the deployment of the Multi-National Force, as well as the election of the Phalangist Amin Gemayel, came to an end. The Amal-army clashes that erupted in Beirut (August 28–September 4) marked the beginning of a reversal in the victor-vanquished relationship brought on by the Israeli invasion. This reversal became even more pronounced when the Druze, supported by Syria, gained the upper hand in the Mountain War brought on by the Israelis' sudden and swift withdrawal. The three-week-long war resulted in extensive massacres and a large-scale displacement of the Christian population. By February 6, 1984, the authority of the army had completely collapsed in West Beirut and roadblocks were reinstated between the two sectors. The administration of Amin Gemayel was facing imminent disintegration, and the American president, Ronald Reagan, announced the withdrawal of the Marines from Lebanon. Gemayel had no one to turn to but Syria.[29]

The time, thus, seemed ripe for Syria's intervention to regulate the Lebanese conflict in its own best interests. At the end of September 1985, the three major militias (the Lebanese Forces, the Progressive Socialist Party, and Amal) represented by their leaders (E. Hobeika, W. Junblat, and N. Berri) met in Damascus to negotiate a comprehensive peace settlement in Lebanon. Notwithstanding the vociferous criticism by the Christians of the section dealing with relations with Syria as stipulated by this tripartite agreement, Elie Hobeika signed what became known as the Tripartite

Agreement on December 28, 1985. The agreement stipulated the end of the war, the gradual abolition of the confessional political system, and an affirmation that Lebanon would be in the Syrian zone of influence.[30] However, with the failure of Hobeika to deliver the Christian constituency and his subsequent ousting from the Lebanese Forces by Samir Geagea, the agreement was defunct.

The wars that ensued (1986–88) were mainly Amal's wars against the Palestinians, against the Druze (Progressive Socialist Party), and against the rest of the Lebanese left. On February 22, 1987, concerned that its most reliable ally would incur heavy losses, Syria entered West Beirut after an absence of five years.

The War of Liberation (1989)

At 11:45 P.M. on September 22, 1988, Amin Gemayel signed his last two decrees: The first dismissed the cabinet and the second appointed an interim government until the election of a new president. His tenure of six years was over. The new government comprised six military officers and General Michel Aoun, commander of the Lebanese army, as prime minister. Selim el-Hoss, prime minister of the previous cabinet, refused to step down. Both cabinets claimed legal status. Aoun governed de facto in the Christian enclave and Hoss, in West Beirut and the areas under the control of Muslim militias and Syrian forces. Thus, the end of the Gemayel regime ushered in, for the first time since the inception of the Lebanese war, the total collapse of all governmental institutions culminating on October 18, 1988, by the expiration of the term of office of the Speaker of Parliament. The parliament was not reconvened. Only one institution retained its unified character, namely, the Central Bank, which continued to finance the expenditure of both cabinets.

The War of Liberation, as it became known, was declared by Aoun on March 14, 1989, against Syria. The devastation in the Christian area due to the long-range attrition bombardment of residential areas was almost complete: Normal life and business came to an end. The heaviest bombardment since the Israeli siege of West Beirut took place on April 13, 1989, the anniversary of the outbreak of the war. Hospitals and grain silos were hit, power supplies were destroyed, and shortages of food and fuel occurred. Aoun retaliated by bombarding West Beirut and Syrian positions in the Biqaa but he was no match for the Syrian army. The War of Liberation continued unabated until September 24, 1989, when a ceasefire was declared and the Saudi government invited the Lebanese members of parliament to convene in Taif.

The conclave commenced activities on October 1, 1989, with the objective of reconciliation and peace. This included not only internal Lebanese conflicts but spelled out the relationship that was to hold between Lebanon and Syria on the military and political levels. The Taif Agreement sanctioned the role of the Syrian army as "helping the Lebanese government to restore its authority," for a period of two years at the end of which the Lebanese domestic reforms would have been enforced. The agreement further legalized the deployment of Syrian troops in the Biqaa region, the mountains, and "other places" for an indefinite period of time and committed the two countries to bilateral treaties consecrating "privileged relationships in all fields." On October 24, 1989, the conclave approved the new Coexistence Pact, which replaced the National Pact and legalized the Syrian presence in Lebanon. Aoun rejected the agreement and announced the dissolution of the parliament.[31]

On November 5, 1989, the new president of the republic, René Moʿawwad, was elected only to be assassinated on Independence Day, November 22, 1989. The following day, his successor, Ilyas Hrawi, was elected. He immediately dismissed Aoun as commander-in-chief of the army and gave him forty-eight hours to leave the presidential palace or face the consequences. A few hours later, tens of thousands of people spontaneously marched to the palace. Tents were set up for them and a sit-in started that was to last for weeks. Speakers, singers, poets, musicians, and others voluntarily entertained the campers. This permanent wake preempted any attack against Aoun whether by air or land.

As the war in Lebanon entered its sixteenth year in the spring of 1990, peace and tranquillity still eluded the Lebanese. The specter of violence grew even more virulent as the fighting shifted from being intercommunal to intracommunal. This is best illustrated by the destructive war that took place in the Christian enclave between the Christians themselves: the army under the command of Michel Aoun and the Lebanese Forces under the command of Samir Geagea. On January 31, 1990, a large-scale military conflagration erupted between these two most powerful military bodies. Violence spread to the heartland of the Christian area exacting thousands of lives, exorbitant material damage, and, most important, the total collapse of the Christian resistance to the Syrian presence in Lebanon. The war lasted eight months, after which the Vatican mediated a cease-fire put into effect on May 21, 1990. At 7:00 A.M. on October 13, 1990, the Syrian air force began bombardment of the presidential palace to force Aoun out, aided by Syrian and Lebanese tanks. At 9:30 A.M. Aoun sought refuge at the French embassy and asked for political asylum.

On December 4, 1990, for the first time since 1984, Beirut was declared a unified city and freed of armed militias for the first time since 1975. The war had finally and truly come to an end. On May 1, 1991, the militias were by and large disarmed and, in early June, 1991, the army took in former militiamen for rehabilitation and training.[32]

The war that raged for sixteen years spelled nothing but tragedy for the Lebanese—thousands of whom were maimed, displaced, became homeless, emigrated, or died.

Effects of the War

Beirut, the home of nearly half the population, suffered the greatest devastation. The harbor, essential to the city's trade and the country's economy, was crippled. Most of Lebanon's tourism infrastructure, including the forty-five most important hotels, was destroyed. The industrial sector was so badly damaged that almost 50 percent of its capacity was crippled. Schools, hospitals, and government offices were hard hit. But worst of all were the devastating blows dealt to the water supplies, telephone installations, and electric power plants, as well as the total breakdown of public transportation. In short, the country's production capacity was reduced during the first two years of the war to 50 percent of what it was in 1974. Before long, Beirut, the bustling center of trade, services, finance, and tourism, known for its freedom and openness to the East and West, famous for its unique atmosphere, became infamous as the center of terrorism, carnage, and violence.

The war turned the Lebanese into migrants, refugees, and displaced persons in their own country. Seven hundred thousand are estimated to have had to flee their homes at least once. Most have not yet returned. It is estimated that about one-quarter of the population emigrated to safer areas and countries. Most of these were skilled workers (industry, construction, hotel, business), doctors, engineers, architects, and financiers. Many firms transferred their activities abroad.

Taking 1974 as a measuring stick, the cumulative losses in the GNP through 1986 alone totaled about $11.6 billion. At the end of that same year the buying power of the government-imposed minimum wage was 13 percent of its 1974 level. The minimum wage in 1974 was 70 percent of the average per capita income; by 1986, it had been reduced to 20 percent. Needless to say, the hardest hit was the middle class, which has now virtually disappeared.[33]

Tabitha Petran, in *The Struggle over Lebanon,* asserts the uniqueness of the Lebanese war: "Indeed, not since the general acceptance of the concept of nation-state has a country disintegrated in quite this way, with the very population held hostage by the rival authority of marauding gangs, not for weeks or months but for years" (383). Joseph Chamie also states, "Without a doubt, this conflict is one of the bloodiest civil wars of the twentieth century in that there are few instances where in so few months such high percentages of a nation's population have been killed and wounded."[34] Kidnapping and massacre became the common feature of the war. However, the ultimate expression of the ugly indiscriminate violence that marked the Lebanese arena, after the Israeli invasion of 1982, was the continuous use of car bombs and explosives that invariably killed more innocents than actually intended victims. The car bomb came to be the militia's weapon of choice. Between January and August of 1986 alone, it is reported that eleven such explosions took place, killing two hundred and twenty-five people and wounding more than eight hundred, many of whom were maimed for life. Explosions in or near supermarkets were timed to go off at peak hours killing mostly women and children. There is no official statistical record of those killed during the war, but the number is estimated to range between one hundred and one hundred and fifty thousand killed during the first nine years of the war, a large figure if measured against the total population. Countless people have been injured or maimed and many more have suffered lasting psychological damage.[35]

The war affected everyday life as well. Fear became second nature and death commonplace. People could not be sure as they left for work in the morning or went shopping or attended schools, whether they or their children would return. Yet life went on—the Lebanese wanted to believe they could cheat death by taking shorter routes to school or business, by watching television and videocassettes instead of going to the movies and socializing with neighbors instead of lifelong friends. In the basements, families claimed small areas for themselves with mattresses, blankets, and candles. Their most indispensable items were the small transistor radios they carried constantly. Everyone knew the frequencies and schedules of news broadcasts of the different militia radio stations.

It was not the fighting alone that weighed on the Lebanese, but the sense of being at the mercy of several parties and gangs: Apartments would be requisitioned for their strategic importance or as accommodation for militiamen or their displaced relatives; cars would be confiscated and their owners robbed; kidnapping became rampant for political or financial gains. Thus terror ruled the day.

Yet, the Lebanese, famous for their resilience, dynamism, and optimism, still managed to see a half-filled glass and waited faithfully for

Godot to bring an end to the incessant fighting, explosions, atrocities, and death. They soon learned to develop a flexible war economy: whenever possible, damage was immediately repaired and houses rebuilt; new factories sprouted in relatively safer areas; and banks, food caterers, supermarkets, and shopping centers were decentralized as provincial towns developed into business centers.

Finally, the unity of the Lebanese, despite all that transpired, is best demonstrated by the desire of the majority for peace and coexistence. This was expressed not only at the individual level but also as mass demonstrations against the war: The first such demonstration took place in November 1975, when tens of thousands of both sectors of Beirut expressed their rejection of the war. In 1982, thousands of West Beirut residents found refuge from the Israeli siege in the Christian enclave, just as in 1990 thousands of East Beirut sought refuge in West Beirut. War cripples protesting the war, on crutches or in wheelchairs, marched from Tripoli, in the north, to Beirut. Trade unions went on strike as homogeneous bodies cutting across confessional and political lines. In 1987, according to police estimates, 60,000 demonstrators from East and West Beirut gathered at the Museum Checkpoint chanting "East and West united" and "national unity."[36]

Although women, on the eve of the war, were a rather complacent lot, generally satisfied with what privileges they enjoyed, they did rise as a group to face the imminent conflagration. The Lebanese Council of Women, convinced of the important role of women in society, formed a delegation of ten women, who, on May 31, 1975, visited the prime minister-designate and presented him with the following statement: "Aware of the awesome dimension of the tragedy that Lebanon is encountering at present, a number of women have agreed on the following:

(1) censure of violence as a means of political action;

(2) appeal to the government to impose security as quickly as possible;

(3) speed up of the formation of a cabinet whose members are known for their moral standards, scholarly qualifications, ability to carry out the law and study the direct and indirect causes of the present crisis for a radical solution."[37]

This was followed by a general assembly held on June 1, 1975, at the Press Syndicate Center to appeal for the imposition of security. A proclamation calling on all women "to emerge from their silence and stand in the face of the tempest" was also issued.[38] The assembly was followed by a demonstration of women calling for love, security, stability, and a better future for all. Half of the demonstrators then proceeded to remove two barricades from both sectors of the city as a symbolic gesture of unity.[39] The Lebanese Council of Women continued its efforts for peace by organizing a series of meetings in various parts of Lebanon to bolster national awareness: Beirut (September 5, 1975), Zahlé (September 19, 1975), Baalbeck (September 26, 1975), Tripoli (October 3, 1975), and Aley (October 10, 1975).[40] In addition, Emily Fares Ibrahim, a pioneer and president of the Lebanese Council of Women, asked the prime minister–designate, Rashid Karamé, to appoint a woman to the forthcoming cabinet as a messenger of peace and love at a time of explosive hatred and violence.[41]

However, the epitome of women's action against the war is best represented by the spontaneous sit-in at the American University of Beirut, on August 1, 1982, by one hundred women of all walks of life, in protest against the siege of Beirut by the Israelis and the shortage of water, electricity, and medications. This lasted for twenty-three days, including a three-day hunger strike, and ended when the siege was lifted.[42]

Many other sit-ins and demonstrations as well as press conferences were held by different women's organizations, separately and in unison, calling for the cessation of all hostilities and the reunification of Lebanon. A new women's organization emerged espousing the cause of the fate of the kidnapped or missing in action, consisting mainly of relatives of the missing.[43] The action of these organizations was not limited to Lebanon: They sent delegations and messages to various countries requesting help in bringing the carnage to a stop.[44] One such action was the three-day sit-in in November 1984 organized by Suad Salloum, president of the Society of the Southern Woman's Home, at the United Nations Headquarters in New York, between the hours of 11:00 A.M. and 4:00 P.M. While fifteen of the delegates returned to Beirut on November 18, 1984, twelve others continued their journey to other American states to explicate the Lebanese-Israeli conflict and occupation of the south of Lebanon.[45]

Emily Fares Ibrahim, president of the Lebanese Council of Women, on Women's Day, 1987, urged all women to unite in expressing their anger and decrying all forms of violence, terrorism, and the starvation and privation of all citizens.[46] However, women's efforts against the war took other forms as well. Thus, the Women's Rights Association, in collaboration with other women's organizations, called on women to join or at least support the resistance against the Israeli occupation of the south, and movements were formed to honor "the mother of the martyr." In fact, Rabab al-Sadr (sister of Musa al-Sadr) said, on the occasion of the birthday of Fatmeh al-Zahra, that "the line of martyrdom keeps us through history revered and honored . . . It is this path in which we find noble sisters accept, full of love, to be mothers of martyrs. They have accepted to draw near to God by becoming mothers of martyrs."[47]

However, the involvement of individual women in the National Resistance Front against Israeli occupation came to a climax with the suicidal missions carried out by seven women belonging to different sects and ideologies. The first to initiate this activity was Sana Muhaidly, who, on April 9, 1985, on the road to Bater-Jezzine, in the south, exploded a car she was driving as she passed an Israeli occupation patrol. The other six were Yasar Mroueh, Wafa Nureddin, Lola Abboud, Ibtisam Harb, Norma Abi-Hassan and Mariam Khaireddine.[48]

Despite this, however, women were allocated a special status symbolizing "family honor," and as such were to be protected by all men and avoided by the combatants. They became, therefore, less likely to become targets and had much more freedom to commute safely from one sector to another. This is best illustrated by Sheikh Mahdi Shamsuddin, then vice chairman of the Shiʿa High Council, when he appealed to human rights organizations against Israel's indiscriminate capture of women and men alike. He described Israel's actions as infractions against freedom, dignity, and the sacrosanct.[49]

Women in groups, however, did not limit their actions to the military and political. Thus, the first demonstration of its kind organized by the Lebanese Union of Women took place on April 4, 1985, in the quarter of Achrafieh in East Beirut, and called for economic and social reforms. The speakers decried monopolies, inflation, and exorbitant medical expenses: "We are hungry, we want to eat, we are thirsty, we want to drink." They also called out for democracy, liberty, and freedom of expression.[50] And on October 7, 1987, a similar demonstration of women, who called themselves Guardians of the Students, called for a revolution in East Beirut against the inflated tuition fees and textbook prices. This time, however, they were fired upon and violence ensued. But this did not stop them. The demonstration was resumed the following day in cooperation with the students themselves. Guardians and students cried for free elementary and intermediate education, subsidy of schoolbooks, support for the Lebanese State University and its professional schools, as well as fuel subsidies for school buses.[51]

Finally, Aniseh Najjar, president of the Congregation of Women's Organizations, described what was happening in Lebanon as the assassination of culture and intellect. She described women as being the primary victims of this senseless war: the kidnapped were the teachers of their children; the victims of explosions, their children; and the destroyed buildings, their life's work, while moral decay killed their children and grandchildren. Women, who constitute half the population, should, therefore, act as pressure groups to become focal points in current events and influence the decision-making process. Women are not to be marginalized any more, not after having proven their worth on the social, political, educational, as well as military levels.[52]

Notes

1. Hourani, *Political Society in Lebanon,* 1.
2. Cobban, *Shiʿa Community,* 2.
3. Halawi, *Lebanon Defied,* 182–83. Matawila is the popular name of the Shiʿa.
4. Ibid.
5. For a full discussion of the Shiʿa community and the birth of Amal, cf. Cobban, *Shiʿa Community;* Halawi, *Lebanon Defied;* Norton, *Amal and the Shʿia;* Wright, *Sacred Rage.*
6. Gordon, *Fragmented Nation,* 38; Odeh, *Lebanon,* 28; Harik, *Politics and Change.*
7. Zamir, *Formation of Modern Lebanon,* 6–7.
8. Hourani, *Syria and Lebanon,* 130.
9. Zamir, *Formation of Modern Lebanon,* 6–7.
10. Odeh, *Lebanon,* 28; Petran, *Struggle over Lebanon,* 23.
11. Snider, "Inter-Arab Relations," 179–80; Khuri, "Arab-Israeli Conflict," 170; Snider et al., "Israel," 91.
12. Hanf, *Coexistence,* 40.
13. For a detailed discussion of the war, see Haddad, *Politics of Revolving Doors;* Petran, *Struggle over Lebanon;* Haley and Snider, *Lebanon in Crisis;* Rabinovich, *War for Lebanon;* Hanf, *Coexistence;* McDowall, *A Conflict of Minorities;* Halawi, *Lebanon Defied;* Kliot, *Territorial Disintegration;* Ball, *Error and Betrayal;* Odeh, *Lebanon;* Bulloch, *Final Conflict;* Deeb, *The Lebanese Civil War;* Hoss, *Agony and Peace;* Lamb, *Israel's War in Lebanon;* Gordon, *Fragmented Nation;* Salibi, *Cross Roads;* Salem, *New Lebanon;* Harik, *Anatomy of Conflict.*
14. Hanf, *Coexistence,* 373–74.
15. For a full analysis of Syria's role, see Rabinovich, "Limits of Military Power," 55–73.
16. Rabinovich, *War for Lebanon,* 36–37.
17. Cooley, "The Palestinians," 30 ff.
18. Hanf, *Coexistence,* 167; Norton, *Amal and the Shʿia,* 65.
19. Kamal Junblat, *This Is My Will,* 78, 94.
20. For further reading see ibid.; McDowall, *A Conflict of Minorities;* Kliot, *Territorial Disintegration;* Odeh, *Lebanon;* Bulloch, *Final Conflict;* Lamb, *Israel's War in Lebanon;* Haddad, *Politics of Revolving Doors;* Haley and Snider, *Lebanon in Crisis;* Rabinovich, *War for Lebanon;* Hanf, *Coexistence;* Binder, foreword to Norton, *Amal and the Shʿia,* vi–xiii; Salibi, *Cross Roads;* Deeb, *The Lebanese Civil War.*

21. Ball, *Error and Betrayal*, 56.

22. For a detailed account of the different political parties, see Deeb, *The Lebanese Civil War.*

23. For a full discussion, see Haddad, *Politics of Revolving Doors.*

24. Ibid., 47; Salibi, *Cross Roads*, 97–98; Snider, "Inter-Arab Relations," 183.

25. Cf. Whetten, "The Military Dimension," 75–90.

26. For a full description, see Kliot, *Territorial Disintegration.*

27. For a full description of the Christian camp, see Phares, *Lebanese Christian Nationalism.*

28. For a full description of the siege, see Bulloch, *Final Conflict;* Ball, *Error and Betrayal.*

29. Cobban, *Shi'a Community*, 8.

30. Cf. Petran, *Struggle over Lebanon*, 368 ff.; Hanf, *Coexistence*, 306–10.

31. Hanf, *Coexistence*, 583–92.

32. For a detailed description cf. Phares, *Lebanese Christian Nationalism*, 154–66; Hanf, *Coexistence*, 597–617.

33. For an extensive discussion with figures, cf. Hanf, *Coexistence*, 350–57.

34. Chamie, *Religion and Population*, v.

35. Petran, *Struggle over Lebanon*, 379; Hoss, *Agony and Peace*, 53–54.

36. Cf. Hanf, *Coexistence*, 638–40.

37. al-Khatib, *al-Harakah al-nisa'iyyah*, 171.

38. *al-Nahar* (Beirut), June 1, 1975.

39. *al-Safir* (Beirut), June 2, 1975.

40. al-Khatib, *al-Harakah al-nisa'iyyah*, 174.

41. *al-Nahar* (Beirut), May 31, 1975.

42. *al-Safir* (Beirut), August 1–23, 1982.

43. Ibid., February 25, 1984.

44. Ibid., November 30, 1983.

45. Ibid., November 18–19, 1984.

46. Ibid., March 8, 1987.

47. Ibid., March 2, 1986; April 6, 1987; March 23, November 24, 1984; March 8/9, 1985.

48. *al-Liwa'* (Beirut), November 25, 1987; *al-Safir* (Beirut), November 14, 1987.

49. *al-Safir* (Beirut), March 9, 1986.

50. Ibid., April 5, 1985.

51. Ibid., October 7, 1987.

52. Ibid., March 25, 1986.

3

Women before the War

There can be no acting or doing of any kind, till it be recognized that there is a thing to be done; the thing once recognized, doing in a thousand shapes becomes possible.

Thomas Carlyle, *Chartism* (1839)

When the first American missionaries arrived in the Levant in 1823, they described Levantine women as "vacant as space" and "lawless as the waves of the sea" and their character a "disgusting compound of childish ignorance, foolish superstition, impertinence and vulgarity."[1] And when the first British missionaries arrived two decades later, Mrs. Bowen Thompson wrote back home, "The females in the East have been so greatly neglected and degraded that it is of the utmost importance to give them a chance to rise above their wretched lot."[2] William Goodell wrote in 1853 that "it was an impossible thing to teach a woman to read" and "we might as well undertake to teach the wild asses of the desert to read, as to teach a woman."[3] And when the first school of girls was to be established in Tyre, the local priest protested to the responsible missionary, Dr. King, that it was better for women to remain ignorant, for they were bad enough with what little they knew.[4]

Women in Politics

In such an atmosphere of ignorance, prejudice, and seclusion during the nineteenth century, some Lebanese women excelled and left their imprint in several domains. On the political level, we know of a few such as Princess Habbusa Arslan, who was appointed by Emir Bashir II, after the death of her husband, as ruler of her princedom which included Shwayfat, ʿAin ʿAnoub, ʿAramoun, Bshamoun, and ʿAin Ksour. She presided as judge (from behind a curtain) over all religious and civil courts. She remained in power for thirty years. Another woman appointed by Emir Bashir II was Umm Mansour al-Khazin, who ruled the region of Kissirwan and was successful in peacefully preventing the Egyptian army from entering her domain. Fatmeh al-Khalil al-Asaad assisted her husband Ali Bek al-Asaad in ruling Jabal ʿAmil. She was so well educated and cultured that the jurists and religious scholars of the time chose her to be the first woman judge. Finally, in 1860, Nayfeh Junblat played a prominent role in the events of the day. When she failed to halt the current massacres of the Christians, she turned her home into a shelter for Christian refugees. She is also purported to have walked the battlefield impervious to danger in an effort to save women and children from certain death and transport them to her home for protection.[5]

In the Arab world, women have attained decision-making positions, such as member of Parliament, minister, and ambassador, yet Lebanon lags behind. On May 29, 1934, Deputy Sheikh Yussef el-Khazin asked for women's right to vote. Only three voted in favor and were dubbed "woman's champions." In 1936, women used the text of the Lebanese-French Agreement, which specified equal civil and political rights to all citizens, to demand the right to run for elections and vote. In 1943, Lebanese women stood side by side with men in their demands for the release of Sheikh Bishara al-Khoury, Riyad al-Solh, and other members of the cabinet from prison and the declaration of Lebanon's independence. They joined in bloody demonstrations for three consecutive days. Although Sheikh Bishara al-Khoury later admitted his debt to the Lebanese woman and asserted his support for her full and equal rights, she was still not granted the right to vote. Women, thus, continued to fight for the right to vote until April 1950, when the Executive Committee of Women Groups was formed. It started its activities by calling for a general assembly on June 10, 1950, to ask for the amendment of Article 21 of the Electoral Law. On February 5, 1951, the committee submitted a petition to the cabinet asking for the amendment of Article 21 to include the word "females," thereby granting women the right to vote in parity with men. This was followed by a mobile demonstration consisting of a convoy of cars to the presidential palace, where women gave impassioned speeches asking for their political rights. On March 2, 1951, another petition was submitted to the prime minister. On March 14 of the same year, the cabinet granted women the right to participate only in municipal elections. This, of course, was rejected, and on March 20, 1951, a demonstration of women from all parts of Lebanon gathered in Parliament Square during the Parliament's weekly sessions to express their dissatisfaction and disappointment, while demonstrations took place in all parts of Lebanon asking for full political rights. And on January 11, 1952, all women's groups and organizations met at the Roxy Movie Theater, under the sponsorship of the First Lady, and asked for full suffrage. On November 24, 1952, the government granted the right to vote only to educated women. This was again rejected by the women's executive committee and finally, in February of 1953, women were granted unconditional political rights in parity with men.

In 1954, a new committee was formed to campaign for the right of financial compensation for children of working women in parity with men. This was granted to women in 1955. On June 23, 1954, they asked for equality in inheritance. On February 24, 1959, a law was passed granting non-Muslim Lebanese equality in inheritance. Women's activism regressed after that, although in 1960 women were granted the right to choose their nationality upon marriage to a foreigner and in 1974, the right of free travel.

Table 3.1. Women candidates for Parliament

Name	Year	Region	Votes
Emily Fares Ibrahim	1953	Zahlé	613 / 27,609
Laure Thabet	1957	Beirut	652 / 34,096
Munira Solh	1960	Beirut	2,165 / 22,692
Renée El-Hajj	1960	Jezzine	601 / 12,047
Myrna Boustani	1963	Shouf	uncontested
Munira Solh	1964	Beirut	999 / 29,584
Ibriza al-Meoushi (withdrew)	1964	Shouf	
Nuhad Seʿayd	1964	Byblos	9,544 / 20,420
Munira Solh (withdrew)	1968	Beirut	
Nuhad Seʿayd	1968	Byblos	10,917 / 21,813
Emily F. Ibrahim	1968	Baabda	944 / 44,423
Nuhad Seʿayd	1972	Byblos	9,863 / 23,736
Nayla Moʿawwad	1991	Zghorta	appointed to replace husband
Nayla Moʿawwad	1992	Zghorta	90,599 / 135,000
Bahiyyah al-Hariri	1992	South	117,761 / ?
Maha Khoury al-Asaad	1992	Byblos	uncontested
Bushra al-Khalil	1992	South	14,677 / ?
Mona Hobeish	1992	Kissirwan	156 / ?
Nayla Moʿawwad	1996	Zghorta	108,631
Linda Matar	1996	Beirut	7,470
Bahiyya al-Hariri	1996	South	141,338
Nuhad Seʿayd	1996	Byblos	7,195

Based on an unpublished study by Fares Saadeh, Nicola Nassif, and Rosana Bou Minsif, "*al-masrah wal-kawalis: Intikhabat 96 fi fusuliha*" (Theater and backstage: Unraveling of the 1996 elections) (Beirut: Dar al-Nahar lil-Nashr, 1996). See also Fadia Kiwan, "*al-Waqiʿ wal murtaja*," 49–59.

Until 1992 no woman was elected to Parliament with the exception of Myrna Bustani, who was elected in 1963 to finish the term of her father, Emile Bustani, who had suffered a tragic death. In 1953, Emily Fares Ibrahim ran for parliamentary elections but was not elected. She ran again in 1957 along with Laure Thabet, Jamal Karam Harfoush, and Maggie Ashkar, but, again, none of them was elected. (See table 3.1.)

The absence of women from decision-making positions was not limited to the legislative and executive branches of the government. Thus, only one or two women have reached decision-making positions in political parties. Instead, women are usually assigned to preside over women's issues or social concerns in their parties. In addition, women are usually isolated from leading positions in international conferences. Thus, in 1975, the Lebanese delegation to the World Conference on Women in Mexico, organized by the United Nations, was headed by a man. To this day there are still no women district governors (*muhafiz*—appointed by the Cabinet to administer the six districts). Women district commissioners (*qa'im-maqam*—appointed by the Cabinet to administer the subdistricts—*qada'*) amount to 4.16 percent of the total number. There are only three women heads of municipalities out of a total of 390, and 15 out of a total of 1,400 members of the municipal councils are women. The duties of the municipal council are normally limited to the city, town, or village concerned and consist of paving the streets, collecting garbage and incinerating it, protecting the environment and public health, and city planning and construction. Out of 1,800 *mukhtars* (appointed by the government in charge of official registries) only two are women.[6] (See tables 3.2 and 3.3.)

Women, however, are well represented in the judiciary but not at all in the Constitutional Council, Supreme Court, or Tribunal. They were first admitted into the judiciary in 1966. In the court of highest appeal, there is only one female assistant judge (*mustashar*) out of a total of twenty-four. In the State Council there are seven women and twenty-six men. In the Of-

Table 3.2. Women in public administration

	1977	1984	1992	1994
First category (total)	83	72	90	135
Women	—	—	3	3
Second category (total)	231	168	242	239
Women	6	6	16	16
Third category (total)	1,153	879	1,414	1,231
Women	59	59	114	91

Based on the unpublished archives of the Civil Service Board.

Table 3.3. Women in the Ministry of Foreign Affairs, 1995

	Number	Women	Percentage
Ambassador	66	1	1.5
Advisor	53	5	9.4
Secretary	46	8	17.4
Attaché	19	4	21
First category	—	—	—
Second category	1	0	0
Third category	15	5	33.3
Total population	282	35	12.41

Based on unpublished material provided by the Ministry of Foreign Affairs.

fice of Litigation there is only one female judge but eleven male judges. In criminal investigation there is only one female judge but twenty-six male judges. In the Court of Arbitration, there is only one female presiding judge but six males in the same position. These figures would be more meaningful if we compared the current number of women in the Academy of the Judiciary, keeping in mind that women were precluded from admission for the year 1994: In the preparatory session, there are seven women and thirteen men; in the second year, there are no women; in the third year, there are eight women and thirteen men.[7]

It thus becomes clear that while women managed, on an individual level, to achieve equality in the different domains, albeit in small numbers, they have been unable to make any headway in the public sector with the exception of the realm of education at the level of instruction. They have been assiduously and methodically kept out of the decision-making machinery of the state. At no time, since the formation of Greater Lebanon in 1920, have there been women presidents, prime ministers, or ministers despite the fact that Lebanon has had thirty-member cabinets at different times in recent history. And in Parliament, only two women assumed, uncontested, the seats of their deceased father (1963) and husband (1991), respectively, for the remaining duration.

The government, unfortunately, is not the only culprit in this matter. The other equally important factor is woman herself. For no women's movement, in the true sense of the word, exists in Lebanon to this day. Even though the Lebanese Council of Women has existed since 1951 and despite the fact that it represents around 130 organizations from different regions, religions, and ideologies, it has failed to carry the banner of women in their struggle for freedom, equality, and the right to be heard in matters of national concern. Thus once they won the right to vote in parity with men, they were lulled into complacency and turned their attention to "feminine" and social affairs. In short, the Lebanese Council of Women has failed to act as a pressure group for the advancement and development of women.

Women, again on an individual level, played an active political role on the national level. Their most active period has always been during their student life, and many young women were recognized for the prominent roles they played in this context. However, once their student years were behind them, they retired to a more sedate life restricted usually to social matters and charity work. Consequently, no women ever reached decision-making positions in any of the known political parties in Lebanon.

It is obvious, then, that while women are symbolically represented, they remain almost completely excluded from decision-making positions.

Women in Education

Education, before the nineteenth century, was limited to the elementary level and to the study of religion. Higher education was confined to two schools, one in Zghorta (1735) and the other in Ain Waraqa (1789), considered the mother of all schools in Lebanon, which, in addition to following the Western method of instruction, taught Arabic, Syriac, Latin, Italian, philosophy, and theology.

With the advent of missionary work, more schools were established. Those founded before the nineteenth century were mostly French and Catholic in orientation. Due to the competition between the French Catholics and British and American Protestants in the nineteenth century, printing, translation into Arabic, and journalism flourished. The first girls' school was founded in Beirut by American missionaries in 1824, and by 1860 they had founded thirty-three schools comprising about one thousand pupils, one-fifth of whom were girls. The Jesuits, in turn, established their first girls' school in 1844, which was followed later by the foundation of the Jesuit (St. Joseph) University in Beirut. The Lebanese were then motivated to establish private schools, one of which is the famous Ain Therèse founded in 1811 for both girls and boys. Five thousand girls were distributed over the new schools all over Lebanon. The overall number of students who graduated from all schools in Lebanon until 1914 is estimated at 70,000. The number of local private schools in Lebanon by 1914 had reached fifty-two for girls and fifty-two for boys.[8] In 1866, the American missionaries founded the Syrian Protestant College, which later became known as the American University of Beirut.

The first woman to seek higher education abroad was Aniseh Saybʿah. She graduated from the medical school of the University of Edinburgh in 1899 and practiced her profession in Egypt. Anas Barakat left for the United States in 1901 and graduated with an M.D. degree from the University of Detroit in 1905. She returned to Beirut in 1907 to head St. George's Hospital. In 1913, Catherine Chamiyyeh graduated from Geneva in physics and chemistry. She became the first Lebanese nuclear physicist.[9] In 1926, the midwife Suhayla Saadeh obtained her diploma from Queen Charlotte Hospital in London. In 1931, Saniyyah Habboub obtained her medical degree from the University of Pennsylvania and, in 1934, Najla Abu-Izzeddin received her doctorate in history from the University of Chicago. In 1942, Saniyyah Zaytoun became the first woman engineer in Lebanon to join the Syndicate. In 1945, Salwa Nassar came from the University of California with a doctorate in physics and joined the American University of Beirut and later went on to head the department.

With the declaration of independence, in 1943, a new phase in the realm of education started. Schools sprouted in all parts of Lebanon so that, by 1972–73, the number of elementary and secondary schools, both private and public, was 2,486. (See table 3.4 for the distribution of students by gender.) The Lebanese (State) University was founded in 1951 and the Beirut Arab University in 1961. According to the educational statistics report of 1972–73, there were fourteen institutions of higher learning containing 32,230 students, 5,600 of whom were girls.

Journalism

Lebanon distinguished itself in the field of journalism and was ranked second only to Egypt in the publication of newspapers and magazines during the period 1858–1929. The number of newspapers published in

Table 3.4. Distribution of students in schools

School	Females	Males
Pre-elementary	52,338	60,197
Elementary	178,295	206,893
Intermediate	59,065	73,086
Secondary	13,769	21,658
Total	303,467	361,834

Source: Department of Statistics, *General Statistics for Education for the Year 1972–73* (Beirut: Educational Center for Research and Development, 1975).

Lebanon during that period is estimated at 400. Women pioneered in this field side by side with men. The first women's magazine, *al-Fatat* (The girl), was founded in 1892–93 and published in Cairo by the Lebanese Hind Nawfal, who was soon followed by Sulayma Abu-Rashid and others. Lebanese women journalists were pioneers abroad as well, like Mary Mokarzil, owner of *al-Huda* (The right path). *Al-Huda* was published in New York and recognized as the oldest Arabic political daily. Mary Mokarzil was followed by her colleague Afifeh Karam, who published the *Woman Magazine of the New World* in New York in 1912. Journalism helped in the spread of women's literature and the proselytization of women's emancipation in the region, especially during the twenties. In 1938, Alvira Lattouf was the first Lebanese woman to publish a political newspaper, *al-Mustaqbal* (The future).[10] The plethora of magazines deteriorated slowly until it disappeared in the forties. The only woman's magazine left was *Sawt al-mar'ah* (Woman's voice).

Feminism

The Lebanese woman realized that her only chance for self-advancement lay in acquiring a good education. She believed that emancipation and autonomy were her birthright and education, the only road to economic independence, equality, and full civil rights. She participated in local, regional, and international conferences and called for marital rights and the abolition of the veil. She also fought for national issues, such as the teaching of the history of the Arabs and the Arabic language as well as the boycotting of foreign products to encourage local production.

Among the first women writers of the nineteenth century was Wardeh al-Yazigi (1838–1924), who wrote mostly poetry. Her poems were collected in the volume *The Garden of Roses*. Zaynab Fawwaz (1850–1914) was known for her rhetoric, poetry, and prose. She wrote mostly on the liberation of women but also delved into social, political, and national issues. She was known as the "jewel of the East," "carrier of the banner of justice," and "authority on women." She struggled for the abolition of the veil and is considered the first Lebanese woman to fight for women's rights. Another pioneer was Julia Tomeh Dimishqiyyeh, a Christian, who defended women's rights from the highest platforms at a time when circumspection was a female virtue. In 1913, following an audacious lecture she gave in support of the establishment of a sanitorium for tuberculosis, she met Badr Dimishqiyyeh, a Muslim, and married him, a revolutionary act against tradition and confessionalism. She published her magazine *The New Woman* in 1921 and made it the platform of her struggle for women's rights—"teach and educate them (women) and they will bring you happiness and glory." She addresses man assuring him she does not want to be his superior, "I am satisfied to walk beside you . . . as a partner. . . . Let me feel I am part of you, not a piece of property to be handled capriciously or a slave created only for housework and motherhood," and in a letter addressing her eighteen-year-old daughter, she says, "Do not be afraid to put your hand in another man's even if he is a villain, for with the strength of your personality and nobility of character, you are bound to raise him to the highest heavens even for a brief moment in his life." Her English daughter-in-law said that Julia taught her to believe "in humanity, in woman, [and] in the East not as a myth but as a truth."[11]

May Ziadeh (1886–1941) was a literary critic who wrote several articles and novels and translated a number of Western works. She wrote poetry in French and rewrote it in Arabic in prose. She mastered French, English, and Italian in addition to Arabic. When she moved to Egypt, she participated in politics and called for national awakening and the sovereignty of Egypt. She fought for the emancipation of women. She dedicated her first collection of French poems to Lamartine and published it in 1911 in Cairo. She established a literary salon in her own home, frequented by the intellectual and political elite. It slowly became the primary literary symposium of the East.[12]

In 1874, Mrs. Mashkur urged women to seek education and learning to be better qualified in bringing up the new generation and to establish for themselves a place in society. Many other women were active in women's organizations, charity work, and social welfare. These were, for the most part, upper-class intellectuals who wanted to help their less fortunate sisters. It was thanks to their efforts that private organizations addressed themselves from 1851 onwards—long before any government—to social, cultural, and health concerns. They founded schools, hospitals, clinics, orphanages, and centers for needy families.

In 1927, Fatmeh al-Rifai was famous for her literary salon, which became known as the Rifai Symposium. It was regularly held on 13, 14, 15 of the lunar nights, which required some women to sleep during the day to be able to stay up till dawn for literature and poetry. She never wore the veil in mixed audiences.[13]

The first Middle Eastern male to address himself to women's issues and their education was Butros al-Bustani in 1849. He believed that the reformation of the family, the community, and the world starts by reforming and educating women, since he believed woman to be mistress of the universe. Education, however, should be limited to religion, language, reading, geography, history, arithmetic, housework, and rearing of children. It is woman's birthright, as a member of society, to enjoy the same privileges of man in seeking learning and development; just as it is her duty to be a good and virtuous member of society. A woman is not a mere ornament or sex object but has an active role to play. Thus, "educating women is a necessity due to the damage their ignorance would incur on the universe."[14] However, a woman should never rise above man in stature, claim all rights and privileges, or have the illusion that she could be independent of man.[15]

Al-Bustani was followed by Farah Antoun (1874–1922), who asserted that the only way to reform society is through the reformation of women: Their education is even more important than that of men, for the ignorance of women is a sign of backwardness and retrogradation. Women, however, are fragile and should be protected and their education limited to marital and motherly duties.[16]

Walieddin Yakan, influenced by Qassim Amin of Egypt, called for the emancipation of women from men's control, the veil, and imposed marriages. Gibran Khalil Gibran also fought against the enslavement of women and called for their emancipation and the liberation of society as a whole.[17]

An organized women's movement, however, did not get seriously under way in the Arab world until World War I. It was in 1914 that the organization Yaqzat al-fatat al-ʿarabiyyah (Awakening of the Arab girl) was established. Although its primary target was cultural, women addressed themselves to national liberation from the Turks or any other foreign power. In 1919, the first women's conference was held at the Syrian Protestant College (today's American University of Beirut). During the French Mandate, women were employed in many public sectors. Salma Sayigh was the first and only woman to sit for the qualifying examination for all government divisions. She was accepted in the translation sector of the French Delegation, and it was she who translated the Lebanese Declaration of Independence issued by General Goureau in 1920.

World War I left its toll on the Lebanese as a whole, and women demonstrated in the streets crying for bread. A committee of prominent women was formed to address the King-Crane Commission in 1919 calling for independence and denouncing the Balfour Declaration.[18] In 1922, Lebanese women addressed themselves to the new parliament demanding amelioration of women's condition, compulsory education for girls and earmarking a budget for that purpose.

Al-Nahda al-nisaiyyah fi bayrut (Women's renaissance in Beirut) was founded in 1924. Its primary target was equality of the sexes. Consequently, it was active in writing petitions to the government, forming symposia on the subject and lecturing on equality with men. It was also active in supporting the national economy and requesting the establishment of more schools especially in the south in the hope of obliterating illiteracy.[19]

In 1924, *al-Ittihad al-nisa'i fi suriya wa lubnan* (Women's union in Syria and Lebanon) was established with Labibeh Thabet as president. It was a union of all women's organizations in Lebanon and remained the main organization representing the women's movement in Lebanon until 1951. It organized several local and regional conferences and addressed itself to issues in the social, cultural, and political domains, such as the strengthening of the Arabic language in schools, reform of the penal institutions, obliteration of begging and homelessness, cleanliness of bakeries, and the safeguarding of moral values.

In 1943, the committee advocating equal rights for women met the president of the republic and the prime minister, to explain the dire working conditions of the Lebanese woman, and demanded shorter hours and comparable conditions and salaries to men's. In 1945, Saada Nassif was the first woman worker to join the labor union. Women marched in demonstrations for equal opportunity and pay and better work conditions. On September 23, 1946, the new labor law, defining the work conditions of men, women, and children, was promulgated. Although, by the fifties, all doors were opened for women on the individual level, including aviation (one woman) and internal security (three women), on the whole, women were restricted to the domains of teaching, nursing, and services. By 1970, women in the labor force totaled 17.5 percent.

In 1951, the name of the Women's Union was changed to the League of Women Organizations in Lebanon, and in 1952 it was changed to the Lebanese Council of Women and has remained unchanged since. It includes about 130 independent women's societies, associations, organizations, and groups. They represent all regions, confessions, and ideologies. The council is affiliated with the Federation of Arab Women and the International Council of Women. Nineteen percent of all women's organizations antedate 1950, and 36 percent were established after 1980. Most of these organizations confined their work to social matters and charity. Consequently, little was done to improve the inferior condition of women.[20] Furthermore, women seemed to bring their subordinate roles at home to these organizations. Thus the work they did was mostly limited to medical aid, public relations, receptions, food preparation, and so forth. The skills taught women were also limited to sewing, knitting, crocheting, embroidery, and so on. Although there were many women's organizations, there were no feminist movements or organizations.

Women in the Labor Force

The Lebanese women entered the labor force at the turn of the twentieth century. This took place slowly and laboriously and more out of financial need than self-realization or fulfillment. Most worked in the silk industry, because it did not require any particular skills, and were paid half the salary of men. In the period between the two world wars, women entered the public sector as typists and secretaries but soon managed to infiltrate all departments. Professional women, in the private sector, started to increase in number as well—pharmacists, physicians, dentists, and lawyers. In 1932, Nina Trad became the first woman to join the bar association. By 1946, women graduates of the American University of Beirut were 14 physicians, 5 dentists, 53 midwives, 11 pharmacists, and 415 registered nurses and 4 nurses with a Bachelor of Science degree. At the same time, women graduates from the Jesuit University comprised four physicians, thirteen lawyers, and five pharmacists.[21]

Notes

1. *Missionary Herald,* 30 (April 1834), 128.
2. Tristram Seedy, ed., *Daughter of Syria; A Narrative of Efforts by the Late Mrs. Bowen Thompson* (London, 1872), 104.
3. William Goodell, *The Old and the New, or the Changes of Thirty Years in the East, with some Allusions to Oriental Customs as Elucidating Scripture* (New York: Dodd, 1853), 89–90.
4. Jessup, *The Women of the Arabs*, 49.
5. Al-Khatib, *al-Harakah al-nisa'iyyah*, 35–39.
6. For further information, see tables 3.2 and 3.3.
7. For a detailed discussion, cf. also Kiwan, "*al-Waqi' wal murtaja,*" 49–59; Moghaizel, "*Musharakat al-mar'ah,*" 212–215.
8. For a more detailed account, see al-Khatib, *al-Harakah al-nisa'iyyah*, 14–19.
9. Ibid., 128–32.
10. Salman, "Dawr al-'i'lam," 67–85.
11. al-Khatib, *al-Harakah al-nisa'iyyah,* 63–108.
12. Ibid., 80–85.
13. Ibid., 57–62.
14. Qubaysi, *al-Mar'ah fi al-tarikh,* 101–5; al-Khatib, *al-Harakah al-nisa'iyyah,* 30.
15. Literally, "nor should she have the illusion to initiate the actions she was allocated or assigned."
16. Qubaysi, *al-Mar'ah fi al-tarikh,* 114–117.
17. al-Khatib, *al-Harakah al-nisa'iyyah,* 30.
18. The promise of England to establish a national home for the Jews in Palestine.

19. al-Khatib, *al-Harakah al-nisa'iyyah,* 119; al-Sayyid, "al-munazzamat al-nisa'iyyah," 2.

20. For a full discussion of women's organizations, cf. Kiwan, *'Amal al nisa'.*

21. al-Khatib, *al-Harakah al-nisa'iyyah*, 135–42.

II

The Public Sphere

4

Women in the Public Sphere

Lamia Rustum Shehadeh

What was the pride we clung to in times of danger and which helped us to struggle against death, to survive, to keep a hold on what life remained to us? The battles had sapped our strength, and melted the fervor in our hearts. . . . I felt that my reflexes had slowed down as the situation deteriorated. The miracle that we were still alive was still the strongest reflex. . . . What was this miracle? . . . The important thing was to be alive.

Leila Usayran

Work is the factor that underpins man's struggle for survival, advancement, and development; it is the guarantor of his humanity and, therefore, civilization. All work, but especially wage labor, comprises a large segment of one's sense of worth. Conventionally, it is an area regarded as distinct from the domestic sphere, with set hours for each day of each week and month. Hence, work is conceived as the opposite of the "home"; it is the "public" sphere of one's everyday life. It is associated with production and the power of exchange in contradistinction to consumption and leisure time. It is, therefore, wasteful to isolate individuals willing to undertake the tasks society needs to be accomplished through an uneven distribution of power and sexual division of labor. Although women have always played a key role in the survival of their families and, therefore, their societies, and although women have worked longer hours for the fulfillment of a wide gamut of responsibilities, their work is neither publicly acknowledged nor privately applauded or acclaimed. For, work becomes regarded as the domain of the male and the home, the domain of the female. Men became the "breadwinners" and women the "hearth keepers," even when the latter ventured outside the home to help economically. Their paid work was often looked upon as an extension of their roles as mothers and wives, normally defined in such familial terms as motherhood, nurturance, care, and warmth.[1] Many experts have erroneously attributed women's plight to cultural traditions and religious constraints.[2] Yet, there is a consensus that women's participation in the labor force is important both at the macroeconomic and the microeconomic levels, because developing women, in parity with men, as a human resource factor in production development, advances society, contributes to the welfare of the family, develops their personalities, and enhances their stature in society.[3] Interest in the role of women in economic development has increased considerably since the United Nations launched the Women's Decade in Mexico in 1975, which resulted in a number of policy recommendations and research priorities through calling for the integration of women in national development and suggesting ways and means for its application.[4]

Development-conscious experts and planners in the Arab world have for some time been giving more serious attention to the integration of women in national development. A number of conferences and seminars have been held to discuss this and related issues, as well as the ways and means through which women could become more actively involved in the economic development of the Arab world in general and their own societies in particular. Efforts were made to improve women's economic condition through legal enactments and other socially oriented changes. However, the continued low economic activity of women and their persistent high fertility rates, in the Arab countries, may reflect the attachment of Arab societies to the traditional role of women as wives and mothers in a patriarchal family system where their activity is limited to the home. This attachment to tradition and resistance to economic change is bound to lead to the widening of the productivity gap between the two sexes and the inevitable limitation of options for women to enhance their condition. Tradition and culture, however, are not the only bastions in the face of women's development and involvement in the labor force. Other factors, such as illiteracy, lack of training in skills, sexual division of labor and the absence of community supportive services, play an important role in their backwardness and underdevelopment.

Sexual division of labor is not confined to the Arab world. All societies exhibit this phenomenon: There are certain tasks that are normally allocated to women and others to men, while still others are reserved for both. As societies change, causing an alteration in the nature of work, a redistribution of tasks between men and women is observed. This division of labor, naturally, varies from one country to another, but it is immutably manifest in one form or another as a permanent fixture of human society.[5]

However, recognition of women's potential for a multiplicity of roles is growing and new forms of labor planning are being developed. Division of labor is not limited to defining the private-public spheres but occurs within the public arena as well. Thus, women's participation in the labor market is seen as an extension of their role at home. Consequently, they are categorized as naturally inclined to fit secretarial, nursing, and teaching jobs. Sexual division of labor goes on to transcend the wage-earning labor market to manifest itself in the fields of farming and urban self-employment in trading, manufacturing, catering, or child care.

Lebanon is no exception to the picture presented regarding sexual division of labor. Thus the few available studies on the Lebanese labor force in 1970 indicate that women made up 17.5 percent of the economically active population and were employed in traditional occupations of the service sector, such as elementary schoolteachers, nurses, secretaries, and housemaids while comprising 56.4 percent of the total population. Women working in industries, estimated at 20 percent of the work force, were mostly unskilled and worked in the textile and clothes manufacturing industries. The rest, estimated at 23.6 percent, worked as agricultural laborers. On the other hand, most women holding university degrees in literature, social science, and law were unable to obtain appropriate work and often opted for positions not related to their fields of expertise, which naturally resulted in overqualified and underemployed women in the administrative sector. In short, occupations readily available to women normally required less education and vocational training and women, regardless of educational attainment, were confined to a limited number of socially acceptable occupations. The vast majority of working women were poorly paid and single. Most women would stop working upon marriage regardless of their socioeconomic backgrounds.[6] Based on a study on the impact of marriage on women's participation in the labor force conducted by the Lebanese government in collaboration with UNESCO in 1973, it was revealed that 64 percent of the working women were single, 30 percent married, and 6 percent widowed or divorced. Among women who did not work, it was calculated that 18 percent were single, 74 percent married, and 8 percent divorced or widowed.[7] As to the age of working women, those between the ages of twenty and twenty-four ranked highest, followed closely by those aged between twenty-five and twenty-nine.[8] Because marriage is a mainstay of life in Lebanese society, a highly educated woman often finds herself simultaneously at the heart of a male-dominated household and society and at the center of economic activity. She is more often than not forced to sacrifice her job and professional aspirations for the sake of husband and family. The position of women in the Lebanese labor force is thus subject to three major socio-demographic variables, namely, educational attainment, marital status, and residence. Keeping this in mind, it becomes obvious that married women in Lebanon work not as a manifestation of emancipation and economic independence as much as out of economic necessity.[9]

For a long time experts in the field have assumed that the impetus for work has always been related to the value of the paycheck in ratio and proportion to the value of leisure time. In other words, the higher the wages the stronger the motivation for work. Does this hold true in times of war?

The aim of this study then is to review women's participation in the labor force during the years 1975–90 and examine the impact of the war on women's performance in the labor market. Did women remain confined to the private sector or did they venture out once the social strictures were removed and society was in need of their productive potential? Did they join the labor force because of economic necessity or were there other catalytic factors brought on by the atmosphere of war? Aware that the results can only be tentative at present due to lack of comprehensive statistical data and the fact that postwar labor participation is still influenced by the effects of the war, this study is designed as a litmus test or checkpoint for future studies once reliable and cogent data are available.

Lebanon's data base ranks among the world's poorest whether in demographic variables, economic indicators, or socioeconomic data. Lebanon's last census was undertaken in 1932, making it thereby virtually impossible to obtain data about women and work. Thus Lebanon today relies mostly on follow-up surveys for its statistical data. Even these have never been part of a consistent comprehensive plan, but simply a response to emerging needs at specific periods of time. Moreover, during the heavy fighting that erupted between 1975 and 1976 many of the relevant data bases were either completely destroyed or damaged beyond repair. In 1986, the Lebanese Council of Development and Reconstruction carried out an ad hoc industrial census in collaboration with the European Economic Community covering the 11,000 industrial establishments in Lebanon. This was followed, in 1987, by an updating survey which included crafts industries. I have, therefore, relied heavily on already published results and field surveys conducted in preparation for the Fourth World Conference on Women held in 1995 in Beijing.

During the war, some women maintained production on family farms as part of their housework. During a field study conducted by Beirut University College (presently known as Lebanese American University), when one woman was asked if she was working, she answered by giving her daily schedule starting at four in the morning and ending at eight in the evening, consisting of working in the field most of the day, and she added, "as you see, my dear, my hands are full and have no time to work"! Other women dressed like men and fought at their side in the battlefield, while still others followed the troops from one front to another, preparing food, shelter, and clothing for the soldiers. In addition to these, others, silently, participated in the labor force.

The sixteen years of war that ravaged Lebanon naturally had an adverse effect on the economy. In 1990, the gross domestic product expressed at constant prices, and estimated at $ 2.6 billion, was less than one half of what it used to be prior to the war. The monthly minimum wage dropped from $245 in 1983 to $70 in 1990, while the minimum expenditure for a family of five was estimated at $313: $150 for food, $123 for fixed expenditures and $40 for miscellaneous expenses. Another cataclysmic effect of the war has been the displacement of large numbers of Lebanese families, estimated in 1991 at 22.5 percent of the resident population (excluding voluntary migration); the high level of emigration during 1975–91, estimated at 520,000 Lebanese, represents 17 percent of the total resident population of 1991. As a result, the Lebanese labor market became fragmented and lost the bulk of its skilled and qualified labor.[10] Furthermore, adding to the damage were the 150,000 war casualties representing about 6 percent of the resident population. This was compounded by lack of electricity and running water, transforming women into experts on water and energy conservation. Women were further affected by the death of male relatives, kidnapping, emigration, detention, and displacement, placing the burden of survival on their shoulders. A field survey revealed that 26 percent of widows were solely responsible for the survival of their families.[11] During the war, when some neighborhoods were transformed into battlefields and neighbors faced one another in combat, many men were obliged to stay home for fear of their lives, while their wives had to go out in search of temporary or permanent jobs. Sewing, handwork, house-sitting for absentee owners and house cleaning, catering, and many other avenues of work became emergency occupations for women, who viewed themselves as homemakers with no experience in the labor market, and who were desperate to find means of survival for their families.[12] Displaced mothers or homemakers struggled to bridge the gap between work in the home and in the marketplace, between life in the private sphere of the family and the public sphere of economics and politics. They had to make this move abruptly and without any preparation. But the entry into the labor market did not relieve them of housework and child care. They simply worked longer hours to fit the added work in.

Simply put, the war made life not only dangerous and hazardous, but extremely difficult. Since the war front was next door, there was a permanent sense of danger and lack of security, and the basic domestic facilities were hit hardest. Food supplies had to be secured under uncertain conditions, water had to be located and then carried to all floors, and electricity became a luxury of the past. Women had thus to rely on primitive and other resourceful means to secure their needs. Sending children to school suddenly became an ordeal for parent and child. Carrying plastic bags to replace their handbags, afraid of mugging, women walked through the danger zones expecting death at every instant. I remember my own tribulations as I walked to work, every day wondering whether I would make it or not; and every day I rejoined my family was a new day, a new life, a new birth. Women's major achievement was to hold together the collapsing structures of Lebanese society. They patched up the lack of adequate social and medical services by volunteering to work in both national and international social welfare organizations. Women reopened schools and resumed education of the children after a long period of closure. They dealt with all traumatic situations and reactions of children and students caused by war conditions.[13] Daily life was thus transformed into a nonending nightmare, the hallmarks of which were fear and anxiety. Violence had gradually imposed its own law in a new reality that had supplanted the older reality of routine and tranquility. Even when the nightmare seemed to recede during periods of illusory peace, the shadow of manifold violence never disappeared. Thus the public space was transformed into a "mine-field,"[14] where car bombs or any other form of explosives were commonplace, shelling developed its own capricious nature, the right of might ruled the day, and the spontaneous eruption of intracommunal fighting made venturing into the public space suicidal. The unpredictability of the future made planning virtually impossible and frequent interruption of activities weighed heavily on efficiency and sense of continuity, leading, thereby, to apathy, discouragement, and lack of productivity. But the Lebanese, especially the women, learned to cope, always ready to improvise and start from scratch. Life was made even more difficult for those, the majority of whom were women, due to the high risk of male kidnapping, who had to cross from one sector of the city to another for the sniper and blind rocket were always waiting. The dread of the struggle in open and unprotected areas during the day and dark streets during the night hung over many workers all the time, adding considerably to the strain of life. After a while, this led many to take lodgings near their work and away from their families. Housing became a problem as many buildings were demolished and lodging became very expensive. In the bitter cold and rain during winter and the scorching heat of the summer, women and children queued outside bakeries and water stations.

Soon the term "accordion day"[15] came to describe the dual role of women very well. They had to fulfill all household chores and adapt themselves to all external duties such as taking children to school and be ready to bring them back at short notice due to shelling or intracommunal fighting, taking them for recreation, shopping for food, providing gas, water and candles, and health services, and, last but not least, going to work. "Accordion day" also implies the virtual impossibility of having a fixed schedule or defining the time that housework entails. What emerges is an incredibly long working day, intensified by family demands and relationships. A woman neighbor once complained to me about the dual role she had to play. When I commented that a woman in those days had to work like an ox, she smiled while strongly disapproving of equating her with the ox. "In contrast to the ox who sleeps at night, my dear, I have to entertain my husband and play the role of his mistress; my day never ends." What I failed to tell her at the time was that it was precisely this ability to adjust to both roles, the attention to basic needs and the trivial details of relationships, that had helped guarantee survival on the physical and human levels. Laura Balbo, through her analysis of how women manage to do their service work and hold together a fragmented society, uses the metaphor "patchwork quilt" to describe how women through their hard work, intelligence, planning, and creativity hold society together by resorting to cheap, flexible, and interchangeable service work, in exactly the same way as design, logic, and order are created out of a patchwork quilt, which in turn entails hard work, long hours, patience, and repetition and is resorted to in times of economic scarcity.[16]

Lebanese women worked tirelessly at their "quilts," trying to produce balance and harmony.

One-quarter of the Lebanese resident population were displaced at least once during the war either transiently or permanently in their search for security and relative stability. By the end of the war 450,000 were still displaced, 52.6 percent of their homes had been completely destroyed, 27.4 percent partially, while 20.1 percent of homes were not habitable. Between 1975 and 1976, 300,000 persons were displaced, 150,000, between 1978 and 1979, 200,000, in 1982, and in 1989–90, 160,000 had to look elsewhere for security.[17] A study conducted by St. Joseph University showed that 43 percent of the houses occupied by the displaced consisted of one or two rooms; 11.7 percent of the families lived in homes that had no running water; while 9.2 percent of occupied dwellings had no kitchens. Other families found refuge in offices, factories, commercial centers, and underground parking facilities. Of all displaced individuals, 29.1 percent had to share their rooms with at least two others, while 8.7 percent had to cohabit with strangers.[18]

Given these economic and social setbacks, the Lebanese woman did not hesitate to enter the labor market in her determination to ensure survival of the family. But although economic need seems to be the primary incentive for women's participation in the labor force, it is important to note that a survey conducted by ESCWA showed that 31.5 percent of the women working in the informal sector did so because they enjoyed working, and 71 percent of the women questioned in the Nabatiyyeh region of southern Lebanon wanted to keep on working because it had enabled them "to secure a place (for themselves) in society."[19]

Education

It is still unclear whether educational attainment is the cause of women's progress or its consequence. But, although education has not helped women obtain social or political gains, it has certainly helped them in invading the economy: The more education a woman has, the more likely she is to be employed. Prior to the war, more Lebanese men attended college than women. Parents were more ready to encourage and finance the education of their sons rather than their daughters. In the past twenty years of war and postwar trauma, the proportion of women going to college has increased considerably (table 4.1). The educational sector in Lebanon involves one-third of the Lebanese population. The private sector has always played a predominant role in education at all levels. Students registered in private schools in 1993–94 comprised about 69.4 percent of the total national student enrollment, in contrast to 58.0 percent in 1973–74.[20] Despite the increasingly high tuition fees for good schools and universities, female enrollment in universities increased from 25.2 percent in 1973 to 48.2 percent in 1993. This increase has been attributed to the opening of branches, by most universities, in the different regions of Lebanon, making it, thereby, easier for female students to pursue higher learning without leaving home. Most of these students, however, study literature, the humanities, education, and the social sciences, which would prepare them for socially acceptable employment in the service sector.[21]

Table 4.1. Student enrollment in major universities

University	1973–74			1982–83			1993–94		
	Male	Female	Total	Male	Female	Total	Male	Female	Total
Lebanese Univ.	10,756	4,070	14,826	14,312	12,835	27,147	16,918	19,585	36,503
American Univ. of Beirut	3,224	1,395	4,619	2,922	2,033	4,955	2,606	2,329	4,935
Arab Univ.	20,036	4,852	24,888	22,352	6,640	28,992	10,021	5,397	15,418
St. Joseph Univ.	1,982	994	2,976	2,485	2,686	5,171	2,282	3,281	5,563
Lebanese American Univ.	0	347	347	880	965	1,845	2,272	1,807	4,079
Holy Spirit Univ. Kaslik	427	109	536	1,577	1,244	2,821	1,101	1,319	2,420
Other universities	1,149	826	1,985	1,299	822	2,121	3,561	2,331	5,892
Total	37,574	12,593	15,827	4,582	27,225	73,052	38,761	36,049	74,810
Percent	74.8	25.2	100.0	62.7	37.3	100.0	51.8	48.2	100.0

Al-Amine, *al-Ta'lim fi lubnan*, 189–91.

The military events that unfolded in 1975 in Lebanon marked a turning point in Lebanese attitudes towards female education and employment. The war seems to have highlighted the importance of developing human resources and the negation of traditional and deeply entrenched beliefs regarding the education of women and their employment. Thus, while female education before the war was limited to the affluent and/or educated families, by the 1980s it had become a necessity for women of all social strata. Major factors in this dramatic change were the reduction of Lebanon's financial resources and the deterioration of the purchasing power of the Lebanese currency, which required the integration of women into the labor force. The Lebanese woman, due to the effects of the war, has become a full partner in family economics and, often, its sole provider. The war also caused many men to emigrate in search of better work opportunities leaving a void in the local labor market, which women tried to fill.

Despite the war, or rather because of it, many public and private schools were opened in the different regions to accommodate the waves of interregional displacement and the consequent creation of new de facto urban centers. The spread of secondary education among girls made college education seem within reach. The mushrooming of more than one campus of private and public universities in different regions helped women, who had been prevented from leaving home for faraway campuses for family and financial reasons, to enter college.

Education in Lebanon is covered by the public and private sectors. Registration figures show that in the preschool stage girls made up 48 percent of the total student population during the years 1981–94 and the same proportion holds at the elementary level (table 4.2). At the intermediate and secondary levels, girls made up 52 percent and 52.76 percent, respectively, while in higher education, the ratio of women students increased from 35.94 percent in 1980–81 to 48.18 percent in 1992–93.[22] This increase in the number of highly educated women has, needless to say, affected the labor market. The proportion of 3.3 percent of highly educated women in the economically active population of 1970–75 increased to 9.3 percent in 1990. Thus, the percentage of highly educated women has risen from 1 percent of the total Lebanese population in 1970–75 to 1.7 percent in 1980, 2.5 percent in 1985, and 2.8 percent in 1990. In absolute terms the number of educated women tripled between 1975 and 1990. What is also of interest is that the ratio of the highly educated of both sexes has dropped from 4.6 in favor of men in 1970 to 1.3 in 1990. With this increase in the number of highly educated women came an increase in the diversity of job availability for women.[23] What also changed during the war years is age distribution. Thus, in contrast to the period before the war, where the heaviest concentration fell between the ages of twenty and twenty-four, the age group had risen to twenty to forty-four years by 1990. The evolution that has taken place in the social and economic conditions of women in Lebanon is further evidenced by the disproportionality observed in the rate of growth of the female population of 1.2 percent per year (1975–90) and that of the economically active population of 2.3 percent per year. The correlation between higher education and economic activity becomes even more evident in the increase of the percentage of highly educated women in the economically active female population from 17.4 percent in 1975 to 50.7 percent in 1990. This increase implies that most newly graduated females are absorbed in the labor market.[24] However, although this percentage grew from 1970 to 1990, the number of highly educated employed females grew from 6.5 percent of the total active population in 1970 to only 24 percent in 1990. This withdrawal of females from the labor market may be attributed to marriage.

Economic Activity

The distribution of highly educated women in the labor market has been observed to concentrate in two sectors: community and social services on the one hand and trade, restaurants, and hotels on the other. The concentration in the first sector may be attributed to the country's needs that tended to rise as a result of the conflagration of violence, namely, in 1975, 1978, 1982, and 1989. Women thus tended to enroll in such fields as medicine, nursing, midwifery, teaching, social work, and other types of civil assistance. The ages of such active women ranged between twenty and

Table 4.2. Registered female students

Level	1972–73			1981–82			1991–92		
	Total	Female	%	Total	Female	%	Total	Female	%
Kindergarten	112,535	52,338	46.51	120,431	57,509	47.75	131,074	63,727	48.62
Elementary	385,188	178,295	46.28	398,977	183,029	45.88	345,662	167,607	48.49
Intermediate	132,151	59,065	44.70	178,908	91,211	50.98	184,926	97,195	52.56
Secondary	35,427	13,769	38.87	71,120	37,099	52.16	63,171	34,157	54.07

Based on Department of Statistics, *General Statistics for Education (1972–73)*, and a field study conducted in 1994 for *The National Report* in preparation for the Fourth World Conference on Women in Beijing. See also al-Amine, *al-Ta'lim fi lubnan*, 177–80.

forty years. The total number of this group grew each year at a rate of 5.5 percent out of a total annual growth of 15.5 percent, reflecting thereby the deep concern of these women regarding their environment. The increase in the number of highly educated women in the second sector of trade (wholesale and retail), restaurants and hotels, in 1990 was estimated at nine times what it was in 1975. Women's participation in the manufacturing sector, however, has not been as dramatic. Although the annual growth rate of their participation was 3.5 percent between 1970 and 1990, the sex ratio was still high at 7.5 in 1990, compared with 10 in 1970.[25]

Due to the political and security instability in the country, highly educated women veered away from the sector of finance, insurance, real estate, and business services. Thus, while the female labor supply had doubled in these fields in 1975, they decreased drastically in 1980 but rose again slightly in 1990. The sex ratio has then decreased by only 1.6 percent—from 5 percent in 1970 to 3.4 percent in 1990.[26]

In the category of professions (medicine, engineering, pharmacy, law, teaching), the economically active population followed a normal trend over the twenty-year period of 1970–90. However, the number of women in this category doubled, particularly during the years 1980–90 (table 4.3). This increase reflects the social, demographic, and economic changes brought on by the war, including, as mentioned earlier, displacement, spread of university campuses across the country, economic hardship, and removal of strictures on female education. The most prominent specialties in this category are medicine, pharmacy, and education.[27] The Order of Physicians in Beirut and in the north of Lebanon showed an increase in the number of women doctors from 6.9 percent in 1980 to 14.36 percent in 1994; the number in the Order of Pharmacists increased from 36 percent in 1980 to 51 percent in 1994; the enrollment of women in the bar association also rose from 5.8 percent in 1980 to 24.3 percent in 1994; but although the number of women engineers and architects rose from 0.2 percent in 1980 to 6.78 percent in 1994, it still remains very low.[28] Although 33 percent of all employees in the Ministry of Education are

Table 4.3. Women in the professions (in percentages)

	1980	1993
Physicians	6.9	14.36
Pharmacists	36	51
Lawyers	5.8	24.3
Engineers/architects	0.2	6.78

women, those registered in 1994 for a teaching diploma at the elementary level in public schools constitute 100 percent of the total body of students, 80.20 percent at the intermediate level and 35.92 percent at the secondary level. Finally, the number of women on the faculty of the Lebanese University rose from 16.73 percent in 1982–83 to 21.21 percent in 1992–93.[29]

The data available indicate that a salient increase in the number of women has taken place in the banking sector (table 4.4). Thus, whereas the rate of female participation in 1975 was 26 percent of the total population, it rose to 37 percent by 1992—the absolute figure being 5,215 women, only 10 of whom are in decision-making positions.[30]

In the commercial and industrial sectors we find an increase in female-owned businesses from 18.9 percent in 1985 to 22.6 percent in 1994, mainly in the clothing industry. Participation in public institutions rose from 6.3 percent in 1985 to 9.3 percent in 1994, the rise being more pronounced in private institutions—from 11 percent in 1985 to 19 percent in 1994. This reflects the ever-increasing female awareness, skills, and training as well as the increasing initiative of private institutions to tap this new developing pool of talent and skills.[31]

Women in Lebanon, as has become evident, are to be found in a number of key positions, from which they are able to wield influence on the quantity and quality of the labor force. They are mothers and housewives in the private sphere and professionals in the public sphere and leaders of nongovernmental organizations; yet they have almost no presence as policy makers in the government or in decision-making positions in the public domain as a whole, including the very important economic one. Thus, of all labor, trade, teaching, and professional unions and syndicates, only two women were elected as heads of unions, namely the pharmacists' and the publishers' in 1994, and only one served on the board of the Order of Engineers, one on the board of the bar association and two on the

Table 4.4. Women in the banking sector

	1975	1980	1985	1990	1991	1992
Number	8,522	10,510	13,993	15,062	15,194	14,075
Females	2,197	3,198	4,785	5,473	5,569	5,215
Percent	26	30	32	36.3	36.7	37.1

Based on an unpublished study prepared by Fadia Kiwan and Fahmiyyeh Charafeddin for *The National Report*.

board of the pharmacists' union amounting to a symbolic representation (tables 4.5, 4.6). This absence from policy-making positions is mostly due to deeply ingrained traditional and cultural values that even the war could not diminish.

Traditional and cultural values, however, are not the only constraints on economically active women. The government, through its legislation of "protective" laws and other laws curbing the work benefits of women in contrast to those of men, has placed obstacles in the way of women to economic independence. Protective legislation, under the guise of helping the fragile woman, has actually made it more difficult for her to compete for jobs or to earn a living wage. Thus the labor law in Lebanon has a special section for women and children: It is incumbent upon every employer to notify the government when hiring women or children. Women and children are further prohibited from working in such areas as mines and quarries, industrial ovens, use of mercury, preparation of explosives, glass production, alcohol preparation, spray painting, extraction of silver from lead, production of aluminum and other such metals, driving equipment with huge motors, cement, tanneries, organic fertilizers, and skinning of animals.[32] While all public employees on tenure are entitled to a pension, which passes on to spouse and children after death,

Table 4.5. Women in executive councils of syndicates, 1994

	No. of members	Females	Percentage
Press Syndicate	12	1 (1990)	8.3
Editors' Syndicate	12	—	0
Total	24	1	

Table 4.6. Participation of women on the boards of professional unions, 1994

	Number	Women	Percentage
Board of Engineering Union	12	1	8.3
Board of the Order of Dentists	12	—	0
Board of the Order of Physicians	12	—	0
Board of the Bar Association (Beirut chapters)	12	1	8.3
Board of the Union of Pharmacists	9	2	22.2

Based on an unpublished study prepared by Fadia Kiwan and Fahmiyyeh Charafeddin for *The National Report*.

a married woman cannot bequeath her pension to her children and husband, unless the latter can prove poverty or physical incapacity. A female employee can receive compensation for her spouse and children only if she is the breadwinner of the family due to the death of the husband, his incapacity, or his absence from the country without any communication for a period of not less than a year, or if she is a divorcée and her ex-husband is incapable of paying alimony. A married woman is granted only 50 percent of medical expenses for her children while her male peer is entitled to 75 percent. The coup de grâce of the Lebanese law against married working women, however, is dealt when she is pregnant. Thus, while a man has to have worked for at least three months out of the six months prior to the date of delivery of his wife to be eligible for maternal insurance, a woman, in addition to the above, has to have been enrolled in the Social Security for a period of not less than ten months before the date of delivery.[33] This discriminatory legislation can only reflect the traditional concept of the male as the only breadwinner of the family.

It is evident from the preceding survey that the participation of women in the labor force rose considerably during the years of the war. Whereas the economically active population in 1970–75 included 17.5 percent of the female population, female participation increased steadily during the war until it reached 27.8 percent in 1990 (table 4.7). While, admittedly, this is still below that of industrialized countries, it is the highest in the Arab world. This rise in the work force may be attributed to three major factors: the wider options opened to women, the imposition of more pressure on them to ensure the maintenance or survival of their families, and the need of the economy for a type of labor women can provide. Although most women had to bring in an income at the end of the day, the job signified more than just survival. Many women, and not only in better-paid and professional occupations, have gained a sense of worth and self-confidence through their work; 38 percent of those questioned affirmed they worked for self-realization and only 37 percent ad-

Table 4.7. Economically active population, by gender

	1970		1980		1990	
	No.	%	No.	%	No.	%
Males	533,000	80.96	571,000	79.96	660,000	72.20
Females	125,000	29.04	171,000	23.04	254,000	27.80

United Nations, *World Demographic Estimates*, 288.

mitted economic necessity. Pressure has increased on women to make up or provide the family wage. A vicious circle of debt, displacement, widowhood, divorce, destruction of homes, kidnapping, or emigration of husbands has placed the heaviest burden on women. As prices rose and incomes fell, due mainly to the catastrophic devaluation of Lebanese currency, women had to work longer hours and diversify their activities to ensure their families' survival.

The Media

The 1865 protocol signed by the Five Great Powers (England, France, Prussia, Russia, and Austria) provided an atmosphere of freedom in Lebanon.[34] This freedom, coupled with the development of the Lebanese educational system and the availability of printing (1610—Syriac; 1733—Arabic), paved the way for Lebanon to become the cradle of Arab journalism. Khalil al-Khuri, a former director of publications in the Ottoman administration, published the first popular Arabic newspaper in Lebanon and the Arab world, namely, *Hadiqat al-akhbar* (The garden of news).[35] Shortly after, a series of Arabic newspapers, edited mostly by Lebanese intellectuals and men of letters, made their appearance in Lebanon and abroad. One such newspaper was *Nafir suriya* (The call of Syria) published by Butros al-Bustani in 1860; another was *al-ʿajaʾib* (The unusual news or events), published by Fares al-Shidyak in Istanbul, which became, for thirty-three years, the most prominent newspaper of its time; a third paper was that of Rashid Dahdah, published in Paris in the same year under the name *Barid baris* (The mail of Paris). All these, however, were weekly publications. The first daily paper, published in Lebanon in 1894, was *al-Ahwal* (The conditions).[36]

During the first period of the Lebanese press, 1858–76, the newspapers' aim was mainly cultural and educational as indicated by the background of their founders and contributors. Between 1876 and 1914, however, the Lebanese press geared itself toward politics, catalyzed by a period of persecution and suppression of freedom during the reign of Sultan Abdul Hamid II (1876–1908), who declared martial law, abolished all existing press regulations, and imposed a strict censorship on the press. Consequently, many journalists fled to Egypt where they enjoyed greater freedom of expression and contributed greatly to the flourishing of the Egyptian press by founding and publishing such important newspapers as *al-Muqattam*, *al-Ahram*, *al-Muqtataf*, and *al-Musawwar*. Others fled to the Americas and Europe, where they founded and published newspapers addressed to the immigrants. Those who remained in Lebanon stressed

Arab nationalism and resistance to Ottoman rule in their publications. With the advent of World War I, journalism in Lebanon came virtually to an end due to the siege imposed by the Ottomans on Lebanon that resulted in famine and scarcity of paper.[37]

By the end of World War I and the French occupation of Lebanon, in 1918, a new era of journalism dawned, and on May 26, 1923, Article 13 of the Lebanese Constitution granted the Lebanese citizen freedom of expression, freedom of publication, and freedom to form societies or associations.

The field of journalism during these three periods, however, was not limited to men (table 4.8). Hind Nawfal published the first woman's magazine, *al-Fatat* (The girl), in Alexandria, Egypt in 1892–93. She wrote, "*al-Fatat* is the only journal for women in the East; it expresses their thoughts, discloses their inner minds, fights for their rights, searches for their literature and science, and takes pride in publishing the products of their pens."[38] In 1906, Labibeh Hashim, journalist and owner of *Fatat al-sharq* (Girl of the east), emphasized the educative role of journalism when she said, "It is indubitable that newspapers are the greatest educators of the nation and the best measure of purity. They are that second school entrusted with enlightening the mind and reforming the rules of decorum and morality."[39] Mary Mokarzil published the first political Arabic daily in New York, *al-Huda* (The guide), and was followed by her colleague Afifeh Karam, who published her own magazine, *al-ʿAlam al-jadid al-nisaʾiyyah* (Women's new world), in 1912.[40] The first political publication in Lebanon, however, was to be published by Rose al-Yusuf, *Roz al-yusuf,* in 1925.[41]

Unfortunately, this plethora of female publications did not seem to last long as may be gleaned from a speech given by Ibtihaj Kaddourah, a woman activist and president of the Lebanese Council of Women, in 1928: "I have no alternative but to mention the lack of support and interest encountered by Arab female journalism during the last five years. This has placed obstacles in its way, depleted its energy and brought it to a stop at a time when each of us should have done her best to pave the way for the development and success of female journalism and to support those in charge to reach their objectives in life."[42] This, however, did not stultify the Lebanese woman and, in 1938, Alvira Lattouf was the first woman to publish a political newspaper, *al-Mustaqbal* (The future), in Lebanon.

After independence in 1943, Lebanon slowly became the economic and diplomatic center of the Arab east. The flow of money and technological development led to the increased importance of Lebanese journalism and it became widespread in the Arab world. Slowly, it became the forum of

Table 4.8. Lebanese women journalists and their publications

Name	Year	Publication	Place
Hind Nawfal	1892–93	*al-Fatat* (Girl)	Cairo
Louisa Hbaline	1896	*al-Firdaws* (Paradise)	Cairo
Mariam Zezher	1896	*Mir'at al-hasna'* (Mirror of the beautiful)	Cairo
Alexandra Afrino	1898	*Anis al-jalis* (The entertainer)	Cairo
Esther Moyal	1899	*al-'Ailah* (The family)	Cairo
Aniseh Atallah	1901	*al-Mar'ah* (Woman)	Cairo
Rogina Awwad	1902–3	*al-Sa'adah* (Happiness)	Cairo
Mariam Saad	1902	*al-Zahrah* (The flower)	Cairo
Rose Antoun	1903	*al-Sayyidat wal-banat* (Ladies and girls)	Cairo
Marie Farah	1903	*al-Sayyidat wal-banat* (Ladies and girls)	Alexandria
Labibeh Hashim	1906	*Fatat al-sharq* (Girl of the east)	Cairo
Malakeh Saad	1908	*al-Jins al-latif* (The gentle sex)	Egypt
Afifeh Karam	1911	*al-Mar'ah al-suriyyah* (The Syrian woman)	Lebanon
	1912	*Murshid al-atfal* (Children's guide)	Lebanon
	1912	*al-'Alam al-jadid an-nisa'iy* (Woman's new world)	New York
Sulayman Abi-Rashid	1914	*Fatat lubnan* (The girl of Lebanon)	Beirut
Salwa Atlas	1914	*al-Karmah* (The vineyard)	Sao Paulo
Mary Yanni	1917	*Minerva*	Beirut
Mariam Zimmar	1919	*Fatat al-watan* (Girl of the homeland)	Lebanon
Afifeh Saab	1919	*al-Khidr* (Boudoir)	Lebanon
Najla Abillama'	1919	*al-Fajr* (Dawn)	Beirut
Julia Tomeh Dimishkiyyeh	1921	*al-Mar'ah al-jadidah* (The new woman)	Beirut
Habboubeh Haddad	1921	*al-Hayat al-jadidah* (The new life)	Paris-Beirut
Rose Antoun Haddad	1922	*al-Sayyidat wal-rijal* (Ladies and men)	Cairo
Amineh Khoury Makdisi	1923	*Mawrid al-ahdahth* (Source of news)	Beirut
Rose al-Yusuf	1925	*Roz al-yusuf*	Cairo
Mariam Zakka	1932	*al-Jami'ah* (The university)	Lebanon
Alvira Lattouf	1938	*al-Mustaqbal* (The future)	Tripoli (Lebanon)

the whole region where political, ideological and economic battles were fought. The coup d'état in Egypt, in 1952, and the consequent political and economic instability hindered the Egyptian print media from reaching the rest of the Arab world losing, thereby, their pan-Arab role. The Lebanese press was quick to take over and assume leadership.

It was not, however, until September 14, 1962, that a new press law clearly defining the role of journalism was introduced. It organized the profession, guaranteed freedom of the press with minimal state censorship, and delineated the boundaries of this freedom. To limit the possibility of state censorship during periods of national crises, a voluntary national association was set up by the Press Council to impose self-censorship. The period between 1962 and 1975 became the golden age of Lebanese journalism as it gained preeminence in the Arab world and was sought after by local, regional, and international trends and movements. This, however, was not a bed of roses for many Lebanese journalists, who, in their attempt to convey information to their readers, lost their lives, such as Nassib al-Matni, Fuad Haddad, Ghandour Karam, Kamil Mroueh, Edward Saab, and others.

This period of journalistic prosperity was not confined to men. Women journalists and reporters were active in the field and exhibited their professionalism in Arabic, English, and French. Some were Mary Dwein who published in French *La femme* (Woman), Aurore Trad Ou-gourlian, owner of the magazine *Phoenicia,* and Dunia Mroueh, editor in chief of the English *Daily Star.* Other reporters were Nelly Helou, Nuhad Azar, Eileen Lahhoud, Eliane Jebara, and Marie Thérèse Abboud. Among reporters writing in Arabic were Edvique Shayboub, editor in chief of the two magazines *Sawt al-mar'ah* (Woman's voice) and *Dunya al-mar'ah* (Woman's world), Nora Nuwayhid, owner and editor in chief of *Dunya al-mar'ah,* Emily Nasrallah, Majida Attar, and many others.[43]

The final phase of Lebanese journalism came in 1975: While journalism until 1975 was aggressively expanding and developing by asking for more freedom and privileges and dominating all the Arab world, the war brought on a new period of withdrawal and self-imposed limitations produced by the political and economic pressures of the war, as well as the shrinkage of its areas of distribution. Many reporters emigrated and many newspapers closed down. However, around three hundred illegal, sectarian and partisan publications were spawned all over Lebanon.[44] By the end of the war, in 1991, Lebanon had 105 licensed political publications (53 daily papers, 48 weeklies, and 4 monthly magazines) as well as over 300 nonpolitical publications for a population of 3 million. Out of the 105, seven are in French, four in Armenian, and three in English. Ten of these are dailies and the rest are weeklies. Some of the nonpolitical publications, of which more than 170 are in Arabic, appear either in French, Armenian, or English. In addition, Lebanon has 28 licensed local news agencies and 10 offices of regional and international news agencies.[45]

As shown in table 4.9, the number of women owners of political publications is very low, while owners of nonpolitical publications represent a greater number. Thus, while the former comprised 1.9 percent of the total number in 1984, the latter reached 8.9 percent in 1989. Both percentages declined in 1995 to 1.8 percent and 8.3 percent, respectively.[46] This decline in percentage and not in actual number could be attributed to women's lack of financial resources in comparison with men. The number of women reporters, however, far exceeds these figures, since they are employees and do not have to rely on personal wealth or inheritance to achieve such positions. Thus, the percentage of women reporters in the five most highly distributed papers is 32 percent as shown in table 4.10.[47]

It is difficult to know the exact number of women reporters or commentators since the only figures we have are those provided by the press

Table 4.9. Women's ownership of publications

Type of publication	Total	Women	Percentage
Political (1984) (daily, weekly, monthly)	103	2	1.9
Daily (1995)	109	2	1.8
Nonpolitical (1989)	604	54	8.9
Nonpolitical (1992)	938	95	10.1
Nonpolitical (1995)	1,300	109	8.3

Najah al-Abdallah, "The Role of Women in the Media" (unpublished).

Table 4.10. Distribution of women reporters, 1994

Newspaper	Reporters	Female reporters	Percentage
al-Nahar	115	35	24
al-Safir	42	12	23
al-Anwar	35	35	50
al-Diyar	125	75	35
al-Liwa'	74	28	27

Based on Nur Salman's unpublished study.

Table 4.11. Women in decision-making positions, 1994

Position	Total	Females	Percentage
Members of press syndicate	1,107	218	19.6
Directors of political publications	109	7	6.4
Editors-in-chief	109	1	0.9
Total	1,325	226	

and few women join syndicates or unions in Lebanon. However, based on these lists, we find that 19.6 percent of reporters are women, 6.4 percent of directors of political publications are women, and only 0.9 percent of editors in chief of political publications are women (table 4.11).

Women's participation in the media was not limited to the written domain but transcended it to the audio-visual as well. The first radio broadcasting station in Lebanon was established by the French in 1938. It continued to be a government monopoly until 1975, when different militias and parties established their own private stations illegally. It was private enterprise, however, that introduced television to Lebanon in the latter half of the fifties: On May 28, 1959, the first television company in the Arab world, La Compagnie Libanaise de Television, SAL, inaugurated its service and began transmission, and on May 6, 1962, the Compagnie de Television du Liban et du Proche-Orient (Tele Orient) started transmission. Bankruptcy due to the war gave birth to a new company, the Lebanese Television Company (Tele Liban), on December 3, 1977, by Legislative Decree No. 770. Tele Liban was given monopoly over television broadcasting in Lebanon. The government owned 50 percent of the company. But, once again, broadcasting did not remain a monopoly for long and, in 1985, the Lebanese Broadcasting Company (LBC) went on the air during the month of October and became the leading television station in Lebanon in terms of technology, variety of programs, news coverage, and size of its audience. In 1990, it was followed by al-Mashrek. After the Taif Agreement, and within a matter of months, forty-two television stations and 186 radio stations were set up. Article 382 of the Law of Information issued on November 10, 1994, legalized private broadcasting.[48]

While the percentage of women in government radio broadcasting and television stations is rather low, though much higher than before the war, the number of women in the private sector ranges between 25 and 50 percent in radio broadcasting stations and 50 percent in television broadcasting. The number, for example, of all employees at the LBC is six hundred (1994), half of them being women, participating in all domains: announcing, news coverage, production and direction of programs, as well as the executive council, which comprises eleven men and three women.[49]

This onslaught by women on the media is best illustrated by the number of women students registered in the Faculty of Information and Documentation at the Lebanese University during the years 1982–83 through 1990–91, where women make up 75 percent of the total number of students (table 4.12). This could be the result of several factors, such as the increase of media outlets in the private sector and the availability of work opportunities, the technological development of the media and consequent importance in society, the impact of the media on individuals, and television stardom.

Conclusion

Although the gap between the occupational positions of men and women is still wide as in all other Arab countries, female progress in the professions has been significantly increased as is apparent from their enrollment in the respective syndicates, which is a requirement for practicing one's profession in Lebanon. This has been due, mainly, to the changes brought about in the level of education made possible by the freedom ushered in by the war. Thus, women, in varying degrees, were found working in almost all fields, including the military, and as parking attendants and mechanics. This was further aided by the increased acceptance, by parents, of their daughters' mobility even before marriage, the wider spectrum of education afforded teenage girls, better educational opportunities due to the spread and diversification of higher education institutions

Table 4.12. Number of registered students at the School of Information

School year	Total number	Women	Percentage
1982–83	589	435	73.8
1983–84	498	400	80.3
1984–85	891	732	82.1
1985–86	1017	821	80.7
1986–87	1058	842	79.5
1987–88	686	562	81.9
1988–89	400	348	87.0
1989–90		Canceled due to war	
1990–91	899	680	75.6

Based on Najah Abdallah, "The Role of Women in the Media."

across the various regions of Lebanon, and the widening of the female employment spectrum.

Unfortunately, although the sexual division of labor in its traditional garb has been greatly relaxed, it has continued to manifest itself in the access to decision-making positions and the higher salary scales. Women are still placed in the less responsible, less secure, and less well-paid jobs; even where an occupation is predominantly female such as teaching, it is men who are found in managerial positions. Women are still underpaid in Lebanon in almost all positions. In fact, the minister of industry, Dr. Asʿad Rizk, in an interview on August 17, 1994, conducted by the *al-Nahar* daily, declared that his problems in the ministry would be partially resolved by hiring women to fill vacant positions, since being accustomed to self-sacrifice, they would tend to accept lower salaries.

Finally, it is evident from the preceding survey that once legal, social, and administrative obstacles are removed, women are capable of penetrating all domains of the public sphere as the equals of men. More and more women have found the courage to step into the unknown, paving the way for others to follow in their footsteps. New pathways have become visible and alternatives to the classical and traditional roles are attractively presented. Together with the emergence of an ideology of equality and the increase of families who treat their daughters as equal to their sons, women will have a strong incentive to plan for careers. In Lebanon, where living well is the goal of the whole society, economic pressures are often strong enough to push families to send their women to work. This exposure to work may help women become interested in lifetime careers, for women who enter the work arena without any plans for a career may continue to work even beyond economic necessity and thus rise within the hierarchy. Factors that may seduce women to work could range from a challenging and self-engrossing job, self-satisfaction, and realization, to high economic rewards and growth of the enterprise with which they had become associated, in addition to growth of self-esteem, pride, confidence, and sense of accomplishment.

One must be realistic, however, and keep in mind the factors that could affect women negatively and make them withdraw from the public sphere. The psychological, social, and physical stresses, brought on by the dual roles of women play a major role in career development. Furthermore, Lebanese women have seldom viewed work as an avenue for self-expression and stimulation; work has always been a means of financial support to be discarded once economic stability is ensured. Moreover, women learn early that most professional jobs are men's jobs and, therefore, are masculine and do not fit their domestic role.

Lebanese women during the war showed what they can do, making it, therefore, very difficult to confine them to their homes or to certain stereotypical occupations. Admittedly, it is still early to determine whether women would retire to their homes once the shadow of the war is completely lifted. But the immense economic and social contributions of women are being recognized and women, through their forced emancipation, are gaining confidence and self-esteem and are, naturally, increasing their control over their lives and acquiring greater strength and power through the work force, as such, and their exodus into the public sphere. Women have, thus, managed to link the private sphere of the home with the public sphere of production, causing what seems to be a structural change in the economy, the media and education, and a fundamental modification of social relations.

While it is still impossible to see the final outcome, and the struggle is far from over, I believe that the momentum built so far by women's awareness and their accomplishments is difficult to reverse. The cumulative effect of changes, brought on by the war, should continue to open new opportunities at all stages of career development. This is enhanced by the growing global participation of women in the labor market. Although the proportion of women in the professions has not increased dramatically, there has been a substantive increase in numbers making them more visible and commonplace. With the reconstruction of Lebanon taking place and the struggle to catch up with technological development in earnest, there is an urgent need for trained personnel (financial and banking sectors), especially as young men have a greater choice of more attractive positions. Educated women are ready to fill this need. With the spread of education to all parts of Lebanon due to the war, more women are getting an education equal to that of men. Once a breakthrough in tradition takes place, the chances are, it will be cemented. Finally, recent ideological changes regarding the role of women in society promise to keep women in the public sphere fulfilling their roles as full citizens.

This has been translated into the repealing of a number of discriminatory laws: In 1983, Articles 537 and 538 of the Penal Code, which prohibit the sale and use of any form of contraception were repealed (Legislative Decree No. 112, November 10, 1983). In 1987, the social security law regarding termination of services due to age was modified to be the same for men and women (Social Security Code No. 2/87, January 6, 1987). In 1993, the law prohibiting women from acting as witnesses in real estate matters was repealed (Decree No. 275, November 4, 1993). In 1994, the law requiring approval of husband for a wife to start a business was repealed (Decree No. 380, November 4, 1994). In the same year, the law requiring a female employee in the diplomatic corps to return to headquarters in case of marriage to a foreigner was, also, repealed (Decree No. 376, November 10, 1994). In 1995, the law equating married women with the retarded and underaged and describing them as "legally incapacitated" in matters pertaining to the soliciting of a life insurance policy for a married woman by a third party was repealed (Decree No. 483, December 8, 1995). Finally, in 1996, the Convention against all Forms of Discrimination against Women was signed, after long travail, and ratified.

Notes

1. Cf. McDowell and Pringle, *Defining Women,* 122.
2. For a full discussion, see Berch, *The Endless Day,* 185.
3. For a full discussion, see Zurayk and Saadeh, "Women as Mobilizers," 35–48.
4. For a full discussion, see Abu Nasr, Khoury, and Azzam, *Women, Employment and Development.*
5. Cf. Mackintosh, "Gender and Economics," 3–17.
6. For a full discussion of female labor in 1970, cf. Chamie, "Labour Force Participation," 73–102; Lorfing, introduction to *Women and Work,* 8–11; Richards, "The Employment Status of Women," 12–37; Lorfing, "Le travail des femmes," 75–80; Azzam, Abu Nasr, and Lorfing, "An Overview of Arab Women," 5–37.
7. Chamie, "Labour Participation," 86.
8. Ibid., 76.
9. Chikhani-Nacouz, "Maternité et travail au Liban," 69–90.
10. United Nations, *Report of the Secretary General, Addendum;* International Bechtel, *Reconstruction and Development;* ESCWA, *Role of Women in the Informal Sector.*
11. The Lebanese National Committee for the Preparation for the Fourth World Conference on Women, *The National Report,* 78.
12. Cf. Chamie, "Labour Participation," 74.
13. For a full description, see Abu Nasr, "Effects of War," 95–99.
14. Kassab, "Paramount Reality," 67.
15. Saraceno, "Division of Family Labor," 195.
16. Balbo, "Crazy Quilts," 45–71.
17. *The National Report,* 78–79.
18. Ibid. For a description of Lebanon's economy before the war, see Iskandar and Baroudi, *The Lebanese Economy,* 11–32.
19. Khalaf, "The Lebanese Woman and the Labor Market," 14–17. Caution here is necessary, because many women might find work for economic need shameful and, therefore, would not admit to it.

20. Khalaf, "Women and Education in Lebanon," 12–15. For complete documentation on education in Lebanon, see al-Amine, *al-Ta'lim fi lubnan* (Education in Lebanon).

21. Schulze, "Communal Violence."

22. *The National Report*, 52–55.

23. For a full discussion of the participation of highly educated women in the labor force, see Chamie, "Labour Participation," 104–7.

24. Ibid.

25. Chamie, "Labour Participation," 108–11.

26. Ibid.

27. Ibid.

28. *The National Report*, 20.

29. Ibid., 57–59.

30. Ibid., 47.

31. Based on an unpublished study prepared by F. Kiwan and F. Charafeddin for *The National Report*.

32. Articles 22, 23, 27.

33. Shehadeh, "Legal Status," 512–13.

34. See the introduction for a full discussion.

35. For more details, see Dajani, *Disoriented Media*, 22–23.

36. Ibid.

37. Ibid., 29–30.

38. Cited in Nashashibi, *Forces of Change*, 49. For a complete list of journalists and their publications, see table 4.8.

39. Viscount Philippe de Tarazi, *Tarikh al-sahafah al-'arabiyyah* (History of Arab journalism) (Beirut: al-Matba'ah al-Adabiyyah, 1913), 1:17.

40. Moulali, "Afifeh Karam," 30.

41. Cf. George Saadeh, *al-Sahafah fi lubnan* (Journalism in Lebanon) (Beirut: Arab Publishing Agency, 1st ed. 1965), 251.

42. Kaddourah, *Language and Nationalism* (Beirut: Sader Press, 1928), 84. This is a speech delivered at the women's conference in Beirut.

43. Based on a study made by Nur Salman in preparation for the Fourth World Conference on Women in Beijing.

44. For a detailed history of journalism in Lebanon, see Dajani, *Disoriented Media*, and "*Wasa'il al-i'lam wal wa'i al-ijtima'i fi lubnan.*"

45. Dajani, *Disoriented Media*, 45–58.

46. Based on an unpublished study by N. Abdallah, "The Role of Women in the Media during the War, 1975–1991."

47. Based on Nur Salman's unpublished study.

48. Dajani, *Disoriented Media*, 45–58.

49. The figures are approximate based on Nur Salman's study.

III

Creative Women

5

Mapping Peace

MIRIAM COOKE

Demain, nos sens de poètes, d'écrivains, d'artistes ou de journalistes se réveilleront pour faire de n'importe quelle manifestation artistique ou littéraire une manière enchantée. . . . Artistes, écrivains, journalistes, penseurs, et poètes . . . notre devenir repose sur le 'Verbe difficile à proférer,' s'il nous importe de ne pas demeurer intellectuels sans histoire!

If we care about not remaining intellectuals without history, we must write the unspeakable. The Lebanese novelist and journalist Nohad Salameh wrote these words for the Beirut French-language daily *L'Orient–Le Jour* on July 25, 1978. The war had been raging for over three years and she was already fearing that its immediacy and intensity, its reality, might be lost if the poets, writers, and artists kept silent until it was over. But it was not over for another thirteen years, and the women and men who were living the violence did write. Their writings attracted international critical attention, perhaps more sustained attention than has any other group or school of Arab writers in the twentieth century. Since the mid-1980s, literature on the war has been translated into English, French, German, Italian, and Dutch; it has been the subject of conferences and their proceedings, scholarly articles, dissertations, and books.

People everywhere have responded to these intellectuals' engagement with their own tortured history, with their need to make sense of what was happening. The women writers invented new nationalisms, imagined new ways out of violence. And so, thirteen years later, in August 1991, when the poet and painter Etel Adnan returned to Lebanon after the peace had been declared she found that

> people have all sorts of stories to tell me. They insist on praising the heroic feats of a war that shouldn't inspire any pride. But for the stories of the women, it's something else. The women have kept

> contact with the earth, if I may say, in the ancient roles of witnesses and memory keepers. . . . It is the women who speak of the war. The men tend to be quiet: they may seek to hide the horror out of shame for their group as much as for themselves. What makes it terrible is that on the rare occasions when the men do speak of the war, they blame it on others; they always plead that they were trapped; they practically claim they had nothing to do with it. Then who committed the crimes, the massacres, the horrors? And if one was merely a pawn, is one not responsible for having accepted to play the role? In this part of the world there seems to be a huge reality-problem! . . . The orgy of violence is over, and now there is amnesia which is setting in and the bill to be paid. Still, I am comforted by the women's stories about the behaviour of other women during the war.[1]

Etel Adnan wrote these words in a letter from Beirut. Two years later, she published the letter in an issue of the international literary journal *Mediterraneans* that was devoted to writings from and about Beirut and Sarajevo. Both capital cities were the sites for their nations' savage struggle over identity and hegemony. In each war, women figured prominently. Beiruti women fought by remaining and resisting the destruction. Sarajevan women were compelled into combat by becoming physical targets; violation of their bodies became the medium of exchange between warring parties. In 1993, the sixteen-year war in Lebanon had been over for two years;[2] the war in Bosnia was in its second terrible year. In Lebanon, women had been writing for a decade and a half. We have yet to receive, at least in English or French, a piece of literature by a Bosnian woman.

In her letter, Adnan celebrates Lebanese women's achievements during the war as well as afterwards. Their stories hold on to the memories of their experiences lest others erase them. Their stories refuse the glorification of the madness but also the amnesia. Their stories provide comfort because they record a moment in the history of human courage and steadfastness. Then, three years later in the 1995–96 edition of *Bahithat,* a journal founded by Lebanese women and devoted to a study of Arab women's writings, Adnan amplified her notion of women's special relationship to words, and particularly during times of conflict. In "Words, Women, Words," she describes women's emotional attachments to language and she writes of herself that she considers

> words like little atoms, like particles emanating from our organism, like audible emanations of our mental and emotional make-up, like creations closest to our being. These little "energies" are similar to

> atoms in the sense that they contain tremendous power. Once they touch our psyche they leave their imprint, their impact, and they seem to affect women most durably, even if it is simply because women traditionally were less in contact with the "outside" world, and remained closer to their inner selves and their memory. . . . In a moment of History where violent action prevails not only on battlefields but also in movies and television, where sexuality seems to be the only expression of desire or love, or of both, let us bring back to our attention that fact of words, their role, their importance, and remember that, like the little atoms that they are, they participate in the energies of Life, and they still have the power to create Paradise or Hell.[3]

Women have the power, what she has called the magic power, to heal societal wounds with the atomic power of their words. Language and literature in such a formulation are not decorative descriptors external to their subject, they are interventions in a political situation.

Etel Adnan is one of a group of women I have called the Beirut Decentrists. In *War's Other Voices,* I described them as "a group of women writers who have shared Beirut as their home and the war as their experience. They have been decentered in a double sense: physically, they were scattered all over a self-destructing city; intellectually, they moved in separate spheres. They wrote alone and for themselves. They would not conceive of their writings as related to those of others, yet their marginal perspective, which gave them insight into the holistic aspect of the war, united them and allowed them discursively to undermine and restructure society around the image of a new center."[4] These women, who include Ghada al-Samman, Hanan al-Shaykh, Huda Barakat, Emily Nasrallah, Nazik Yared and Nur Salman, testify to the power of language to create Paradise or Hell. It should be used to overcome evil and to fashion a new nation, another kind of nationalism that I call humanist nationalism. This Lebanese nation, sometimes defined as the extended village or even family, becomes an adopted child that demands constant care. In the process of giving such care, these nurturers paradoxically become the one nurtured. The Beirut Decentrists assigned women nurturing, preservative, resistant roles. They wrote of staying in Lebanon as being part of their duty as mothers to a child who was being torn apart by its careless fathers; they wrote of ordinary women walking up to militiamen and chiding them as naughty sons for wreaking such havoc. As scolding mothers they undermined the glory of gun-toting and for a period put themselves into a position of authority over the implementers of the violence. In other words, they became involved, assumed responsibility for trying to stop the war. It would seem that for some of them not to do so would have signified madness. In her 1980 novel *Tilka al-dhikrayat* (Those memories), Nasrallah described isolation and abstention as madness: "How wonderful to be mad! You erect a wall between yourself and the world, and you can relax. Or you can construct that tough cocoon, and you can stay in it, so that the poisonous breaths cannot reach you."[5]

The Beirut Decentrists put themselves in charge of the construction of meanings. They questioned the binary epistemology that organizes war into neat dichotomies like friend and foe, victory and defeat, front and home front. They revealed the artificiality of the Lebanese War Story, as it has generally been told, that forced order on to the chaos of emotions, motivations, and outcomes of war. The Beirut Decentrists highlighted the fluidity of the structures of the war. They exposed abstractions and called the war a chaos, a vortex of love and hatred, *not* a revolution.[6] They pointed out that the periods of calm were not peace but different degrees of being at war. They established different criteria of belonging, of being Lebanese that required individual commitment to the country. They used the manipulation of language and experience inherent in the writing of the War Story to change interpretations of women's behavior from passive to active, from mad to creative. They put to rest the lie that men go to war for women, and that women, although inherently peace-loving, prefer their men dead to defeated. The dynamic, reciprocal relationship that the Beirut Decentrists write themselves as having with their nation is at the heart of what I call humanist nationalism. This loyalty is to be contrasted with statist nationalism. I call the latter "statist" because of the insistence by its advocates on the overlap between an imagined community—the nation—and a public entity—the state. Whereas statist nationalism is absolute and constructed within a binary framework of differentiation and recognition, positing the nation "out there" from time immemorial and awaiting discovery by those who "naturally" belong to it, humanist nationalism construes the nation as dialectic, as both produced and productive. Lebanese women's writings thus redefine nationalism and extend it to reveal its humanist dimensions.[7]

The Beirut Decentrists' literary constructions of the nation in civil-war Lebanon emerged in response to a sense that not only had statist nationalist projects failed but that they had been responsible for the carnage of the civil war. Musing about how the war had driven her to write, Jean Said Makdisi described her surprise to find herself able to articulate in writing her own and then others' strong reactions to the absurdity of the war. With time, the surprise gave way to defiance:

> I became more and more aware of myself as a rebel spokeswoman, as though a member of an underground movement. I became more and more aware of my own anger: I was angry at those who conducted the war, and at those who wrote about it, the journalists and the historians . . . they made it sound rational, logical. Whether political leaders or writers, they seemed to me to be members of a very clearly patriarchal order, from which their authority, which in my heart I denied, stemmed . . . [they] made sense of things in their own way. That, after all, was their raison d'être, to explain the inexplicable, and to make order out of chaos. . . . Early on, it already seemed clear to me that leaders were not saying the truth about the war: and that, almost without exception, the very ideals in the name of which the war on either side had been undertaken, were being betrayed.[8]

She understood how important it was to write so that she should not continue to be duped by others' naming of a situation that she was living but could not recognize in such namings.

Like most of the Beirut Decentrists, Makdisi rejected people's need to tidy up the mess of the war into the neat and unchanging binary scaffolding of the War Story. She used writing to authorize herself: "the great lesson of writing about the world [is that] writing about it made it mine."[9] She had constructed links with a piece of land, the geopolitical dimensions of which she does not define, that then became instrumental in her self-definition. Makdisi's focus on individual agency in constructing political selfhood shows how nationalism, when it is humanist, may become a meaningful and dynamic way of belonging and caring, rather than of dominating, as is the case for statist nationalism.

I

The literature produced in Lebanon between 1975 and 1982 suggested that women had evolved a different relationship with Lebanon than had the men. For someone like Nasrallah, staying on the land was more important than fighting for the polity. During the last ten years of the war, the years that followed the Israeli invasion, most of the women continued to write and a few new voices came to be heard. Emigration and staying as well as the refusal of the War Story remained central.

Emily Nasrallah, one of the major exponents of the emigration theme, wrote many short stories during the post-invasion period. She first published in magazines and then she collected the stories into three volumes:

al-Mar'ah fi 17 qissah (Women in 17 stories, 1984); *al-Tahunah al-da'i'ah* (The lost mill, 1985); *Khubzuna al-yawmi* (Our daily bread, 1990).[10] Most of them revolve around the importance of staying in Lebanon despite the trials of the war, because, although the "whole world can be a homeland, yet one needs a very tiny place into which to sink one's roots."[11] But this is not so easy to do because this small place is unstable, it has erased the traces of its past. What are these roots? Are they ancestral or contingent? Andrée Chedid in her 1985 *La maison sans racines* (The house without roots) provided one answer. After asking whether roots are found in the land of origin or are formed in the city of residence, she responds that they are both. Her heroine, a grandmother who witnesses and then succumbs to the ruthlessness of a sniper, knows that her roots are both ancient and modern, that she is thus a hybrid. She is not anguished but delighted by that mixture that allows her to remain open to, and in touch with, others' perspectives.[12] Since these roots are new and dynamic, not just lying in wait to be uncovered, they may be changed. In pointing back but also forward, they signify the present. Those who live by such roots can build a strong future, for they live close to the land and understand its rhythms, as Nasrallah writes: "The storm seems more violent when we stand on the lookout tower. But when we confront it, it dissipates, disappears."[13]

In Nasrallah's stories, it is the women and the children who unroot and reroot themselves so as to create new spaces where they can imagine alternatives. In "al-Nafidhah" (The window), the child in the basement-shelter turns the concrete underground dungeon into a fertile land by painting a brilliant window on the blankness of the wall. She gives the people hope that their confinement is over, because she has been able to "dive into the depths of human nature, to extract its best and to give it to you (the reader)."[14]

Nazik Yared's *al-Sada al-makhnuq* (The stifled echo) examines the consequences of emigration.[15] In contrast to earlier literature that portrayed men who leave and women who stay, Yared's novel describes a man in Beirut whose wife has emigrated to Paris "for the sake of the children." As in most fiction about Lebanese war emigrants, the one left behind does not at first censure the one who leaves. With time, however, the hero resents the Lebanese who live easily and far from the war, and he justifies his love affair and his alienation from the distant wife. Only one of the characters in this novel has been able to leave with impunity. Loyal to her family ties, Najla stuck by her husband when he decided to go to Paris. Yet even while distant, she can never banish her country from her mind. Najla is staunchly loyal to Lebanon, and she fosters in her children the same kind of loving loyalty. Najla remains connected to her nation through love. By teaching love of nation to others, in this case to her children, Najla is involuntarily a long-distance yet still humanist nationalist.

Unlike most of the Beirut Decentrists who chose women as their main characters, Huda Barakat told her two 1990s novels through the eyes of a male narrator.[16] *Hajar al-dahik* (The laughing stone, 1990) and *Ahl al-hawa* (People of passion, 1993) probe the psyche of men who stayed during the war. Their stories demonstrate how the war forced many men who stayed to make impossible choices that drove them into militias or out of their minds. In *Hajar al-dahik,* Huda Barakat examines the ways in which nationalism creates an alternative family out of a military matrix. Adopted parents are more real and loving than are the natural ones. These self-made nationalists censure laughter until they create their new families that give them the security to do what they like even if their desire is to rape and pillage. Khalil is a homosexual who at first embraces the feminine in himself. He is serious and deeply sensitive until he loses the two men he loves to the war. After his losses, he gives up the deadly seriousness of nationalist demeanor and has an affair with a militia leader. Now he can convince himself that morality and nationalist sentiment are meaningless in this city, and that what really matters is to love oneself even if that love means hating others. By the end of the novel, Khalil has taken this new philosophy so far as to have raped the woman who lives upstairs from him. He has yielded to the temptations of the drugs and arms trade and to the lure of the group—the real family—that makes him one of the boys. The war has masculinized him.

Barakat may mock but she does not trivialize the compelling attraction of statist nationalisms. Khalil is now the "laughing stone,"[17] the polar opposite of his own conception of how a nationalist should feel and act. As a stone he feels nothing, but he laughs nonetheless. Khalil joins a nationalist unit, but in defiance of what he had believed to be the necessary conditions for nationalist sentiment. When I read this novel, I was shocked by its ending. Relentlessly optimistic to the end, I had hoped to read of a man who was sufficiently in touch with his femininity that he might have different choices. For example, he could stay in Lebanon during the war, make a stand and not become involved in the fighting, immorality, and violence. I immediately wrote to Barakat asking her why. Why, having started to do so, could she not have constructed a model for humanist nationalism that would not be undone by its own project? Less than two weeks later, I received her reply. She was happy the novel had made such a strong impression, but I had to understand that this war was different from any other war, even the Spanish civil war that had two clear sides. In other wars, in which the enemy is clear, "*hiss watani* (nationalist feeling) can develop as a kind of defense of identity and belonging. But what I wanted to say was that in the Lebanese civil war, all the fighters were corrupt, and violence and hatred had reached the point of absolute evil, so that all claims to defend a cause—whatever it might be—became a lie and a crime." In such a situation, Barakat's letter continued, individuals had the "choice between being the executioner, which Khalil rejected at the beginning, or the despised victim. In the latter case, the outcome is *madness* [my emphasis], drugs or escape. I wanted to write an accusation, a complaint. I wanted to understand how an entire people turns into criminal fighters. What human resources do we draw on when legal protection is withdrawn and the body consumes itself from within? I wanted to convey the deepest impact of the civil war on human society and how it changes and rots when the only enemy is ourselves."[18]

Barakat's next novel, *Ahl al-hawa,* which was written in 1993, a year after the war ended, explores one of the outcomes of victimization: madness. Unlike Nasrallah's state of blissful ignorance within the cocoon of indifference, this madness is an intensely conscious state of irrelevance. The narrator had been kidnapped and tortured and upon his release his sister finds him unbearably changed. She commits him to a psychiatric hospital run by nuns, whom he upsets with his singing and his crazy perspective on the world outside. At times of danger, the patients flock to him, however, "believing that I was their father. They would crawl under me as though I were a great hen."[19] Mother and father to the patients, he is to himself a political and sexual failure. He has lost his reason because he can no longer function morally in his society. The reference to laughter, the theme of the previous novel, may provide a key. He and his friends are uncontrollably amused—antinationalist?—whenever they hear the word "society." The doctor tries to calm them down by suggesting other words, like *ahl* (people of the family) or *nas* (people) or *al-kharij* (the outside). But the preferred words are *ummah* (state) or *qawm* (nation, or tribe) or *shaab* (populace). The patients do not like these alternatives and assure the doctor that there is really no need to find another word because they like the word "society" very much. Why else would they laugh? Yet it is not for joy because these are tormented, emasculated men cared for like children. They cannot—perhaps, will not—do all the lethal things that real men are supposed to do, and so they have become useless to their nation. Their only home is an insane asylum.

In this later literature, poetry played a greater role, both as a separate genre and as part of prose fiction, in the cases of novelists like Andrée Chedid and Evelyne Accad. Poetry transforms the anger of the prose into a plea for another way of thinking and of acting. In *Coquelicot du massa-*

cre,[20] Accad urges the power of love, especially when it is lyrically articulated, to resist the destruction and somehow to resurrect the human spirit. We can read this in a passage that decries the war as being not about glory but about *wastah,* or nepotistic influence-mongering. The anger at this realization is interrupted by the following:

> Etoile filante
> Rayant le ciel de larmes rouges
> Cartilage d'un monde qui craque
> Trous qu'on creuse pour faire un cimetière
> Coupe de sang qu'on leur donne à boire
> Pas effacés sur le rivage.[21]

It was not until eight years later, in her "Writing to Explore (W) Human Experience," that she meditates on the meaning of poetry to her life and writings:

> Writing also helped me heal the wounds. It reconciled me with my past. When expressing what upset me, I exorcised the anger, the pain, the suffering, and could move on. I started composing songs in 1975 when the war broke out in Lebanon. My grief was so overwhelming I could not sleep nor lead a normal existence thinking about what my loved ones and the country I cherished were going through. Songs—music and words—came out of my body like a long plaintive shriek. . . . When I witnessed how some of the audiences, especially in Lebanon, cried when I sang, I was overcome with the realization I could really move them. And the question came: what if it moved them so much they decided to change the wrongs in Lebanese society? . . . And perhaps, in the end, when all is said and done, when life's experiences have given us the rounder, sharper vision, one is able to see writing, singing, art, culture as a fuller, more complete hopeful picture, ways to recreate the hidden face of the world, the lost image of one's childhood.[22]

These songs were not so much separate creations but had grown organically out of the prose texts of *L'Excisée*[23] and *Coquelicot du massacre.*

Then there was a form of epic poetry. Nur Salman published her 220-page *Ila rajul lam ya'ti* (To a man who did not come) in 1986.[24] The narrator accuses men of leaving and warns them that those who have kept faith with the land have been transformed and may even be dangerous. Throughout, the poet summons and then immediately repels *Ya baʿidi,* (My distant one). Again and again, she calls to him. Yet, almost in the same breath she warns him not to come. He, like the others who left, is not safe in this land of martyrs, prophets and poets who are the bedrock of the new nation. The poets "plant the nation in the earth / Master creators. They fertilize our history with fire /. . . . The earth holds its head high because of them and is called nation."[25] She is trying to survive in a death world that has destroyed the possibility of parenting and so she turns the dream of *Ya baʿidi* into a reproductive instrument. The dream makes her at once mother and father; his return might render her body sterile, unable to love and produce her nation, which in turn loved and thus produced her. What is the nation? For Salman, as for Nasrallah, the nation is the grief of the people who have stayed and survived and whose staying has allowed them to push down roots that are both old and new into the soil, the earth of the nation. This grief of the survivors is an empathy that links and creates a community out of those who have experienced it.

The writings of Huda Barakat, Evelyne Accad, Andrée Chedid, Emily Nasrallah, Jean Said Makdisi, Nazik Yared, and Nur Salman write the nation not as an ideological construct, despite its discursive nature, but rather as an individual sense of belonging and then of responsibility, which radiates out from multiple centers. It is first of all personal, it may become collective. This nation is the context within which each individual constructs a center for her/himself, the new citizen. Citizenship is neither a birthright nor a reward for military service; it is an affective identity that becomes a building block in the construction of the nation, the center of another humanist nationalist. The process is circular and keeps renewing itself in terms of itself. For those who are humanist nationalists, there is no single polity but multiple, fragmentary projects that are continually disassembling, but also reassembling and self-regenerating, because they foster, above all, survival.

II

This is a hard-hitting literature that gives a unique insight into how people can live sixteen years of war and survive and not necessarily go mad and even retain their dignity and self-worth. In 1995, *Al-Raida* published a double issue on women in postwar Lebanon that contained many interviews with women, most of them professionals, who had lived through parts if not the whole of the war. The interviewers, who reported to the Institute for Women's Studies in the Arab World of the Lebanese American University, concluded their sessions with the same question, which went something like this: "If you could sit and talk with women in other war-torn societies, such as Bosnia, Rwanda or Chechenia, what would you advise them about surviving a war and its after-effects?" The answers were consistent: prevent the men from fighting; commit yourselves to humanity; teach the children to be patient and strong; never give up nor even only remain passive, even after the war is said to be over; if you can do nothing directly about the fighting, move away from the place where it is at its most intense; never leave your country; some recommended that women train themselves in self-defense since women so often are the primary victims of violence. The lawyer and peace activist Laure Moghaizel said: "I can't say we stopped the war, but even though we were a minority, it helped us overcome the war."[26] These women knew that they had participated and that their participation mattered sufficiently that it might constitute a lesson from which others might learn. Their message was that women have a special role to play in the war theater and that if they do not do so then they, their families and the nation as a whole will suffer. Ghena Ismail conducted interviews with several young women after the war, asking them what women had contributed to or gained from the war. Most of them, she writes, "believe that war has set a new course for women. They held more responsibilities, both inside and outside the home. It is in the hands of us young women to carry this progress a step further, to improve the status of women on the political, economical [*sic*] and social levels."[27]

These post–civil war Lebanese women see themselves, and others also see them, as models for a new way of entering into the *politikon*. Unprecedented and sustained attention has been paid to what women are doing in what was considered to be men's space. Ironically, and yet perhaps not so strangely, this self-assertion comes at a time when the academic focus on what women are doing in war is being attacked as a form of essentialism. Critics, many of whom are women, argue that even if the project of singling out women as a discrete object of study is based not in nature but in culture, not in biology but in learned behavior, it is unhelpful at best, harmful at worst. The nation that is sundered with strife cannot sustain such a splitting that pits women against men. Particularly problematic is the position of the outside observer, particularly when she is a woman. She is liable to the charge of using women's problems in a troubled nation to attack the men and thus to further disable the nation. Were she to take these criticisms seriously, this critic would be compelled to silence, at least about those women whose lives and writings interested her. Her silence would not be a form of passivity but rather a deliberate choice not to speak so as not to offend. That choice, however, runs the risk of making her complicitous in a system that silences women who want to talk about war because it is believed that people can only talk about what they have experienced and women do not experience war (even when they do) and therefore they should keep silent.

I thought long and hard after Lamia Shehadeh asked me to participate in this volume on what women had done during the Lebanese civil war. Why? It was not as though I had not written about the subject before. In 1988, I published *War's Other Voices,* a book about the writings of over fifty women that had been produced between 1975 and 1982, the year of the Israeli invasion. The discovery of a quantity of neglected writers and of the quality of much of what they had written was less important to me than the dawning awareness that together these women were telling a new story about the war. They were recording their experiences and their reactions as they happened and then turning these experiences and reactions into riveting stories of strength, resistance, and love.

I read this literature not as isolated literary products but rather as a whole. It is this whole that provides us with a counternarrative. I became fascinated with this counternarrative. It was different from any story I had read about any war anywhere. The Beirut Decentrists took for granted that war and peace is a senseless construct and that at best the condition they were living was one that moved along a continuum between war and not-war. They also took for granted that they were as much participants in this violence as were those who carried the guns and reaped the benefits. The Beirut Decentrists were unequivocal about the need for all to bear responsibility for the war, not only for its beginning but also of course for its ending. They wrote out of war and about war, but most of all they were writing *against* war. And as I wrote about this story, I assumed that my story would be read as I had read theirs: against their war in particular, and against all wars in general. I analyzed and dissected their emancipatory strategies, how they transformed meanings of words and interpretations of actions, how they opened up space for new actors who had no stake in the maintenance of a violent status quo. Like them, I did not try to imagine a utopian condition outside the one they were living. Peace was not an available option. I tried with and through them to talk about how the ways in which the war was survived and described contributed to the construction of an alternative vision, what might be called a narrative of peace politics.

Some critics objected to my thesis that proposed that women wrote of themselves as humanist nationalists, as more loyal to Lebanon than the men, except when the men acted as women and stayed. I had presented their humanist nationalism to be exclusive also, not of members of another political group but rather of all, regardless of political or religious persuasions, who perpetuated the violence. I read the Beirut Decentrists as saying that citizenship in the Lebanese nation was earned through individual evidence of loyalty to the land, an entity that was at once concrete and amorphous, because it is never delimited or even defined. As long as people left the country and allowed it to self-destruct, the war would continue. The Lebanese had to stay, loyal to the land, if they were to stay Lebanese. The Decentrists called for a collective sense of responsibility that does not point the finger of blame and then smugly shrug, for, as Ghada al-Samman writes, "there are no innocents in an unjust society."[28] This sense of responsibility was not backward but forward looking as it demanded that each person participate in the effort to end the violence. How could this loyalty to the land be recognized? It manifested itself in the impossible decision to stay in Lebanon, and to write of the staying as transformative; those who left forfeited their citizenship. Through fiction writing, women came to understand their decision to stay. Their discourse then became part of the new social and civic contract between the Lebanese and their nation, as defined by these same texts.

Others dismissed my conclusions as being relevant only for Lebanon because Lebanon was sui generis. My purpose had not been to set up a universal model, but these criticisms convinced me that it might be worth a try. That is what I have been doing over the past eight years. I have been filling in the context, arguing that Lebanon is not so different from the Intifada in the West Bank and the Gaza Strip, not so far from Bosnia and the American inner city gang wars. These are all postmodern wars that refuse the dichotomous ordering of the confusion of war experiences into the clear-cut certainties of the conventional War Story. Above all, they are wars that have implicated women as much if not more than men.

Women have a stake in interpreting their war experiences. I, a woman literary critic who is deeply suspicious of just war arguments, have a stake in making sense of these interpretations. Across borders and boundaries, we have to learn how to talk about and with each other. As I put pen to paper I know that I am writing with those who know that if we do not stop the intertwining, swirling circles of violence into which we are all everywhere being sucked, we shall destroy ourselves and our children. We cannot stop war with talk of peace, with examinations of scriptural sources for the discovery of age-old prescriptions for or against the implementation of violence to resolve conflict. In a world grown tolerant of violence, we must understand how its assumptions shape our daily lives. We must try to reveal the links between hidden, interpersonal violence and that which is played out at the community and state level. We must expose the abstractions and deceptions.

I want to plait the multiple strands of a narrative of non-war. I have always looked for women's ways of combatting the silence that has traditionally been their lot in war. I have tried to understand how women have sought to participate in ways other than those prescribed since time immemorial; how women have improvised ways of retaining this kind of participation as equivalent to that of men in war; how they have inscribed an oppositional consciousness and alternatives that may have existed before but were always written out of the War Story; how they challenge what some have claimed to be the inevitable disempowerment of women in the aftermath. In light of the new wars that we have observed and lived in the postcolonial period, I refuse the fatalism of the double helix.[29] Some counter that such an attitude betrays approval of war as helpful to women. Be that as it may, I am convinced that to describe women as having combatant roles that are not cross-dressing complicates the notion of the warrior and allows the observer to imagine participation as more complex than quite simply combat.

When I grouped the women who had written on the war and called them the Beirut Decentrists I wanted to draw attention to the fact that these women had something in common. They were all opposed to the violence. By creating a school of women writers resistant to violence, I wanted readers to come to terms with the fact that political allegiance—and its corollary statist nationalism—is not the primary force shaping all lives in war. The stories these women told and continue to tell affirm that there will always be conflict, that conflict is not in and of itself bad, but that there are multiple ways in which conflict can be addressed and resolved. By challenging the self-perpetuating discourse that justifies the use of violence, they seem to threaten to destabilize coherent group identity. I say "seem" because that, of course, is not the intent. Far from it. Women have long known that violence does not eliminate violence. That once violence has been dubbed "sacred" it consumes its practitioners. They know that successful opposition to domination depends on survival—physical, psychic, and social—and that survival in turn depends on overcoming domination. This dialectical proposition refuses violence as an instrumentality. Women in Lebanon write their awareness not to undermine but rather to strengthen opposition to domination.

I have written about the women who have written and struggled in Lebanon as a group because I feared with Sheila Rowbotham for the fate of individual women in war: "An individual woman who appears as the spokeswoman for the freedom of all women is a pathetic and isolated creature. She is inevitably either crushed or contained as a sexual performer. No woman can stand alone and demand liberation for others because by doing so she takes from other women the capacity to organize and speak for themselves. Also she presents no threat. An individual 'emancipated' woman is an amusing incongruity, a titillating commodity, easily consumed."[30] The Beirut Decentrists are not amusing incongruities, titillating commodities, they are not easily consumed. Together they threaten statist nationalists because they have given others, women and humanist nationalists, the capacity to organize and speak for themselves.

Notes

1. Etel Adnan, "Letter from Beirut," *Mediterraneans* 5 (1993):107–10.

2. Some dispute the date and even the fact of the war's ending. Claire Gebeyli told Wafa Stephan Tarnowski that "even five years after the cessation of armed conflict, the war is still continuing on the intellectual level. . . . Currently, we have a war against the after-effects of the war . . . the struggle to prevent a repetition of what happened before, a campaign to tell others about the sacrifices made and to guarantee that those sacrifices were not made in vain." Tarnowski, "Interview with Claire Gebeyli," 40.

3. Etel Adnan, "Words, Women, Words," *Bahithat* 2 (1995): 159–60.

4. Miriam Cooke, *War's Other Voices*, 3.

5. Emily Nasrallah, *Tilka al-dhikrayat* (Those memories) (Beirut: Naufal, 1980), 225.

6. Daisy al-Amir, *Fi duwwamat al-hubb wa al-karahiyah* (In the vortex of love and hatred) (1979).

7. Cooke, *Women and the War Story.*

8. Makdisi, "Speaking Up," 133–35.

9. Ibid., 138.

10. Emily Nasrallah, *al-Mar'ah fi 17 qissah* (Women in 17 stories) (Beirut: Naufal, 1984); *al-Tahunah al-da'i'ah* (The lost mill) (Beirut: Naufal, 1985) and *Khubzuna al-yawmi* (Our daily bread) (Beirut: Naufal, 1990).

11. Nasrallah, *al-Tahunah al-da'i'ah* (The lost mill), 16.

12. Andrée Chedid, *La maison sans racines* (Paris: Flammarion, 1985), 79.

13. Nasrallah, *al-Tahunah al-da'i'ah* (The lost mill), 120.

14. Ibid., 237–38.

15. Nazik Yared, *al-Sada al-makhnuq* (The stifled echo) (n.p., 1986).

16. Huda Barakat, *Hajar al-dahik* (The laughing stone) (London: Riad el-Rayyes, 1990), and *Ahl al-hawa* (People of passion) (Beirut: Dar al-Nahar, 1993).

17. Barakat, *Hajar al-dahik*, 250.

18. Paris, October 28, 1992.

19. Barakat, *Ahl al-hawa*, 19.

20. Evelyne Accad, *Coquelicot du massacre* (Paris: L'Harmattan, 1988).

21. Ibid., 102.

22. Evelyne Accad, "Writing to Explore (W) Human Experience," *Bahithat* 2 (1995):114–15, 121.

23. Evelyne Accad, *L'Excisée* (Paris: L'Harmattan, 1980).

24. Nur Salman, *Ila rajul lam ya'ti* (To a man who did not come) (Beirut, 1986).

25. Ibid., 103.

26. Osseiran, "An Interview," 15.

27. Ismail, "Young Women," 57.

28. al-Samman, *Kawabis bayrut* (Beirut nightmares) (Beirut: Ghada Samman Publishing House, 1980), 315.

29. Higonnet and Higonnet, "The Double Helix."

30. Rowbotham, *A History of Women and Revolution.*

6

A Panorama of Lebanese Women Writers, 1975–1995

Mona Takieddine Amyuni

A bomb falls in the garden
a man falls inside
a child screams
Darkness blinds me
silence deafens me
time stops
My wild heart
bleeds
aches
beats
and does not die . . .

Indeed, my heart did not die. The healing process took its natural course and I, as well, took up my pen. Writing soothed me, linked me back to reality and to my people. Somehow, we emerged from the nightmarish war which decimated Lebanon, our country, between the years 1975 and 1991. Those of us who managed to survive, nevertheless, felt absolutely shattered. We licked our wounds, started to reconstruct our homes, and took stock of the devastation.

Today the whole country is in reconstruction. Beirut's city center has become the most important archaeological site in the world. International teams are participating in the excavations and have, so far, unearthed an amazing number of layers of civilizations taking us back to 60,000 years before Christ.[1]

Today, a new kind of awareness grips our imagination, together with a renewed feeling of responsibility. Bearers and carriers of a unique heritage, Lebanese women struggled during the long war to preserve a semblance of humanity in the midst of savagery. The majority of women, in fact, did not carry arms. Instead, they queued for bread, gas, gasoline, and water; they cooked, organized shelters, made provisions of candles, transistors, first aid medication, and were always ready to meet emergency situations.[2] They were propelled to the foreground at home and outside. They took upon themselves domestic, economic, and social responsibilities, when men fought, went away, or simply died. So many testimonies of displaced families speak of the stamina of women, in a country where one-sixth of the population was displaced.

Mere survival on the one hand, the need to be heard on the other. New voices emerged. Talents exploded. Women spoke up. Women wrote.

To draw a panorama of women writers in war-torn Lebanon and beyond is a daunting task. Fiction and poetry flourished in the three languages, Arabic, French, and English, often used by the intelligentsia of Lebanon. The women writers to be considered here belong to Lebanon's middle class; they are highly educated, broadly read, and quite cosmopolitan in a city, Beirut, which has traditionally been the platform of the Arab world, its conscience, its experimental space.[3] It is well known that the cosmopolitanism of prewar Beirut rested on the fact that about 40 percent of the overall population, estimated then at around three and a half million inhabitants, were foreigners. These clustered around the American University of Beirut and its hospital creating an Anglo-Saxon tradition, and around the French St. Joseph University and its hospital, Hotel-Dieu, reinforcing an old-time Francophone culture, while the Lebanese University drew a large segment of the Arabophone youth.

Moreover, in creating a framework for this paper, a rich body of literature written by Lebanese women who live and publish in the West had to be eliminated. Well-known to the public, writers such as Andrée Chedid, Vénus Khoury-Ghata, Hanan el-Shaykh, Evelyne Accad, Dominique Eddé, Huda Barakat, Ghada al-Samman, and Etel Adnan, to name but a few, have been recognized and have often received prestigious awards for their poetry and fiction. A later study will analyze their works and try to discern parallels and contrasts with those women who wrote under the bombs in Beirut and who will be presented in this paper.

Finally, it is hoped that the present choice of women writers, while not exhaustive, will be indicative enough of their main concerns and preoccupations since the year 1975 and up to 1995. Indeed, the Taif Agreement reached between the fighting parties in 1990 had technically brought the war to an end. The postwar writings, however, strikingly reflect the impact of two dramatic decades in Lebanon, as will be exemplified by Thérèse Basbous and Renée Hayek in this study. The mode of writings to be examined is both specific and varied, and each of these women, whose works will be looked into, has written in isolation, pursuing her own inner journey in the language in which she is most skilled. Hence, the affirmation that language is a mere tool in the hands of these women who are Lebanese in their sensibilities and outlooks whether they were born and grew up in Lebanon or chose Lebanon as their new home. Such is the case of Daisy al-Amir of Iraqi birth, Claire Gebeyli of Greek origin, Jean Said Makdisi born in Palestine, and Huda al-Naamani from Syria. These women remained in Lebanon when so many Lebanese left the country during the war. They felt a new kind of allegiance to their country of adoption and a deeper attachment to the land and the people. They also wrote in Beirut.

This study shall be divided up into the various genres adopted by the authors to be analyzed: Starting with Makdisi's autobiographical *War Memoir,* then to short stories by Daisy al-Amir, Emily Nasrallah, and Renée Hayek, to Nazik Yared's and Thérèse Basbous's novels, reaching finally the poetry of al-Naamani, Aghacy, Gebeyli, and Tuéni.

A War Memoir (1990)

Jean Makdisi wonders: "How can I write about Beirut? How can I collect it all into one volume: the years of pain; of watching a world collapse while trying to stave off that collapse; the layers of memories and hopes, of tragedy and even sometimes comedy, of violence and kindness, of courage and fear? Above all, how can I express my strange love for this mutilated city; how to explain, both to myself and to others, the lingering magic of the place that has kept me and so many others clinging to its wreckage, refusing to let go, refusing to abandon it?"[4]

This is the opening of Makdisi's *War Memoir;* she subtitles her autobiographical book *Beirut Fragments.* She goes on to say that she feels more committed than ever to Beirut, that she grew up and matured during the war, that a new woman was born in her, a woman who took the pen to speak up for herself and other women. When asked about the function of writing in her life she gives its genesis a new voice, with great sincerity. Her testimony sums up that of other women writers, for it speaks of commitment, responsibility and self-liberation through writing. Makdisi entitles her testimony "Speaking up: Why I Wrote" and describes a moment of anger which functioned as a catalyst in her life. She was serving dinner to friends while Beirut was being shelled and she asked a colleague of her husband "Who is fighting whom, and why?" a question we all asked during the war. With contempt, the guest turns to her husband and wonders what the matter was with her. Where was she living, he asked!

Slowly but surely, in anger and great secrecy, Makdisi started to keep a record in writing of all that the Lebanese around her as well as herself were going through. Slowly and surely, her friends knew of her enterprise and started to use her as spokeswoman for what they were enduring. She, herself, came to realize that until the moment when she took up her pen, she was never an individual woman living an individual life. She was wife of . . . , mother of . . . , daughter of . . . , a passive spectator, a mere watcher of events.

A new awareness of her political alienation invaded her. She called herself a noncitizen of the Arab world, of the third world, where governments were imposed from above and the people had no voice in any decision making. A second reality struck her, that being a woman and a mother with "confirming and restricting domestic responsibilities," imposed on her a "further degree of alienation," added "to the already alienated non-citizen," who had no say, whatsoever, in public affairs.

Indeed, Makdisi considered her writing to be subversive, for she was doing something different, something male journalists and writers did not do. She was not recording the events of the war, nor conflicting political allegiances. She was recording the lives and reactions of human beings, which meant that she was challenging the roles of politicians, militias, and parties as definers of reality. She was proclaiming her own reality, articulating for the first time her own vision of the world and of herself in the world. Exhilaration possessed her, together with the fear of this new commitment to writing. Indeed, writing is dangerous and telling the truth is not easy: "writing is like gambling: you have to put your money down, and take your chance." She was ready for the dangerous adventure and she tells all women that unless they speak up nothing would change: "for in the absence of our voices, we who form half the population, how can life possibly become better?"[5] In fact, the women discussed in this study have had the courage to speak up and with a different voice.

Makdisi's *Beirut Fragments* is a vibrating testimony of the increased fragmentation of our country, while writing about it joins the fragments together with deep love, compassion, and piety. Makdisi singles out key events in her life spent between Palestine, Egypt, the United States, and Lebanon, as well as key events in the Lebanese war. The Israeli invasion of Lebanon, and the Beirut siege, in the summer of 1982, formed one of the climaxes of the war, and Makdisi's treatment of those happenings is masterly as she mixes the realistic, cruel details of the relentless bombardment of Beirut with a universal kind of mourning, and a frightening self-reflection. Instead of focusing on the horrible violence of the enemy, she wonders whether man, all men, are just as horrible: "Standing there watching, I felt I could see all the tragic, cruel history of humanity concentrated: all the wars, the inquisitions, the persecutions, the wickedness, crimes great and small . . . evil in all its forms," and in a dreadful self-revelatory moment, she adds: "it is easy here in Beirut to look at every passing stranger and see the face of a potential murderer. . . . Yet it is when I look at my own face in the mirror that I am most frightened. Is mine the face of one of the damned?"[6] The writer's question underlines here a communal guilt shared by a fallen humanity in the universe at large.

Finally, when Makdisi tries to sum up the implications of all this horror and what it meant to have stayed on, she believes that she, together with all those who stuck it out, had reclaimed and redefined their humanity since they had salvaged life while the fighters had sowed death. They had experienced fraternity in the midst of hatred, and had grown more tolerant of humanity. Similar to the end of a Greek tragedy, Makdisi suggests that people emerged from the war richer human beings, by becoming more humble, more vulnerable, and more tolerant. She closes her *War Memoir* with a prayer for the creation of a new alphabet running in reverse from *Z* to *A* in which the last letters would be a new *B* for Beirut, *poor, ugly, stricken Beirut,* that would be redeemed by a new *A* far from *any army.*

Short Stories

Similar to Makdisi, Daisy al-Amir is also concerned with human beings rather than with a chronicle of the war as such. She makes it clear in her introduction to the collection of short stories entitled *In the Vortex of Love and Hatred* (1979), where she immediately tells the reader that it is the "humanity of man" which she wants to examine: "In all that has happened, she wonders, in the midst of the political, military and international fighting, where is man, the loving, noble, generous, social, tolerant, wise human being?"[7]

In several of her collections of short stories written during the war, mainly *In the Vortex of Love and Hatred* and *Promises for Sale* (1981), al-Amir explores in realistic style many of the situations lived by the Lebanese under harassment: electricity and telephone cuts, the terrible isolation and loneliness, the fear and anguish, the loss of family and friends, of apartments and locality, exile abroad or displacement within, the will to remain and not to leave, together with the protecting love of friends and the solidarity of people. Love and hatred actually coexist, as the title indicates, and love redeems a totally distressing plight.

Reading al-Amir's short stories one understands much better the stamina of some people as well as the savagery of others. The tone is authentic, her style is pure and vivid, with great simplicity. What is worth noting, as well, is her rendering of women's condition in Lebanon and the Arab world at large. In the first short story of the collection *Promises for Sale,* for example, titled "Future, Present, Past," a man is talking to his fiancée assuming she speaks the same language, yet he is totally taken up by his own voice, his words, and future plans, while she is drifting further and further away. Each in his own orbit is creating his own world. Very subtly, in impressionistic style, al-Amir suggests the alienation of her protagonist until she tells him at the end of the story: "I am sorry I cannot marry you." The story closes with her lucid statement that she knew she would feel terribly alone but tomorrow will be a new day.[8]

Another short story, which has often been translated into foreign languages and published in journals abroad, is titled "The Mirror of Eyes." A true story, apparently, in which the heroine is on a professional trip to participate in an international conference. She finds herself in the restaurant of her hotel for dinner. Self-conscious, she chooses a faraway table in the corner of the dining-room which was, to her horror, fully packed with men. Not a single woman, she remarks, totally shattered! As she sits at the table, she realizes that a thousand eyes are staring at her through the mirrors that walled the dining room. She feels awful, and in an inner monologue technique she justifies her presence: "I'm an honest woman, dressed up modestly, I'm here on a professional trip, stop staring at me! stop staring at me!" She then takes flight and sleeps without dinner.[9]

Later she dedicates her collection *In the Vortex of Love and Hatred* to her colleagues who helped her reach her office in bomb-shelled Beirut. They also provided her with food, candles, and matches when she could not leave her apartment. They constantly took risks to help her, which makes her wonder about the amazing mixture of violence and generosity in mankind. Similar to Makdisi, as shown above, she subtly underlines the guilt one feels in a war situation. She thus says through her narrator: "She drew the cushion away. She put down her feet. She could not sit comfortably at home . . . when so many, out there, had lost their homes and did not know what would become of them and of their beloved ones."[10]

Through such domestic details, al-Amir captures Chekhovian scenes where the settings reflect states of being as life was stripped down to mere survival. Her writings, on the whole, are concise, go straight to the unique crisis each short story suggests, depict it realistically from within, and leave the rest to the reader's insight. She could seem out of tune with her epoch if one compared her to a Renée Hayek, for example. Yet she shares with many other socio-realistic Lebanese writers the sorrow for the breakdown of Lebanon and the disintegration of the values that had made it unique. Those values spoke of tolerance, respect for the other, freedom of the individual, and a deep love for the community. The Lebanese people were nurtured by these values while growing up in the fifties and sixties. They fought to keep them alive during the war, as testified to by al-Amir, Nasrallah, and Yared (who are discussed later in this essay). The war generations, on the other hand, to which Renée Hayek belongs witnessed the collapse of such values and tried to convey totally different moods in different styles, as will be seen.

Emily Nasrallah, like Daisy al-Amir, has been writing since the early sixties. She was one of the first female journalists in Beirut. Author of many novels and short stories, as well, a few available in translation, Nasrallah has become a classic writer in her own lifetime. She is read in schools for the purity of her style, which remains classical, simple, and crystal clear, and she has been introduced into the doctoral programs of St. Joseph University in Beirut and the University of Damascus.

Nasrallah has been deeply committed to the cause of women since the beginning of her career, and her novel *The Hostage* (1974) encapsulates the tragic plight of women especially in the rural areas of Lebanon. In it, Rania, the heroine, is betrothed by her poor parents since her birth to a rich man, and remains his prisoner throughout despite all her efforts to leave the village, fly away to the city and liberate herself. Namrud (that is, the "angry man") holds his whip over her head, everywhere, and tightens his grip on her soul until she realizes, in horror and despair, that escape is impossible. She will remain his hostage forever after: "Protest and rebellion ran through my veins, through my nerves, she says, and mobilized every cell of my being. I wanted to push him away and escape from his tight grip."[11] But she realizes that she will remain his *hostage* from birth to death.

This early novel foreshadows much of what Nasrallah develops in her later writings, where her heroines refuse to remain hostages. They become mature human beings who study, take up a profession, often get married, and cope naturally with their various roles in life. The short stories Nasrallah wrote during the war bear many parallels with al-Amir's, as mentioned above. In a socio-realistic style, they record life in an urban atmosphere in which men and women, mostly professional women, live and react to the prevailing violence in war-torn Beirut. The women Nasrallah creates are creatures of love, stamina, and heroism. Their skins are glued to the skin of their city and they remain vigilant in the midst of bombardments and massacres. They are often intellectuals and artists whose self-awareness and willpower insert them into a new epoch in the Arab world. Family and city revolve around them, and when they are displaced within their own country, one of them says "exile became our daily bread," hence, a collection of short stories titled *Our Daily Bread* (1990).[12] Under such tragic conditions, it is the wife and mother who quickly re-creates the semblance of a new home in the most dire of places. She carries with her large "spaces of love and tenderness,"[13] where the family takes refuge.

In another collection of short stories recently translated into English under the title of *A House Not Her Own* (1992), Nasrallah, like so many other Lebanese writers of the period under study, depicts herself as scattered and fragmented: "I become disjointed . . . my parts scattered . . . I am scattered in the corners . . . I have no throat, no vocal cords." Further on, "the rubble and the debris of the city" recur, in the "broken times" when "little holes" are "in the memory," and "rockets explode inside the brain."[14]

Suffering, nevertheless, is redeemed by hope in everything Nasrallah writes. Along with Makdisi and al-Amir, she deeply identifies with the wretched humanity that she describes and stands as both actor and observer through her shifting narrative points of view. Her first-person narrator takes part in the action described, while an omniscient author, elsewhere, recounts what they observe. Moreover, as seen above, women are deeply involved in the tragedy of their city. They perceive the shock and the horror of so much violence. They react by clinging ferociously to life in the midst of the shambles and debris of Beirut.

In a completely different vein comes the collection of short stories ironically titled *Portraits for Forgetfulness* (1994) by Renée Hayek.[15] A young journalist, Hayek reached maturity during the Lebanese war, hence the grayish color she creates. Her collection certainly belongs to a postwar atmosphere and gains when read in the wake of what had been written since 1975. Hayek, however, was very much surprised when she was awarded the first literary prize at the annual book fair held in Beirut in 1994. In several interviews she gave on this occasion, she confessed that she had published her short stories with great reluctance, being overpowered by a deep sense of futility at such an endeavor. Her title, in fact, suggests that her short stories would better be forgotten!

Indeed, the collection announces a new sensibility on the Lebanese literary scene and an original rendering of the inner climate of the female narrator. The eleven short stories that form the collection reduce time to the present moment within which "the author does not create a *work* (a thing made to last, to connect the past with the future) but one current event among many, a gesture with no tomorrow."[16]

Bathed in an urban, grayish atmosphere, all external objects and events reduced to minimal happenings reflect the mood of the female narrator. The latter is invaded by boredom, vacuity, and anguish. She seems to expect nothing of life nor of people around her. Isolated, she lives alone, sits alone in a café where she drinks coffee, smokes, wishes the man facing her would speak to her, and stubbornly bites her nails. She then stands up, leaves the café, and goes to work with no expectation whatsoever. She returns home at the end of the day, has a drink, watches TV and goes to sleep with the full awareness that tomorrow will be like today, gray, empty, boring: "Nothing happens, but that nothing has become a heavy, oppressive, threatening something." Hayek's short stories represent "an entire human existence which has no issue," in a destroyed country and a besieged epoch.[17]

A passage chosen at random from the short story titled "Boredom" captures well the prevailing mood of Hayek's collection: A young woman goes into a café early one morning and sits alone smoking and drinking nervously several cups of coffee. Later, "she bites her nails with stubborn insistence. If only her colleague showed up . . . though she neither liked nor disliked her. She used to look forward to college life . . . She does not like it any more. She fears the next day . . . Several hours will go by, she will feel tired for waiting so much. Nothing happens. A bitter taste fills her mouth."[18] The absurd has certainly invaded Hayek's world.

The Novel

It would have been simpler to conclude that the difference in the writing of short stories between al-Amir and Nasrallah on the one hand, and Hayek on the other, indicates an important generation gap and a new vision of life conveyed in a different style. Things, however, are not so simple, as exemplified by two authors who belong to the same generation as al-Amir and Nasrallah, and who write novels in completely different styles. Nazik Saba Yared is a professor of Arabic literature, a literary critic, and a novelist. Her Arabic novels, starting with the early seventies, faithfully reflect the realities of life in Lebanon. In classical socio-realistic style, she creates feminine protagonists around whom revolves the narration of events as lived daily by the Lebanese, mainly in Beirut.

On the whole, Yared, in her fiction, is eager to defend a few theses. She takes position and creates events drawn from reality, which support her points of view during the war: that woman fights today to gain professional independence, that the professional woman is fulfilled while the one at home is frustrated, that families during the war shouldn't have separated, that the result of separation is a severe gap between those who stuck it out in Beirut and the others who went abroad, that the single professional woman is still the prisoner of a backward mentality which prohibits her from enjoying her financial independence and newly conquered autonomy. These themes are developed by Yared and reflect changing behavioral patterns in a society at war. Interestingly, war seems to precipitate such changes in the life of women while men are busy fighting. During such difficult times, her young protagonist Layla, for example, in *The Point of the Circle* (1983) creates for herself a beautiful position in a prestigious newspaper. She is one of the earliest professional women, in the literature under study, who sacrifices her love for her career.

Indeed, Layla loves Usama and hopes to make him appreciate the importance of her career and how deeply committed she is to her nation and her people. She tells him, following their engagement, as he expects her to go with him to Saudi Arabia where he works: "Usama, your goal in life is your profession for it fulfils you. Indeed your work is the point of the circle in your life. Do you think it is different for me?" Later she adds: "In the last few months my work made me feel how deeply committed I am to my country and my people. I have to carry on to safeguard my personality and my identity."[19] Shattered, Usama leaves the scene unable to understand her.

In contrast with al-Amir's introspective moods and vignette-like stories, Yared often describes scenes of heavy shelling in Beirut. The streets become suddenly empty, children scream, families leave their apartments and take refuge elsewhere, looters and squatters invade the area and take possession of anything they find, and other wartime realities. Under such hard conditions Nagib sends his family to France and suffers from the separation. As expected, he falls in love with Nuha, his colleague at work. Nuha supports her old mother and comes from a traditional background. She finds it extremely difficult to have an affair with a married man and the novel ends as she questions, with irony and bitterness, her freedom in life. Indeed, in reality, she does not feel free at all and refuses to be the mistress of Nagib.[20]

Such situations recurred during the Lebanese war. Yared does not attempt to bring in any moral lesson but just records what she observes, implying or allowing her reader to draw a few basic conclusions about human relationships under duress. In her semi-autobiography *Variations on a Lost Chord* (1992), Saada, her heroine, is sick in a hospital in Beirut and recapitulates her life story. Parallel to Jean Makdisi's narrator, Saada was born in Palestine, was educated in Cairo, then came to Beirut with her mother and sister following the 1948 Arab debacle and the creation of the state of Israel. Hence, the novel dramatizes so many confrontations of cultures since Saada grew up in Palestine and Cairo with girls from the West as well as from the Arab world. Then she was thrown in the midst of religious conflicts when she lived the war in Beirut and she deeply resented all kinds of fanaticism as she was extremely broad-minded.

A bright student, Saada excels in Arabic literature and becomes an academician in a school in Beirut. Her students and friends love her dearly and the author depicts the Lebanese society during the war through her heroine's eyes. Saada is set in contrast to her sister who gets married and has a child. The latter feels deeply frustrated because she cannot carry on with her vocation as a painter; this allows the author to create parallels and contrasts between the sisters' plights. Thus, Saada's, her expertise in Arabic language and literature makes her feel deeply rooted in her heritage. She denounces the sectarian conflicts that prevailed during the Lebanese war and the fanaticism that succeeded in separating former friends: "I do not want to hide anything, Saada says. I neither proclaim my identity [as a Palestinian] nor hide it. Roots, identity, belonging. . . . Words which carry today, dramatic implications."[21] Deeply compassionate, Saada shares many traits with Makdisi's narrator. In both autobiographies, there is a poignant plea for human understanding and respect of the *other.* In short, Yared, in her novel, pleads for tolerance, for a more authentic rootedness in one's language and heritage, for the basic humanistic values defended, as well, by al-Amir and Nasrallah among others. Her personal narrative shows, as in the case of Makdisi's *Beirut Fragments,* the need to take stock and to assert one's place in the universe. Finally, Yared vividly renders the mosaic of Lebanese society as it lived at the edge of annihilation.

This sharp edge between life and death is taken up by Thérèse Aouad Basbous and rescued through the art of writing.

Thérèse Aouad Basbous has been writing plays, poetry, and fiction in Arabic and French since the late sixties. Irony, ambiguity, and a surrealistic imagery define her style. Her most recent "novel," *Mon roman* (1995), which stands in sharp contrast with the autobiographical narrative of Yared's *Variations on a Lost Chord,* will be singled out for analysis. The French title of Basbous's story *Mon roman* is highly ambiguous. Is it "My Novel" in the sense of a piece of fiction that would be new and original? Is it her own story as the possessive pronoun suggests? To feed the ambiguity even further she says, "My title bears no relevance to me. I who is writing . . . A snowy white birth during the seated position I take as I am writing,"[22] the same seated position of women in labor, "My life interests nobody."

And the reader literally witnesses the birth of words on a white sheet of paper. Words come together or dissolve, construct a story or deconstruct whatever was said a moment ago. The author starts thus: "I am scattered. You can't write when you're fragmented . . . this feeling of being divided up. Cut off everything. One's self. The world. Life."[23] The author, then, picks up the fragments of herself and personifies each according to her whims and fantasies. She sets a stage in front of her reader's eyes, gives a role to each of her fragments and fills the scene with pen, paper, and people who start talking, mixing, quarreling or making love. The pencil likes or dislikes what the author is doing, while she adds up or erases whatever she pleases, goddess of her own funny creations. Pathos is cut short by humor, the desire to die is quickly replaced by childhood memories and lifetime loves. Words take shape, stumble, stagger, while the country is afire, bombs fall down like rain, and lovers burn up their passions as the city consumes her inhabitants.

Finally, it may be ventured to say that Basbous's real subject matter is writing itself, writing in the making. She mentions, for example, the white manuscript, the dry piece of paper, then she turns to her audience and takes them as witnesses of her task. She wants to catch the magic of the moment, she says, so she creates a seductive Leila, daughter of the night. Leila asks her, "when is the time for love?" she answers, "when you write," and writing becomes clearly a recuperation of the evanescence of life. She demonstrates in many instances the difficult birth of writing that, nevertheless, is essential to life, part of the flesh and sinews of the artist.

With great originality, Basbous allows her writing to run freely, widely, with exuberance, with pathos, and a streak of madness. She breaks down all barriers of sex, of social taboos, of a strict education in a nun's school. She also breaks away from classical styles in French and Arabic, the two languages she has used equally in her writings since the sixties. Her syntax is syncopated, her sentences very short, often unfinished, her characters intermix as in a Georges Schehadé play, and her prose is highly poetic. It moves by image, pattern, and rhythm on several levels simultaneously, in counterpoint.

Thus, invention and imagination are pushed to frontiers that become the subject matter of the work at hand. The Lebanese postwar reader has witnessed such aesthetic creations in Abdo Wazen's *Garden of the Senses*

(1993), for example, or Rashid al-Daif and Elias Khoury's novels.[24] In such works, stories dissolve and are made up again building up different spatiotemporal relations while the work is bathed in an oneric atmosphere and moves within the mental landscape of the author. Scenario within scenario constantly mystify the reader.

Basbous seems to tell us, in fact, that nothing exists beyond our sensual perceptions, that nothing would exist if we did not fix it down in writing. Wittgenstein warned us, in the very early years of the twentieth century, that the mind's workings are not in the consciousness but in the articulated language. Postmodernism, a vague concept quite difficult to define, would follow this philosophic statement. More specifically, in literature, postmodernism would designate the end of the mimetic model, exemplified above in the socio-realistic short stories and novels, and would usher in the eruption of the autotelic work, the work that revolves on itself, a work whose purpose is purely itself.[25] The writer would write or die, and Basbous assumes this stance.

Finally, one would situate *Mon roman* as an experiment in writing, similar to modern films in the making by a Fellini, a Truffaut, or a Marguerite Duras. One thinks as well of Pirandello's play *Six Characters in Search of an Author,* Joyce's *Finnegans Wake,* Gide's *Les Faux-Monnayeurs,* or Paul Auster's works. In fact, the bulk of what Basbous has written—plays, poems, and fiction—is highly experimental and original on the Lebanese scene. It often reaches the archetypal as in the following example where Pen asks the narrator, "Why Woman? Why you?" (we notice the capital letters that transform the woman in question into all Women). She answers: "I affirm to you, Pen! It is a deep cut, and fracture, and blood, which flows drawing the itinerary of seasons, opening up footpaths and roads towards new upheavals. Life is a hand-vice. Like the light and the candles of my body. Desire is under the skin. And the earth cracks down."[26] Surely an archetypal vision of the cycles of life.

Poetry

In her elegiac ode *I Was a Point. I Was a Circle* (1995–97) Huda al-Naamani also reaches out to the archetypal, the universal. In an impassioned, highly cumulative style, with overcharged images and the building up of symbolic plurals, the Beiruti war scene captures elemental basic historical references that transform the real agonizing city into a Jerusalem of the imagination, an allegorical atemporal space.

A poet and a painter, al-Naamani presently lives in Beirut, after much traveling, and wrote her elegy in Beirut between 1975–77, as she clearly indicates at the end of her long poem. The eleven parts of the poem have individual titles and capture many echoes from T. S. Eliot's *Wasteland* and N. Kabbani's "Beirut" poem, which was sung by Fayruz during the war in many places.[27] Al-Naamani writes in free verse, with a juxtaposition of many jarring elements, a telescoping of time and space, mixed with realistic descriptions that imprison her and choke her being.

Her words, however, reject the prison. Her voice speaks up:"Beirut . . . you are the scream / . . . We die, ah, how much we die!" Archetypes take shape as surrealistic images accumulate:

> I pluck suns from between your eyes,
> I pluck thorns,
> I kindle the twigs of dreams,
> I melt the years, the bloodgroups,
> The conditions of war and peace,
> I cordon off a blue volcano from the right and the left
> It watches me with its white fangs.
> Twilight, is it a calamity that brings you or a flood?
> The desert is turning black,
> The desert is turning green.
> Orbits, expand beyond time, beyond weapons, beyond vipers.[28]

At the beginning of her poem, a doomsday atmosphere is created: "Despair swelled into darkness / Bullets wove an umbrella / . . . The parched earth seeks to imprison . . . your voice." And she resolves all tensions at the end in a mystic prayer to God: "Peace, peace / He is the Creator / . . . He is the just / . . . Peace, Peace."[29]

In sharp contrast stands the poetry in English of Samira Aghacy. Chairwoman of the Humanities at the Lebanese American University of Beirut and a literary critic, Aghacy discovers poetry as she hides in a corridor of her apartment under heavy shelling. In an essay titled "The Carnival of Poetry and the Prison of Facts," she vividly describes how she took pen and paper to kill the time and drown her anxiety. She meant to start a diary, yet, suddenly, she saw, she almost touched words coming together, then verse, then poems. Released, totally self-immersed, she wrote poems for six months completely oblivious of the raging war outside. She also expresses, in her testimony, how she had been totally imprisoned in her daily life by a patriarchal system that stifled her voice, her whole personality.[30]

In the wake of Ezra Pound's imagism, Aghacy writes short, concise, incisive poems where she liberates herself of intense emotional repression, recollected, with anger and passion. The title of the collection *A Spike*

Unleashed (1993) suggests immediately a metallic release as sharp as a point. But the "unleashed" point is contained within the structure of each poem, stark, naked and strictly framed. The mood of release is conveyed through a highly controlled imagery, icy in its violence, yet tragic:

Shocked with the biting smell,
The veins blast.
The bursting deluge
Dashes the
Skeleton form,
On rocks and icebergs
Of a drowning world.

A bursting out of one's innermost being violently arrested by the "hard rocks and icebergs" in a "drowning world"; a powerful poetic rendering of the violence of the times through the accumulation of onomatopoeic words such as "biting," "blast," "bursting": Indeed, a poet is born with a great mastery of her craft. Self-liberation through language, the exorcism of hatred, the breaking down of "the idols of the tribe," be they mother, father, husband, or child, all is tightly encapsulated in such verses as, for example,

A butchering Knife,
My mother,
Digs at my skin,
Slashes the veins
Until blood spews
A stagnant bog.

or

Little round faces,
I place in a bag.
My babies in a trash bag.
No room in the leafy, rotty flat.

and

Like a piece of cloth
In a pail of water,
I shrink
My mind a wart,
A shriveling piece of flesh
In the rays of his obsessive mind.

Let me cool my searing skin
In the depths of a wholeness ocean,
And emerge a launce,
Pacified, released,
In the bracing sands of the shore.[31]

The mother is cruel, there is no room for babies, while man's obsessive mind tragically reduces the female narrator's own mind into "a wart" and a "shriveling piece of flesh." A return to the elemental ocean, however, pacifies her. Released, she unites with "the sands of the shore."

Similar to Aghacy, the poet, novelist, and journalist, Claire Gebeyli kept vigil in her burning city, Beirut. Her faithful readers waited with great expectation for her weekly *Billets*, in the Francophone daily *L'Orient–Le Jour*, a genre she created in journalism, a kind of short poems in prose transforming daily dramatic events into works of art. Part of her *Billets* were later collected in a volume she titled *Dialogue with Fire; Lebanese Notebooks* (1985). Andrée Chedid writes in the preface of the "burning centre of the universe" and states that the author keeps open the question as to the reasons that push men to death in a world that "traffics with human lives."[32]

In a later testimony on the function of writing in her life, Gebeyli confesses that she draws her artistic material, be it journalism or poetry, from the raw stuff of life. She titles her article "Two Functions for the Same Cult," meaning the "cult of writing," and gives the following example of a particularly "black Saturday" in the Lebanese war, transformed into a poem of deep sadness and desolation:

I saw fear face-to-face
Saturday September twenty-nine
The old shop . . .
. . . the parking lot
The broken window
And that sky
So blue so new
That sky which looks
for its place
on Saturday September twenty-seven.[33]

In this particular instance, as in her poetry as a whole, the city is starkly delineated, vibrating at a distance, helpless, desperate, like a human being:

On every roof a bond
in every star a scream
under every coarse gown a city
with every vigil a birth.
And the aching inability
to draw a single branch[34]

A screaming star, an awaited birth, the absence of greenery: The texture of the poem conveys with deep emotional control life sharply arrested yet ready to leap, aching with expectancy, paralyzed by its inability to draw a single branch. The last two lines are arrestingly set off, the end has no punctuation, and the whole is built up on the antithesis between the awaited birth and the incapacity to draw a single branch.

The poem is an epigram chosen to illustrate Gebeyli's symbolist technique. The poet's consummate art ties in her epigram with the title of her collection, *Memorial for Exile* (1975). The existential feeling of loss and exile has traditionally recurred in urban literature, as if men had created a superb artifact, the city, and keep on losing it. The poetry examined here certainly perpetuates this universal tradition. Gebeyli did not leave the city at war but the poet as an exile in her own city is underlined here.

Thus Gebeyli's poems are grafted on the daily events of her city. The difficulty of writing in a city at war, again a recurring theme in the wartime literature examined here, is rendered in a frozen metaphor: "A frozen ice-bank between me and my sheet of paper, between the world and me. There is no more room for a single word, a single letter."[35]

Yet Gebeyli continues to suffer the pangs of labor, as she gives birth to vivid images of a dismembered city. (The metaphor of child labor is immediately suggested in the title *La Mise à jour* [1982], literally meaning "to give birth" and was used by Basbous.)

Gebeyli starts by creating a series of dynamic images pushed wildly into the wind by her need "to name." The city slowly dissolves, carried away by the succession of metaphors. She conquers her space and writes:

A Porch
I had to name
I had to cross . . .
Lost seed on the line of hardened eyes
Set like a kitten
On a dying dance
Heart broken

Burnt up
I had to belong again
Stretch out my arms
To the light strips
Run wild in the wind
I had to write.[36]

Exile for poetess Nadia Tuéni is more specifically women's plight. Thus, she promises women to create for them "a new language, a new world, a new path," for, up to the present moment, women have been exiles in a world not made for them. Tuéni stands as the precursor of so many women who are discovering "in a new voice" that they can start to tailor cut the world to their own "measurements," their own vision. This vindication was encountered above, in the context of Makdisi's "speak up" outcry. Nadia Tuéni started her career writing in the cultural pages of *L'Orient–Le Jour* and then devoted herself to poetry. She died prematurely of cancer in 1983, leaving an important number of collections of poems, which won her several prizes in France and in Lebanon.

Tuéni identified wholly with her decimated nation. To the women of her country, she says:

Woman, I shall create for you something else, a different language, a world, another path.
Woman, I shall reclaim our path, under dormant sands.
Woman, this world is not yours.
Alien are you in it though you try, with such grace, to belong.
Woman let your world be.[37]

And the miracle of language operates. Tuéni unfolds it generously and women step in.

For this brief analysis, Tuéni's volume on the Lebanese war titled *Sentimental Archives of a War in Lebanon* (1982) will be singled out. Previously, her *Beirut* poem (1979) had been rich with political overtones, as she situated her city at the heart of all the crosscurrents of the Middle East. With high concision and allusiveness, she referred to the worshipping of many idols, their breaking down in wars and the never-ceasing flood of people into Beirut's generous heart. At the beginning of this essay there was mention of the cosmopolitanism of Beirut, and Tuéni adds here that "Beirut is in the orient the last sanctuary, / Where man is clad in the color of light."[38] Tragically, however, the freedom of Beirut gave way to sheer political anarchy, says the poet.

In *Sentimental Archives*, Tuéni frees her verse and constructs a three-part dramatic poem that projects the agony of her cherished "sanctuary" on the forefront of the urban stage. The verse quickly runs from past to present and future, while a narrator digs into the deep layers of the city. The "archives" unveil the cruelty of history, the vanity and solitariness of man, while the stage is set for the drama to take place. A shock technique often operates in cubist form, in the midst of a city "white like a tomb." Irony, satire, and black humor punctuate the sequence of vignettes, while deep love for her city makes Tuéni's verse vibrate with renewed life and hope. A striking light imagery renders the mad rhythms of Beirut, a city she loves unto madness as the title of this sequence, "Mad Land," suggests:

> . . .
> I love
> these ashes that taste of a city which was
> more of a city than Antioch or even Babylon;
> words turn my city red-hot
> . . .
> I love
> that a segment of light be called a shriek
> and nova, the madness of men.

A *Nova* is a star that shows sudden and great increase of light and energy for short periods. In one compressed image, Nadia Tuéni seizes the essence of all cities that consume themselves in every recurring outburst of energy and fire kindled, of course, by the madness of men. Once again, a surrealistic imagery projects multiple perspectives on the urban stage, while the poet dies of incoherence in the full glare of the sun. When the poet digs into the archives of her city, the atavistic fights among men are thus bound to provoke rifts of the deepest sort, a total collapse of comprehension.

To sum up, the selection of detail in Tuéni's *Sentimental Archives* is governed not by the logic of verisimilitude but by the demands of the decor necessary to enhance the symbolic significance of the characters' drama, and the tragedy of their city. A feeling of complete identification operates between the poet and her city.[39]

"I belong to my mad land," she confesses, "I create it when I die." A sacred reintegration operates and the poet closes the curtains of her urban stage on a mystic tone which was felt at the closure of al-Naamani's elegiac ode. Tuéni affirms:

Therefore, I held tightly under my tongue a country
Cherished like a host.

Conclusion

I must confess, in conclusion, that I was not fully aware, when I started this essay, of the talent and the breadth of the writers under study. Each text lived from within, in the critic's eye, revealed itself as a dynamic field with many affiliations to author, reader, the historical situation, and other texts, past and present. Moreover, I was personally reacting to every text and author, with mind and heart, since I had lived those same dramatic events while they were being recorded in the midst of a cruel war. Thus, slowly, the body of literature I was analyzing formed a vital aesthetic and cultural whole that mirrors in an arresting way the tragic situation in the Lebanon of 1975–95.[40]

What has come out of this body of literature is a renewed sense of womanhood and citizenship articulated in sober and courageous fashion. The women writers I have considered have certainly grown in maturity and independence as they voiced their opposition to the prevailing violence. They have affirmed their need to be heard and to become active members of their society instead of being merely subservient to men.

The female protagonists dramatized in the works under consideration are, mostly, professional women who are fully involved in the life of their city. Independent, self-aware, and responsible, they articulate much of what educated Lebanese women felt as the war increased in savagery. Thus, the novels, short stories, autobiographies, and poems, written between the years 1975 and 1995, are precious documents of the Lebanese society and its rapidly changing patterns of behavior.

Today, this corpus functions as the memory of war-torn Lebanon between 1975 and 1995, a firsthand rendering of a developing process whereby women write fiction and poetry and register the changing patterns of their lives and of their world vision. Emotions, aspirations, frustrations, and achievements are conveyed in increasingly frank and experimental modes. The complexities of life, the feelings, the agonies, the fragmentation of self and nation, and above all, the courage "to speak up," constitute a recent phenomenon in our country. Lebanon, indeed, has always stood at a crossroads of religions, languages, and culture. East and West meet in Beirut and give birth to a multidimensional body of writings expressed in several languages and techniques, written equally by men and women.

The fragmented self of women is healing in the process.

Notes

1. See, for example, *Le Monde* (Paris), June 2, 1995; *L'Orient–Le Jour* (Beirut), June 13, 1995; and the Beirut press of this period.

2. See Amyuni, "And Life Went On," 1–14. See also for the role of women within displaced families, Hazzaz, "Le défi à la guerre," 59–74. Several participants in this Colloquium later founded the Lebanese Association for Women Researchers, whose yearly publication *Bahithat* is mentioned in this essay.

3. See the leading Arabic newspaper *al-Nahar* (Beirut), which did a questionnaire for the artists who remained in Beirut during the war. Writers, painters, photographers, actors, and playwrights testified for this leading role of Beirut amongst all the Arab capitals. *al-Nahar* (Beirut), August 8–October 25, 1990.

4. Makdisi, *Beirut Fragments.*

5. Makdisi, "Speaking Up," 127–39.

6. Makdisi, *Beirut Fragments,* 185, 203.

7. Daisy al-Amir, *Fi duwwamat al-hubb wal-karahiyah* (In the vortex of love and hatred) (Beirut: Dar al-Nidal, 1979). I owe the title in English to Miriam Cooke in her sensitive study of what she calls the Beirut Decentrists, those women who wrote during the war and spoke "in a new voice," in *War's Other Voices.* Cooke devotes several sections to Daisy al-Amir, Emily Nasrallah, and Claire Gebeyli, among others.

8. Daisy al-Amir, *Wu'ud lil-bay'* (Promises for sale) (Beirut: Dar al-Nidal, 1981), 7–18 (excerpt is my translation).

9. Ibid., 19–26.

10. Al-Amir, *Fi duwwamat al-hubb wal-karahiyah,* 97.

11. Emily Nasrallah, *al-Rahinah* (The hostage)(Beirut: Naufal, 1974), 139.

12. Emily Nasrallah, *Khubzuna al-yawmi* (Our daily bread) (Beirut: Naufal, 1990), 17–26.

13. Emily Nasrallah, *al-Tahuna al-da'i'ah* (The lost mill) (Beirut: Naufal, 1985), 149–60.

14. Emily Nasrallah, *A House Not Her Own; Stories from Beirut,* trans. Thuraya Khalil Khoury (Charlottetown: Gynergy Books, 1992), 21, 43, 44, 45, 85, 87.

15. Renée Hayek, *Portraits lil-nisyan* (Portraits for forgetfulness) (Beirut: Al-Markaz al-Thaqafi al-Arabi, 1994).

16. Milan Kundera, *The Art of the Novel,* trans. from the French by Linda Asher (New York: Grove Press, 1988), 18–19.

17. I have borrowed these two sentences from Auerbach's brilliant discussion of Flaubert's *Madame Bovary* in *Mimesis: The Representation of Reality in Western Literature* (New York: Doubleday, 1945), 431.

18. Hayek, *Portraits lil-nisyan,* 8–13.

19. Nazik Saba Yared, *Niqtat al-Da'ira* (The point of the circle) (Beirut: Dar al-Fikr al-Lubnani, 1983), 227.

20. Nazik Saba Yared, *al-Sada al-makhnuq* (The stifled echo) (Beirut: Naufal, 1986), 12, 35, 36, etc.

21. Nazik Saba Yared, *Taqasim ala watarin da'iʿ* (Variations on a lost chord) (Beirut: Naufal, 1992), 146.

22. Thérèse Aouad Basbous, *Mon roman* (My novel) (Paris: L'Harmattan, 1995), 6–7 (excerpts are my translation).

23. Ibid., 5.

24. Abdo Wazen, *Hadiqat al-hawass* (Garden of the senses) (Beirut: Dar al-Jadid, 1993); see M. T. Amyuni's interpretation in *Beirut Review; A Journal on Lebanon and the Middle East* 7 (Spring 1994):145–52; Rashid al-Daif, *al-Moustabid* (The obstinate) (Beirut: Dar Abaad, 1983); *Fushah mustahdafah bayna al-nouʿasi wal-nawm* (Trapped between drowsiness and sleep) (Beirut: Moukhtarat, 1986); see M. T. Amyuni, "Style as Politics in the Poems and Novels of Rashid al-Daif," *International Journal of Middle East Studies* 28 (1996):177–92; and Elias Khoury, *Abwab al-madinah* (The city doors)(Beirut: Dar Ibn Rushd, 1981); see M. T. Amyuni, "The Image of the City: Wounded Beirut," in *The View from Within: Writers and Critics on Contemporary Arabic Literature*,ed. F. J. Ghazoul and B. Harlow (Cairo: The American University in Cairo Press, 1993), 53–76. See also M. T. Amyuni, *La ville source d'inspiration, le Caire, Khartoum, Beyrouth, Paola Scala, chez quelques ecrivains Arabes contemporains* (Stuttgart: Franz Steiner Verlag, "Beiruter Texte Und Studien," Band 63, 1998).

25. See, for example, Hamadi Qdissi, *Post Modernité, Philosophie, et Esthétique* (Post modernity, philosophy, and aesthetics) (Tunis: Editions Alyssa, 1993), 3, 4, 8, where he quotes Wittgenstein.

26. Basbous, *Mon roman*, 91.

27. Fayruz is the foremost Lebanese singer whose role in her society as spokeswoman for her people is comparable to Oum Kulthum's in Egypt. See my translation of Kabbani's poem, "Beirut," in *Literary Review*, a special issue titled "Bearing Witness: Recent Literature from Lebanon," 37, no. 3 (Spring 1994):498.

28. Huda al-Naamani, *I Was a Point. I Was a Circle*, an elegiac ode translated by the author and S. I. Sara (Georgetown University: Three Continents Press, 1993), 3.

29. Ibid., 1, 66.

30. See Aghacy's testimony written in Arabic in *Bahithat* 2 (1995):23–32.

31. Samira Aghacy, *A Spike Unleashed* (Germany: Al-Kamel Verlag, 1993), 5, 6, 15, 17.

32. Claire Gebeyli, *Dialogue avec le feu: Carnets du Liban* (Dialogue with fire: Lebanese notebooks) (Paris: Editions du Pavé, 1986) (excerpts are my translation).

33. "Two Functions for the Same Cult," *Bahithat* 2 (1995):51–59.

34. Claire Gebeyli, *Mémorial d'éxil* (Memorial for exile) (Paris: Editions Saint-Germain-des Prés, 1975), 9.

35. Claire Gebeyli, *Dialogue avec le feu*, 19.

36. Claire Gebeyli, *La mise à jour* (Giving birth) (Paris: Editions Saint-Germain-des-Prés, 1982), 9. This collection of short poems was earlier awarded the first prize in the literary competition of the Agence de Coopération Culturelle et Technique in Paris in 1980. Parts of this passage on Gebeyli and later parts of the discussion of Tuéni's poetry are inspired by my essay in *The View from Within*, "The Image of the City: Wounded Beirut."

37. Nadia Tuéni, *La Prose, oeuvres complètes* (The collected works in prose) (Beirut: Dar al-Nahar, Collection Patrimoine, 1986), 242 (excerpts are my translation).

38. Nadia Tuéni, *Les oeuvres poétiques complètes* (The collected poems) (Beirut: Dar an-Nahar, Collection Patrimoine, 1986), 278. See my translation of this poem in "Wounded Beirut," 56–57, and in *The Literary Review*, 527–28.

39. Nadia Tuéni, *Les oeuvres poétiques*, 323, and for the verses cited below, 323, 314, 326, 303, respectively.

40. I was impressed for these last few lines by Edward W. Said in *The World, the Text, and the Critic* (Cambridge: Harvard University Press, 1983), 157.

7

Lebanon Mythologized or Lebanon Deconstructed: Two Narratives of National Consciousness

Elise Salem Manganaro

I spent April 1996 in Lebanon, and one of the first things I did upon my return to the United States was rent the John Ford movie *The Grapes of Wrath,* starring Henry Fonda and based on the classic Steinbeck novel. As I watched the film, it was very clear to me that the forced evacuation of farm dwellers in Oklahoma and then the depiction of overcrowded and poverty-stricken slums in California recalled the fate of Palestinians and Lebanese terrorized off their land to be housed in refugee camps or Dahia slums outside Beirut. To me, the tractors that bulldozed the farms, the police that shot the slum dwellers, and the entire organized corporate technocratic powerful machine was Israel itself dominating, expanding, controlling our region. The fact that Israel would choose that title (also drawn from the biblical Revelation and the American "Battle Hymn of the Republic") to describe their military operation in Lebanon was beyond irony.

I begin with *The Grapes of Wrath* because it is a startling and relevant example of how mythic/cultural sources can proscribe a historical/political event. My work is concerned with the relationship between the cultural (specifically the literary text) and the political (particularly the evolving nation in Lebanon), and I would like to examine how two contemporary female authors, Emily Nasrallah and Hanan al-Shaykh, negotiate that relationship differently. As I've made clear from my opening, however, one's positionality determines, to a large extent, one's reading. It is necessary, therefore, to acknowledge how texts might resonate differently in different contexts.

"The Grapes of Wrath" in Lebanon has a certain ring to it these days! The discrepancy of this cultural/political assignation is repeated Sunday nights on Hizballah's TV al-Manar station in Lebanon. Then, an American film is shown, not as mindless entertainment but to provide rich material for a continuous critique (sort of like a somber Islamic "Mystery Science Theater 3000").[1] One can only imagine how a Western audience might respond to Hizballah-produced TV footage. The point, of course, is that our very diverse worlds do not often intersect, but when they do (in a political/military operation or in the reception of a foreign cultural artifact) the opportunities for misunderstanding are high indeed. Part of my work in the United States is to reduce that misunderstanding, and contextualizing the cultural artifact is helpful if useful reception is to take place. In this paper I will be "reading" two contemporary female Lebanese authors against a broad sociopolitical backdrop, but a quick contextualization is in order before I proceed.

Since 1991 and under a Syrian-imposed government, Lebanon's sixteen-year-old internal war virtually came to an end. Israel remained an occupier of one-tenth of the country, however, effectively justifying the continued military action of Hizballah—all other militias were disarmed. The Lebanese nation went about the business of reconstruction despite occasional military exchanges in the South. Something like normalcy was returning to the lives of most Lebanese. One now had the luxury to debate strategies of nation building, on whether to focus on infrastructure or funnel monies toward human resources, on how best to institute electoral and judicial reforms, promote civic and national awareness, revise the educational curriculum, reconstitute Beirut's downtown financial district, and, less publicly, to wonder about Syria's continued hegemony over the country. Intellectual and cultural activity, especially through Lebanon's free press, guaranteed that the debate would enter the public domain. Beirut was the publishing center of the Arab Middle East, Lebanese newspapers were amazingly blunt in their political assessments, new TV talk shows thrived on openly discussing previously taboo subjects, and theater was popular and bold again. Despite Syrian hegemony and occasional government censorship, Lebanon's cultural output was vibrant and varied.

Then in April of 1996 Israel launched its "Grapes of Wrath" sixteen-day offensive supposedly against Hizballah fighters but literally against Lebanese civilians, villages, and infrastructure. The effect was devastating. In Qana, where Jesus supposedly turned water into wine, over 100 Lebanese were killed by a succession of Israeli rockets that even UN peacekeepers and foreign reporters knew could have been no accident. Lebanese newspapers, flooded with gruesome photos of the massacre, also made room for narratives, and not just the typical political editorial.

Al-Safir and *al-Nahar* papers, for example, relegated much space to poems, tributes, drawings that captured something of the misery wreaked upon Lebanon. Qana quickly became a rallying cry for all Arabs resisting Israeli aggression; the wine was now transformed into blood; for every victim a flower would grow, creating a renewed Lebanon, and so on. The narratives are symbolic, grief-stricken, angry, and, amazingly, patriotic. They bespeak an unusual solidarity among Lebanese.

Already Qana has become a pilgrimage site, Lebanese officials are holding meetings there, and the government has announced plans for a commemorative stamp and museum. Four days after the massacre, Lebanon held an official day of mourning that saw Christians and Muslims surprisingly united in tragedy. The incident at Qana is prime material for the myths upon which nations are built. Ernest Renan, one of the first scholars to write on the concept of nationalism, claims that perhaps the most crucial criterion for the formation of a nation is the need for a common "rich legacy of memories." In fact, he continues, the sharing of a past is made all the more poignant through common suffering: "Where national memories are concerned, griefs are of more value than triumphs, for they impose duties, and require a common effort."[2] The myths and instantly produced literary texts resulting from tragedy are hence useful gauges of the cultural climate and circulate, like popular song and TV shows, in the public domain. And it is here where, as Gramsci taught us, potential cultural/political work can be done.[3]

My interest lies primarily in how cultural production enters and resonates within that domain; how the intellectual, the author, shapes her discourse to effect and/or respond to the huge challenges that shape the nation-state. I read the texts of contemporary writers with an eye for a suggestion, a solution, a transformation (aesthetic or social or political). I wonder if these texts can be "transformative agents" in the Gramscian sense; are they sufficiently embedded in the popular culture; who do they speak for and to? How can they contribute towards a discourse on national consciousness?

Because of the recent tragedy in the South, I thought it relevant to focus on two authors from the South who write about the South. Lebanese recognize the full import of the South, *al-Janub.* Ever since the 1969 Cairo Agreement, which legitimized Palestinian resistance against Israel from Lebanon, it is the South that has suffered the consequences of Israeli reprisals. And after the 1982 Israeli invasion, with its purpose of destroying the PLO in Lebanon, it was the Shiʿa of South Lebanon who became displaced when Israel established its so-called Security Zone there. Hizballah was formed as a military resistance force to the Israeli occupation and has usually concentrated its attacks (with antiquated Katyusha rockets) on Israeli positions within that "zone." As a region, the South has been traditionally underfunded by weak Lebanese governments. The people of the South, generally poor, underrepresented, and victims of Israeli aggression, have been labeled *al-Mahrumin* (the deprived) and have generated entire political, cultural, and intellectual movements.

A group of poets, *shuʿaraʾ al-janub* (poets of the South,) is writing some of the most innovative and important poetry in Lebanon today. Popular singers like Marcel Khalife and Julia sing the plight of the South calling for resistance, honor, and revolution. Many organizations, presses, and councils (like *al-majlis al-thaqafi li-lubnan al-janubi*, the Cultural Council for South Lebanon) devote all their activity to the plight of the South. Both Amal and Hizballah are powerful Shiʿa political and military movements that represent the South. The South, in other words, is Lebanon's current cause célèbre. It would be impossible to be in a public gathering where the South is proclaimed without there being an outburst of applause. It has generated a rhetoric of defiance and solidarity and something like national fervor.

During the 1975–91 war years, Nasrallah (like most other Lebanese authors) wrote about the war: She graphically describes how car bombs rip families apart, how Lebanese are forced into a life of miserable exile abroad, how Beirut women survived the Israeli invasion, and other effects of the war.[4] I was curious, though, to see what she was writing about after 1991, when most of Lebanon was at peace but the South was still smoldering, when social and economic rehabilitation proceeded apace despite serious political inequities. Lebanon was experiencing a new phase of nation-building and search for identity—now was the time to assess the damage and begin a program of recovery. Intellectuals, journalists, artists, and authors, as I've mentioned, were doing a good job of keeping the central issues alive in newspapers, the press, drama, and TV.

After 1991, Nasrallah published many short stories in *Fayruz*, a woman's magazine, and a collection of her stories, *Mahattat al-rahil* (Stations of departure, 1996), has recently appeared. In 1995, she published her first novel in eight years, *al-Jamr al-ghafi* (Sleeping embers), to positive reviews. Although she writes "literature" (often considered an elite form of cultural production), Nasrallah's work is relatively popular. She is the only Lebanese female author whose work is regularly anthologized in textbooks, and because her stories are often first printed in popular magazines, her audience is considerable.

Perhaps the most striking aspect of her post-1991 works, however, is that they do not overtly confront the reality of the long war or deal with the predicament of the South or any other social/political cause. Could her work be culturally constructive or socially active? Was there anything here to forward a discourse on identity and national formation, so crucial to Lebanon at this juncture?

The novel *Sleeping Embers* is set in two pasts: the first, between the two world wars when emigration from Lebanon to the United States was heavy; the second, some twenty-five years later (pre-1960) as one of the emigrants, Nuzha, returns to the southern village to "stir the sleeping embers."[5] Reading this 350-page novel this past April in the context of Lebanon's recent history (and literally as the South was undergoing its most major pummeling since 1982) was rather extraordinary. Not a single opportunity for political or social elaboration on then-important (and still current) issues is developed. A secondary character, Fares, feels resentment because he is an outsider to the village; from Maronite Mt. Lebanon, he questions the legitimacy of the larger nation. But his resentment and political musings are only fleetingly mentioned and come to nothing. The motivation to emigrate, supposedly every villager's dream, is left unconvincing since everyone seems to be a rather satisfied landowner. Yet feudalism, political oppression, and poverty were more the rule than the exception in these villages. Muslim/Christian coexistence and tension in the South (as across all of Lebanon) is never a reality in this novel. The Lebanese Christian migration to the Americas would soon be followed by Muslim Shiʿa emigration to West Africa, yet the incredible wealth accumulated by a minority Shiʿa and the social transformation resulting from the returning multi-confessional immigrants is left unbroached.

I searched as well for a potentially liberating feminist agenda. In 1962, Nasrallah wrote *Tuyur aylul* (September birds), a novel that inaugurated her concerns for a female consciousness. Most of her works since then have focused on women and she has earned a reputation as an Arab feminist author. Perhaps a political agenda could be discerned through gender issues, but I was disappointed here as well. The novel *Sleeping Embers* is dedicated to the "spirit of Lea," a character who is humiliated in the village when she is supposedly discovered not to be a virgin on her wedding night. We later find out that her husband was impotent and that she suffered a great injustice, but her character is neither central nor is her gendered plight elaborated on. The main character, Nuzha (the impotent man's second wife), promises at first to be a feminist heroine. She returns to the village as the successful immigrant searching for a groom (a reversal of the usual gendered formula), but she remains hopelessly in love with a confirmed bachelor and coward who is unmoved by her flirtatious attempts. The book's cover, in fact, is graced by that same bachelor, presented always as a man of conscience, wisdom, and great restraint. He seems to represent the novel's moral core and whatever feminist concerns exist are left trailing in the book's wake.

In her other recent stories, feminist issues are totally dissociated from their socio-political contexts. Repeatedly, Nasrallah undermines the realities of the *watan* (homeland) to focus on the private lives of her female protagonists. In "*Sahwah*" (Awakening), for example, a middle-aged woman, unhappily married to a sick man she no longer loves, fancies herself in love with another. She reflects upon her marriage which has declined like her nation after sixteen years of war. A brief paragraph then describes the ravages of war and the postwar time; this is the "reality that surrounds her . . . the reality of her nation," she muses.[6] And yet in a flash all that reality is erased as she recalls the face of her lover.[7] She later feels guilty at being so immersed in her own feelings, but this is not the central conflict of the story. The point of crisis that leads to her "awakening" is when her supposed lover comes to visit her at the end of the story and surprisingly introduces her to his young fiancée! The plight of the nation not only does not consume the protagonist, it is hardly a factor in her very being. This is not to say that thwarted love is not a legitimate crisis, but it is worth noting that the personal is so disconnected from the social that it is especially challenging to detect a pragmatic political (including gender) discourse.

Other stories in the same collection, *Mahattat al-rahil*, introduce female characters like Hanan in "*Sik Bara'a*"—(Document of innocence) or Selma in "*Wa yabki al-zahr*"—(And the flowers weep) who have emerged from sixteen years of war totally unaltered. The author deliberately, in fact, states that all outside forces left no impression on them. But this is not elaborated on as a philosophical point. Social and political forces are simply not formative in Nasrallah's discourse; they exist to temporarily impinge upon supposedly insular human lives. They may or may not disrupt one's routine, initiate new thoughts or feelings, but they do not take center stage as constructing a base or superstructure that might determine all subsequent human action. Consequently, Nasrallah the humanist, who has chosen a feminist (or more accurately a womanist) mission, constantly prioritizes the internal voices of women as legitimate and worthy metanarratives. It is a syndrome I find quite reminiscent of earlier twentieth-century Western feminist discourse when the incentive was to de-marginalize female voices. The prioritization of this mission has often led to de-politicization, a condition then countered by certain First and Third World women feminists who reclaimed a feminist agenda from within a broader nationalist cause.[8]

But I don't intend to just dismiss Nasrallah's fiction. She has consistently provided a much needed discursive space for women's consciousness, even though that consciousness is generally severed from its sociopolitical source. When one considers the dismal record of women's rights in countries like Lebanon, any foregrounding of women is important work. The fact that Nasrallah's texts are popular also insures that they have entered the public domain and reach a wide audience.

The real impact of her post-1991 texts, however, lies in her ability to recreate a mythology of national consciousness, a collective memory of a past, idealized Lebanon. One cannot but be jolted in *"Dhahiba ila bayrut"* (She is going to Beirut) as the author carefully describes Sahat al-Burj (Burj Square, Beirut's downtown) with its cinemas, hotels, and souks—a district ravaged in the first two years of the war (1975–76) and now totally leveled in the Solidère project to rebuild the downtown. In *"Sanduq al-firji"* (The wonder box), Nasrallah recalls the chants of the gypsy-like travelers of her childhood; they came to the village with the box of wonders and called for the kids to take a peep inside and relive the glories of the great epics.

The nostalgic quality to these stories is captured as well in her novel, *Sleeping Embers*. Like the stories, this novel's inspiration comes from Nasrallah's remarkable ability to evoke some of the nuances of her childhood culture in the South. Almost ethnographic, the novel records customs and values, describes homes and the church, and, perhaps most important, foregrounds the dialogue between the villagers, giving the reader a good chance to "hear" the numerous proverbs, expressions of greeting and hospitality, and overall cadences of the colloquial rural southern Lebanese Arabic language. These were the good old days and there is almost a desperate sense to record them before they disappear forever from the nation's collective memory. The nostalgia reinforces the sense that the past was better, simpler, and purer than our present. In interviews, she has stated that she has wanted to educate a new generation, to give them solid values and a secure sense of the past to offset the anarchy of the war years.[9] This same incentive continues to drive the Lebanese Baccalaureate curriculum and help shape much of the cultural reproduction of the nation. Gramsci talks at length about the role of education in fostering a thinking citizen within the evolving nation.[10] Education is intrinsically linked to cultural production, so how has Lebanon's educational program promoted critical inquiry? How have school texts been transformative tools? What function has the culture of education served within the political culture of Lebanon?

Even a quick glance through elementary Arabic textbooks reveals an interesting selection of texts. While there are many excerpts from Lebanese authors of the twentieth century, they are mostly defanged of political, economic, or social issues. The great majority are descriptive pieces, often on the village and almost always set in a previous generation. Quasi-nationalistic poems praise an idealized Lebanon no one has ever experienced, but there is no conscious irony, dialectic, or humor. Khalil Gibran's glorification of the Lebanese peasant and mountainside are represented, as are Maroun Abboud's unproblematized pro-independence stories, and Emily Nasrallah's quaint portrayal of the southern Lebanese village. This is a curriculum that still, in some schools, uses a geography textbook with pictures of downtown Beirut taken in 1970 (the downtown no longer exists—not a single building was left intact!). Most history books make absolutely no mention of Lebanon's recent wars (and the revised book, I was told, will only make nominal references to the sixteen-year war, focusing on leaders' names and dates of treaties only). These ludicrous omissions are deeply entrenched as well in the rhetoric of our political leaders who deliver tiresome speeches that every Lebanese recognizes as lies. But that tension between what is said and what is known is also part of the culture. It is that gap between the mythology, if you will, and the reality (whatever that may be) that allows for irony, humor, and a playful dialectic that we witness in some cultural productions. While the text might be inherently devoid of irony, its reception might, on the contrary, highlight that irony. Then again, it might not. It depends, partially, on positionality.

Ernest Renan wrote that "forgetting" and "historical error" are actually essential qualities to any nation formation.[11] Benedict Anderson would later develop the theory that nations exist partially as the result of the narratives that "imagine" them.[12] Hence myths, stories, folklore—exaggerated and only marginally historically relevant—cannot be dismissed as mere sentimental wishful thinking. They too can serve a purpose in creating a popular philosophy of the people. Gramsci advocates taking folklore seriously as it could bring about the birth of a new culture.[13] Although national myths and symbols can be (and certainly have been) harmful, they can also reinforce positive feelings of national solidarity. I am suggesting that Nasrallah's work may function at this level, providing something like national memory—even though the memory is of no real time or place.

I am also suggesting that even when one admits to constructionist theories of nation, the power and impact of national myths are real, and that's where Nasrallah's work primarily resides. I'm trying to refrain from passing easy critical judgment here and to expose something like the experience of being part of the Lebanese nation. And, like all nations, there seem to be entire cultural industries in Lebanon intent on preserving a distorted national memory. It is the Lebanon of Gibran, the dabke dance, and the glorious singer Fayruz; the Lebanon of snow-capped mountains, red-roofed village homes, the "holy" cedars, and Phoenician coast. One of Lebanon's recent big "hits" is the Caracalla dance troupe's production of *Elissa,* story of the ninth-century B.C. Phoenician princess of Tyre (just a few kilometers from Qana in south Lebanon) who kills herself after founding Carthage rather than be wedded to a man she does not love. The drama then shifts to "present Lebanon" and the upcoming wedding of a village couple. The bride-to-be, initially refusing her groom, is quickly seduced (unlike the virtuous Elissa) by his wealth. Instead of being a damning critique of Lebanon (which has seemingly lost its pristine Phoenician values), the production concludes with the festive marriage and a riveting traditional dabke dance. Clearly described as "present Lebanon" in the program, this last scene is actually set in an undefined static past neither Ottoman-dominated, nor during the French Mandate, nor under Lebanon's postindependence government. It is the Lebanon of so many of our songs, our stories, our myths.

I attended this production, very hesitatingly, on April 18, the day of the Qana massacre. We weren't sure they would perform that night; phones were down due to the Israeli bombardment of Beirut's two major electrical plants, so we had no luck calling the theater and just appeared, rather certain the audience would be miniscule. It was huge—a somber full house! The last number, the incredibly joyous dabke of the entire troupe (linked arm to arm in a human line across the stage), was being performed to an audience that had just come from watching the evening news, which showed the most graphic footage of any massacre anywhere, anytime. This was present Lebanon. But the glowing dancers on the stage, the rhythmic music, the gorgeous costumes. . . . That night we knew we wouldn't give up that dabke for the world!

The power of myth to invoke national sentiment needs to be acknowledged in any theory that attempts to study culture in conjunction with politics. Nasrallah's contribution to the discourse on national consciousness exists, I believe, at the level of folklore. And especially while the nation is in crisis, the folkloric or the mythic can take on special poignancy and significance. The devastation brought upon the social fabric of Lebanon has resulted in a special need for healing. Narratives that assert an uplifting value-laden mythic Lebanon can certainly assist in that healing process.

Hanan al-Shaykh, another Lebanese fiction writer from the South, provides a very different kind of discourse from the nostalgic, myth-invoking

Emily Nasrallah. Whereas Nasrallah presents a relatively static and positive Lebanon entity, Shaykh intentionally demystifies Lebanon, constantly undercutting and dislodging her subject so that it is virtually impossible to formulate a fixed, let alone a positive, sense of the nation. I would like to focus on Shaykh's 1992 *Barid bayrut*[14] (Beirut mail, translated as *Beirut Blues*, 1995) as an important example of another post-1991 extended narrative by a Lebanese southern woman (and an interesting contrast to Nasrallah's stories and *al-Jamr al-ghafi*).

At first glance there may seem to be some obvious points of similarity between the authors. Both focus on women, deal with the South, and recall a past Lebanon, and yet so drastically opposed are these two writers in their perspectives on each of these issues that it would be pointless to dwell on extended similarities. A careful look at Shaykh's novel will uncover, I believe, significant points of difference with Nasrallah on questions relating to national discourse.

Unlike Nasrallah, Shaykh's fiction is overtly political and conscious of socio-economic factors. Her novel is set in 1985 as rival Shiʿa militias were vying for dominance in Beirut. As Hizballah gains ground in the Dahia, the Syrians intervene on the side of Amal. The PLO, evacuated after the 1982 Israeli invasion, are replaced by other groups. The Christian factions, Lebanese government, Iranian fighters, and Israeli army are all players in the arena as well. But this military and political reality is not merely a backdrop for Shaykh's fiction; it is an intrusive and transformative reality. No one has been left unaltered by the events of the war. Everyone and everything has changed. Beirut is a divided city and its people no longer know how to relate to each other. City and landscapes have been forever transformed by bombs, by ugly rebuilding, by cannabis and opium poppies. The very lives and values and thoughts of Shaykh's Lebanese have been altered, unlike Nasrallah's characters. In a recent interview, Shaykh responds to a question on whether the war wounds have started to heal: "I believe that the Lebanese people don't want to look back and discuss the war or even think about it. They don't want to understand it; they don't want to analyze it so that they can live peacefully with it. They are putting it in a dark closet and saying 'We don't want to deal with it'."[15] One of the objectives, or certainly one of the consequences, of reading Shaykh's fiction is that it forces the Lebanese reader to re-confront the war. I mentioned previously that there is an active Lebanese cultural and educational industry that blatantly denies the complicated and messy internal Lebanese reality. Shaykh's cultural output is an example of an opposite industry that attempts to keep the difficult issues alive and in the public domain.

Unfortunately, Shaykh's fiction is not especially well known within Lebanon. Despite excerpts and positive reviews of her work in leading local newspapers and journals, her output remains rather isolated within intellectual circles. She herself admits that she is more popular abroad than within her own country; most of her fiction has been translated into English and she has achieved a reputation as a leading Arab woman writer, an assignation, by the way, that she dislikes.

The point of all this is that, despite her populist intentions, Shaykh's work is unpopular, or at least not well known. She does not fulfill a folkloric criterion deemed suitable for the government educational curriculum, nor has she been able to claim a voice from within the larger public. Constantly aware of her position as a writer living in London away from the community she writes about in *Beirut Blues,* she tackles this question of positionality in her fiction. Asmahan, the narrator and writer of the letters that constitute the novel, is very careful to distinguish herself from another observer and writer/photographer, Jawad. Especially toward the end of the novel, as Asmahan gradually realizes that she will not leave Lebanon, she criticizes her lover Jawad for recording, as if for some scientific experiment or a folkloric project, everything he observes in Lebanon. Fresh from Paris and thrown into the tumults of war, Jawad is fascinated by the experience. Asmahan notes that we are "specimens under your microscope," "you regard us with a foreigner's eye. . . . You see us as folklore."[16]

The folkloric is that which supposedly identifies Lebanon for the outsider; it can be defined, labeled, studied, appropriated, passed on. It also, as we saw with Nasrallah, resides in a past and has static qualities that need to be remembered and commemorated narratively and mythically. With Asmahan as her mouthpiece, Shaykh seems scornful of any attempts to crystallize the past or reduce Lebanon to a folkloric mythology.

Asmahan is especially bitter when she realizes that Jawad is using Lebanon as material for his novel: "I'm irritated at the way he continues to look at everything as if he is turning it into a work of literature" (276). Almost like a vulture, his art thrives on the death of his subject. He admits: "I pick the bitter fruits of war and write in a Western language about the emotions which lie between my language and my conscience. The more successful I am, the more my conscience troubles me, because I always used to long for this country to be destroyed" (359).

Jawad's remarks capture a generally unspoken and insidious consequence of Lebanon's wars: the capitalization on the tragedy by outsiders. We are all aware of the numerous foreign journalists' accounts, artistic renditions, scholarship, and documentaries, that have created saleable products inspired by Lebanon's demise. Shaykh fears that her own work might be regarded in this way: "I was terrified when [*Beirut Blues*] was published in Arabic in 1993 as to whether or not the Lebanese were going to judge my novel as being from the point of view of a voyeur writing about 'their' war" (6). Although her positive reviews in Lebanon dispelled those fears, they are still warranted.

In one of the most revealing admissions in the novel on this subject, Asmahan, at the end of the novel, declares: "[Jawad] only sees what is in his camera lens and recorded in his notebook. I don't want to become like him, collecting situations and faces and objects, recording what people around me say, to give my life some meaning away from here. I don't want to keep my country imprisoned in my memory. For memories, however clear, are just memories obscured and watered down by passing time. There are many empty corners between remembering and forgetting. I want things to be as they are, exposed to the sun and air, not hidden in the twists and turns of my mind" (360).

Asmahan decides to remain in Lebanon and live out the days rather than attempt to capture/reduce the experience while living abroad. Jawad's art, like her own memory, will end up imprisoning/limiting/simplifying the reality of Lebanon, and this she will refuse to do. Not coincidentally, in her own art, Shaykh does all she can to counter the impulse to reduce Lebanon in any way. By providing many voices, differing perspectives, intricate details, conflicting scenarios, unresolved emotions, and other pluralities, Shaykh presents a vibrant and lived reality. It is not static and not comforting. On the contrary, Shaykh's Lebanon is disturbing and fluid. Asmahan notes: "The country was as hard to grasp as beads of mercury" (89). People and places were not what they seemed; even the language had changed. The nation could not be held in the palm of one's hand, could not be recalled by memories of an idyllic past, could not be identified by its traditional folkloric practices.

One of Shaykh's most effective means of accentuating the very fluidity of the nation is in her depiction of the various political parties within Lebanon. Not only is every group undermined and demystified, but the communities (and hence the individuals) linked to those groups are also implicated and, by association, undercut. The overall effect is an unsentimental portrayal of citizens, institutions, societies, and the larger nation.

Many of Shaykh's political barbs are bold and confrontational in that they go against public political discourse in Lebanon. The Palestinians, depicted mainly through flashbacks linked to Asmahan's *fida'i* (Palestinian commando) boyfriend Naser, are only reservedly praised. Though their "cause" against Israel may be just, and their expulsion after the 1982 invasion tragic, they are also presented as damaging to Lebanon. Asmahan suggests that perhaps the Palestinians should leave Beirut so that Israeli retaliations would not destroy the city she loves (74); Asmahan's grandfather, like many Shiʿa from the South, detests the Palestinians who have occupied and abused his land (108, 134); their "cause," in other words, has not always been clean. In fact, Asmahan confronts Naser on exactly this point: "You confused the words for wealth [*tharwah*] and revolution [*thawrah*], which sound similar in Arabic, and I said it was not a slip of the tongue, but a slip of the soul" (79).

Shaykh's depiction of Hizballah is equally disconcerting. While she describes the Dahia in all its vibrancy with its many shops, narrow streets and inhabitants, and she presents characters, like Fadila, who praise the social services provided by Hizballah (303), Shaykh does not hesitate to voice criticism of their cult of kidnapping and desire for martyrdom. A veiled Shiʿa woman in Asmahan's village in the South lashes out at the young men so eager to become famous martyrs, painted before their suicide missions: "Well, Asmahan, did you see those madmen's pictures? See how stupid they are. They're the death of their families. Their mothers put up with all the pain of giving birth to them, sweep up cowshit for their sakes, and raise them. The fathers die a thousand deaths to keep their mouths stuffed with food, and go out begging to make sure they have an education. As soon as they're old enough, they say, 'Bye bye. We're off now" (156).

Whatever ideologies the various militias might have espoused, they are almost totally overshadowed in this novel by a desire for a quick buck. Drugs, ransom, theft are the order of the day. The fields in the South are overrun by cannabis and poppy plants, militiamen (counseled by foreign drug experts) manage the drug trade, and the villagers partake actively in the daily work of cultivation, manufacture, and packaging. It is a thriving business that involves all Lebanese denominations and factions: "Here each party, each sect, needed the other. Who would distribute these sacks of hashish apart from the Christians with their connections with the outside world? Who would plant the cannabis, irrigate it, and harvest it, other than the Shiʿites? Who would handle the cocaine if the Druzes didn't?" (250).

In the English translation of this novel, Shaykh also implicates the Syrians in the drug trade. One of the American-educated sons of a drug family designed a small plane to use for "short runs into Syria" (113). The Syrians are feared and need to be placated. They enter the Dahia to assist the Amal movement against Hizballah and bring terror to the inhabitants. But an interrogator, who kidnaps and then releases Jawad, lectures him on the many benefits the Syrians have brought to Lebanon: They succeeded in releasing the hostages, stopped fighting between internal Lebanese factions, and were intent on restoring Lebanese sovereignty (340). Could anyone question that?

Although the political players might be the most obvious target of moral degeneration in the novel, few of the ordinary citizens come off as much better. People are primarily motivated by self-interest, but the presentation is not overly judgmental and steers clear from any sense of moral superiority. The overall effect of reading Shaykh's fiction is of a refreshing honesty in the depiction of human nature. Characters, thoughts, and feelings are trivial, funny, concrete, and constantly undermine sentimental and abstract grand notions of self or other.

Asmahan herself is perhaps the most vividly drawn. Her self-portrait is highly ironic, humorous, and self-involved. And it is defiantly so. When her friend living abroad questions Asmahan about the import of the war and assumes that she is immersed in large sociopolitical issues, she has no way of knowing that, in fact, Asmahan (as she herself admits) is "absorbed with the trivia of love and sex, and at the moment with the rat" (3). Later, as she is being evacuated from Beirut in a tank, she worries not about the gravity of the precarious situation at hand, but about her failure to attract. The militiaman has ignored her: "I must have stopped being attractive. He hadn't responded to my smile" (64). Even when she makes one of her most insightful comments in the novel criticizing Jawad's regarding "us with a foreign eye" (225), she pauses to reflect on her own motives for attacking him. "Is the heart of the problem that you [Jawad] are not attracted to me? Am I jealous of Juhayna and her youth?" (225–26).

The extent to which Shaykh undermines political discourse is matched by her willingness to undercut all forms of traditional Lebanese discourse. Nothing, not even the land, not even memory, is sacred. All is subject to review, to exposure. Shaykh intends to stir the waters, not to leave them safely unperturbed. I mentioned above the refusal of the educational curriculum to confront harsh Lebanese realities in recent textbooks. Here, on the contrary, we meet a schoolteacher who can no longer teach the expected history and geography classes: "He could no longer stand the hypocrisy of explaining with apparent objectivity how the administrative districts of Lebanon had been reorganized, found himself unable to ramble on about its snowcapped mountains and ski resorts when there were armed men at the top of the runs keeping the skiers in line" (228).

Shaykh is not interested in preserving a distorted national memory or identity. Her direct approach has the effect of discomforting readers even while they recognize the truth of what they read. It's an honesty that we occasionally see in TV talk shows like *al-Shatir yihki* (Let the clever one speak) that do not hesitate to expose some of the most taboo subjects in Lebanese society; it is a directness matched in recent drama by Ziad al-Rahbani or Rafiq Ali Ahmed; it is a discomforting style that we witness in the writings of Elias Khoury and Abdo Wazen. It is part of a cultural opposition (*mu'aradah*) that has not yet met its match in a sociopolitical transformative movement, but its power resides in its potentiality to invoke change.

At the 1994 MESA (Middle East Studies Association) convention in Arizona, Shaykh spoke about how she attempted to capture something of the Beirut she remembered before the war altered it forever. In *Beirut Blues*, one of the letters is addressed to Beirut and, before revisions, was over 300 pages long.[17] Cut down to about 65 pages in the actual Arabic publication (and English translation), the letter to Beirut is only marginally in a reminiscent mode. The flashbacks to Sahat al-Burj, for example, are not purely nostalgic descriptive pieces that serve as sad contrasts to Beirut in ruins. Not at all. The city now has soul, Asmahan notes: "Even the alley cats have become real cats, catching flies, missing an eye or a leg . . . my city . . . had begun to pulsate with life like cities with long histories, Cairo for example. Characters emerged who seemed eternal and had some kinship with the half-collapsed wall; apartments which previously dreamed only of the smell of food and the rustle of soft dresses became houses for convictions, ideas, where people could breathe freely and make love . . . I was like a bee, discovering the honeycomb city with you [Naser]. I sat facing the sea, the hookahs bubbling around me, and found I was not distracted by the images of devastation and dead bodies the way I used to be."[18]

There is no time or place in Shaykh for nostalgia, for fixating on a past era that never was (or could have been) ideal. Hers is a narrative that proceeds with the irony, dialectic, and humor that we do not encounter in Nasrallah. It offers not solutions, per se, but potential discourses of transformation that, perhaps alongside the national myths, can also serve a function in Lebanon's search for meaning. By refusing to store memories and events in a "dark closet," by insisting on wanting "things" to be "exposed to the sun and air," Shaykh forces the Lebanese to confront who they are and what their nation has become.

With Qana and "The Grapes of Wrath" as recent national memories, Shaykh's fiction seems to steer a course away from pure sentimentality and an ideology of victimization. The South that she presents is complex, containing within it some of the seeds of its own destruction. The Lebanese have a knack for placing the blame elsewhere, but Shaykh is not willing to let them so easily off the hook. Her narrative deconstructs the nation with all its trappings and poses a great challenge to the reader/ citizen who must then endure the glare of painful recognition. With myths and tributes set aside, perhaps national reconciliation and nation building in the spirit of a genuine civil society can then become a reality.

Notes

1. I am referring to a parodic cable program in the United States where two aliens and a human observe and provide constant hilarious commentary on a film, usually a trashy one.

2. Ernest Renan, "What Is a Nation?," trans. Martin Thon, in *Nation and Narration,* ed. Homi Bhabha (London: Routledge, 1990), 19.

3. In his *Selections from the Prison Notebooks* (ed. and trans. Quintin Hoare and Geoffrey Nowell Smith [New York: International Publishers, 1971]), Antonio Gramsci argues that culture, especially popular culture, has a crucial sociopolitical role to play. For a national literature to reach its potential as a transformative agent, it must be deeply entrenched within a popular culture that circulates in the public domain (333–42).

4. I am referring here to a selection of Nasrallah's work like *al-Iqla' 'aks al-zaman* (Departure against time) (1981), *al-Mar'ah fi 17 qissah* (Women in seventeen stories) (1984), and *al-Tahunah al-da'i'ah* (The lost mill) (1985).

5. Emily Nasrallah, *al-Jamr al-ghafi* (Sleeping embers) (Beirut: Naufal, 1995), 307, 316.

6. Emily Nasrallah, "*Sahwah*" (Awakening), in *Mahattat al-rahil* (Stations of departure) (Beirut: Naufal, 1996), 105.

7. Ibid.

8. Gayatri Spivak, Chandra Mohanty, Nawal al-Saadawi, and Benita Parry are just a few examples of feminists who have sought to theorize on Third World literature in broad political terms.

9. Cooke, "The Globalization of Arab Women Writers," 184.

10. Antonio Gramsci, *Selections from the Prison Notebooks,* 37–40.

11. Renan, "What Is a Nation?" 11.

12. In his *Imagined Communities,* 26–46, Benedict Anderson argues that narratives (popularized and disseminated through the advent of print capitalism) help construct the cultural communities that become the modern nations.

13. Antonio Gramsci, *Selections from Cultural Writings,* ed. David Forgacs and Geoffrey Nowell Smith, trans. William Boelhower (Cambridge, Mass.: Harvard University Press, 1985), 191.

14. Hanan al-Shaykh, *Beirut Blues,* trans. Catherine Cobham (New York: Anchor Books by Doubleday, 1995).

15. Paula Sunderman, "Between Two Worlds: An Interview with Hanan al-Shaykh," *Literary Review,* in press.

16. Al-Shaykh, *Beirut Blues,* 207, 225. Subsequent page references are in parentheses in the text.

17. Sunderman, "Between Two Worlds," 8.

18. Al-Shaykh, *Beirut Blues,* 81–82.

8

Art, the Chemistry of Life

Lamia Rustum Shehadeh

Pitiful, indeed may seem the lot of Man whose little days end in a black night of nothingness; yet though humanity may mean so little in the scheme of things, it is weak, human hands that draw forth images whose aloofness or communion alike bear witness to the dignity of Man: no manifestation of grandeur is separable from that which upholds it, and such is Man's prerogative. All other forms of life are subject, uncreative, flies without light.

André Malraux, *Voices of Silence*

Throughout the Renaissance, art was only a means to an end, be it social, ecological or religious, but never an end in itself. It was not until the nineteenth century that there emerged an art whose end was art itself, and declaring itself, henceforth, the mouthpiece of the artists. Thus, the modern artist, dedicated to freedom and self-expression, was born and slowly became the judge, mentor, and critic of his society. The aura surrounding artists and descriptions of artists as creators of the representational arts has portrayed the modern artist as possessor of mysterious supernatural powers that set him apart from other humans and elevate him to the rank of divinity since he can create out of nothing.[1] The term "artist" before the eighteenth century was limited to that of craftsman or someone who displayed taste. It was F. D. Maurice, in *Prophets and Kings* (1853), who first used the word to mean "one who cultivates one of the arts, in which the object is mainly to gratify aesthetic emotions by perfection of execution whether in creation or representation."[2] Artists thus came to signify certain distinctive characteristics, such as "different," "exotic," "eccentric," "imaginative," "creative," and so forth. An artist came to be seen as a combination of genius and social influences. This transformation in the conception of the artist reached a peak during the Romantic period, when he came to be regarded as a prophet, a divine creator. Today, the artist is still regarded as special, a fountain of creativity and genius.[3]

It was at this point in time that Arab art, from the Western perspective, made its appearance. Until the nineteenth century, the Arab aesthetic experience had been deeply rooted in Islam, manifesting itself mainly in calligraphy and architecture. In 1799, Napoleon conducted his Egyptian expedition accompanied by French savants and artists. Other artistic influences stemmed from the French occupation of Northern Africa and the foreign missionaries sent to all Arab countries, and, most notably, to Lebanon. This was followed by the occupation of the Arab world at the end of World War I and the imposition of the Mandate, resulting in the Western aesthetic acculturation of the local population. All of these factors led to a new Arab artistic awareness and creativity enhanced by the prevailing Age of Arab Renaissance. Al-Khidawi Ismail, of Egypt, was the first Arab to attempt the Westernization of Arab thought and art. But, constrained by tradition and religion, Arab artists could not adopt all of the themes and motifs current in the West and sought, instead, to learn new artistic skills and techniques.[4]

Of all the Arab countries, Lebanon was the most liberal and, therefore, best prepared to deal with the various forms of Western art. In 1613, Fakhreddin II, ruler of Mount Lebanon under Ottoman hegemony, visited the Medici court in Florence and was highly impressed by the art and architecture of the period. Upon his return to Lebanon, he imported Western civilization and culture to his country, marking, thereby, a new era in the history of Lebanon.[5] In the eighteenth century, the Gothic school of religious painting became popular in Lebanon through the church—churches and convents all over the mountain were filled with icons, portraits of patriarchs, and paintings of religious themes. Secular art from Italy and Austria was also introduced. Orientalists, such as David Roberts, William Bartlett, Horace Vernet, Sir David Wilkie, Edward Lear, Carl Hagg, and Amadeo Preziosi, came to Lebanon and painted the landscape and the ubiquitous ruins and monuments.[6]

During the nineteenth century, Western artists continued to come to Lebanon and, by the second half of the century, an increased number of Lebanese youth traveled to Turkey to study art. The first Lebanese art trend came to be known as the Lebanese Marine School of painting. It was characterized by depictions of beach scenes, historical representation, and ships. Most of these paintings have, unfortunately, been lost, but those still extant show the Lebanese artist as amateurish and lacking in academic training and technical skill.[7]

By the end of the nineteenth century, Beirut had already established itself as the bridge between East and West and developed an active cultural life. Thus, the theater, public libraries, book publishing, newspapers, and journals flourished and proliferated. Most of the Lebanese pioneers of modern art went to European cities—Brussels, Rome, London, and Paris—to study art and further their education. The most prominent of this generation of artists was Daoud Corm (1852–1930). He studied at the Institute of Fine Arts in Rome under Roberto Bompani, the official court painter of Victor Emmanuel II, and was influenced by such artists as Raphael, Michelangelo, and Titian. Official recognition of his work took place when he was commissioned to paint the portrait of Pope Pius IX and asked to join the Belgian court of Leopold II. It was not long, however, before he returned to Lebanon to paint the portraits of distinguished personalities. He also produced a wealth of religious paintings that brought him international acclaim.[8]

With the turn of the century a new generation of artists came to the fore. They were no longer interested in religious themes. Yusuf Howayyek (1883–1962) studied drawing and sculpture in Paris and Rome under Henri Bourdelle and others. In 1932, he returned to Lebanon and devoted himself to sculpture and teaching and was dubbed the father of modern Lebanese art.

It was during the French Mandate, however, that the most important artists made their appearance in Lebanon. Artists such as Mustafa Farroukh (1901–57), César Gemayel (1898–1958), Omar Onsi (1901–69), Saliba Dwayhi (1915–94), and Rashid Wehbi (1917–90) laid the foundation of modern art in Lebanon. A spirit of freedom and originality pervaded their work. Their style, always realistic, served to pass on to posterity the beauty of the landscape and the details of Lebanese architecture as well as local dress and customs.

During the Mandate, Beirut soon became a cultural and artistic center targeted by Lebanese, French and other artists from all over the world. Art exhibitions became common and Beirut was catapulted from relative obscurity to being the center of Arab and Francophile art. In 1937, the Académie Libanaise des Beaux Arts was established by Alexi Boutros in Beirut, which contributed further to the cultural standing of Beirut and provided an opportunity for the Lebanese to study art in Lebanon. Beirut continued to flourish in the artistic world and, in 1954, the American University of Beirut opened its department of fine arts with the help of two American artists as instructors. The Department of Fine Arts did not limit its activities to instruction but contributed to the community by initiating a series of public lectures and demonstrations.

By 1960, Beirut had become the home of several art institutions and art galleries exhibiting the work of internationally renowned artists. Thus, Beirut, with its free intellectual atmosphere, became firmly established as the cultural center of the Arab world. The existence of a sophisticated public led to a dynamic and fruitful relationship between it and the artists as well as the critics and art dealers. Publishing houses, literary salons, journals, theaters, and art galleries were spawned everywhere.[9]

It was not until the thirties that women artists in Lebanon made their public appearance. In 1931, l'École des Arts et Metiers in Beirut organized the first group exhibition of contemporary art in Lebanon, and right alongside the works of the leading male artists were exhibited the works of women artists, such as Blanche Ammoun, Marie Haddad, Gladys Choucair and Mrs. Bart. An art critic wrote in the French monthly *Tout* (Beirut, January 1931), "Another observation is that the only painters who succeed in being very good, who have done interesting things and remain original, are the women."[10]

A second generation of women artists made its appearance in the mid-forties, encouraged by the first art school in Lebanon, the Académie Libanaise des Beaux Arts (ALBA). Women students at the time made up 50 percent of the total student body. [11]

It is, I believe, important at this point to mention that although great male artists, such as Farroukh, Onsi, Corm, Dweihy, and Salibi, abound, art was never considered a serious male occupation. This attitude, on the part of society, facilitated the entrance of women into the domain of art. In her role as artist, woman is offered a chance at independence, freedom, and creativity while remaining within the fold of the existent traditional patriarchal society, as art is accepted as a domain of the female and part and parcel of her private sphere. She was, therefore, never a threat to man's world. The image of the Lebanese woman artist can best be described as that of the educated, cultured, and financially secure. She is a daughter, a wife, a mother, or a grandmother. Rather than portraying a bohemian image, she is almost always conventional in behavior and dress.[12]

In a cursory survey of their work, one finds women to be bold, ready to experiment with different techniques and materials and to explore new terrains. Men, in comparison, are more traditional and conservative, possibly because their livelihood depended on their art being more marketable. Thus, Salwa Choucair, in 1947, was the first abstract artist in Lebanon, Nadia Saikaly, the first to work extensively in kinetic art, and Juliana Seraphim and Huguette Caland, the first to exhibit explicit erotic themes. Etel Adnan, poet, literary critic, and painter, experimented with mixed media, and her poetic stance was always present in her calligraphic paintings, ceramics, and tapestries. Most of her works are thus abstract representations of her poetry.[13]

Furthermore, women artists are found to be normally more meticulous and patient in their attention to detail and more aware of the physical properties of their medium than their male peers.[14] One such artist is Lulu Baasiri. An art critic pointed out, however, that there is no male qua male art just as there is no female qua female art. "In essence," he says, "art is asexual and there is no criterion of male or female; there is only good or bad art."[15]

The aim of this paper is to give a cursory description of the impact of war on women artists and their work, and, due to the enormity of the material for study and the difficulty in locating all artists concerned, to concentrate, arbitrarily, on the life of one particular artist, her unique work, and the multifaceted metamorphosis of her persona effected by the war.

On April 13, 1975, war broke out in Lebanon and the cultural atmosphere became electrified as cultural life went into shock and the most flourishing art movement in the Arab world came to a standstill. The state patronage of the arts, as well as the patronage of the affluent middle class and the intelligentsia, came to an end. Foreign cultural centers and art galleries closed and many established and renowned artists emigrated to Europe or the United States. As soon as the shock started to wear off, people anticipated a speedy end to the war. But with the dawn of the eighties, the Lebanese realized they had to adjust to the war and learn how to cope with it. Slowly, life became concentrated only on the present, divorced from the past and oblivious to the future. The war generation was thus cut off from Lebanon's golden age and all it had to absorb was death, destruction, and devastation.

It was not long before the Lebanese artistic spirit surfaced. Most of these artists, however, designed marketable, decorative pieces emphasizing realism and Islamic motifs. This trend replaced the prewar individualistic and expressionistic style. Another trend, fostered in isolation, drew, also, on calligraphy and traditional forms but from a more original and innovative perspective, putting on modern garb.

The style of some of the prewar women artists, who stayed in Lebanon, was overtly modified by the war. Thus, Seta Manoukian was torn away from her obsession with the self and her solitude to depict street scenes, destruction, violence and people. Her heroes were the victims of the war—anxious and distraught. The work of Nadia Saikaly was not affected much, but she published a book entitled *Nawafidh ala al-watan*

(Windows on the homeland) in which she decried all forms of violence and condemned a war that destroyed the innocent and guilty alike. Odile Mazloum painted a collection in which she expressed the devastation of the war.

The intensity and the violence of the war drove many women to portray some of their most intimate and traumatic experiences. Breaking out of their silence, women resorted to art as a form of exorcism. The war thus spawned a plethora of female artists in need of expression. The act of painting became, for some, an addiction or a haven, an ivory tower away from the revulsion and disgust that consumed them—a form of catharsis. This new generation of painters, the war generation, had no anchor, no previous point of reference other than the war itself. Thus their work was drawn exclusively from war experiences—tragedies, fear, deficiencies, and instabilities—and reflected them. Thus, Najat Taher worked in the realm of children—warmth, love, compassion—perhaps to express what was missing from real life; Gretta Nawfal concentrated on the realm of the family—father, mother, child—representing woman's fear for her endangered domestic world; others produced works that manifested emotional stress and melancholy as a direct result of the war.[16]

And yet, the war affected different artists in different ways. For some, such as Rima Amyuni and Samia Osseiran, the carnage resulted in a form of hopelessness and despair reflected in their use of large canvases, vivid or dark gray colors and savage strokes or slashes of the brush or palette knife yielding desolate landscapes, deformed shapes and forms, violent eruptions, and broken-down humanity. The former, oppressed by the war, found her panacea in large canvases, filled with beautiful landscapes, constructed by heavy brush strokes and with wild screaming colors. Looking at Osseiran's paintings, one is struck by a palpable tension, enclosed in a small space about to explode, inhabited by dark colors, forlorn individuals, and sterile landscapes, mourning a lost life and disfigured beauty.

For others, however, the war experience was more merciful, even salutary and redeeming—resulting in a joyful affirmation of life. This is best illustrated by the odyssey of one artist who was actually transmuted and enriched by the war.

"What woman essentially lacks today for doing great things is forgetfulness of herself, but to forget oneself it is first of all necessary to be firmly assured that now and for all the future, one has found oneself."[17] Such a woman is Houry Chekerdjian who ran away from home at the age of seventeen to marry a man thirteen years her senior. She was beautiful, intelligent, carefree, and independent. She left the comforts of her wealthy parents to escape the strictures imposed upon her by her traditional and conservative family. Her husband was also wealthy, well-established, and the descendant of a highly conservative family, but he provided her with the love and freedom she yearned for; he catered to her every need: sports cars, designer clothes, parties, and all the help she needed at home—two maids and a cook. It wasn't long, however, before she became pregnant and gave birth to a beautiful girl. Her hedonistic life lasted for three years, at the end of which she lost her father and, shortly afterwards, her husband filed for divorce. For justification, he cited her liberalism, eccentricity in behavior and dress (although he himself bought her clothes for her), and her refusal to cook and behave like a traditional, conservative housewife.

Houry, without any preamble, found herself, at the age of twenty, at war with her husband, her family, her church, and her society. She fought ferociously for her freedom, dignity, and autonomy, but more so for her daughter, whom they threatened to take away. In a symbolic gesture of resistance and defiance, she took to wearing army fatigues from Vietnam with a wide leather gun belt and a stiletto for self-defense against any male predator. Thus, Houry's private war started about half a decade before the war in Lebanon erupted; it was a war against tradition and female suppression; it was a war of liberation and independence. But instead of using force, as she put it, she decided to take up the palette knife and start painting. Painting with a palette knife, she believes, helped her rid herself of the pent-up anger and violence that had consumed her. Characteristically, she used such colors as red, black, and white. The canvas became at once her battlefield and panacea.

Her choice of weaponry was made following a trip to Paris to get over the shock of divorce. She visited the Orangerie Museum which was showing, among others, Van Gogh's self-portrait. She immediately sensed his suffering as expressed by his palette knife, his only mouthpiece, to a world deaf to his needs and anguish. Thus, in rebellion and rejecting the idea of having men teach her the art of painting, she started, like Van Gogh, to paint without any formal training. For, it is through suffering that the knowledge to paint unfolds and expresses itself. She relied totally on that newly discovered internal power to direct her hand. Hence, life for her became a race toward death, which she equated with the sun toward which the horse (mankind) would gallop steadfastly, unwavering, looking neither left nor right. Painting became the stage from which she would proclaim her sanity and worth; a woman is man's equal in intellect and dignity even if she does lack the culinary arts. She believes that being a woman in the Middle East "is worse than contracting the HIV virus!"

And, what men, in the Middle East, do not seem to understand, is that no matter how hard they try to enchain women, they can never control their soul or subconscious, which will forever remain free.

Houry entered the second phase of her painting after going to Spain, where she was introduced to the work of Jerome Bosch, who had also suffered greatly in life. It was he who inspired her to start her journey into the labyrinth of the unconscious and deconstruct herself in an effort to find and understand the inner self. Her imaginary shelters, created in her labyrinthine tunnels, provided her with illusory security and safety from a hostile external world of patriarchal society intent on destroying her ego and sense of worth.

While still blindly exploring in her "tunnels" to establish a safe haven, war erupted in Lebanon on April 13, 1975, to last for sixteen years. With the conflagration of the war, divorce proceedings, the custody suit, the private investigators, gossip, and church and family interference, all came to an end, thus, eliminating the incentive for Houry's private, personal war. While Lebanon and the Lebanese were plunged into the bloodiest war of the region, Houry, on the contrary, found herself, for the first time in six years, totally at peace, liberated, free to do whatever she wanted and to be her own woman. She said to me, "When your war started, mine stopped, and when everybody was seeking safety in the shelter, away from the random bombing, shelling and shooting, I was reveling in my newly won freedom on the terrace of my penthouse. The shattering noise brought on by the explosions and constant shooting was music to my ears blending perfectly with Bach's Suites, which always gave me a sense of warmth and protection against the mad world outside." Thus, instead of carrying a gun or fighting or getting inebriated, Houry decided to stay home and paint. All the tension that had existed before, due to the strictures of society, had been lifted. Houry was free at last to become one with the cosmos, thus ushering in a period of huge surrealistic paintings of cosmic eggs with flying wings symbolizing the rebirth of her soul. Painting gave her a sensation of power and tranquillity, which engulfed her so completely that she became oblivious to the mad world outside, the world of violence, blood, and death. It was as if this feeling of power assured her that as long as she was creating nothing could happen to her, nothing could harm her.

Feeling liberated by the war, the latter became her ally, her companion, her protector against society, infusing her with a feeling of invulnerability. She would thus go out at night driving her Porsche at high speeds, secure in her invulnerability, in defiance of society, the combatants, the snipers, the shelling and the dead bodies strewn on both sides of the highway. It was as if she was telling the universe, "Now that I am free, no one can touch me, no one can harm me, I can live forever"—she was taunting death itself. It was five A.M. one morning, when she decided to go out in her sports car to buy lamb chops, after having spent the whole night drawing behind a couch as the facing wall came tumbling down at her feet.

All of a sudden, however, and after six years of war, Houry discovered that death was lurking around the corner, after all, and she was not as invulnerable as she had thought: Two of her friends lost their legs as they were leaving her apartment. In twenty-four hours she was packed and on a plane to Paris, where she stayed until the end of the war. She rented an apartment in the basement of a building, which she turned into a cocoon, isolating herself from the ravages of the world to revel in a strange sense of security and tranquillity. For two years she refused to buy a television set or have a telephone installed in the hope of keeping the world at bay. Her only excursions were to buy food and attend the religion and philosophy classes at the Sorbonne, and in the evenings she would haunt the concert halls and theaters. She stopped painting and developed an interest in dreams and their interpretation, which in time became the source of information for her paintings.

It was not until 1985–86 that she finally emerged from her seclusion and started to paint again. This time, she concentrated on geometric designs, trying to create order out of the chaos she inhabited. She believes chaos is the mode of life on earth brought upon it by man himself whose only salvation rests in a form of equilibrium imposed from above. She also discovered a love of nature, which she tried to capture by painting mineral stones with a rarely encountered transparency and colors filled with music, as well as plants of all shapes and colors. Nature brought Houry back to reality, down to earth, creating thereby a harmony between them. It was then that she created her rich deep blue cosmic mountains representing another planet, a planet of dreams guiding and inspiring her creativity, the deep blue color being the "psychological laboratory" bestowing a healing power. This newfound harmony was further cemented by the beautiful, "free," colorful fruits she went on to paint. The culmination of her journey into the world of the unknown, however, came with the birth of her "personages." Her main figure has always been the female—the cosmic woman, beautiful, serene, tranquil, peaceful, and fertile. She calls her *Sophia*, "wisdom," the mother of philosophers. This cosmic woman, present in all the paintings of this period, has two universal features: big beautiful eyes full of life reflecting a stern reality, or radiating love and compassion for mankind. The second feature is the mouth, seldom fully expressed, representing woman's silence and frustration. She is invariably represented as a mother with a small boy: the mother protecting and supporting her offspring, mother earth nurturing mankind. Another variation on this theme is the cosmic woman with a third eye in the center of her forehead. This is the cosmic eye that sees all, knows everything but is unable to speak or wisely remains silent.

Climaxing this period, however, are the paintings in which Houry tries to portray the role women played during the war. The cosmos here is represented by a series of clouds possibly representing the smoke of explosions, out of which a woman's face emerges, half hidden by the smoke but becoming gradually more distinct. Thus, women, hitherto hidden and marginalized, are being liberated by the fires of war to assume a more active role in society. Woman is also the mother of the world, full of love and compassion. What is fascinating about these figures is that even males share this female aura, which makes it difficult at times to differentiate the sexes in her paintings. Looking at her personages, Houry allows you to catch a glimpse of her innermost soul, a soul that has finally found peace, making her impervious to the outside world and, therefore, invulnerable. One art critic described her work as "peaceful and serene," giving the impression that she has found peace of mind—"une œuvre apaisante et douce à travers laquelle l'artiste donne l'impression d'avoir accédé à une paix de l'âme."

Houry has learned that the only permanence in life is one's inner tranquillity nurtured by following Kipling's advice to his son—to be ready to lose everything in life in a second and not to cry. To be true to herself has become her goal in life as she realized that she did not exist as a real person but was merely the personification of a fantasy: She represents different things to different people—sex symbol, martyr, sister, mother, whore (to her husband). Thus, by being true to herself, Houry believes, she can keep her true identity.

As soon as the war, in Lebanon, came to an end, Houry returned to Beirut, because, as she put it, she did not want to die in Paris and be buried there; she wanted her own earth, the source of her energy and essence.

Houry Chekerdjian has had several exhibitions in France, Lebanon, and Japan. Her working habits in the disordered atmosphere of her apartment studio fit the ideal representation of the bohemian artist at work. She moves through this confusion with assurance and grace. When she paints, her whole body, almost nude, moves like that of a dancer to the rhythm of Bach's music. Having never had any formal training in the art of painting, she believes her art to be instinctive, pushing itself out from within and unfolding just like giving birth. This brings to mind Maurice

Schroder, who, in 1961, compared artistic creativity to male sexuality and cited Flaubert as having described the artist as "a 'fouteur' who feels his sperm rising for an emission."[18] Painting is thus completely spontaneous and self-perpetuating. A painting, according to Houry, breathes and moves as a result of the cosmic energy that grows out of her, enters the painting, and becomes a separate living being. She says, "The images in my paintings come from deep within me; they are surreal and beyond any explanation." Her art has a metaphysical quality, whether in the form of an apple, a pear, an onion, a mountain, or a face. Her paintings impress themselves upon the beholder as being free and unconstrained by the finitude of space and time. There is a literal as well as a visual luminosity about her paintings expressed by the absence of lines, making them thus appear light, almost weightless. In the abstract domain of geometrics and pure color and form, she discovered the absence of language barriers and sociocultural differentiations. This discovery became her new faith, which she embraces with the joy and passion of a religious convert. Her involvement in the study of Far Eastern and Egyptian religions and philosophy during her stay in Paris stimulated her vision to perceive the mystic qualities of life. The art critic Joseph Tarrab described her work as originating from an intermediary world, where the spirits materialize and the corporeal is spiritualized.

It is evident from her work that, in exploring her own psychological depths, the images that emerge are invariably the archetypal symbols of the female unconscious. Through these images, Houry maintains, she is expressing a feminine sensuality and an emotionalism that are the essential core of all women. Yet, she insists that when she begins to paint, she does it spontaneously without a preconceived plan, relying upon images "stored in my memory." In short, painting, to her, is a way of communicating with life, with one's feelings, with one's psyche. When she started painting, Houry explains, it was in response to an intense need to transcend her physical isolation. But now her work has, in turn, responded and given meaning to her existence. If it were not for her painting, Houry says, "I would have lost my sanity." She speaks with intensity about her work, describing it as the only thing in her life that she could really call her very own. It provides her with an incomparable sense of joy and vivacity; instead of taking, it gives by revealing her inner self to her; it confirms her identity and renders it strong and whole. This brings to mind what Van Gogh once said: "In life and painting I can quite well dispense with God. But, suffering as I am, I cannot dispense with something greater than myself, something that is my whole life: the power of creating."[19]

Her life today is inseparable from her art; she cherishes her independence and sees no room in her life for marriage. She believes that men not only do not understand women but, in the guise of giving, they invariably take, never really ready or willing to give women what women actually need. She believes herself totally equal to man in society although far superior in maturity and cosmic awareness. Houry, however, does not hate men; she enjoys their company and has had several intense relationships bound, however, by carefully and clearly drawn lines beyond which men could never trespass, safeguarding her identity and autonomy. Houry would thus sing with Ghada al-Samman in "To Catch a Fleeting Moment,"

> They'll never steal my freedom
> They'll never put their horseshoes on my feet
> Never put their reins on my neck. . . .
> I'll retain my ability to dream and fly high.[20]

Houry, indeed, personifies André Malraux's claim that "the history of art, so far as genius is concerned, is one long record of successive emancipations, since while history aims merely at transposing destiny on to the plane of consciousness, art transmutes it into freedom."[21]

Houry thus saw in art a means to find her way through the contradictions and limitations of society and discover a new language infused with her own meanings. She says, in French, "l'art est comme une transmutation de l'esprit humain et l'alchemie de la vie." Has this transmutation prepared her to enter yet another phase in her life, a phase where she can converse with the other world? Indeed, Joseph Tarrab wrote: "au point de confluence des deux mondes, dans cet entre-deux séminal, lieu des échanges et des métamorphoses, Houry Chekerdjian, tel un thérapeute cosmique, transmet médiumniquement ses images et messages d'intégration et d'harmonie à un monde en proie au grand désordre des fins de cycle. C'est le seul peintre New Age du Liban."[22]

Notes

1. Cf. the skepticism of Nochlin in *Women, Art, and Power,* 153–54.
2. Cited in Parker and Pollock, *Women, Art and Ideology,* 82.
3. Ibid.
4. Al-Soufi Assaf, "Historical Overview," 12.
5. Mikdadi Nashashibi, *Forces of Change,* 79.
6. Ibid.
7. Ibid.
8. Ibid.

9. Ibid., 82.

10. Khal, *The Woman Artist in Lebanon*, 25–28.

11.Ibid., 28–29.

12. For a discussion of feminine or feminist art, see Nochlin, *Women, Art, and Power*, 148–49; Parker and Pollock, *Women, Art, and Ideology*, 17–99.

13. Khal, *The Woman Artist in Lebanon*, 34; Nashashibi, *Forces of Change*, 87.

14. Khal, *The Woman Artist in Lebanon*, 34.

15. Ibid., 35. See also Nochlin, *Women, Art, and Power*, and Parker and Pollock, *Women, Art, and Ideology*.

16. Sobh, "al-Intaj al-thaqafi," 28–30.

17. Parker and Pollock, *Women, Art, and Ideology*, 110.

18. Ibid., 83.

19. André Malraux, *Metamorphosis of the Gods* (London: Secker and Warburg, 1960).

20. Cited in Cooke, *War's Other Voices*, 49.

21. Malraux, *The Voices of Silence*, 623.

22. *L'Orient–Le Jour* (Beirut), April 17, 1993.

IV

Women at War

9

Women in the Lebanese Militias

LAMIA RUSTUM SHEHADEH

It is not because of woman's cowardice, incapacity, nor, above all, because of her general superior virtue that she will end war when her voice is finally and fully heard.

Olive Schreiner

Masculinity and femininity have for long been conceived as polar opposites: women, passive and dependent; men, active and dominant; women, emotional and expressive; men, rational and stoic; men, the breadwinners and women, the homemakers. In 1974, Michelle Rosaldo distinguished between women's domestic sphere and men's public sphere and argued that this dichotomy in social roles is due to socialization rather than natural differences as commonly believed.[1] This link between gender stereotypes and nature still persists today among feminists and antifeminists.[2] The question is what happens to women in times of political or armed conflict? Do they remain confined to their domestic sphere or do they venture out? Do they perceive themselves immersed in the national struggle or as mere bystanders, victims of powerlessness and passivity imposed upon them by traditional and societal conventions? Do women gain greater freedom of expression during periods of war or remain addicted to the status quo? Can one speak of a constant trend in women's relations to war throughout history? In other words, have women held a distinctive attitude and/or role in times of war? What has the experience of women in wartime been like?

When war invades society, it may be difficult to maintain traditional social mores such as gender boundaries.[3] Women have generally been regarded as nonaggressive and innately self-sacrificing and nurturing, and, therefore, more predisposed to conciliation, cooperation, and compromise than men who are "naturally" aggressive and confrontational. Women are, therefore, the "gentler sex." While women brought life into the world, men destroyed it. The concept of peace was slowly feminized and that of war and violence masculinized. Jean Bethke Elshtain believes that "the image of woman . . . as the Goddess of peace" is used by patriarchy to symbolically define the limits of war and provide guarantees for continuity of prewar normalcy in war's aftermath.[4] Thus, men and women, according to Elshtain, "locked in a dense symbiosis, perceived as beings who have complementary needs and exemplify gender-specific virtues—take on, in cultural memory and narrative, the personas of Just Warriors and Beautiful Souls. Man construed as violent, woman as nonviolent, offering succor and compassion."[5] Laura Kaplan, on the other hand, while agreeing in principle that equating women with peace is a patriarchal manifestation, traces the roots of "woman as caretaker" to the patriarchal aim of containing women.[6] But the mere fact that women are conditioned to believe that their role in society is that of "caretaker" makes them complicitous in the act of war by fulfilling their duties toward those involved in the fighting and by assuming roles left vacant by men, to keep society going. Thus, women under the rubric "caretakers" and lovers of peace stand alongside men in the newly militarized society.[7] Women are designated "noncombatants," and, yet, they are placed as nurses on the front ready to help and soothe the wounded.[8]

It has been reiterated for centuries that war is the domain of men: It is fought by men, defined and planned by men for male purposes and ends. Women remain mostly absent from policy making and debates regarding war and whether wars are morally justifiable.[9] Hector, addressing Andromache immediately before he goes out to meet Achilles and his certain death, says, "Go therefore back to our house, and take up your own work, the loom and the distaff, and see to it that your handmaidens ply their work also; but the men must see to the fighting." (Iliad 6: 490–494). Two thousand years have elapsed and women are still traditionally viewed as "Beautiful Souls." Yet, all wars, especially those of the twentieth century, have shown the falsehood of such statements. Women have been equally mobilized for civilian as well as for military action. Their work has ranged from caretakers at home (mothers) and the field (nurses) to espionage, terrorism, and actual combat, not to mention their involvement in food shortages, rationing, evacuation, and displacement. It was, thus, virtually impossible for most women to ignore the violent and politically charged atmosphere in which they lived.[10] Whatever battles are fought, women are found on both sides of the battle lines supporting the military involvement of their male relations—son, husband, lover. Increasingly, however, women are fighting alongside them and just as fiercely.

Women have always been described as aligned with peace and pacifism and against any philosophy propounding just war theory and the potential morality of war. Women's role in the military has been obscured among other things by sexism and feminism. The former excludes women from the military on the ground of their physical inferiority rendering them unsuitable for combat. The latter either emphasizes their special qualities of nurturance, creativity, and pacifism—and, therefore, women's unsuitability for combat—or emphasizes the war machine as a patriarchal institution, predominantly male, which not only excludes women from its ranks but victimizes them as well.[11] But a careful study of available data shows that not all women are pacifists, not even the feminists among them.[12] Thus Jane Addam maintains that "the belief that a woman is against war simply and only because she is a woman and not a man, does not, of course hold. In every country there are many women who believe that war is inevitable and righteous, and that the highest possible service is being performed by their sons who go into the Army."[13] In wars, typical male attributes, such as aggressiveness, ruthlessness, and violence, permeate the scene in juxtaposition to the traditional feminine attributes of nurturance and caretaking. Women have been described as brave and fierce in their defense of children and home, in wearing uniforms as auxiliaries in noncombatant duties, even as spies, given their traditional image of seduction and deceit, but what about women in actual combat? Are women capable of showing the same aggressiveness, violence, and ruthlessness men are famed for in times of war? "Resolved to conquer for her husband, armed with the sword in the midst of Vitellius's soldiers, she flung herself, now here now there, on those unfortunates, in the darkness of night, as they stumbled in total confusion and the darts rained down amid blood and the groans of the dying. It is told that when the city was re-conquered she, following the iron law of war, was pitilessly cruel with the enemy, with extreme ferocity."[14] Such women fighters are considered the exception rather than the rule and the "Ferocious Few are routinely eclipsed by the enormous shadow cast as the Non-combatant Many step into the light."[15] Can this traditional image of femininity coexist with that of a woman wielding a gun and ready, like a soldier, to kill on command?[16]

The aim of this paper is to address some of the questions raised so far by describing the role women played in the four major militias during the sixteen-year war in Lebanon.

The War

The Lebanese War (1975–91) set the pace for later wars in human violence and carnage. "The war was the explosion of anger, hatred, and fear that penetrated every corner of people's lives; it tore into the calm of the boudoir and the kitchen. No space could provide shelter against the ubiquity of danger. There was no longer any difference between the experiences of the home and the street. Private and public merged; more they were wrenched into each other."[17]

This war has been variously attributed to economic, religious, political, local, and international causes. Economic, because of the alleged growing chasm between the rich and the poor; religious, because of the spreading dissatisfaction among the various religious communities with regard to alleged inequitable political representation along confessional lines; political, because it represented a power struggle between multifarious political units or parties; civil, because it involved all the Lebanese with the consequent paralysis of the government and the national army and the latter's final dissolution; and international, because it pitted the Palestinians against their Lebanese hosts and turned the country into an arena in which foreign powers waged their own battles. A war that had been called civil and Lebanese, in 1975, was finally acknowledged to have been neither. Etel Adnan, in her *Sitt Marie Rose,* says "All the quarrels of the Arab world have their representatives here. . . . The wretched and the downtrodden are terrorized."[18]

After the Israeli invasion in 1982, the different conflicts assumed more strictly religious markings. Society was fragmented into autonomous groups that found it very difficult, if not impossible, to communicate, much less, of course, cooperate.

The involvement of Lebanese women in the destruction was almost nonexistent. They had nothing to do with the eruption of the war nor did they ever encourage it. Women were excluded from all decision-making processes, whether in the initiation of the war or in bringing it to an end. "Their roles were those of the recipients of the consequences and the outcomes of the war on the one hand, and the makers and manufacturers of the laws of survival on the other."[19]

It was impossible, however, for many women and noncombatant men to ignore the highly charged political atmosphere in which they lived. In most areas, the war was being fought around the homes, on rooftops and balconies, or around the corner, and fighters moved easily through civilian property, marching through one's farms, confiscating homes, or even raping one's neighbors. Heavy artillery was used within residential areas.

It is, therefore, not surprising to find political expression by women not so much as a radical challenge to the mores of the time, but, rather, as the natural response to the reality that surrounded them all. Men and women were no longer definable by the spaces they traditionally occupied, for fighting could erupt at any time anywhere. The home front was no longer sacred. Thus, fighters (men) and non-fighters (women) were no longer distinguishable. In Lebanon, where neighborhoods have been on the front line for many years, women on all sides took part mainly by providing food to combatants, sewing hospital sheets, knitting sweaters, administering first aid, and even donating blood.

Women suffered greatly in their traditional roles as homemakers, mothers and caregivers during the Lebanese conflict. They lost the support of their husbands and sons who had joined the fighting or were taken hostage or kidnapped or migrated for greener pastures or, worst yet, killed. They saw their young children and elderly parents go hungry when food supplies ran short and other necessities, such as electricity and water, were lacking and even bread simply unobtainable. Work had to be attended to, the family held together, and the children helped through a very irregular education. Daily life seems to have been transformed into a never-ending nightmare marked with fear and anxiety. The Lebanese women, in particular, were suddenly thrown into a permanent state of emergency in their daily lives.

As the war continued, women of all communities staged peace marches, hunger strikes, and sit-ins. They submitted petitions to national and international peace organizations; they even stood on occasion in the line of fire to bring the waves of kidnapping to a stop and, at other times, tried to dismantle the militia checkpoints dividing the city of Beirut into two sections. Moving from one checkpoint to another and from one headquarters to another, they "were speaking in the name of spouses, mothers, and sisters. They wanted the butchery to stop."[20]

Not *all* women were pacifists: Some were driven by a desire to take an active part in shaping the present and future of their communities. Women were encouraged to display their commitment to the "cause" by sending husbands and sons cheerfully into the conflict so the problem of mobilization would be eased. But others displayed their commitment more directly: They underwent self-mobilization by contacting the parties or militias with whom they shared the same ideologies and goals. The women belonged mainly to the urban lower and middle classes or to the university educated class. Women were affiliated with the militias in a number of ways: as friends, members, auxiliaries, and actual fighters. They were thus active at all levels—the military, political, administrative, and social. Their highest concentration, however, was in the social fields, such as mass work, education, information, and health, and in the lower echelons of the administration as secretaries, clerks, telephone operators, and the like. They appeared in fewest numbers in the military and higher level political positions.

The Militias

As soon as the war erupted in April 1975, the Lebanese army was confined to its barracks through a political decision of the government. The vacuum created led to the mushrooming of several militias representing the different political trends in the country at the time. Indeed, not since the development of the nation-state had such a disintegration of a country taken place and the population held captive by gangs and parties competing for authority.[21]

Although there were four major Lebanese militias active during the war—Progressive Socialist Party, the Lebanese Forces, Amal and Hizballah—I shall limit my discussion to the latter three in which women played an important role at all levels. The Progressive Socialist Party existed as a political party comprising members of the different confessional sects long before the outbreak of the war. However, it gradually evolved into a primarily Druze institution in the aftermath of the Israeli invasion in June 1982.[22] Needless to say, women rallied to support their husbands, brothers, and sons. They comprised roughly 5 to 10 percent (no accurate figures available) of the fighting corps. Their function centered on sociomedical aspects: preparation of food at home and its distribution to the fighters, assistance in paramedical and field-hospital activities, knitting sweaters for the fighters, and attending to storage and distribution of ammunition. Many joined the office of recruitment for clerical work while others joined the sector of communications. Although a small number received light military training, they were not allowed to fight for fear of captivity, which would demoralize the fighters—since women represent male pride and honor.

Amal and Hizballah

At the death of the Prophet Mohammad in 632 A.D., a number of his companions looked to Ali, Mohammad's cousin and son-in-law, to be his successor, or *khalifah* (caliph). However, the majority of Muslims rejected the claims of Ali's supporters and entrusted their leadership to Abu Bakr al-Siddiq, Mohammad's father-in-law and one of his closest companions.

The ensuing conflict ignited the major schism that was to take place between the Shiʿa, "partisans of Ali," and the Sunnis. The Shiʿa, in turn, adhering to different doctrines split into a number of different groups, the most important of which are: Twelver Shiʿism to which the Lebanese, Iranian, and Iraqi belong; Zaydi Shiʿism; Ismaili Shiʿism; and Alawi Shiʿism.[23] The Twelver Shiʿa get their name from their belief in the succession of twelve imams, the last of whom disappeared in 874 and is to reemerge at the end of time to reestablish the reign of peace and justice.[24]

In 1960, Musa al-Sadr, born in 1928 in the Iranian theological center of Qom, was appointed *ʿalim* (scholar), or clerical leader, of the Shiʿa community of Tyre in the South of Lebanon. From the beginning of his tenure, he addressed himself to what he considered to be social injustice. By the early seventies, he had successfully established himself as the "preeminent Shiʿa political voice, the main figure of the national reform movement, and the focus of an inter-communal dialogue that was without parallel in the country's history."[25] In 1974, Musa al-Sadr formed the Movement of the Disinherited to mobilize the Shiʿa and to improve their social standing, and, in a press conference on July 6, 1975, he announced the formation of Amal, symbolizing the sacrifice of those "who responded to the call of the wounded homeland."[26] Amal is an acronym for *Afwaj al-muqawamah al-lubnaniyyah* (Lebanese resistance battalions), and also denotes "hope" in Arabic.

During the first phase of the war in Lebanon, 1975–76, Amal played a marginal role. Three major events seem to have brought it to life: Israel's invasion of southern Lebanon in 1978 prompted Amal to define its position vis-à-vis the Palestine Liberation Organization, the disappearance of Musa al-Sadr while in Libya in 1978, and the Iranian revolution in 1979.[27] It achieved its greatest power in the early eighties in the aftermath of the Israeli invasion of 1982. It had grown from 5,000 to 30,000 members and, with the help of the Druze artillery, it was able to drive the Lebanese army from West Beirut in February 1984.[28]

During the eighties, the Shiʿa community witnessed a rapid social mobilization and a variety of radical movements found support among its younger generations. A second and looser group emerged under the name of Hizballah. Its emergence in 1982 was prompted by the arrival of the Iranian Revolutionary Guards in the Biqaa Valley to repel the Israeli invasion. Hizballah is not a monolithic organization but an assembly of various groups with two common features: transformation of Lebanon into an Islamic republic after the Iranian model and the influence wielded by the Iranian government due to a common ideology and enormous material support.[29] Hizballah, which means "The Party of God," is derived from a verse in the Qur'an, which promises triumph for those who join "the party of God." It is modeled after a militia group of the same name in Iran. Hizballah rapidly won numerous followers as whole families joined en masse—men and women.[30]

As both Amal and Hizballah are Shi'a, have some common politico-religious beliefs, and have similar views of women, I shall treat the role of women in both as one. Women were mobilized gradually in a step-by-step approach. Whereas men volunteered readily, women were recruited slowly and gradually in an effort to overcome social barriers that hindered activities outside the home. Women's participation remained limited as a result of different forms of social control and values entrenched ideologically in the family, the community, and the religious laws. The war, however, opened a range of new possibilities for political activism by politicizing the traditional role of women within the family. Family relationships proved especially important in mobilizing women because members of militias were primarily recruited through family and sociopolitical channels. This was particularly true for women because they needed the permission of the men in their families to venture outside the home. It was Musa al-Sadr who encouraged women to join men in the resistance movement. He maintained that a woman complemented a man's role and his struggle, for she equaled him in heroism, nobility, and glory. He said, "We, in our contemporary society, are in urgent need of fully realizing the message of the Prophet. We need women who strengthen the will for we need to enlist all our resources to achieve what God has ordained for us."[31] He actively relied on his sister Sayyidah Rabab to encourage and enlarge the social involvement of the Shi'a women and their ultimate visibility. Musa al-Sadr's aim was to reveal the important role of women by making her role public but even her public role was always within her traditional role. It was his intention to awaken the silent half of the population and introduce it to the political arena.[32]

It is important at this point to stress the two fundamental tenets of Islam the Shi'a leaders refused to transcend: women's subordination to men as explicitly expressed in the Qur'an, "Men are the managers of the affairs of women for that God has preferred in bounty one of them over another" (Sura 4:34) and "women have such honourable rights as obligations, but their men have a degree above them" (Sura 2:228);[33] and natural sexual division of labor.[34] Women as potential and actual mothers enjoy reproductive power at the expense of physical and intellectual prowess. Their duties are to create a harmonious atmosphere at home and to promote their children's growth and husbands' success. Subordinate to their husbands, they expect economic and physical protection. Although there are no legal barriers to prevent women from participating in the political sphere, it is deemed more virtuous if they refrain. However, should the political situation prove it necessary, women are to leave the domestic sphere and support the men and the cause they are fighting for, but always within the traditional role that the Qur'an has prescribed. Ayatollah Khomeini maintained that women were the "manifestation and realization of the desires of humanity, the trainers of society and the nourishers of valuable men and women alike."[35]

Consistent with the Muslim tradition, there is total segregation of the sexes. Women had their own Women's Affairs Department, which was subordinate to the Executive Council and received instructions through a male liaison officer, thus reducing the mixing of the sexes to a bare minimum. The tasks assumed by the women in the militias were often extensions of the traditional feminine roles in the home. They involved not only the provision of necessary support services to the fighters but also the care of needy families. The aim of involving women was to mobilize the community to support the party and to raise the levels of political awareness and, at the same time, to see to their needs and provide for them. Members refuse to call Hizballah a political party but refer to it as *'amal jamahiri* (popular work), thus fostering good relations between the militia and the masses, making them feel part of the movement that, in turn, took care of them. Women of Hizballah visited all the families of their communities, informed them of all social and political events, and saw to their educational, medical, or financial needs. They also acted as official mourners, lamenting the destruction of the war, afraid of defeat, yet never regretting having sent their husbands, brothers, and sons to their death. One such woman said to me, "We mothers will never tire of producing martyrs;"[36] and another said, "We wish we had more children to send them to battle [and, therefore, martyrdom] and make us proud [literally, 'raise our heads']." Posters with the martyr's picture were usually distributed in the neighborhood with a verse from the Qur'an, consecrating martyrdom and assuring immortality for the deceased, imprinted beneath it: "Count not those who were slain in God's way as dead, but rather living with their Lord, by Him provided, rejoicing in the bounty that God has given them" (Sura 3:164). Martyrs' funerals brought together a large segment of the community in a show of solidarity and compassion. Community expressions of grief were manifested by women's mournful wailing and, at times, ululation (as used in weddings), manifestations of the glory that martyrdom brings, engendering a sense of profound emotions and sharing. Eulogies by prominent men and women (separately) lent stature to the dead and the significance of martyrdom. There was no despair in martyrdom and bereaved mothers did not wear black and only wished they had more sons to send to war to bring them more glory.[37]

Women may not have been the model citizen-soldiers in Amal and Hizballah, but they were the home front helpmates, they were the "Spartan Mothers"[38] whose civic duties and identities were inseparable from their fighting sons. Many women accompanied the combatants to provide them with food. The main duty of women, according to one woman from Amal, was to prepare their sons for the Jihad (Holy War), for the *jihad* (struggle/endeavor) of the woman is to make her family virtuous and, in so doing, make society virtuous as well.[39]

In addition to teaching other women the arts of embroidery, home economics, sewing, aesthetics, and social edification, women members were to lecture in mosques, workplaces, factories, and even in private houses as part of a systematic program of ideological indoctrination and Islamization of Lebanon. Lectures and seminars were not limited, however, to politics and religion—dogma, divine law, and jurisprudence—which are intertwined in Islam, but covered a wide range of topics from child care and health to current events. These seminars served as a link between women and their problems of daily life and the wider concerns of the militias.

On the politico-religious level, steadfastness and perseverance were considered political statements. Many women refused to leave their homes and go to safer areas. Others joined demonstrations and political rallies and delivered speeches, albeit to audiences segregated into men and women, and still others helped displaced families find refuge, provided them with food rations and blankets, and tried to find them work or ways and means of subsistence.

Although women in Amal and Hizballah seem to have been liberated by the war, shedding their invisible domestic role to participate actively in the public sphere, albeit veiled and segregated, they were not allowed to join the military, because, according to one woman I interviewed, the capture of a woman by the enemy would cause the greatest humiliation and dishonor. Women, therefore, represented the "second line of defense," as the first line was occupied efficiently by men. Their main role was to send their husbands and sons to war, while they stayed behind.[40] Another stricture imposed on women's participation involved barring them from occupying positions that required "perpetual bodily and mental vigilance,"[41] such as religious authority, leadership of the *ummah* (the Muslim community), supreme judge (*qadi al-qudat*), and head of the army, because of natural hormonal and physical "impediments" that deter such vigilance.

The Lebanese Forces

The Lebanese Forces was created in 1976 by Bashir Gemayel, the son of Pierre Gemayel, founder of the Phalangist Party. The Lebanese Forces was comprised in large part of lower- and lower-middle-class Maronites of the eastern sector of Beirut as well as intellectuals and professionals, who rejected, in most cases, the politics of the older generation. Lewis Snider described the Lebanese Forces as a political ethos that rejected traditional politics as practiced by the Christian and Muslim establishments.[42]

Three periods can be distinguished within the war in Lebanon (1975–91) to characterize the inception and development of the Lebanese Forces: inception and birth (1975–80), organization (1981–85), and institutionalization (1986–91). In the first period, the Lebanese Forces (LF), as it came to be known in 1981, had not been formed yet. There were groups of partisans comprising all Christian forces: Phalangists, Guardians of the Cedars, National Liberals, Tanzim, and independents.[43] During this period, women, as was the case in their involvement with the other militias, participated in the preparation of food for the fighters, paramedical activities, communications, administration (secretaries, clerks, telephone operators, and so forth), news media, and care centers for children.

The participation of women in the LF, however, was not limited to traditional feminine domestic tasks: Some were actively involved in the fighting. The years immediately preceding the war witnessed a dynamic political engagement among the younger generations, and many, males and females, either joined political parties or were simply sympathizers. With the eruption of the war in residential areas, all felt threatened, and, aware of the danger involved, wanted to defend their way of life and their country. Several factors encouraged women to join the military besides partisanship: Many were girl guides or engaged in the Lebanese Red Cross or other social and religious youth organizations; others sought military training because they liked the discipline and the uniform; still others joined because they wanted to overcome the fear and anxiety that pervaded them by learning to use arms; and many others joined the military for patriotic reasons, or because their male relatives or friends were involved. For many, however, joining the military was a rather gradual process, which started by preparing sandwiches or running errands for the combatants whose barricades were down the street or in the same neighborhood, or even helping maintain weapons or serving as substitutes in guard duty for short periods of time. Some even attended training sessions, which brought them in contact with other women fighters.[44]

The female combatants came from all social classes. The professions of their fathers ranged from physician and lawyer to peasant or unskilled laborer, and the majority of their mothers were housewives.[45] They were born between 1950 and 1965 with the heaviest concentration between 1957 and 1962. The youngest, eleven years of age, had accompanied her father and older thirteen-year-old sister, thinking the war would be over in a matter of months. They came from all districts of Lebanon, as they were repeatedly displaced and sometimes within the same neighborhood.[46] The degree of their participation was at its peak during the first years of the war (1975–76), before the Christian fighting forces were united and organized into one militia. During those early years, there were three all-female units: two in Beirut and its suburbs and one in Bikfayya in the Matn district. In all, around three thousand young women received extended military training during the war, and around two hundred and fifty to three hundred participated actively in combat over a substantial period of time. Most of them took part in the fighting as members of the female units but others joined the male units to fight side by side with their fathers, cousins, brothers, uncles, husbands, or neighbors.[47]

The core of the downtown Beirut unit consisted of thirteen girls, most of whom were born and raised in the downtown area and all of whom were politically active or members of a party. They participated in combat not only in the downtown area of Beirut but went to Chikka, other areas of the North, and the mountains.[48] The second unit was founded by one of the downtown group members whose brother had been severely wounded in the fighting and had to be evacuated. Her family, who had given her permission to fight as long as her brother was in the vicinity, ordered her to go back home. Thereupon, emulating the downtown group, she organized her own unit in her own neighborhood and obtained her family's approval.[49] The third unit, of Bikfayya, once again, was comprised of local girls, girls from this mountain resort and girls originally descended from there. They took part in the battles surrounding the town and other fronts of the North-Matn district.[50]

The three units zealously guarded their independence vis-à-vis their relationship with the regional command. This was facilitated by the partisan character of the first two years of the war, when all units were fighting with their own private weapons (mostly hunting rifles and handguns), and the belief that their military engagement was temporary in contrast to what the future might have held for the male partisans. These factors played an important role in defining the role of female combatants, in determining which battles and under what conditions they would participate.[51] With a few exceptions, they were trained with the rest of the men in the use of light arms. Heavy weaponry was naturally more prestigious but was usually reserved for male combatants, either because it was felt that female participation was temporary or because of the limited number of such weapons or both. This distinction in the use of weaponry, however, did not stop the female combatants from taking an active part in the fighting. Thus, the first unit in the downtown area was assigned the protection of the Phalangist Headquarters. They were barricaded in Martyrs' Square, the center of town, which came to be regarded as the demarcation line between the two sectors of the city. They kept their post, an unfinished concrete building occupied by them against orders, from autumn 1975 to October 1976, when the Syrians entered the area. As mentioned, they also participated in other battles outside of Beirut.[52]

Since 1985, while the two other units continued their struggle, the downtown unit of Beirut distanced itself from the military and formed a pacifist movement. Their cause remained unchanged, but they no longer believed war to be the answer to the problems of Lebanon. Rather, they emphasized education, coexistence of the different communities, and self-sacrifice.

During the summer of 1980, the Phalangists under the leadership of Bashir Gemayel completed the campaign begun two years earlier for the unification and control of the Lebanese Front (all Christian parties). On July 7, Gemayel attacked and destroyed the military power of the National Liberal militia, his only contender, and announced the official birth of the Lebanese Forces, thus initiating the second phase of the LF. However, the Lebanese Forces did not start functioning formally as one organization until April 1, 1981, when the war against the Syrians in Zahlé took place. Service in the different militias, once a matter of choice, became mandatory for male students in 1981.[53]

The female members of the LF were still referred to as Nizamiyyat (Regulars) and participated in all fields mentioned earlier, including care of the handicapped.

During the war in Zahlé, they were in the field administering first aid and evacuating the wounded. In 1982–83 another surge of women joined the LF as the Mountain War erupted. They constituted 7 percent of the whole force: 3.7 percent were involved in full-time military activity, while the rest were concerned with logistics and administrative matters.[54]

In 1985, a coup d'état took place within the LF and the third and last phase of their history started. The LF became "institutionalized." In 1988, the doors of the newly instituted military academy were also opened for females. The program was divided into three stages, each comprising a period of one year. The first year included what is referred to as the "Hell

Cycle," when recruits, totally isolated from the rest of society, underwent hardship training for a period of forty days. Twenty percent of those accepted for the 1988 session were women ranging in age between eighteen and twenty-five.

Although both males and females operated under extreme physical hardship and although men on the whole fared better on the physical level, it was some of the males who dropped out but none of the females did, and the second in total rank among the graduating class was a female. She had fractured her pelvis due to hardship training, but, despite the severe pain, continued her training to prove that she was as worthy of being an officer as any male. She described those days as "the most beautiful." She found herself stimulated, even euphoric, by the constant "challenge, defiance, exhaustion, coercion, sheer force and ferociousness"; "We never knew when the sun rose or set." They would get up at 6:00 A.M. and start their rigorous training, which included running, hand-to-hand combat, walking in boiling oil, plunging in septic tanks, carrying full gear on their backs, wearing woolen clothes in the heat of the summer, running while carrying sandbags, doing push-ups, climbing walls and ropes, high and broad jumping, and more.

This severe training, however, resulted in fractures, as mentioned earlier, especially due to the weight of the sandbags that had to be carried and so the female cadets had a reprieve, when the military command, aware of the problem, ordered them to carry 30-kilo sandbags instead of the 40- or 50-kilo sandbags required of the males.

Women infiltrated almost all branches of the military. Thus, they were not limited to the infantry, but joined the artillery as well. Because the artillery demanded more physical prowess than any woman could muster, women were assigned to command posts, where they acted as trajectory calculators and directed the artillery barrages. The only service women were excluded from was the tank corps on the assumption that it required more physical hardship than the females could endure.

Women also excelled in the field of communications. This demanded not only expertise in the field but patience and perseverance as well as courage to go out to the front lines, day or night, to repair transmitters, replace cables, or deliver needed equipment.[55]

The only time women, during this last phase, participated in active combat was during the fighting that flared up in 1990 between the Lebanese army and the LF: Some of them were placed in the front lines and one was taken captive. The Supreme Command, afraid that more would have the same fate, transferred them from the front to staff some of the most strategic checkpoints. Again, according to their male superiors, the women showed a great deal of perseverance, self-control, patience, and, above all, unwavering commitment in the face of danger.

I have described so far the role(s) played by women in the Muslim and Christian militias. The question that presents itself at this point is the manner in which these women fulfilled their roles. Needless to say, where the role had to do with the traditional female domain, such as provision of food, sewing, caring of children, teaching, medical aid, nursing, mourning, and other social functions, the behavior of women was naturally that of the traditional woman—nurturant, loving, and emotional. The question, however, assumes a different dimension when it addresses the militant role that some of the women had adopted.

The behavior of the female combatants of the LF revealed the following: Although they were never assigned traditional female chores by their superiors or peers, they manifested, despite their young age, traditional female skills such as cooking, sewing, and cleaning. Thus, the downtown unit, Nizamiyyat (Regulars), organized their barricade as if it were their home: they had separate places for eating and sleeping; they arranged a special corner for praying with the statue of the Holy Virgin in place; while in still another corner, they installed a bookshelf which contained books they had brought from their homes. Often, to kill time, they would read aloud as an act of sharing or simply prepare their homework, which was assigned to them before the schools closed. Their home economics was best exemplified when they used electrical bulbs and strewed pebbles on the pathway leading to their barricade in an effort to economize on ammunition by minimizing unnecessary shooting.[56]

Another characteristic was the rationalization of their involvement, which was shared by the Shiʿa women. They described their involvement as being of a defensive nature. Thus, whenever they referred to their strategic movements, they described them as "defensive" or "repossession," but seldom as "conquest" or "occupation." Their distaste for killing may be best exemplified by their refusing, at one time, to enter a building harboring a sniper when they heard the cries of a baby, since they knew they had to kill all moving objects on sight.[57] Both the Christian and Shiʿa women involved in combat denigrated aggression and both groups saw their participation as temporary and for the duration of the war.

Women combatants were quick to learn and master the martial arts. They competed easily with their male compatriots and sometimes even bested them in all-military training as well as in the speed and thoroughness with which they dismantled and cleaned their weapons. Some, though never encouraged, excelled at artillery practice when six of them manned a major artillery station during the war in Zahlé (1978). Their professionalism, however, came to the fore during their training at the military academy as mentioned earlier.

Combat and military discipline, according to those interviewed, taught them how to face difficult situations and exercise self-control. But most important, it provided them with a sense of empowerment, new self-worth, and confidence. Military training "polished" them and prepared them to meet all the vicissitudes of life. One of the women interviewed equated joining the military with entering the convent. She maintained that military training produces simultaneously the soldier and the monk in the individual. Military life, however, had its negative consequences as well. One such consequence was the pressure to perform well at all times, having to prove their worth every step of the way. This affected them not only psychologically but physically as well. Many women failed to report physical injuries, such as fractures and other ailments, for fear of expulsion or of not performing up to expectations.

Women at no time lost their "femininity." Their reaction to this question, however, differed. One of them blushed as she confessed that she never lost her femininity. In fact, she looked forward to her home leave to take leisurely baths, go to the hairdresser, wear makeup and perfume, and put on her miniskirt. But this, she claimed, never made her forget what she learned in the military or the self-confidence she had acquired. Another maintained that, while she was in the military, she had to forget her femininity and be "like a man," otherwise, "I would not have been able to shoot." Yet, as soon as she went home, she resumed her feminine role. A third felt that femininity was a weakness and she had to show the same commitment and show of force as the males, but that had never kept her from manifesting her femininity when called for.[58] One of the female officers interviewed admitted that her boyfriend broke off the relationship on the eve of her joining the military academy, because he did not want his son to wake up in the morning and say, "*Bonjour, mon colonel,*" instead of "*Bonjour, maman.*" In contrast, some of the girls during the first period of the war arrived at the training camps with rollers and hair dryers.[59]

The relationship between the male and female combatants varied; it ranged from sexual harassment and resentment to a complete sense of solidarity. Thus, in the downtown area, male combatants resented the females and refused to have their barricade behind the females' barricade, some in the military academy refused to take orders from female superiors, and still others tried to flirt. But on the whole, and according to all those interviewed, men and women, a sense of solidarity prevailed. This may be attributed to three factors: They were all fighting for a common cause, which created a special bond between them, contrary to women's experiences in professional armies; there was a closeness imposed by familial relationships and previous friendships especially during the first phase (1975–76); and there was also the traditional protective stance males usually had toward females, which lent the relationship a familial atmosphere. Furthermore, the men interviewed looked favorably at the participation of women for a number of reasons: Because there was no front as such and fighting could erupt anywhere, anytime, some welcomed the opportunity to have their wives or daughters next to them, thus alleviating any anxiety or fear regarding their unknown fate. Another reason was the warmth and security provided by the feminine element; a third reason, the dedication of women to their duties and their self-sacrifice. Women would bring supplies to the battlefield under fire, when men would not. Furthermore, the presence of women at the front line made the men fight harder and with greater dedication.

Impact of Militarization on Society

The impact of the militarization of women on Lebanese society varied. From a Western perspective, Lebanese society is still characterized by a traditionally clear sexual division of labor. Women are encouraged to remain within the domestic sphere, although they enjoy equal opportunities for education, circumstances permitting. Their occupations in the public sphere are usually of a social or cultural dimension. The Lebanese of all communities praise the mild, sweet, virtuous girl whose goal in life is to be the perfect wife and mother. She is expected to be obedient and have a low profile. It is easy, therefore, to imagine the reaction of parents, whose society defines war as masculine activity, to the militarization of their daughters, which could be implicitly seen as unsettling to the social order. In addition to their fear for the lives of their daughters, they were worried about the reaction of the community and the negative influence this would have on their prospects for marriage.[60]

The attitude of parents, however, varied, although all shared the same fears and anxieties. Those who related best to this situation were themselves involved in the fighting or ideologically committed. But even they had some misgivings, because they still felt that fighting was the domain of men. Other parents personally escorted their daughters to the front and trained them in fighting. But there were others who categorically refused to allow their daughters to join the militia. While this may have stopped some girls from joining, it did not stand in the way of others, who joined the LF in secret and explained their absences as simply helping in some "innocent" chores far behind the lines.[61] This, however, left them in a state of solitude, anxiety and guilt, and without any moral support for having disobeyed their parents. Thus one of them said to her companions just before battle, "Tell your mothers to pray for me, because mine does not know where I am." To alleviate feelings of guilt, these girls would immerse themselves so completely in domestic life as soon as they got home that a chasm was created between their military and civil lives.[62]

This, of course, was not the only obstacle faced by women fighters, for they had to defend against rumors regarding their reputation and accusations of sexual license and immorality, especially when they had to spend nights, and sometimes weeks, away from home. Many of them sought an education because military life was deemed temporary, but more important, and for the sake of their families, to underline the fact they were serious normal young women intent on developing and enhancing their role in society.

Conclusion

It is evident from the preceding survey that both Christian and Muslim militias—inherently traditional, patriarchal, and sexist in orientation—called upon and encouraged women to join. Politicized religious ideologies transformed Muslim women into one-dimensional symbols of cultural purity and religious virtue. Thus Shiʿa women, who before the war were living in the rural South, were neither educated nor politically or economically active except in the agricultural domain. But in the early seventies, called upon by Musa al-Sadr, Shiʿa women found themselves mobilized to serve in whatever capacity they could.[63] They soon came to personify the struggle of the Shiʿa by wearing the veil or chador, symbolizing resistance to the West and its allies.[64] The patriotic woman, whether carrying a machine gun or wearing the veil or playing the perfect wife and mourner or working as nurse or teacher, became a model of partisan propaganda to satisfy the needs of the military. Thus, even if women were to be excluded from the military, they could not be described as pacifists or bystanders watching men destroy life and stone. The figure of the patriotic woman in all the different roles she played was just as militarized as the one who carried the gun.[65] What is important, therefore, to remember is that neither group entered the political or military arena in demonstration of women's rights or in support of equality between men and women. Their participation sprang from a purely patriotic perspective. Feminism and women's rights were the farthest things from their minds. They perceived themselves as part and parcel of the national crisis, oblivious to any other concern. Hence, when asked, both groups perceived themselves as emancipated, albeit for different reasons: The Christian female of the Lebanese Forces, having actualized her emancipation and realized equality of opportunity with the males of the same militia, refused to believe that any woman could be in chains unless self-inflicted; and the Shiʿa female of Hizballah and Amal, acquiescing to male superiority in certain domains, saw herself just as emancipated within these bounds and says: "We [women] represent half the population of the world and we rear and cultivate the other half." Thus, woman, according to her, is effectively in control of the whole world, albeit indirectly. Hence, while national revolutions or crises may help emancipate women, total liberation cannot be achieved unless political unrest is married to a sexual revolution.

The final question is whether the gains achieved in broadening the sphere of women during the war could or would be transferred to civilian life where sexism and sexist attitudes are still deeply ingrained in the subconscious of patriarchy. In an interview, one of the women of the LF, who was very active all through the war and who is now married to another LF combatant and pregnant, was enthusiastically describing all her military feats during the war and the skills she had acquired. In answer to a question about her relationship with her husband and whether he accepted her or was resentful of her accomplishments, she answered spontaneously, "Why should he? With my skills I can save him a lot of household problems including fixing the car when it stalls. But, of course, I always know my place and keep within my limits."

It is still too early to determine whether the women of the militias will sustain their independence and liberation in the external world now that peace is achieved and the militias disbanded. The experience of other women involved in revolutions or resistance movements shows that women are usually summarily sent back home once they are no longer needed. Thus the Palestinian Soraya Antonius is quoted to have said: "I have progressive ideas but I can't implement them fully. . . . Men are my comrades but deep down they don't believe I'm really their equal. Socially we haven't caught up with our political development. . . . I'm 36 and I haven't yet met a man who has really shaken off the old conventions about women. . . . At public meetings they [leaders] talk about liberating women but they really believe, and some of them say it openly, that a woman does her revolutionary duty by ironing her husband's shirts, cooking his dinner and providing a cozy and restful ambiance for the warrior."[66] Yet, Janice Yoder maintains that, in accord with what social psychologists have known for quite some time, the inevitability of change produces a positive reaction when one relates to it positively, creating thereby a more favorable atmosphere for women.[67]

In conclusion, the preceding survey of the role(s) women played in the Lebanese militias has shown that while women's "peaceable" nature may be acclaimed universally, women's attitudes toward war and active participation in it vary substantially from one period to another, from one geographical area to another, and from one culture to another. There are moments when women's behavior challenges facile assumptions regarding women's nature and their involvement in politics. The Lebanese experience has shown that just as both men and women are victims of war and violence, so are they both responsible for military activities. It is true that women did not participate in the decision to wage war, but they contributed to the building and maintaining of war machinery. There were those who actively participated in the fighting, but they were no more patriotic or involved than those who raised, encouraged, and drove their husbands and sons to go to battle. Women, thus, as combatants, military personnel, protesters, demonstrators, civic organizers, mourners, paramedics, and political sympathizers, fully demonstrate the range of their roles and the extent of their participation in war and society, thereby putting an end to such speculations as the facile statement made by Muammar Gaddafi that "Events in Lebanon have shown how necessary it is to know how to defend oneself; there all the women were able to do was weep and mourn," as quoted by Maria Graeff-Wassink.[68]

Notes

1. Ridd, "Powers of the Powerless," 2.

2. Cock, *Women and War,* 234.

3. Ridd, "Powers of the Powerless," 3; Macdonald, "Drawing the Lines," 1–26.

4. Higonnet et al., *Behind the Lines,* 1. See also Kaplan, "Woman as Caretaker," 124.

5. Elshtain, *Women and War,* 4.

6. Kaplan, "Woman as Caretaker," 124.

7. Ibid., 129–31.

8. Elshtain, *Women and War,* 181–84.

9. Peach, "An Alternative to Pacifism?" 152.

10. See also Vickers, *Women and War,* 19; Higonnet, "Not So Quiet in No-Woman's Land," 205.

11. Cock, *Women and War,* 231.

12. Peach, "An Alternative to Pacifism?" 153.

13. Ruddick, "Rationality of Care," 230–31.

14. Boccacio, *De mulieribus claris,* cited in Russo, "The Constitution of a Gendered Enemy."

15. Elshtain, *Women and War,* 173–80.

16. Addis and Russo, eds., *Women Soldiers,* xv.

17. Cooke, *Women Write War,* 3.

18. Etel Adnan, *Sitt Marie Rose* (California: Post Apollo Press, 1982), 12.

19. Abu Nasr, "Effects of War," 96.

20. Schulze, "Communal Violence."

21. For a full discussion, see introduction.

22. For the history of the Druze, see introduction.

23. Halawi, *Lebanon Defied,* 21–22.

24. Ibid. For the history of the Shiʿa in Lebanon, see introduction.

25. Halawi, *Lebanon Defied,* 182.

26. Ibid., 155. See also Wright, *Sacred Rage,* 51–57; Norton, *Amal and the Shiʿa,* 10.

27. Cobban, *Shiʿa Community,* 4.

28. Kliot, *Territorial Disintegration,* 22–23.

29. Hanf, *Coexistence,* 315–16. For more information, see introduction.

30. Wright, *Sacred Rage,* 82; Reeves, *Female Warriors,* 17; Norton, *Amal and the Shiʿa,* 202.

31. Halawi, *Lebanon Defied,* 180.

32. Ibid., 181.

33. Arberry's translation.

34. For a detailed description of women's role in Islamic fundamentalism, see Bizri, *"al-Mar'ah al-lubnaniyyah,"* 65–87.

35. Reeves, *Female Warriors,* 12.

36. Compare a similar statement cited in ibid., 13.

37. Interviews I conducted with female members of Amal and Hizballah.

38. Elshtain and Tobias, *Women, Militarism, and War,* ix.

39. Personal interview I conducted with her.

40. In contradistinction to this statement, Reeves cites in *Female Warriors,* 7, a suicidal attack against Israeli soldiers carried out by a sixteen-year-old Shiʿa girl of the National Lebanese Resistance, whose mainstay is Hizballah, as reported by Reuters, April 10, 1985.

41. Personal interview I conducted with two women of Hizballah.

42. Cited in Norton, *Amal and the Shiʿa,* 10.

43. Ibid.

44. Karamé, "Girls' Participation in Combat," 381–82; see also the essay in this collection by Jocelyn Khweiri, "From Gunpowder to Incense."

45. Karamé, "Girls' Participation in Combat," 380.

46. Kari Karamé, "L'Expérience des jeunes militantes," 180.

47. Karamé, "Girls' Participation in Combat," 379.

48. See Khweiri, "From Gunpowder to Incense."

49. Karamé, "Girls' Participation in Combat," 383.

50. Khweiri, "From Gunpowder to Incense."

51. For a detailed description, see ibid.

52. For details see ibid. and Karamé, "Girls' Participation in Combat," 384.

53. Rabinovich, *War for Lebanon,* 114–15.

54. This information is based on several interviews I conducted with the previous military command of the LF and ten female officers.

55. Ibid.

56. Cf. Khweiri, "From Gunpowder to Incense"; Karamé, "Girls' Participation in Combat," 385.

57. Ibid.; Khweiri, "From Gunpowder to Incense."

58. Cf. Elshtain, *Women and War,* 243.

59. Karamé, "L'Expérience des jeunes militantes," 183; cf. Macdonald, "Drawing the Lines," 6.

60. Karamé, "Girls' Participation in Combat," 387.

61. Ibid., 380.

62. Ibid., 388.

63. Schulze, "Communal Violence."

64. Cf. Ridd, "Powers of the Powerless," 5.

65. Cf. Addis and Russo, eds., *Women Soldiers,* p. xvi–xvii.

66. Accad, *Sexuality and War,* 24; cf. also Steven Hause, "More Minerva than Mars," 102.

67. Yoder, "Women at West Point," 529. For a full discussion of the socialization of women, see Lipps, "Gender-Role Socialization," 197–216; Vickers, *Women and War,* 43–44, 107; Warren and Cady, "Feminism and Peace," 4–20; Berkman, "Feminism, War, and Peace Politics," 141–60.

68. "The Militarization of Woman and 'Feminism' in Libya," 141.

10

Lebanese Shiʿi Women and Islamism: A Response to War

Maria Holt

According to popular legend, the mother of one of the Lebanese suicide bombers, a seventeen-year-old youth who destroyed the Israeli military headquarters in Tyre in November 1983 with massive loss of life, reacted with joy and pride to the news that her son had become a martyr in the war against Israel. She declared her fervent hope that all her sons would follow his example. Was this woman an unnatural mother? Had she been brainwashed into believing that any sacrifice, even the lives of her own children, was desirable for the greater good? Have other women who relate this anecdote as an example of admirable female behavior fallen victim to brainwashing? Or is her attitude an inevitable consequence of the Shiʿi history of sacrifice and martyrdom?

Introduction

In their struggle, the Lebanese Shiʿa, like other Lebanese groups, have recognized the unavoidability of violence as a means of conflict resolution. Although it threatens the community and is certainly destructive to the individual, they are aware that violence also possesses the power of catharsis. But violence for its own sake cannot be justified for very long; it must be supported by a framework of meanings. Any situation depending on violence demands "the forging of mythologies that aim to justify the death of innocent people. The mobilization of aggressiveness for war is first of all an ideological mobilization."[1]

To solve the riddle of the "unnatural" mother and to appreciate the frequently contradictory roles of men and women in the violence of Lebanon, we need to untangle the strands of Shiʿism as an ideology of protest from the particular experiences of the Lebanese Shiʿa, and to study the practical effects of ideology on the position of women. We know that, on the whole, men and women differ in their reaction to violently cataclysmic events. They have diverse needs and priorities, especially in their relationship with the state. Yet, despite striking disparities between male and female coping mechanisms in the face of upheaval, a key argument of this paper is that occurrences that threaten the survival of the community have the effect of drawing its members together and eliciting common purpose in their response.

Under normal circumstances, males in Shiʿi society, like any other society, are brought up to believe that their actions are capable of having an impact and that aggression can be an acceptable way of dealing with a problem. Females, in contrast, are taught to be dependent. Much of their dependence focuses on the family and particularly on their fathers, brothers, and husbands. In the era of the modern nation-state, women have also begun to look to the authority and institutions of the state to provide a modicum of protection. The state has become "a site of strategic importance to women. . . . It is here where (they) gain or lose crucial legal and political protection against other political communities, patriarchies, and religious and secular non-democratic forces. Often women have nowhere other than the state to turn for protection from domestic violence, familial coercion, discriminatory religious practices, and the oppression of oppositional political parties or movements."[2]

In the case of Lebanon, of course, the state as an effective source of authority disappeared during the war and women were, therefore, compelled to depend fully on the actions and decisions of men. This lack of a functioning alternative, with its implications of potential powerlessness, undoubtedly influenced women's range of responses and, even though their instincts may have tilted toward balance, conciliation, and the preservation of life, they were forced into a routine dominated by violence. At the same time, one should bear in mind that, on the one hand, the violence was part of a life-and-death struggle to protect the Shiʿi identity and, on the other, it was closely bound up with communal religious practices that were viewed as empowering rather than "discriminatory."

Therefore, in order to survive the period of intense trauma brought about by war and to enhance their own position within the Lebanese political system, the Shiʿa adopted an assertive form of political Islamism. This legitimized the limited—and carefully controlled—participation of women. A closer identification with Islam empowered the Shiʿa on two levels. In terms of formal politics, it could be argued that Islamism—or more precisely the use of Islamic symbols—has provided a vehicle to correct the imbalance in Lebanese politics. But, more important as far as women are concerned, it has also furnished a means of coping with the horror of war.

Lebanese Shiʿi women took part in the civil war and the numerous Israeli attacks upon and occupations of their country in a wide variety of ways and displayed qualities that were not merely innovative but occasionally even seemed to challenge notions of acceptable behavior. In the process of this learning experience—or prolonged act of survival—women assumed a number of less-familiar roles, suffered, lost family members, homes, and any notion of security, and supported their menfolk in the struggle for fairer representation within the system. Their conduct, I would like to suggest, proceeded from a mixture of desperation at the descent into chaos, lack of any coherent alternative, the perceived threat from outside as a communal binding mechanism, and, on a deeper level, some sense of Islamism as a source of female assertion.

This paper seeks to analyze the actions that Shiʿi women took in response to the war and the reasons behind this particular set of actions. I propose to argue that, although the character of the war was wholly masculine and the principal protagonists all men, Shiʿi women benefited in unexpected ways. One would imagine that women's experience of prolonged and all-consuming violence would be an entirely negative one, striking as it did at the very heart of family and community. An unforeseen outcome, however, was to create conditions whereby Shiʿi women were able to push forward the boundaries of what was previously regarded as permissible. In a prevailing atmosphere of anarchy, women had the opportunity to explore what could be described as the "revolutionary potential" contained in their lives and to discover hitherto unimagined avenues of opportunity. At the same time, the fact that this upheaval took place within a highly traditional and conservative society that was in the throes of a violent civil war imposed certain constraints on women's progress. What I hope to illustrate in this paper is that the combination of a pious population, the ravages of war, and the influence of an activist political ideology had the effect of creating an entirely new form of female participation in the Middle East.

The notion of female empowerment within the context of war raises a number of questions. Firstly, what were the precise outlines of this apparent change in female behavior and in what ways has it proved "liberating" for Lebanese Shiʿi women? Secondly, how much, in real terms, have they benefited from the war and its aftermath? Finally, what is likely to be the effect, both on Lebanese women in general and on future generations within the Shiʿi community itself, of the transforming experience through which these women have passed?

One cannot help wondering to what extent Shiʿi women—even those who were politically active—felt part of such a protracted struggle. As war is traditionally—and in most cases solely—a male arena, it is likely that women were, on the whole, excluded from it. Apart from support activities, such as tending the injured and maintaining the family, their participation would have been either abnormal or highly circumscribed. The mystique of Shiʿi religious discourse, too, tends to be jealously guarded by males, who retain the right to define the spaces in which women may move and the scope of their activity.

It is not, of course, so simple. While we can talk, on one level, of a male conspiracy to control women's behavior, more complex issues soon begin to emerge. The first is the attitude of women themselves. When encountering the women of the political groups Amal and Hizballah—or even the ordinary village women of southern Lebanon—one by no means gains the impression of an oppressed or downtrodden segment of the population. On the contrary, these women seem to have made a very clear choice and are content in their identity. This identity, nonetheless, is still a relatively new one. It emerged from a war situation, forged by a mixture of adversity, violence, and religious revival.

A second complexity involves the nature of the war. Within any belligerent situation, the mode of warfare has a direct effect on women's ability to participate. As the Lebanese war was more precisely a series of interfactional squabbles, women experienced shifting levels of involvement and loyalty. In the south of the country, there was an added dimension that may well have helped to legitimize women's efforts. The local Shiʿi population had long been waging a struggle against aggressive Israeli encroachment, first in response to the Palestinian resistance movement and then against the indigenous inhabitants themselves. Here, in particular, Islam has come to be associated with the national liberation struggle and, in this sense, it has been instrumental in mobilizing the members of a previously victimized community. In the southern battlefields, "it was the women's policy of 'non-departure'—refusing to leave the land whatever the cost—that played a crucial role in encouraging resistance."[3]

The third complicating factor is the question of whether Lebanese women, as a group, share an awareness of their disadvantaged position in society. What they have in common as women, in other words, might be greater than their sectarian differences. During the course of the war, there were few opportunities for the development of a feminist consciousness. Although some women crossed the factional divide in order to engage in antiwar demonstrations or to minister to the casualties of war, the majority had little choice but to seek refuge in their own sectarian strongholds.

Women and the Contemporary Islamist Movement

The move by the Lebanese Shiʿa toward Islamism as a favored form of political expression by no means occurred in a vacuum. It was part of a larger trend within the Arab world and beyond. Social changes in the Middle East and North Africa "have given rise to an ideological movement of a specific type, sometimes called fundamentalism or political Islam," but that might more accurately be described as "the Islamist movement, advocating reconstruction of the moral order that has been disrupted or changed. Islamist movements have arisen in the context of socioeconomic crisis, a crisis of legitimacy of the state and political order, and the weakening of the patriarchal family structure."[4]

While Islamism is not perhaps a surprising response to the problems of modern times, its effect on Muslim women has been criticized. Islamic resurgence "exemplified by movements as varied as Jamaat-i Islami in Pakistan, Ikhwan al-Muslimin in Egypt, the Islamic Republic in Iran, and the Islamic Salvation Front (FIS) in Algeria, insists on singling out women's relations to society as the supreme test of the authenticity of the Islamic order."[5] While this certainly seems to be the case among certain groups, one should distinguish between the plethora of antiwomen practices that have attached themselves to Islam over time—and inevitably have an effect on modern interpretations—and the genuinely revolutionary spirit of Islamism that seeks to enhance the position of women.

Islamic "fundamentalism," suggests one critic, has been, "in part, a response to 'Westernizing' processes by using women's bodies as sites for assertions of cultural authenticity, further reinscribing women's symbolic and real importance in definitions of the nation. . . . The symbolic equation of women with nation often leads to the subordination of actual women through calls for the preservation of 'traditional' families, codes of ethics, values and conduct. At times, the preservation of the nation results in moves to assume greater control over women than had existed in some imagined past."[6] The key concept here is the "imagined" or idealized version of history, in which the Islamic *ummah* lived in harmony, flourished, and controlled its women. A yearning to impose the blueprint of "simpler" times onto the crude competitiveness of the modern international system has led certain over-zealous adherents of the Islamist movement to equate the repression of women with an orderly and balanced society.

Nonetheless, the assumption of coercion is only partially accurate. It would certainly be fair to say that pressures are placed on women to conform to the Islamist model, in terms of dress and behavior, and that such pressures remove the element of choice. But one must ask what "choice" means in this context. Many women have their own reasons for opting for Islamism. The adoption of Islamic dress, for example, expresses "an affirmation of ethical and social customs—particularly with regard to mixing with the opposite sex—that those adopting the dress and affiliation are comfortable with and accustomed to. For women, Islamic dress also appears to bring a variety of distinct advantages. On the simplest, most material level, it is economical. Women adopting Islamic dress are saved the expense of acquiring fashionable clothes and having more than two or three outfits. The dress also protects them from male harassment."[7]

The question of the veil, in the Lebanese context, is a fascinating one. Lebanon, particularly Beirut, remains a cosmopolitan and Westernized society. Many women do not wear headscarves and some even sport relatively revealing garments. There is certainly no pressure in the broader societal framework to conform to a particular version of womanhood. However, if we take revolutionary Iran as a model, we can see that women chose to rebel by adopting the veil precisely because it represented a strong anti-Western statement. The same pattern is repeating itself across the Arab and Islamic worlds as women put on the veil as a symbol of authenticity and identity. It can also be seen as a way of confronting a situation of potential uncertainty.

Although the Islamist movement is by no means monolithic, it always contains a pronounced political tinge and frequently has a tendency to use women in ways that seem to represent a reversion to traditional practices. In general, "family affairs and women's subordination are . . . recognized as the reflection of Islamist movements' definition of identity, and laws are passed or modified in order to meet their demands."[8] In the new ideological construction of Islamist movements, "women are presented as symbols and repositories of religious, national, and cultural identity. In the context of fear and loss of economic and social status, the link between the honor of the family and the honor of the community leads men to attempt to control 'their' women."[9]

However, despite the rigidity of male interpretations, one begins to see the possibility of political Islamism being used as a tool for women's liberation. If we take "original" Islam as a starting point and interpret the modern Islamist movement as a yearning to "return" to the revolutionary beginnings of the religion, combined with a program to transform these feelings into a political project for reform, we can suggest that men have used their control over the movement to corrupt it and exclude women from it. Muslim women, by engaging in their own movement for reform and return, have been able to reclaim important elements of their religion and to use them to achieve their own ends. These women see no contradiction between Islamism and full participation in public life.

Shiʿism in Lebanon

The Shiʿa are by no means newcomers to the Lebanese sectarian mosaic. On the contrary, there has been a Shiʿi presence for many centuries. The Lebanese Shiʿa, it is claimed, "are as old as Lebanon itself. They have participated with the other communities in cultivating its plains and mountains, developing its land, and protecting its frontiers. The Shiʿa have survived in Lebanon in prosperity and adversity. They have soaked its soil with the blood of their children, and have raised its banner of glory in its sky, for they have led most of its revolutions."[10] Despite its proud history, however, the Shiʿi community "has always been and largely remains to the present the poorest and least-educated among Lebanon's religious groups."[11] Until the French Mandate period in the 1920s, the Shiʿa—who mainly inhabited the mountainous regions of Jabal ʿAmil in the south of the country and the northern Biqaa were not even recognized as an official community distinct from the more numerous Sunnis. After Lebanon gained its formal independence from France in 1943, the Shiʿa continued to be overlooked in the political arrangements of the new state.

During the 1960s, "increasing numbers of dispossessed and uprooted Shiʿi migrants"[12] were forced to move to Beirut, where they settled on the southern fringes of the city. But this group lacked even elementary organization and "could not, by virtue of the electoral laws, mobilize their collective protest or vent their grievances."[13] Neither were the community's religious institutions in any position "to reinforce substantially its cohesion and political effectiveness. The Shiʿi clergy was weak, materially deprived, fearful and under the reactionary influence of the traditional Shiʿi leaders."[14] This situation began to improve as a result of the efforts of Musa al-Sadr, a particularly energetic Shiʿi religious scholar. In late 1967, by an act of the Lebanese Parliament, the Shiʿi Supreme National Islamic Council was created and, in 1969, Imam al-Sadr was elected as its president. The following year, he "was instrumental in setting up a Council of the South to develop the Jabal ʿAmil region."[15]

Unfortunately, in the highly unstable environment of southern Lebanon over the past few decades, any attempt to create a better society must have been both uneven and circumscribed by various imperatives, such as resistance, survival, and the management of fear. Southern Lebanon, it is said, lies "at the root of the Lebanese political problem. It embodies the basic elements of the Lebanese crisis caused mainly by the Israeli occupation, but also a confessional political system lacking equality and social justice. . . . It is the base of the noble and heroic resistance holding the torch of confrontation before the aggressors."[16] Under such conditions, it is likely that simplified options were sought that relied on the primordial sentiments of the mass of the population. By appealing to Islamic belief, it was possible to mobilize the community. Shiʿi solidarity was facilitated by the shared values of religion and reinforced by poverty and alienation. In this sense, the teachings of Musa al-Sadr, which applied to women as much as to men, were revolutionary.

In Lebanon, after 1975, the entire social order collapsed into chaos and violence. The population saw that this state of affairs demanded a response. The various sects and groupings identified the need for a clearly articulated alternative towards which members of a group sharing common characteristics can strive. The Lebanese Shiʿi community, with the example of their coreligionists in Iran and a proud history of Shiʿism as a form of social protest, perhaps inevitably turned to Islam. The Amal movement was the first step but, for many Shiʿis, it proved insufficient. These people then sought a more radical form and, thus, Hizballah and other more extreme groupings came into being.

But, while a retreat into comforting confessional certainties was no doubt a natural response to the insecurity of the situation and the vulnerability of the population, it also brought its own dangers. By withdrawing from the national project, the various sects risked "eroding civility, increasing distance between groups, and sharpening further the segmented character of society."[17] This is particularly acute for the women of the community who depend to a larger extent than men on the mechanisms and controls of civil society.

Three events in 1978–79 "accelerated the mobilization of the Shiʿi community." The first was the massive invasion, in March 1978, by Israel; secondly, in August of the same year, Musa al-Sadr disappeared during a visit to Libya; and, thirdly, the Islamic revolution in Iran succeeded, in January 1979, in overthrowing the Shah and creating an Islamic republic.[18]

One starts to gain an insight into a community, the Shiʿa of Lebanon, which is slowly finding a sense of self, a confidence previously lacking. It is also a community that—paradoxically—feels itself an integral part of a united Lebanon. There seems little desire to follow the Iranian model of an Islamic republic. Instead, intense national pride may be discerned, although members of Hizballah admit they anticipate an Islamic state at some point in the future "when people are ready for it."

Women in the Shiʿi Community

When a Shiʿi girl is nine years old, she may begin to participate in the daily prayer ritual of the community. She should also assume the *hijab* (veil). As this moment in her life is associated with a transition from the world of childhood into the world of adults, it is eagerly awaited. Small girls play at being grown up by putting on a head covering. They are taught that this act is symbolic of dignity and responsibility. To choose not to wear the *hijab*, on the other hand, is regarded as a sign of rebelliousness and, therefore, much frowned upon. In actuality, one could argue that it is a subtle form of conditioning whereby young girls actively participate in their own oppression. But, to develop this idea further, we must separate the strands of what might be termed "fundamental oppression" from the societal norms as dictated by the Qurʾan and the special conditions imposed by war.

Encountering young Shiʿi women in Lebanon, one is struck by their confidence and fluency. Many use their headscarves almost as a fashion statement. Theirs is far from the drab uniform of the Iranian revolution. On the contrary, they are proud of their smart clothes and color-coordinated scarves, and give the impression of a more modest version of fashion-conscious young women in the West. Of course there are variations and, while a minority of devout Shiʿi women have opted for the austere and all-encompassing chador, the more secularized members of the community have abandoned the veil altogether.

Lebanese Shiʿi society is rooted in the belief that man "is a slave of his basic urges and woman is a captive of her love. What causes man to stumble and lose his footing is his basic motivational urges. According to psychologists, woman has more patience and endurance in the control of her passions. However, that which imbalances woman and enslaves her is the sweet voice of affection, sincerity, fidelity and love from man."[19] Thus, although women and men are regarded as equal in religious terms, "woman is a human being with particular conditions, and man is a human being with other conditions. Man and woman are equal in their being human, but they are two kinds of human being with two kinds of characteristics and two kinds of psychology. . . . Nature had a purpose in these two different conditions."[20] Men and women, in other words, are designed to occupy separate "spaces" in the world. Yet, although their functions and their "societies" differ, both are deserving of equal respect.

The writings of the late Ayatollah Mutahhari on "the rights of women in Islam" are much respected in the Shiʿi community. He produced a theory that argues in favor of seeing women's rights in a new light. By illustrating the flawed and ethnocentric reasoning behind Western philosophy and feminism and the weakness of the Universal Declaration of Human Rights, Mutahhari sought to prove that an alternative Islamic model indeed exists whereby "despite the fact that Islam acquainted woman with her human rights, gave her individuality, freedom and independence, it never induced her to revolt and mutiny against, or be cynical towards the male sex."[21] The Islamic women's movement, in Mutahhari's view, is a "white" movement, untinged by the "black, red, blue or purple" of some particular "man-made ideology."[22]

He developed two arguments to support his hypothesis. The first asks whether equality or identicalness is preferable; while the second reveals the extensive and revolutionary rights enjoyed by women in Shiʿa Islam. Equality, accordng to Mutahhari, "is different from being exactly the same. What is certain is that Islam has not considered there to be identicalness or exact similarity of rights between men and women, but it has never believed in preference and discrimination in favor of men as opposed to women. . . . Islam is not against the equality of men and women, but it does not agree with the identicalness of their rights."[23] For the sake of practicality, and also on the basis of their different personalities, there must be a division of rights although, as Mutahhari admitted, "many rights that have been given to women by Islam and have in practice been ignored should be restored to them."[24] But he advises Muslims against blind imitation of the Western model of equality between men and women for, as he pointed out, despite the lofty pronouncements of numerous Western philosophers and the wide acceptance of the Universal Declaration of Human Rights, the reality of sexism, male power, and the denial of a spiritual dimension remain. The Islamic system attempts to remove hypocrisy and to celebrate the differences between the sexes.

The claim that women are "different but equal" is a crucial one and brings to mind some of the heroic female figures of Shiʿi history, such as the Prophet Muhammad's first wife, Khadijah, his daughter Fatima, who was married to Ali, the first Shiʿi imam, after whom an entire dynasty, "the Fatimids, initially ruling in North Africa from 909 and then in Egypt and Syria up to 1171 A.D., took their name from the daughter of Muhammad, their founder reinforced his claim to power with the assertion that he was a descendant of Fatima."[25]

The question of female leadership is a contentious one. But, while Shiʿi history has accommodated a handful of women in positions of political and even military leadership, modern Lebanon evidently does not encourage women to aspire to such roles and many people even claim that they would be "inappropriate" for women. Although women are allowed to occupy certain influential positions within the Lebanese Shiʿi community, these tend to be of a social, family-oriented nature. On the whole, women are not found in the ranks of political leadership and certainly never become religious leaders. This appears to confirm the argument that male religious leaders have appropriated the words of the Qurʾan and also the traditions of Shiʿi history and made use of them for their own ends. Seeing the posters and huge pictures of religious luminaries on the roadsides in the southern suburbs of Beirut and in southern Lebanon, one gets the impression of total female invisibility. Religion, in this sense, has the appearance of a male-controlled space that excludes women.

Nonetheless, much has changed over the past few years for Shiʿi women. They are now better educated, frequently have jobs, a choice of marriage partners, and fewer children. Yet, at the same time, they are experiencing a religious resurgence, which expresses itself in dress, behavior, and attitudes. On one level, it is an expression of defeat. The war has succeeded in eroding a natural desire for freedom. It has distorted the people's longing for a more just order and channeled it into safer manifestations of rebellion. But on a deeper level, as in Iran, this "rebellion" must be recognized for what it is: an authentic expression of empowerment, a way of shaking off unwelcome Westernization.

The two movements most closely associated with the Shiʿi renaissance in Lebanon are Amal and Hizballah. Although both are rooted in Shiʿi religious symbolism and make extensive use of Islamic terminology, it would be fair to say that only Hizballah can now claim to be an "Islamist" organization, according to the definitions set out above. After the disappearance of Musa al-Sadr, Amal has gradually shifted to a more "secular" approach, although one should, of course, use such terms with caution.

The Amal Movement

The Amal movement, which started life as a militia attached to *Harakat al-mahrumin* (the movement of the deprived or disinherited), was founded by Iranian-born cleric Musa al-Sadr in 1974. The original social protest movement on behalf of the powerless and largely ignored Shiʿi community of southern Lebanon turned to violence when its demands for justice and a larger share of the communal pie were ignored. Shiʿi dissatisfaction had grown as the result of a number of factors. As newly independent Lebanon flourished, the Shiʿi community was languishing "under the domination of a relatively small number of *zuʿama* (political bosses), whose political power stemmed from land wealth and the political ineffectualness of their clientele."[26] At the same time, the Shiʿa "were exposed to wide-ranging economic change and social disruption."[27] Gradually, as a result of "changing agricultural patterns, increased access to the media, improved internal transportation networks, internal and external migration, and a deteriorating security environment, traditional political leaders became less capable of meeting the escalating needs and demands of their constituents."[28] The Shiʿa, in other words, were ripe for social mobilization.

Musa al-Sadr "vowed to struggle relentlessly until the security needs and social grievances of the deprived . . . were satisfactorily addressed by the government."[29] He was a charismatic and widely revered figure and, although he mysteriously vanished in 1978, "his aura still resonates in almost mythic proportions."[30] When he began his work in southern Lebanon in the early 1960s, it was with the objective of improving the lowly and impoverished status of the local Shiʿi population. He approached this in two ways: by endeavoring to persuade the central Lebanese government to devote more resources to the south of the country, and by founding local institutions to address basic needs. To start with at least, he sought to operate within Lebanon's complex confessional system and "to tackle the immense social needs of his community by filling the role left vacant by the state and the politicians."[31] Very soon, however, it became apparent to him that the Shiʿi problem "had to do with deprivation and degrading physical conditions, the lack of spiritual and cultural guidance, and the sociopolitical reality of being a part and yet not full participants in a country."[32] Gradually, he began to adopt a more militant stance.

With the growing militancy of Amal, it has been argued, the military and social arms of the movement began to diverge. The social aspects of Musa al-Sadr's teachings are still promoted by the Imam al-Sadr Foundation, based in Tyre, southern Lebanon, which is run by his sister, Rabab al-Sadr Sharaf al-Din. The foundation comprises a number of projects, including a kindergarten, an elementary school, an orphanage for girls, and a nursing school. Approximately 300 girls live at the foundation; until the age of nine, they are taught there and, after that, attend local schools while continuing to reside at the foundation. If they wish to attend university, the foundation assists with funding. Imam Musa's declared objectives were to take a girl from an impoverished background, to endow her with power and dignity and, in the process, to remove from her any feelings of inferiority or victimization. He wished, in other words, to produce model female citizens for the Shiʿi community and, in this respect, the foundation remains faithful to his principles. However, while its staff were promoting his work on behalf of the more deprived members of the population, the Amal militia embarked upon a campaign of violence or—perhaps more precisely—joined in the general violence taking place in the society.

As in every patriarchal society,

> Lebanese Shiʿa politics was a man's world. The woman merely represented an additional vote which the male head of the household had at his disposal to support his candidate of choice. . . . With Sayyid Musa's efforts, this was substantially altered. After his arrival in Lebanon, the Sayyid actively relied on his sister, Sayyidah Rabab, to widen the social involvement and visibility of the Lebanese Shiʿa woman. The commitment to bringing women to the forefront of Lebanese social and political life was symbolic of the cleric's leadership as a whole. The change that was effected was not revolutionary in any way, nor was it intended to be. The aim was to make public the role of the ordinary woman within the traditional mold, to involve her in a world that complemented the domestic private sphere in which she operated. It was Sayyid Musa's intention to inspire to action what had until then been a silent and silenced population and to hasten its entry onto the political scene.[33]

This was no Western-inspired ideal of "women's liberation" but rather an attempt to perfect an alternative and—in the Shiʿi context—more universally respected model. To a large extent, Sadr's dream has been fulfilled.

How, one wonders, can the ideals of Imam Musa be put into practice in an environment of such relentless brutality? The staff of the foundation—many of whom are from southern villages whose populations are only too familiar with the mind-numbing violence that has characterized Lebanon since 1975—explain that they follow his example by adhering to Islamic principles and creating an appropriate moral environment. There is a genuine air of enlightenment, although one might speculate as to how much choice a child is permitted and whether an education of this nature might not produce an overly conformist society.

According to Rahmeh el-Haj, director of the al-Zahra school at the Imam al-Sadr Foundation, there have been far-ranging changes in women's education in southern Lebanon over the last few decades. When the Israelis originally invaded the country, many southerners fled to Beirut or even left Lebanon altogether. Such experiences contributed to a heightened awareness of the world. The curriculum at the school is a balanced one. It includes Arabic, English, mathematics, science, geography, history, art, sports, and religion. Regular prayers and leisure activities are also features of daily life for the orphans and impoverished girls being educated by the foundation. There is a strong emphasis on communal activities in the belief that, if the girls respect and live in harmony with each other, they will be confident and more capable of flexibility in their future lives.[34]

Before his untimely disappearance, Imam Musa's efforts were aimed at removing the oppression being suffered by the people of the South and to create a more enlightened civilization for the Shiʿa. His teachings applied as much to women as to men. He was determined that girls should receive a comprehensive education and gave special attention to girls from poor backgrounds. His attitude raises the question of breadth of vision. Undoubtedly a pious and widely admired individual, Musa al-Sadr possessed an uncompromising vision of Islam. For him, it meant liberation through the education and religious devotion of *all* citizens, male and female.

At the foundation, the girls are raised to be good Muslims by a combination of example and education. The foundation works rather like an extended family in which young people seek to imitate their elders in order to receive praise. For an orphan, one might imagine that the impetus to conform would be even stronger, as failure to do so would have the effect of isolating the child from her community. Every attempt is made to prepare the girls for their future life in the larger society. Each girl is warned that she might encounter "bad things," that others might try to persuade her not to wear a headscarf, or that she might be tempted by pleasures formerly forbidden to her.

Although Shiʿi women are brought up to believe that there is equality between men and women, they also learn that men are responsible for the material well-being of their families and are physically stronger. Therefore, in the resistance movement, it is men who must take the initiative in confronting the enemy. Women's role is to supply the men with ammunition, to gather news and information for the men, and to care for them. Islam, according to Rahmeh el-Haj, insists that the woman's job is to build a new society rather than to fight on the battlefield. But, in a war-centered society, it seems clear that the honor and glory must lie with those who engage in combat. They are the heroes while those who support them are not usually remembered.

On the other hand, it has been suggested that, in contrast to Islamist movements in, for example, Egypt and Algeria, which have had the effect of inhibiting women, the Islamic revival in Lebanon has encouraged women to be active and outgoing.[35] Amal women claim that, as a result of the desperate conditions caused by war and occupation, together with their role within the resistance movement, there has been "a rebirth of the fundamental character of women."[36] Some activists report that it became "quite normal" for Amal men to marry women who devoted all their time to the movement. Said one woman: "We never imagined that our men would reach this stage of understanding women's position—even in a hundred years' time."[37] Another felt "our traditional life and women's confinement to the home didn't generate anything but injustice and a stupid acquiescence towards it." But after Musa al-Sadr began his work in the South, "we started to raise our voices; as women we started forming groups in which women were educated and encouraged to rebel against our unfair conditions."[38]

The village of Maarake in southern Lebanon used to be a center of Amal resistance during the Israeli invasion in the early 1980s. Zaynab Jaradi, widow of Amal leader Khalil Jaradi, who was murdered by the Israelis in 1984, told me about her husband's death and her present life. Khalil Jaradi, she explained, was a religious man and defended his country as a matter of honor. In his dealings with the Israelis, he had developed powers that sounded almost magical; he could, it seems, appear and disappear at will. Although the Israelis had tried many times to capture him, they were always unsuccessful and so, in exasperation, they placed a remote-controlled explosive device in a local *husayniyyah* (religous meeting place), where they knew the leaders of the area would gather to discuss future strategy. In what has been described as "the most notorious incident" during Israel's "iron-fist" policy in southern Lebanon, fifteen people, including Khalil Jaradi, were killed and over fifty injured.[39]

Mrs. Jaradi, too, had been involved in the resistance. She had worked as a nurse and had smuggled ammunition to the fighters under her clothing. At night, she recounted, women would sit in groups on hills or on the tops of buildings to keep watch for the Israelis; they would warn the men whenever the enemy approached. Sometimes women and girls made barricades out of burning tires in order to block off streets so that the men could escape. Children were also encouraged to confront the Israeli troops. On occasion, women would be hurt or even killed by the Israelis. Zaynab Jaradi proudly evoked the familiar image of the heroic mother, a baby in one arm and a gun in the other. According to the Qurʾan, she said, it is a matter of pride to die for one's belief, but a woman's primary role is to wait for her husband and for God's will to be revealed. Nowadays she is no longer involved with the resistance but, instead, teaches children. Her hope is for a unified Lebanon, with Israel back behind its own borders.[40]

Another potent image is that of tender plants in inhospitable places. Against the odds, they survive and even flourish, and this could be said too of the women battling Israeli oppression in the south of Lebanon. Their determination to survive is impressive. They have endured torture, imprisonment, the threat and reality of rape, the terrorizing of their children and the blowing-up of their houses and destruction of their villages—an Israeli act of collective punishment intended to flush out the fighters. In order to intimidate local people, the Israelis have invaded the personal space of women and, as a means of resisting such violations, women say that the preservation and strengthening of their faith has been essential. It has helped them to face the enemy boldly and to bring their children up to do the same. The vivid mythology of martyrdom that thrives among the Shiʿa has done much to aid this effort. According to one woman: "All Southern women urged their children to join the Lebanese resistance and give their blood for the liberation of the land. Here, it is no longer the habit of women to mourn their dead children; instead they celebrate their death and hand their guns on to their young brother or sister."[41] Once again, we glimpse the specter of the "unnatural" mother.

During its years of participation in the general violence and civil unrest, the Amal movement was accused of supporting the Israeli invasion. It has been claimed that the Shiʿa of southern Lebanon initially welcomed the Israelis who, they hoped, would rescue them from the arbitrary power and high-handedness of the Palestinians. The local Shiʿi community, more than anyone, suffered from the ongoing border scuffles between Palestinian *fidayeen* (commandos) and Israeli troops, their villages becoming war zones. Whenever a Palestinian military operation took place against Israel, the Israelis would retaliate by attacking the villages of southern Lebanon in an indiscriminate manner. As a result, countless innocent Lebanese civilians, including women and children, were killed and wounded, and an atmosphere of fear and insecurity created in which family life grew increasingly difficult.

Amal's reputation among sections of the Shiʿi community is far from spotless. The movement has been accused of selling out, hypocrisy, and seeking power for its own sake. In response, the ideologically more extreme Islamic Amal movement was founded in the early 1980s by Husayn Musawi. While the other rival Shiʿi organization, Hizballah, insists that armed resistance is the only practical tactic to use against the Israelis, who continue to occupy a narrow strip of land in southern Lebanon, Amal calls for a political settlement. In consequence, many Shiʿa, particularly young men, are drawn to the seemingly more wholehearted ideology of Hizballah, and Amal has lost some of its support. A number of defectors report that, had Amal remained true to the teachings of Musa al-Sadr, they would not have abandoned it. As it is, they find its present, more pragmatic approach unconvincing. Since the ending of the civil war, the Amal militia has transformed itself into a political party. Led by Nabih Berri, it gained several parliamentary seats in the 1992 general election, and Mr. Berri was appointed Speaker of the Lebanese Parliament.

During the years of war, many women participated in the struggle. They regard it as a religious duty, but explain that, according to the Qurʾan, the tasks of men and women in war are different. In the words of one Amal woman, "our arms are our thoughts and words. We have first to understand where we are and where we stand before we carry arms. If we have to carry arms, then of course, we will; otherwise our role is primarily social and educational."[42] While men must act as the primary defenders, women too are permitted to fight if the situation becomes desperate. Otherwise, they are obliged to protect their homes and children and, as we have seen, may perform support roles. These, as Mrs. Jaradi explained, include the smuggling of food and weapons (pregnancy was a popular disguise), keeping watch for the enemy, and creating a diversion so that men can get away. In one village, so the story goes, elderly women threw boiling oil over intruding Israeli soldiers. In addition, women have had the task of explaining "to families and neighbors what was going on." One woman describes the ways in which "we taught them how to face grave situations bravely. We offered them various services and ran special courses for mothers to teach them how to cope with the war situation. We also taught them religion and the place of women in Islam."[43] In return, though, the women of southern Lebanon have suffered a variety of humiliations at the hands of the invading Israelis.

It is clear that these women regard themselves, and are regarded, as an integral part of the resistance movement. By being a good wife and mother, a woman is contributing to the defense of her country. But Amal women also possess qualities of courage and defiance and the ability to speak out against injustice. They describe their roles with profound conviction, believing that their position in society is religiously sanctioned. It is tempting to accept that, since the women themselves are evidently content with their lot, it is not the business of outsiders to criticize. Aware of the available options, the women of Amal have committed themselves to a particular course. Another view would be that it is a successful and not particularly cruel form of indoctrination, although one might wonder about its ultimate objective.

The Amal movement now has a new set of certainties, the most pressing of which are to expel Israel, to reconstruct the country in a way that provides for intercommunal harmony, to participate fully in the Lebanese system, and, most important, to remain true to Islam.

Hizballah (the Party of God)

The name "Hizballah," with its associations of unrestrained violence and religious fanaticism, still strikes alarm in the minds of many in the West. In order to discuss the impact of this political movement on the Lebanese Shiʿa, we must separate the myth from the reality. Hizballah was founded in 1982 in response to two pressing crises: the invasion and occupation of Lebanon by Israel, and the Amal movement's perceived departure from "the true path of Islam." During that tumultuous period, many in the Shiʿi community, especially "among the young generation, who did not find in Amal a cogent response to their fervor and their desire to launch a *jihad* against Israel and bring about a change in the Beirut regime, left Amal and joined Hizballah."[44] Another influential factor, of course, was the recent stunning success of the Islamic revolution in Iran.

Deriving its ideoligical inspiration from the political writings of Ayatollahs Ruhollah Khomeini and Muhammad Baqir al-Sadr,[45] Hizballah declared "frankly and clearly that we are a nation that fears only God and that does not accept tyranny, aggression, and humiliation. America and its allies and the Zionist entity that has usurped the sacred Islamic land of Palestine have engaged and continue to engage in constant aggression against us and are working constantly to humiliate us. Therefore, we are in a state of constant and escalating preparedness to repel the aggression and to defend our religion, existence, and dignity."[46]

Hizballah's boldness of vision proved irresistible to many in the Shiʿi community who had been disappointed by Amal's moves toward accommodation within the Lebanese system and sought a more wholehearted course of action. Particularly inspired were the large numbers of young Shiʿi men alienated by poverty, dispossession, and defeat. The group rapidly developed centers of support throughout the Shiʿi heartland: primarily in the southern suburbs of Beirut, in the Biqaa Valley, particularly the town of Baalbeck, and in the Jabal ʿAmil area. But there is evidence to suggest that Hizballah has modified at least some of its positions. Since 1989, it has entered a "new phase," described as the phase of "political *jihad*" (holy war).[47] Although the organization is regarded with apprehension in the West, it has many supporters in Lebanon, and its popularity, particularly as a result of its fierce resistance to the Israeli occupation, is now believed to have overtaken that of the Amal movement.

But there are a number of common misconceptions about Hizballah based on the popular mythology that grew up in the 1980s and continues to cloud the group's existence. The first is that Hizballah is unduly influenced by the Islamic Republic of Iran. In 1982, contingents of Iranian Revolutionary Guards came to the Biqaa Valley to assist in the training of Hizballah fighters. Large sums of money have also been made available by Iran to Hizballah. In the opinion of one analyst, the founders of Hizballah, led by Sayyid Abbas Musawi and Shaykh Subhi al-Tufayli, "acknowledged the Imam Khomeini as their religious and political leader and identified with Iran's striving to make Lebanon part of the Islamic Republic."[48] Nowadays, for practical as well as ideological reasons, the relationship with Iran is recognized as being a religious rather than a political one. By professing allegiance to Iranian leader Ayatollah Ali Khameneʾi, Hizballah members are not putting the interests of a foreign country above Lebanese national concerns but, rather, deferring to the international concept of a Shiʿi hierarchy, of which Khamanei is at present the head.

A second misconception is that Hizballah is solely a fighting group. While it is heavily involved in resistance activities against Israel, since 1992, it has also been developing an active parliamentary role and, with the benefit of its considerable financial assets, has been able to put into practice a comprehensive social program, specifically aimed at the disadvantaged members of the Shiʿi community. For example, the Martyrs Foundation takes care of the families of Hizballah "martyrs"; the Campaign for Reconstruction Institution is responsible for renovating houses and roads; and the Resupply Committee provides money, food, and clothing for the needy. In addition, Hizballah has established two major hospitals—one in the southern suburbs of Beirut and the other in Baalbeck, a network of schools, and numerous other services.[49] Some critics argue that there is an element of manipulation in these activities. "Good works" such as these, they suggest, are frequently utilized by radical groups like Hizballah as an effective method of gaining the sympathy and support of a population which otherwise might be less enthusiastic. It is certainly the case that, by contributing practically to the communal good, Hizballah has been able to win new adherents as well as enhancing its overall popularity, but it is true too that the social aspect of its work has, since the beginning, played an integral part in its general ideological stance. This is particularly relevant when considering the position of women in the Hizballah structure and their "natural" inclination towards welfare activities.

A third point of contention is the fear that Hizballah is plotting to impose Islam by force in Lebanon. However, although Hizballah members call for the creation of an Islamic state because it is in line with Qurʾanic teachings, most realize that this is unlikely to be achieved in the immediate future. The group's so-called "spiritual mentor," Sayyid Muhammad Husayn Fadlallah, is similarly realistic. While acknowledging that he would much prefer to live in an Islamic state, he concedes that this will be a slow process, requiring "dialogue, education, and mutual understanding." In the meantime, he recommends "intercommunal toleration."[50] It is forbidden to impose Islam by violence or terrorism. Instead, advises Sheikh Fadlallah, Islamists should proceed by way of "wisdom and good advice" and in accordance with the will of the whole Lebanese people.[51]

The final misconception concerns the role of women in Hizballah ideology. It is clear that their role is regarded as being significantly different from that of men. In an "Open Letter to the Downtrodden of Lebanon and the World," dated February 1985, Hizballah states: "Through their Islamic resistance, the strugglers—the women with rocks and boiling oil for their weapons, the children with their shouts and their bare fists for their weapons, the old men with their weak bodies and their thick sticks for their weapons, and the youth with their rifles and their firm and faithful will for their weapons—have all proven that if the nation is allowed to manage its affairs freely, it is capable of making miracles and changing the imaginary fates."[52] But, at the same time, there have been reports that Hizballah fighters have been known to engage in *mutʿa* (temporary marriage), which, although it is allowed by Shiʿi Islam under certain conditions, is often compared by oher Muslims with prostitution or, at the very least, the selective use of religion by men to achieve their own pleasurable ends. Thus, although appropriate female participation is recognized, men have been left with room to maneuver.

According to Shaykh Fadlallah, a woman's highest achievement is located in motherhood. But this does not mean she must act as a domestic drudge for her husband and family. In a contract drawn up before marriage, a woman agrees to perform certain household tasks. She does them of her own free will and can even extract payment from her husband if she so desires. Islamically speaking, such duties cannot be imposed on a woman. Marriage partners are exhorted to be "loving and merciful" towards each other within a framework of clearly defined functions, which cover day-to-day living as well as abnormal situations such as war: For the woman this is the bearing and raising of children, while the man is obliged under Islamic law to provide for the material well-being of his family. He has no choice about this but the woman, in contrast, is by no means confined to a purely household role. In Islam, she has the right to be educated, to have a career, and to pursue an involvement in the wider political and social environment, as long as this does not interfere with her primary mothering function. But it is important to remember, as Sheikh Fadlallah points out, that men, as much as women, are bound to abide by the moral code of Islam. As far as prohibitions and duties are concerned, there is no discrimination between the sexes.

The women of Hizballah are in no doubt about their role, both in the family and in the larger society. They speak in positive terms of the achievements of Imam Khomeini and the eventual certainty of the global triumph of Islam. Their role in the conflict is equally clear-cut. One Hizballah woman explains the situation in the following manner: The Islamic revolution in Iran, she says, awoke the "sleeping Shiʿa of South Lebanon," thus initiating a revolution in the mosques. When the Israelis invaded in 1982, women and children fought back with stones. Then, slowly, the people in the area obtained weapons and began to form themselves into a resistance movement. In Islam, according to this woman, there are two ways: either to kill the enemy or to die oneself—the concept of martyrdom being a crucial one in Shiʿi oppositional ideology. Men bear the primary responsibility for waging war. However, if the enemy enters one's country, women too may fight and, therefore, are liable to become martyrs.[53]

But there have been few examples of the female warrior in Hizballah's short history. In line with their understanding of the Islamic message, men seem to prefer to keep the weapons of war for their own exclusive use. If one equates control of the means of warfare with overall control of the power in society, it is clear that men are consciously preserving these privileges, including power over women's sexuality, for themselves. Needless to say, Hizballah members, male and female, would dispute this analysis.

In 1982, during the devastating Israeli invasion, Hizballah women, like the women of Amal, performed a number of vital functions, the most important of which was to support their husbands and children and to inspire the men with strength and courage to fight the enemy. This activity is reminiscent of the early days of Islam and before, when women used to accompany their menfolk to the battlefield in order to urge them on with songs and inspirational words. Hizballah women, as well, occasionally smuggled weapons under their voluminous garments, guessing, very often correctly, that the Israelis would be unlikely, or unwilling, to search a modestly clad female.

In the view of the women of Hizballah, women are accorded a strong role in society. They are permitted to acquire education, to work, to become leaders, and to have a political input. At the same time, however, a woman must not attempt to usurp the position of men in the society. It is important, they stress, to maintain a balance. One of the heroines of Islamic history, most often cited as an example by Shiʿi women, is the daughter of the Imam Ali. Zaynab, who fought alongside her brother Husayn on the battlefield at Karbala, is regarded as the prime example of female behavior during times of war: There should be a balance between the instinctive defense of one's country and the appropriate modesty of one's sex. In more recent times, Ayatollah Khomeini is said to have given permission for women to work in military activities during times of war. Afterwards, of course, they were expected to return to more traditional roles.

Hizballah's ideology includes a strong critique of the West and particularly the United States, which it sees as an unmitigated evil. The appropriate role of women and importance of balance in society is presented as a contrast to unbridled Western freedom and female promiscuity. According to one Hizballah woman, the cause of rape and adultery in the West is that women do not cover themselves; they wear scanty clothing and, thus, encourage men to lose self-control.[54] At no point, it would appear, are men expected to take responsibility for their own behavior.

Even Hizballah women, though, admit that changes have occurred in the last ten years or so. Before the war, Lebanese society was strongly influenced by Europe and was following a particular path toward modernization. The Shiʿi community, as a disadvantaged group, lacked cohesion and organization, but this changed with Musa al-Sadr who galvanized the Shiʿa into action. Although the action was military, it also represented a return to religion. Younger people started to reclaim their religion and, as a result, discovered a new pride. But religion, in the opinion of one woman, is not simply praying and fasting; it structures one's entire life, politically, socially, and economically. Their newfound religiosity, for many women, was an act of rebellion. In many cases, their mothers had become secularized and were shocked at the feelings of resurgent religion displayed by their children. One hears stories of parental disapproval and dismay when teenage daughters suddenly decided to adopt full Iranian-style chador. This is a revolution indeed and something that women appear to have chosen for themselves. These women are well-educated, articulate, and decisive. They have witnessed the horrors of war, the utter dislocation of their society, and have come to the conclusion that religion is the only way to restore a sense of moral rightness to their lives. This accounts for the purity and fervor of their vision.

After the Taif Agreement (October 1989), when a sort of peace descended on Lebanon and parliamentary democracy was reinstated, Hizballah amended its tactics. While its principal objectives remain to rid southern Lebanon of the Israeli occupation and to encourage an Islamic state, it was sufficiently pragmatic to offer itself as a participant in the reborn Lebanese governmental institutions. In the parliamentary elections of August and September 1992, Hizballah candidates won a surprising eight seats. In this way, it is able both to gain political experience and to have some influence over the direction of government policy. According to Secretary General Sheikh Hasan Nasrallah, "If parliamentary elections contribute to a new formula for the system that renounces political sectarianism and lays down the foundation for the state that embodies the will of the Lebanese people, Hizballah's decision to take part with its brothers and friends in these elections will remain based on the essential political principles it has always demonstrated by the sacrificed blood of its martyrs; the sacrifices of its *mujahidin* (fighters); the pains of its prisoners, detainees and wounded; and the cries of the oppressed and the families of its martyrs."[55] It is worth noting the language used in this pronouncement. Typical of statements by Hizballah leaders, it tends towards confrontation and triumphant masculinity.

Although the politics of Hizballah present an uncompromising agenda for the future, women are still excluded from the centers of power and accorded a status secondary to that of men. Nonetheless, by combining religious zeal with resistance, social welfare activities, and a blueprint for an ideal society, the party has been able to attract large numbers of supporters, including many women. One wonders whether its program is realistic or merely another desperate response to the apparent meaninglessness of Lebanese political life, and even whether some of the more uncomfortable extremities might be tempered by the balancing voices of women. It is quite possible, of course, that a synthesis will eventually emerge whereby Hizballah's more unacceptable policies are moderated by engagement with day-to-day politics and, at the same time, the moral standards of the entire community are lifted as a result of exposure to the group's social platform.

Conclusion

In this paper, I have explored three themes. The first considered the nature of Islamism and its impact on the Shiʿa of Lebanon. The community has traveled from a position of political marginalization and virtual irrelevance in the early days of national independence to its present more assertive role in the postwar reconstruction of the country. It has done so by a skillful mixture of force, social programs, and religious fervor. As it grew and became better educated and politically sophisticated, the community began to see the need for a stronger voice in Lebanese affairs. Starting as an opposition movement on behalf of the oppressed, the Shiʿa have created an ideology of resistance and dignity that, on the one hand, has served to empower both men and women and, on the other, has drawn attention to their devalued status. Having played a vigorous role in the civil war, the Shiʿa, who are now believed to be the largest single sect in Lebanon, are seeking a stake in their country's future. Given the intricacies of the Lebanese political system, however, their influence remains limited.

My second theme took war itself as a galvanizing factor. While some view the Lebanese civil war solely as destructive and devoid of deeper meaning, others see it in a somewhat different light. According to one commentator, the civil war "was not a war of suicide, but a war of survival."[56] Far from being an exercise in anarchy, it contained its own careful logic. Indeed, if we look at the war in terms of power, survival, and national identity, a pattern of response begins to emerge. Many Lebanese citizens, perceiving their political system to be corrupt and unrepresentative and unable to reform it by peaceful means, embarked upon a battle to alter the balance of power. One should bear in mind, of course, that the attitude to "power" varied according to one's tribe or sect, the disparate groups were not fighting for an abstract notion of "justice," and the issue of male control at no point entered the picture. Women had little choice but to fit as best they could into the general chaos that rapidly developed. In the process, they learned strategies of survival but, equally important, sought to rationalize their own roles. They discovered that it was not enough merely to survive; meaning had to be found within the motivating frameworks of liberation, national identity, and communal honor.

As far as the Shiʿa were concerned, their religion—for reasons of history and habit—became the primary motivating factor. It legitimized the movement of women from traditional to revolutionary modes of behavior and even justified the use of violence. Yet, if women have extracted a degree of empowerment from their involvement in long-term violence, one wonders whether they might exhibit an ambition to restore to society the female element of "tenderness" that is now effectively absent.

A final theme speculated that the masculinity of war, combined with the beneficial effect it evidently had on Shiʿi society, contributed towards a reordering of gender relations. If we take as a starting point the traditional character of Shiʿi society and women's expectations within it and add to this some notion of radical transformation, we can see two somewhat contradictory outcomes. One could argue that the long period of violence, together with a triumphant commitment to sectarian identities, has created stark divisions between the sexes. In the belief that female "immorality" is the main cause of disruption and instability within society and having failed to conquer each other, men must apply themselves anew to controlling the weaker members of society, namely women; within such a resolutely masculine culture, women have little option but to submit to a male "grand plan" if they are to survive. On the other hand, they too have passed through the experience of violent upheaval within their community and their country. Far from sitting idly by and letting the men fight, they have acquired new skills and embraced unfamiliar roles. In the process, this traditional society has embarked on the road to what might loosely be described as a form of modernity, which includes a meaningful Islamically appropriate and frequently activist role for women.

Given the available evidence and one's particular standpoint, it is possible to draw two quite separate and contradictory conclusions. The first assumes that Shiʿi women as a group share the aspirations and ideological convictions of their menfolk, subscribe to a vision of Shiʿi militancy, and are prepared—on the basis of choice—to adhere to the dictates of the brand of Islamism being practiced in Lebanon. Women's acquiescence suggests that, not only have they internalized the world view and the constraints of women's behavior that this model involves, but also that they themselves are convinced of the rightness of this path and the potential empowerment it is able to provide. Seen in this light, the "unnatural" mother of the martyr is an inevitable outcome of deeply held and communally experienced religious conviction.

The second conclusion, in contrast, takes a broader perspective. Beginning with the suggestion that women's rights are a global issue, it reviews the evidence of Shiʿi women's experiences in Lebanon in relation to the Islamist movement. There is a strong argument that Islamist ideology is flawed in the sense that it is rooted in patriarchal assumptions that have no basis in Islam and that it tries to put into practice an idealized and unrealistic version of the religion as it was originally conceived. Women are thus disadvantaged in the sense that neither the egalitarian spirit of the Qurʾan nor international human rights declarations are taken into account. The female members of the traditional Shiʿi community are treated as second-class citizens and neither their voices nor their aspirations respected.

Now that the war has ended and the state is reasserting its authority, we can begin to assess the gains that women—as a group, as components of sectarian units, and as citizens of a Lebanese entity—have made. In order to do this, it is helpful to locate the discussion within larger debates, such as the competing claims of Islam, nationalism, and democracy, and the conflict between Western and Islamic interpretations of feminism.

It is clear that, for Shiʿi women in Lebanon, the goals of citizenship and democratic participation are by no means incompatible with a vision of the state that is in harmony with Islamic principles. Critics argue that the modern Islamist movement is both antidemocratic and antiwoman, that it seeks to limit women's freedom of choice by imposing restrictive dress codes and by substantially reducing the space in which they are permitted to move. In reality, however, such curbs have come about as a result of traditional practices. As we have seen from the statements and actions of both Hizballah and Amal, women are not excluded from playing a meaningful part in communal affairs. But, they readily admit, this is not the same as the role played by men. Until now the situation has been unbalanced by war. Yet, while the accomplishments of Shiʿi women during the long period of upheaval, in terms of support, resistance, and perseverence, were impressive, one wonders, in the absence of war, whether their achievements can be sustained. This seems to be a viable question in light of the characteristically bellicose masculinity of Hizballah's official statements: Although it is not particularly surprising under battlefield conditions, one would expect them now to reflect the reassertion of civil society, with all its masculine and feminine nuances and subtle shadings.

A final conclusion takes into account the element of pragmatism, which characterizes Lebanese Shiʿi society. Despite pronouncements in favor of an Islamic state by the supporters of Hizballah, the Shiʿa are also part of the complex sectarian Lebanese mosaic and, as such, they are acutely aware of the need for coexistence. They are influenced by the wider society and identify being "Lebanese" as their primary affiliation. The women who profess a sympathy for the political groupings claim to enjoy the benefit of choice. They feel themselves to be an integral part of a larger reformation project and are sufficiently motivated to accept as necessary the impositions this involves, particularly in matters of dress and behavior. To these women, veiling is not an imposition but something they, as much as the men, recognize as an authentic element in the Islamist project. They have also internalized the necessity for violence as a political weapon. To understand these women and what they see as a revolutionary venture, one needs to take into account the possibility of interpretations other than the liberal Western view of human rights and women's liberation. But one should also remember that the majority of Shiʿi women are not political activists; they simply feel more comfortable with a more Islamic lifestyle.

Lebanese women across the sectarian spectrum continue to suffer a variety of discriminatory practices and there is no reason why women as a whole cannot benefit from the liberation that Shiʿi women have experienced and the strength they have derived from their experiences. Once we distance ourselves from notions of exclusivity, it is possible to welcome the pooling of resources from the disparate religious and political groupings who all share the profound conviction that "Lebanon" as a national, cultural, and geographically distinct entity must survive.[57]

Notes

1. Corm, "Myth and Realities of the Lebanese Conflict," 258.
2. Joseph, "Gender and Citizenship," 4.
3. Shaaban, *Both Right and Left Handed*, 81.
4. Moghadam, *Modernizing Women*, 135.
5. Afkhami, *Faith and Freedom*, 1–2.
6. Joseph, "Gender and Citizenship," 6.
7. Ahmed, *Women and Gender in Islam*, 223.
8. Ibid., 144.
9. Ibid., 146.
10. Halawi, *Lebanon Defied*, 19.
11. Momen, *Introduction to Shiʿi Islam*, 264.
12. Khalaf and Denoeux, "Urban Networks," 187.
13. Ibid., 188.
14. Ibid.
15. Momen, *Introduction to Shiʿi Islam*, 266.
16. el-Khalil, "The Role of the South in Lebanese Politics," 305.
17. Khalaf and Denoeux, "Urban Networks," 197.
18. Norton, *Amal and the Shiʿa*, 49.
19. Mutahhari, *Rights of Women in Islam*, 69.
20. Ibid., xxviii.
21. Ibid., 65.
22. Ibid.
23. Ibid., 116.
24. Ibid., 126.
25. Walther, *Women in Islam*, 108.
26. Norton, *Amal and the Shiʿa*, 15.
27. Ibid., 16.
28. Ibid.
29. Ibid., 47.
30. Halawi, *Lebanon Defied*, 126.
31. Ibid., 135.
32. Ibid., 138.
33. Ibid., 181.
34. Interview, Tyre, January 1993.
35. Shaaban, *Both Right and Left Handed*, 95
36. Ibid., 86.
37. Ibid.
38. Ibid., 89.
39. Norton, *Amal and the Shiʿa*, 207.

40. Interview, Maarake, January 1993.

41. Shaaban, *Both Right and Left Handed*, 92.

42. Ibid., 86.

43. Ibid.

44. Shapira, "Imam Musa al-Sadr," 128.

45. Hamzeh, "Lebanon's Hizbullah," 323.

46. Hizballah, "An Open Letter Addressed by Hizballah to the Downtrodden of Lebanon and the World" (Beirut, February 16, 1985), 6.

47. Hamzeh, "Lebanon's Hizbullah," 321.

48. Shapira, "Imam Musa al-Sadr," 124.

49. *The Lebanon Report* (Beirut: The Lebanese Center for Policy Studies, March 1993), 7.

50. Norton, *Amal and the Shi'a*, 103.

51. Interview with Sheikh Fadlallah, Beirut, May 1994.

52. Ibid., 181.

53. Interview, Beirut, January 1993.

54. Ibid.

55. "Voice of the Oppressed," reported by Summary of World Broadcasts, August 10, 1992.

56. Cooke, *War's Other Voices*, 123

57. Even though the analyses and conclusions contained in this paper are entirely my own, I would like to express my deepest gratitude for the patience and generosity of the many Lebanese women who took the time to tell me about their lives, beliefs, and hopes for the future.

11

Maman Aida, a Lebanese Godmother of the Combatants: Fighting without Arms

KARI H. KARAMÉ

It has become commonplace to see women's place in war literature limited to the symbolic defenseless victim, "The women for whom men must fight and men must die." This does not do justice to the great number of women, who either by personal choice, or under the dictates of events, play a very active and often decisive role, both in civilian life and in war-related tasks. It also limits our notion of what war actually is. Thus, Paula Schwartz calls for a broader definition of resistance "habitually equated with actual combat" to include also those who hold supporting roles in housing, feeding, clothing, and actual protection of the combatants, of whom the majority are women.[1]

Introduction

When war breaks out, people react to the new situation in different ways according to sex, age, social level, political affiliation, family situation, education, cultural norms of behavior, health, and also, to a large extent, personal factors, like courage. Most adult men will go to war, leaving women to replace them in civilian life, assuming new tasks in addition to their ordinary obligations. On their own, women will have to face the responsibility of raising children and taking care of the aged. Thus, war opens "a range of possibilities for political activism by politicizing the traditional role of women within the family."[2] In resistance movements, in civil and ethnic wars, the gap between military and civilian life is smaller than seen in conventional wars among various states, where there are—at least in theory—clearly defined front-areas. As Helga Konrad, the Austrian minister for women's affairs, said when she opened the Seventh Symposium of the International Association of Women Philosophers at the University of Vienna in September 1995: "Modern wars do not primarily differ from the wars of the past because women are at the front, but because the front is where the women are." This is very much so in the Lebanese war of 1975 to 1991, which left no area untouched, and where the central parts of Beirut became a vicious battlefield and most of the over 150,000 casualties were civilian.

In a forthcoming paper on women in the Lebanese war, Kirsten Schulze states that "Women of all communities were caught up in the conflict and were faced with the choice of actively becoming involved or trying to avoid the fighting. Active involvement took on two forms: fighting for the respective nationalist cause or protesting against the communal violence. Each involved risking their lives in defense of their country."[3] Active involvement must not be understood solely as bearing arms, even though women were engaged in combat on all sides in the conflict,[4] but should also include the great number of women who were engaged in supportive activities, essential for the male combatants' efficiency.

The Godmothers

Aida, who was to become known as Maman Aida or Maman Ghanime[5] to the combatants of East Beirut, earned this title because of the limitless devotion she showed them from the first days of the war in April 1975. She opened her home to them, fed them, and cared for them in every way. Little did she know that by so doing she joined the ranks of the Godmothers renowned from the days of the American Civil War, the resistance and the Foreign Legion in France, the resistance in northern Norway, and now Beirut. The resemblance of these women, separated by time and space, clearly indicates the existence of a general framework within which they all fit. They all have common characteristics manifesting one more role played by women during wars that is least talked about. It is this phenomenon of women caring for soldiers or fighters on the front as mothers care for their children that will be examined in this paper with special emphasis on "Maman Aida" during the war in Lebanon.

Literature concerning the American Civil War—academic and fictional—presents a gallery of captivating women on both sides of the conflict. In May 1861, the small town of Pulaski, Tennessee, decided to send a company of men "for Confederate service."[6] One of them was John Sullivan, and when he left for the front, his wife, Betsy, accompanied him. As they had no children, she "determined not only to go to the war, but also to 'mother' the entire company as well." From the first day she was known as Mother Sullivan and "there was nothing the men would not dare for her and for what her presence represented to them—their wives, their mothers and their homes."[7] She followed the First Regiment in campaigns to West Virginia, to Northern Virginia, Kentucky, Mississippi, and back to Tennessee, sharing the same conditions as the soldiers, marching on foot and sleeping on the frozen ground. "In return, the soldiers loved and reverenced her, treating her at all times with the same courtesy they would have shown their own mothers. No rude speech or improper word was uttered in her presence."[8] On the battlefield she nursed the wounded and stayed with the dying. The regiment suffered heavy losses, and Mother Sullivan brought the bodies of the dead back to their families in Pulaski. Finally, in October 1862, her husband sustained a severe head wound and shortly after, the whole regiment was taken prisoner. Mother Sullivan went with them to prison, "where she continued to serve her husband and the other members of the company as long as she was able."[9]

Mrs. Bettie Taylor Philips became Mother of the "Orphan Brigade," the nickname given to the Fourth Kentucky Regiment after the death of their heroic commander Hanson. The daughter of a doctor, she married at the age of seventeen, but had no children. Her husband joined the Confederate army at the very beginning of the war, and in the fall of 1861,

> Mrs. Philips, having no children, determined to follow her husband through weal and woe. She remained at his side through all the stern vicissitudes of war, in camp, on long marches, often under shot and shell of the enemy, but ever at hand as an angel of mercy, ministering to the sick, wounded, and dying of her beloved brigade, each man of whom she seemed to love as if bound by ties of blood, and each, in return, giving her the affection and reverence due to a mother. At Shiloh, at Donelson, and many other hard-fought fields of the South, her slender form might have been seen bending over the cots of the wounded and dying, receiving their last words, writing down their last messages, faintly whispered by dying lips—messages of love to the far-away dear ones at home.[10]

Two years later she tried to return to her home for health reasons but was turned back through the lines, to her base camp. Here a warm welcome awaited her, "Every man in the command begged the honor of shaking her hand; the band played 'Home Again,' and strong men wept."[11] She remained with them until the end of the war, and devoted her remaining years to ease the life of the returning soldiers and to the cause of the South. She was in Georgia with President and Mrs. Davis just before their capture and received the president's mess cup as a token of his gratitude. This became a valued relic to her.

In occupied France, toward the end of World War II, a letter of protest was sent to the newspaper *La Marseillaise* from a group of resistance soldiers before they left for the front, because it had failed to mention their "Mother." This letter is kept in the archives of the Bibliothèque Marguerite Durand in Paris: "We want to repair the regrettable omission of her who was really our Mother during these tragic moments. That is why we will speak today about this extraordinary woman who was, and still is: The Mother of the Maquis."[12] She was then fifty years old, a widow of World War I left with five children. Of these at least one was in the French resistance, and the others helped their mother in her assistance of the maquisards: She collected food for them from neighbors she could trust, gave them shelter, and provided them with false identification papers. She even hid weapons in her own vegetable garden. "The Mother of the Maquis considered all of us as her own children." With three faithful helpers she made foot-bindings, to protect the feet of the soldiers during their long marches. On one occasion she made badges in French colors for up to 500 soldiers. "This piece of ribbon made of us real soldiers of the regular army, with it we were no longer 'terrorists' for whom the Germans showed no pity." She was threatened by the occupation powers on several occasions but never let her "boys" down. Another letter in the same archives tells the story of Madam Laurent, called "Mémé"—Grandmother—"by all her children, the resistants," and who turned her home into a refuge for soldiers, "always smiling, always ready to cheer up and drive away the blues, known by everybody, even the strongest." Finally, two Mothers of the Patriots are mentioned by Paula Schwartz, and of whom testimonies can be found in French archives.[13]

Even professional soldiers may need a Godmother. Christmas celebration is very important for the men of the Foreign Legion, and has in many ways come to symbolize the unity of *la grande famille* (the family of the legion). The other feasts on the legion calendar are marked by balls to which the consorts of ranked men are invited. But not for Christmas when officers stay with their men, because the legion is their home. The First Regiment at Orange is singular in this context because they have allowed the presence of a woman, the Comtesse Ladislas de Luart, who was appointed Commander of the Legion of Honor in 1944, and who was known as the *marraine,* the Godmother, of the regiment. "She is the godmother, the spiritual mother, quite different from those who are waiting alone for their men to come home. Completely removed from the sexual and procreative role of wives that threatens the central core of Legion ideology, the essence of her spiritual role is enhanced by her aristocratic background and military honors, dignifying the Legion's creed for purity and elitism. Despite the fact that it would be difficult to imagine a personage less like the stereotype of 'legionnaire's woman'—or rather because of this—she plays the symbolic role of mother within la grande famille perfectly."[14]

During World War II, high up in northern Norway, a woman was to become "Mother Karasjok" to hundreds of prisoners of war from former Yugoslavia, who were sent to this Sami village as slaves working on the construction of roads in the mountains.[15] Mother Karasjok's real name was Kirsten Svineng and she belonged to a family of both sedentary and nomadic Samis. Her father owned a horse, which was considered a sign of prosperity, and her mother worked as a midwife and cared for the sick. Kirsten, who was born just after 1900, went to the school for Sami migrant children, six weeks in spring and six weeks in autumn. She learned a little Norwegian in school and had the opportunity to become more proficient when she worked in the house of senior Norwegian civil servants. As time went on, she started to care for the sick, like her mother before her, but had to abandon her training for midwifery. When her parents became elderly she moved back home to help them. She never married, though many courted her. Back in her own village, she was held in high esteem because of her knowledge of the Norwegian language and her work as a nurse.

"Even the war came late to the people in the mountains. In June 1940, the fighting against the German troops was over in Northern Norway, but it was not until some months later that the people of Karasjok saw a unit of Hitler's soldiers."[16] The presence of German troops among them led to closer relations between the Sami population and the Norwegians. The situation in the village changed radically in July 1942, "when hundreds of starved, ragged and tortured men arrived in Karasjok." Most of them came from Yugoslavia, and most were Serbs. Many of the inhabitants tried to help, but for Kirsten it became an obsession, she could not think of anything else. She spent all her time gathering food from people she could trust, and also used her own money to buy whatever was available. Every day she would prepare small packets of food to hang on trees and fences for the prisoners to find. It was strictly forbidden to help prisoners, but Kirsten soon found out that some of the German guards turned their back on what she did, but others did not. She had to be careful. One woman told her she did not have the courage to help the prisoners in the same way. To this Kirsten answered: "You have to care for your own folks, while I have neither husband nor children. If something happens to me, it will be to me only, and the doors of heaven are always open."[17]

She even helped some of the prisoners escape. The first attempt was made in August 1942. The men came to her house, and called her

"Mamma," and she, risking a death sentence, helped them to escape. Other prisoners gave her small letters to deliver to their families. Of the 450 prisoners who came to Karasjok in July, only 150 were still alive on Christmas. Fifty of these were shot, and 100 were transported to other camps. In autumn of 1944, the Germans burnt down the whole village, except for the church, as they did in all of northern Norway, to leave nothing standing in case of a Soviet invasion. The population was deported to the southern parts of the country, but many avoided this by hiding out in the mountains or on isolated islands. Kirsten and her family chose to stay in the mountains close to the village. In 1957, she was invited, with thirteen other persons from different parts of Norway, to Yugoslavia, where she met with President Tito, and received an important medal in recognition of her efforts to help the Yugoslav prisoners in Norway. When Tito paid an official visit to Norway in 1965, Kirsten was among those invited by the king to the official reception. "I always include Yugoslavia in my prayers" she told Tito.[18] Only a few Norwegian women were rewarded for their efforts during the war. The recognition of what Kirsten did for the prisoners of war is, therefore, even more interesting, as she was both a woman and came from an ethnic minority not yet well integrated in the Norwegian national society at the time of World War II.

By the end of May 1990, the region of Ofoten and the town of Narvik, also in northern Norway, commemorated the heavy fighting that took place there fifty years earlier between the Germans and the Allied Forces. Among the veterans who were introduced to the late King Olav V, was an eighty-four-year-old woman, Alfhild Dalas. "Meet 'Mor Gratangen' [Mother Gratangen]" said the ten-year-younger veteran, Arvid Akersveen, who accompanied her, "We just called her 'mother.' She nursed the wounded, cooked and made coffee. She lived with her family in the middle of the battlefield, and without considering the risk of attacks or reprisals from the Germans, Mother Gratangen and her family opened their home to the Norwegian soldiers."[19]

Maman Aida

When the war broke out in Lebanon in April 1975, Aida was around forty-five years old. She had a comfortable life in a cozy flat with a wonderful view on what was soon going to be the Green Line, dividing the city into a western, mainly Muslim, part and an eastern, mainly Christian, part. Aida's house was situated close to one of the main crossing points, at Tabariz.

She was born in Homs, Syria, into a Greek-Catholic family, but her mother was from Zouk-Mikhael in Lebanon. When she grew up, the family moved to Beirut, where she went to school and passed the French Baccalaureate or Secondary School examination. She was a happy, extroverted young girl, who loved the cosmopolitan lifestyle in Beirut. As a well-behaved girl, she went out either in the company of her older brother or with a group of girlfriends.

Still, despite this easy life, she felt insecure. The newborn state of Lebanon, which obtained its independence from the French mandate-power in 1943, had not yet found its place between a Mediterranean and an Arab orientation. After the creation of the state of Israel, and in the wake of decolonization of the Arab world, the ideology of Arab nationalism became part of the struggle for national identity in Lebanon. In 1958, a civil war broke out, which came to an end shortly after because of the intervention of the U.S. Marines. Most Christians were opposed to Arab nationalism because they feared the loss of their Christian identity and religious freedom in a huge and massive Arab-Muslim surrounding.

In the Mediterranean, and more so in the Arab world, the female arena is defined as the private sphere, traditionally identical to the household. The public sphere is the arena of men, and national security and politics constitute two major activities of this arena. Lebanese women obtained their political rights in 1953 but have never played an important role in the formal political structure of the country. In fact, during the elections of 1992, three women were elected as members of Parliament for the first time. And even then "it can be argued that all three women can be seen as an extension of the politics of a male family member, brother or husband."[20] The country has never had a female cabinet member.

On the other hand, many women have been members of political parties and worked in different sections of the party systems. It is said that women carried secret messages and explosives in their handbags or on their bodies during the short civil war. Aida's own mother participated in the conflict of 1958. She "was in the streets before me. It is she who gave me the will to do something." "She was a resistant! She had a stick with nails on one end, with which she slammed the cars of the army."[21]

For Aida, the main issue was to save Lebanon, which for her, above all, was an idea of religious freedom and expression. In 1958, she had already been close to the Kata'ib (Phalangists) for some time, but she had not yet become a member of the party. She admits that she even found it unwomanly to be a member of a political party. This attitude changed because of the events in 1958, and together with several other women she joined the party in 1959, where a woman's section had already been established in 1948 by Laure Moghaizel.[22] This section has since had its own seat in the party's central committee.

In private life she continued a rather easygoing and comfortable existence. She married and moved into a nice flat at the top of a six-floor building close to the center of Beirut. To the couple's great sorrow they had no children. Even though she was educated, Aida never worked outside her home, like most women of her class in Lebanese society, before the war. She spent much time with her parents, and one of her favorite occupations was to prepare good meals for their numerous friends, always assisted by a maid. She also liked to play cards in a private club not far from her home.

Aida distinguished herself from most of her female friends in that she was a member of a political party. She never personally held any political position, and probably never had any ambition to do so. She was content to be active within the party's section for women, where she worked in election campaigns, fund-raising, and participating in organizing social and political gatherings for the party. She did this as member of an informal group of women who were particularly active in this kind of party-work, and whom the men respectfully called "comrades." They came to hold important positions in the medico-social service of the party during the war, especially during the years 1975 to 1985.

Her Own Story of Her Life as Maman Aida

"I will tell you how I have lived this war. We, the women, what did we do at the beginning of the war? Each one took on her responsibility. We felt that the situation was not good, and we gathered in small meetings. It was also the location of my house which was close to down-town Beirut, and from where there was a good view on nearby West-Beirut and one of the main-crossings." The location was difficult, but it was possible to enter the building from behind without being seen. Her home soon became a permanent base and observation point for around twenty young people, mostly men along with some young girls who were fighting in the Christian militias.[23]

No doubt the war was poorly planned on the Lebanese Christian side. The combatants most often fought with their private arms, and no arrangements were made to feed and lodge them. From the first day of the war, Aida, like many other women in the same area, prepared sandwiches that they sent out to the nearest fighting points. She was assisted by her maid, Yasmina, whose son was with the combatants. She also called on friends and neighbors for assistance and food.

One day, one of the combatants told her that he longed for something sweet, a cake, for instance. Aida called on her friends again, those who had left for the mountains and those who stayed in the neighborhood, and received more than twenty cakes. She loved to please her young comrades and take their minds off the fighting.

Fighting usually took place at night, and during the daytime it was difficult for the combatants to find suitable quarters to rest and sleep, especially those whose homes were not in the neighborhood. Some slept on the floor in the party headquarters, others found some shelter behind a wall, in a shop, and so on. Aida offered her house as a hostel. Some came regularly, others only now and then. She is proud to report that nothing was ever stolen from her home during this time.

As the war progressed, combatants started to complain about the food. They wanted to eat something else besides sandwiches. Aida immediately complied and started to offer hot meals daily, which she served at home or sent out to the other posts in her neighborhood (called Saifi) and all the way to the front. During the fighting in the hotel area she used her skills and power of persuasion and managed to send food to the besieged combatants. In fact, she once convinced an officer of the Lebanese army, who was posted nearby, to use his tank to transport food to isolated combatants. On the return trip, the tank was used to transport the wounded back for medical care, thus, saving several lives.

Combatants were all aware of, and thankful for, her efforts on their behalf. On the day a shipment of cakes arrived, one of them said to her: "You must love us very much to do all this." "I love you like you were my own children," she answered, "I do not have children of my own. I do not know why I love you, but I do. I consider all of you to be my own children." "Well, then you must allow us to call you Maman Aida?" Tears come to her eyes when she recalls this moment, especially because both this young man and his best friend were killed in the downtown fighting. Thus, she became known as Maman Aida or Maman Ghanime among the combatants, and also among the civilians of her neighborhood. Many people still use this name to this day.

Her care went far beyond the provision of food and shelter. Fighters also needed comfort and sense of security: Because of the kidnapping that was rampant at the time, what they feared most was to disappear in combat without a trace. Many took up the habit of passing by Aida or one of the other women who worked in the medico-social service on their way to the front. They would complain of pains in the stomach or the head, but what they really needed was to be seen and listened to before they engaged in combat. Many worried about their families, security, and the need for food and milk for the children. And Aida used her savings to provide for the needy families, but never on a regular basis, because she did not want it to be considered as payment for military services, and also because one day, maybe, she may not be able to go on providing.

Her reputation and her responsibilities grew. She was asked to cook for party leaders who stayed permanently in party headquarters. At the beginning, she relied on contributions, but as the war went on, she was given her own budget, and no one refused her when she asked for provisions for the combatants. Bashir Gemayel asked her if she could also take care of Zakhra, where he was then in command. This was another part of the front close to Saifi. She accepted and had to engage several women to assist her. In fact, she had never cooked once in her whole life, and she did not do it now. She was a manager and a planner.

In the meantime she had been forced to leave her house, which was damaged by shelling. The war went on, and the situation became precarious for many civilians, above all those who had lost their jobs. Many of them had helped Aida in the beginning but now found themselves on the needy lists. Aida went on to provide for them as she did for the combatants, and she did so discreetly to save them embarrassment.

Another sad result of the war was the growing number of the handicapped and orphans, and Aida engaged in fund-raising for institutions created to take care of them. It is a tradition in Lebanon to collect money for the church during marriage and funeral services. When somebody close to the Kata'ib Party or the Lebanese Forces married or died, Aida was there at the entrance of the church—she felt that this money should go to the victims. This competition was not always welcomed by the clergy, but Aida never feared untraditional solutions.

Although she lived and worked in the front area for twelve years from 1975 to 1986, she never changed her lifestyle. Even though other women, for understandable reasons, started to wear more practical outfits like jeans and sneakers, this was a concession she refused to make. She continued to wear high heels, nice suits, and flowered dresses, went to the hairdresser, and used makeup. "Finally, a woman!" was her comrades' reaction. Her own explanation is: "Me—I like a woman to be feminine, in the way she dresses, in everything. I don't like women to dress like men. It is not my way." One may wonder why this was so important, both to herself, and to her comrades, who, years later, still reminisce about her. Did it represent refusal of the war, and therefore, a semblance of normalcy?

Although she was met with positive reactions in the party and among the combatants, the situation was not the same in her family. Her husband told her that she was free to do what she wanted, but he left for the mountains, where he stayed for four years. Aida admits that this made her feel free and grateful to her husband. Her only brother, who had moved to Germany, wanted her to join him there, very much encouraged by their mother who wrote to ask him to send for his sister, "because she has gone completely mad." Aida's mother could in fact never accept that her only daughter was exposing herself to all the dangers of war. Aida herself is more inclined to explain her mother's reaction on the basis of Lebanese family traditions: "We have this mentality that the children belong to the parents, until the end of their days. The children live their parents' life until they die. My mother reacted out of love for me, and for herself. Who was going to take care of her if something happened to me?"

Aida continued her work until just after the elections of the Kataʾib Party in 1986. Military affairs had by then been completely taken over by the Lebanese Forces, and she did not feel comfortable with the new leadership. The office of medico-social affairs also lost its importance. To Aida this was a hard blow, because she was no longer able to help the handicapped, the displaced, and the orphans of the combatants who had a very special place in her heart. But she continued to assist through the network she had established when she was working for the party. And few people refused Maman Aida. In 1996, several years after the end of the fighting in Lebanon, she went on defending the rights of the handicapped and the orphans.

What has all this meant to Aida? When she looks back to the first years of the war, she thinks, above all, of friendship and solidarity. "For me this is a great satisfaction—I am happy when I think about it. People say to me: you have given so much. I do not feel that I have given anything, because everything I gave has been returned to me with affection and esteem. That is great, it is a lot. That is all I ever want."

The Godmothers' Contribution to War

One of the great heroes of the Norwegian resistance during World War II, Gunnar Sonsteby, pointed out in an interview in 1993,[24] that he and his comrades could never have carried out sabotage activities against the occupation forces had it not been for a network of helpers, most of whom were women. Well aware of the risks they were running after several arrests and even deportations, they provided the men of the resistance with hiding places, new clothes, and identity papers, and often accompanied them during transfers.

As we have seen, the Godmothers added to this vital assistance their almost permanent presence and consideration for the welfare of the soldiers or prisoners. This seems to have had a direct impact on the men's morale. Maman Aida observes that it seemed to her that food was sometimes as important as weapons to the combatants, and that their only preoccupation was to fight and eat.[25] Further—and more important—was that these grown-up women among them, who were placed above any sexual consideration, as they were called and treated as Mothers, were constant reminders of the life back home, the normal one. In short, what they were fighting for. To the men of the Foreign Legion, their *Marraine* symbolized the unity of their troops, while Mother Karasjok, an ordinary, civil woman in a hostile and alien surrounding, kept alive a fragile hope of seeing the homeland once more.

The presence of the Godmothers among the combatants influenced their behavior in many ways. When Mother Sullivan was around, "No rude speech or improper word was uttered."[26] From 300 to 350 young girls participated on the so-called Christian side in the combat in Lebanon. To be present at the battlefield meant that they had to leave the close control of their parents and stay several days, even weeks and months, away from home. This became for many of them an obstacle to their normal activities.[27] Some of these girls came to Aida's house and slept there, and her presence among the young girls and boys was looked upon as a guarantee of decent behavior. This influence on the men's conduct is not only related to the presence of Godmothers, but of women in general. In Lebanon, too, the male combatants avoided swearing, they shaved and washed themselves, and behaved in every way in a more normal manner, as in times of peace, in the presence of girls or women.[28]

They Did It Their Way

Nobody can decide to become a Godmother; it is obviously a status that is bestowed upon a woman out of recognition and gratitude by the group, usually men, to whom she has devoted herself. Even Mother Karasjok can be said to have sided with the Yugoslav prisoners against the Nazi forces, their common enemy. What makes the Godmothers interesting, beyond each of these extraordinary life stories, is that they occur under distant skies and in different kinds of war. Yet they share several distinctive features.

First of all they are mature women, in contrast to most female soldiers. The youngest was thirty-one years old, and the oldest, well over fifty, whereas Maman Aida was forty-four when the war started in Lebanon in

1975. Except for Mother Karasjok from northern Norway, they were all married and settled when they started their work of support for the soldiers or prisoners of war. They were all childless, except for the "Mother of the Maquis" who was assisted in her work by her grown children, and her fellow citizen Mémé who had two adult sons in the French resistance. In other words, they were adult women, but without responsibility for younger children. This gave them a freedom of action that other women, who also wished to help, might have lacked. "I have neither husband nor children," said Mother Karasjok. The parents might protest, though, as did Maman Aida's mother. This will probably occur in cultures and times when parents depend on their children for subsistence and care when they grow old.

Information regarding their social background is poor, but it seems these women were of good economic means. This gave them more freedom to help because they could tap their own resources for provisions.

Only Maman Aida was a member of a political party. But in war, any action in favor of one of the parties may be considered a political act, "even women who held supporting roles, who took other resisters into their homes and fed, clothed, and protected them, performed political acts and made political choices."[29]

Conclusion

Thus, operating within the framework of the traditional role of women within their own culture and time, defined by age, social status, and class, these women fought for their cause side by side with the men and were recognized by them. They did not carry arms but engaged in supportive activities which were of vital importance for the men's capacity to fight. Further, their status as Mothers gave a symbolic content to their presence among the combatants or prisoners of war. Their devotion went first to the soldiers or the prisoners of war, but then through them, to the cause; they were fighting for a way of life in the American South, opposing the Nazi invasion forces, or, as in the case of Maman Aida, for a certain idea of multi-confessional Lebanon.

Author's note: This chapter is Maman Aida's life story told during field research on the social reintegration of Lebanese combatants. The project was funded by the Catherine T. and John D. MacArthur Foundation (Chicago), to which I am deeply grateful.

Notes

1. Schwartz, "Redefining Resistance," 143.
2. Ibid.
3. Schulze, "Communal Violence."
4. Karamé, "L'Expérience des jeunes militantes"; Karamé, "Girls' Participation in Combat"; Maksoud, *Les adolescents libanais*; Schulze, "Communal Violence"; Shehadeh, "Women in the Lebanese Militias."
5. Maman Aida's life story is based on several interviews carried out by the author in 1992 and 1993 with Maman Aida and her comrades.
6. Mathew Page Andrews, *Women of the South in War Times* (Baltimore: The Dixie Books of Days, 1924), 111.
7. Ibid., 112.
8. Ibid., 114.
9. Ibid.
10. Ibid., 123.
11. Ibid., 124.
12. Letter in the archives of Bibliothèque Marguerite Durand, Paris.
13. Schwartz, "Redefining Resistance," 146.
14. MacKechnie, "Living with Images of a Fighting Elite," 132.
15. *Dagbladet* (Norway), May 28, 1990, illustrated with a large photo showing King Olav V, Mor Gratangen, and the veteran Arvid Akersveen.
16. Hansson, *Mamma Karasjok*, 165.
17. Ibid., 172.
18. Ibid., 162.
19. Interview with Gunnar Sonsteby, Oslo, October 10, 1994.
20. Schulze, "Communal Violence," 25.
21. Maman Aida's life story is based on several interviews carried out by the author in 1992 and 1993 with Maman Aida and her comrades.
22. Schulze, "Communal Violence," 26.
23. Cf. Karamé, Shehadeh, and Schulze.
24. Interview with Gunnar Sonsteby, Oslo, October 10, 1994.
25. Interview with Maman Aida, November 1992.
26. Andrews, *Women of the South*, 114.
27. Karamé, "Girls' Participation in Combat," 388.
28. Observation made by several combatants in interviews 1988, 1992, and 1993.
29. Schwartz, "Redefining Resistance," 143.

12

From Gunpowder to Incense

Jocelyn Khweiri

I was born in Beirut in 1955 and brought up in a house directly facing that of the Phalangist central office, in al-Saifi district, on Charles Helou Street near Martyrs' Square. My family comprised ten members: my parents and eight children (six boys and two girls) of whom I was the fourth. Ever since my childhood, I had become attached to a daily ritual, which I awaited every morning and evening: the reverent raising and lowering of the Lebanese flag by the Phalangists across the street. In the early seventies, my three eldest brothers started to frequent the Phalangist center and attend party meetings for students. Soon afterwards, I was invited to join the Women Comrades' Branch of the Students' Welfare Division and thus became a Phalangist myself. We were organized into cells present in most secondary schools and universities all over the country. We used to hold regular ideological and organizational meetings during which I was introduced to such popular slogans, at the time, as "Democracy," "Marxism," "leftist" and "rightist" movements, "students' needs," and "social justice."

In 1973, the Phalangist Party started military training during regular summer camps, and my eldest brother, Sami, became a prominent military figure. He played a decisive role in convincing my parents to allow me to join the military circles. Our training included the use of firearms, military transport, camouflage, and defense tactics.

Preliminary Training (1973–75)

Our military training was not intensive at first. Girls were trained for two to three hours every Saturday afternoon in the Phalangist headquarters gymnasium. We were taught the handling of various firearms, hand-to-hand combat, and self-defense. During the holidays, training was held in special camps in the mountains and became more rigorous and extensive: It included live ammunition exercises, the use of grenades, field movement, and patrolling. At night, we were trained in guard duty, night patrols, and ambush tactics. Our training then was less rigorous than that of our male comrades especially in the areas of military maneuvers, high jumping, and patrol duty in the woods. I remember how impatient I was to perfect all those tactics and how invigorated I was after each training exercise—quite unlike my days at school. There, the hippie movement was starting and for a while I was torn between this new lifestyle and that of the rigorous military life of the camps. I never dreamed, however, that I would ever be involved in actual combat despite the portents of an inevitable conflagration between ourselves and the Palestinians, who were slowly being transformed from an armed force with powerful Lebanese alliances into a state within a state.

As a member of the St. Maroun's parish of the Gemmayzeh district, I joined the Legio Maria, the Legions of St. Mary, an international Catholic Miriamite organization. Meetings were held every Saturday afternoon, and due to my constant absenteeism for training purposes, the Mother Superior asked me to choose, as she put it, between Jesus and Lebanon! After a brief hesitation, I told her I would choose Lebanon and left.

The year 1973 brought about a pivotal change in my life. It was my third year with the Students' Welfare Division, and I was in charge of the Phalangist girls' cell in the Shahrour Secondary Girls' School in Achrafieh. In the summer of that year and during the clashes between the Palestinians and the Lebanese army, I spent two months in rigorous military training in Faytroun in the Kissirwan mountain district, where the Phalangist fighting core was born. With a group of twenty girls, I started to train alongside hundreds of young men. The atmosphere was brotherly and comradely and many of us were training alongside our actual brothers. Parents used to visit our camps every Sunday afternoon, and everyone knew everyone else. They admired and encouraged us while some outsiders, and even some party members, considered us unfeminine and man-like.

In the summer of 1974, the major training camp was held in Qihmiz under the leadership of my brother, Sami, and the famous P.G. Division was founded (a commando unit sixty men strong named after the Phalangist founder, Pierre Gemayel), which later played a vital role in the initial rounds of the two-year war in the downtown area, the hotel district, and the Karantina region.

During that year, my women comrades and I prepared a training program for girl volunteers, who came every weekend for military training, while my own group and myself trained at times with the P.G. unit. At this time, our training had become highly specialized and hazardous—charging through flames, mine fields, high jumping, balancing on and crawling along strong ropes, mountain climbing, and other advanced exercises.

The Explosion: 1975

I was in my first year at the Faculty of Information at al-Musaytbeh, and in charge of the secondary school girl-comrade office of the Students' Welfare Division. I was also in charge of training three regular girl divisions every week. At that time there was no unified organization of militia-women in existence yet and the girls were scattered in various divisions in Bikfayya, Beirut, and Kissirwan. In college, I participated in the burgeoning political life and noted the formation of a student communist, Palestinian, Syrian-Socialist-Nationalist alliance that influenced college life as a whole. The university noted the harbinger of war as its various faculties witnessed violent outbursts and the academic year, 1974–75, witnessed a fateful students' election in which the alliance of the Phalangists, Liberals, the Awareness Movement (*Harakat al-wa'i*), and the Youth Labor Union came face to face with the alliance of the communists, the Syrian nationalists, and the socialists—supported overtly by the Palestine Liberation Organization. The latter coalition won the elections in most faculties except for the faculties of law and information. The Maarouf Saad assassination in Sidon, early that year, led to two opposing student demonstrations: one against the Lebanese army spearheaded by the leftist alliance and another in support of the army spearheaded by us. This led to violent confrontations involving the use of firearms between the opposing student factions in several faculties of the university, which was followed by besieging the Faculty of Law by armed Palestinians and socialists. As a result, Phalangist students demanded military training for defense purposes. This was started in earnest that same year.

I used to attend almost all general assemblies of the different student factions, but what hurt most was the total absence of any reference to Lebanon, not only while saluting but even from the long list of Third World countries covered in their speeches. Simultaneously, we were accused of being isolationists and reactionaries because we preached allegiance to Lebanon first and foremost instead of looking for unity and alliances with neighboring Arab countries. As such, we were looked upon as enemies of the Arab nationalist cause. The last time I visited the Lebanese University was just before April 13, 1975 (the date of the outbreak of the war between the PLO commandos and the Lebanese in Ain el-Rimmaneh). My friends had already decided not to attend any more classes to avoid further clashes. It was thus that I found myself alone in the university cafeteria and was invited by the late Anwar Fatayri (a member of the Socialist Party and head of the Students' Union in the Lebanese University that year, and who played a very important role later on in the war) to attend a meeting against the Lebanese army and in support of the PLO in southern Lebanon. As I was returning by bus from the UNESCO district to Martyrs' Square afterwards, I was surprised to see a relative returning from the same meeting, especially on discovering that he was a member of the Communist Party. A sharp interchange ensued between us regarding Lebanese sovereignty, Palestinian license, and the role of the army, which soon spread to involve other passengers who were split between support and opposition of my stand. A forty-five-year-old Lebanese soldier, seated right across from me, shed silent tears, while a Muslim passenger from the Basta district of Beirut shouted after me as I was disembarking: "Listen to me, Miss, your green Cedars are going to become blood-red soon." "Over our dead bodies," I retorted, as I stepped off the bus, and I burst into tears as soon as my mother opened the door for me.

It, thus, became quite clear that we would have to defend our homes, streets, and towns against an imminent Palestinian-leftist onslaught. At the time, my parents disapproved of my prolonged absences from home and my neglect of my education, and our relationship became rather tense, despite the fact that my two older brothers were members of the Phalangist Party. However, as soon as hostilities broke out on April 13, 1975, and a state of national emergency was declared, my parents became quite frightened, especially so when my brothers turned our home into a makeshift barracks for the young men of the P.G. Unit, and the Phalangist headquarters across the street streamed with men at the ready. Our street gradually became the security barometer of the country.

The first round of hostilities lasted fifteen days during which my role was limited to guard duty much to my father's disapproval, who regarded my carrying arms as audacious and beyond my limits as a girl. This, however, did not sway my resolve.

At the end of the first round of hostilities, I returned to college to find that political problems and verbal clashes among students had become a daily practice. These clashes focused on the bus incident, which had sparked the clash between the Palestinians and the Phalangists and was responsible for the outbreak of fighting two weeks earlier, and the incident of the Bashoura Barricade, where several Christians were killed because of their confessional adherence. Such tirades, taking place even during classes, led the professors to suspend their classes, on several occasions, to avoid further escalation.

I spent the summer of 1975 in the camp at Qihmiz on military maneuvers with the P.G. Unit during the week and training groups of girl-comrades coming to us from the regions on weekends. A campaign to buy new weapons was launched in the party and each of us bought his/her gun on an installment basis.

In September 1975, the second round of hostilities began, and this time the fighting was heavy and fierce. We left the camp directly for our house in Beirut. My brothers with their comrades left first and I with my comrades followed afterwards. We passed through the Karantina district of Beirut very cautiously under heavy sniper fire to reach home, which had by then been transformed into a real barracks in the presence of my parents and younger siblings. We started working as Nizamiyyat (Women regulars) by procuring food and women's clothing for the fighters and taking daytime guard duty at the various barricades overlooking Martyrs' Square in downtown Beirut. I used to accompany some fighters on their sojourns to other fronts in Beirut, like the Karantina, Birjawi, and hotel district. I still remember vividly the first time we were asked to secure the defense line extending from Martyrs' Square to the Beirut harbor area (consisting of four barricades) because the P.G. Unit was on a military mission in the Ras Beirut area. We secured the area quite well and for the first time took pride in our worth as women fighters (there were fifteen of us), and we earned the respect and confidence of our leadership. This was the beginning of a new phase for us—the phase of the downtown campaign and the birth of the "Nizamiyyat Building."

The Downtown Area: 1976

The Phalangist military command now looked upon the Nizamiyyat Division (thirteen girls in addition to another twenty who used to work with us on a part-time basis on barricade duty) as experienced fighters to be depended upon. With the widening of the front and the defense lines, the need for the Nizamiyyat increased, and the military command assigned us the "Rivoli Barricade"—a sandbag barricade on the roof of the Rivoli Building overlooking Martyrs' Square. We were to keep a lookout on the Square and silence any sniper fire from other buildings across from the Square—particularly the Azariyyeh Building. The building next to us was the Regent Hotel, which had not yet become one of our defense stations, and facing it, an unfinished concrete building (now demolished) that could be entered from the square and from the rear, through a back alley that reaches the old Jewelry Market and St. George's Church. Near us also stood the partially demolished Royal Hotel. At night, the Palestinians used to sneak into the concrete building to cover the main street where the Phalangist central office was. The concrete building was a thorn in our side and we asked permission to occupy it and thus strengthen our defenses, but permission was denied. We then decided to take the initiative and mount an unauthorized occupation of the building. We did so during the daylight hours when it was empty, made a clean sweep of all seven floors, cleaned the building, and rearranged the barricades into better defensive positions. We then moved our gear and supplies (military blankets, old and new rifles, sponge mattresses, and food cans and bread), together with our icon of the Virgin Mary to our new position. Thus started our four-month, twenty-four-hour-a-day sojourn in the concrete building. To this day we remember the backaches we developed from transporting the sandbags, backaches that we continue to suffer from today. We slowly improved and increased the number of lookout stations in our new quarters in order to control both the square and all the rear alleys and approaches. To confuse the enemy and give an illusion of a large defense force in the building, we would shoot from one floor then run to shoot from another. Furthermore, due to the proximity of buildings occupied by the enemy, we used to make hourly rounds of all seven floors starting from the top down by day and night every day. Frequently, while patrolling the area, we would venture outside our territory and would come face to face with the enemy, who, in turn, were trying to sneak into nearby buildings, and gun fights would erupt, resulting in a quick withdrawal of the infiltrators. We called our tactics "offensive defense"—the venture into enemy territory for the sake of surprise and prevention of hostile attacks.

To improve our efficiency and save ammunition, we brought in electric wiring and some lightbulbs to light up the dark approaches to our positions at night with the light switches situated in our barricades. Thus, we would light up any area where suspicious shadows or movements were noted to avoid shooting at random and thus save on supplies and ammunition.

I divided my unit into two groups of six girls each on twenty-four-hour duty. We received, occasionally, part-time help from the Nizamiyyat of the Kissirwan (Mount Lebanon) area. At night we would light a candle to the Virgin Mary and shield it so as not to betray our position. In those days, I had very little sleep, usually for a short while in the early hours of the morning, as I was wary of the responsibility accorded me, coupled with fear because two of the fighters were only fifteen and had not told their parents of their whereabouts. The way to the concrete building, known since as the "Nizamiyyat Building," was also full of danger, so much so, that even the male fighters were afraid to take that path. Slowly our station in that building became a daily account reported by male fighters and civilians of the region, which prompted many inquisitors among the male fighters to come and see for themselves, just as it became a source of annoyance and insult to others, who refused guard duty on barricades set behind the barricade of the Nizamiyyat. This, however, was soon to change.

The Attack

It was on a night during the month of May, in the light of a full moon, that the Palestine Liberation Army decided to infiltrate the downtown front lines ostensibly to secure an effective cease-fire. Several days earlier, a correspondent of *ʿAmal* newspaper published an article describing the Nizamiyyat Building, and giving accurate details of our numbers, supplies, and ammunition. After that, the Palestinian officer in charge of the front lines raised a green flag signaling his desire to negotiate with us. I moved toward him in the direction of St. George's Church, while he, in turn, walked toward me accompanied by a man, whom he claimed to be the owner of one of the shops adjacent to our building, from which he wanted to withdraw his goods. My girl comrades had already spread out behind me to ensure protection. I allowed the owner to empty his store, while the Palestinian officer started to question me, amazed that we were all girls.

At dusk the following day, while I was reconnoitering the roof of our building on my usual daily rounds, I was suddenly seized by a feeling of impending danger. This was so gripping that I immediately fell on my knees and supplicated the Virgin Mary to help us ward off whatever was to befall us. On my way down to the first floor, I suddenly saw a group of Palestinians by the wall of the Regent Hotel building—but they immediately disappeared. I remained uneasy, however, until the attack took place: At exactly a quarter to ten P.M., the wall near our inner barricade was shelled and one of my comrades was wounded. A few seconds later, all our outlying electric bulbs were shattered and the attack began. I asked my comrades if they wanted to withdraw, but none did. The girls split into groups of two to man the barricades. One girl alone manned the third-floor barricade firing at tens of Palestinians moving towards us only a few meters away. At that moment, a tank approached from one of the alleys facing our barricade, but it was unable to advance because the alley was too narrow. I only had a few Molotov cocktails, which I hurled at the tank to delay it or force it to retreat. The Martyrs' Square was peppered by mortar shells to preempt any support for us. The shelling was so intense that the girls manning the outer barricade would fall down at the pressure caused by the falling shells. I ran from one barricade to another to encourage the girls, but we were quickly running out of ammunition. I had only one grenade and sixteen rounds left. I ran up to the fifth floor from which I jumped to the roof of the Royal Hotel building and found myself looking down at about one hundred Palestinians in the opposite street. Their commander was calling me by my name to surrender and shouting orders to intensify the shelling to frighten us. The scene was terrifying and any wrong move could have cost me my life. I would have to throw the grenade into their midst without any error. With a silent prayer, I pulled the pin of the grenade, aimed carefully and threw it at them, immediately prostrating myself on the roof for protection. It exploded among them, and I followed up by firing my remaining rounds at the group. Loud cries were heard followed by orders to retreat immediately. . . . I returned quickly to our building before being discovered and informed the girls of what I had done. We had some refreshments as the shooting and shelling ceased. It was half past two in the morning and the attack had ended after four hours of hell. My wounded comrade was still bleeding but refused to relinquish her position. However, by now, we had completely run out of ammunition and had to make plans to retreat. At that moment, help arrived: Young men from the Rumayl region came to our aid, and we made our way back, sanitizing the area anew as we did. I took the wounded girl to the hospital.

Early the next morning, I was summoned by our leader Pierre Gemayel, who congratulated the Nizamiyyat for their heroic stand of the previous night. A feeling of exhaustion coupled with exhilaration and gratitude prevailed the following day. I sensed that the premonition that warned me the previous night may have been divine providence, and my faith in the Lord was fortified. This incident had a great effect on my life and that of the whole group. It opened wide the doors of true faith, and I started to perceive things and events with new eyes. The relationship between my friends and me was strengthened and enriched and a feeling of solidarity developed. As for the young men fighters, the Nizamiyyat of the Pierre Gemayel Unit, as they used to call us, had become an ideal to follow and look up to.

Unfortunately, rumors spread among the populace that the Nizamiyyat were able to resist and prevail because they were using stimulants. But these rumors slowly evaporated and we were left with unblemished reputations and a way of life that we still enjoy today.

During the summer of that year, hundreds of girls came to train with the Nizamiyyat of the Pierre Gemayel Unit. My brother was martyred in June 1977. At that time I left the barricades and went to Qihmiz with my group, where I started cycles of intensive training for the Nizamiyyat. The training cycles were now more professional, reinforced by a year's experience in actual fighting, and ended with maneuvers with live ammunition.

The Battle of Chikka

In the period between the downtown events and Qihmiz camp, at the beginning of the summer of 1976, the Palestinians attacked the city of Chikka in the north. Our young men in the area sped to repel the attack, after the attackers had slaughtered the civilians, and corpses, demolished cars, and fire lined the streets. The following morning, my comrades and I made our way to Chikka and arrived at our command center, where Sheikh Amin Gemayel was directing the battle to regain the city with the help of my brother Sami. The head of the Phalangist Party, Sheikh Pierre Gemayel, asked me to take charge of security and discipline in the city following the battle, but I declined, preferring to fight and man barricades on the front lines, the work we became proficient at. He finally agreed and we were put in charge of the Don Carlos (name of restaurant there) post at the center of town, which had just been liberated. Before we could do that, however, we had to wash away the blood.

Our position at Don Carlos consisted of three horizontal barricades facing the Palestinian positions about fifty meters outside town, and I was also in command of a group of fighters manning one of the three barricades. The area was not completely secure yet, and I, therefore, conducted systematic rounds of all the barricades to keep abreast of the situation, meet my comrades' needs, and study the movements of the enemy ahead of us.

Al-Kourah

After Chikka, we returned to Qihmiz to supervise the graduation of forty new Nizamiyyat of the P.G. Unit, and to take them for a week's tour of duty in the downtown area in Beirut, including our famous building. I was devastated, however, to see our former position in which we had stayed for four months, in a state of disrepute and poorly guarded—on the one hand, it was very dirty and, on the other, the Palestinians were allowed to come very close to it, using passageways they had bored through semi-demolished buildings. Furthermore, our young men never practiced the policy of "offensive defense," as we had, but were content to guard their positions from behind the barricades. Their negligence may be attributed to the fact that they came from outlying areas and had no particular attachment to this place and its inhabitants and to the fact that they were on duty for twenty-four hours consecutively. In this way, they were unlike us girls, who gave our all anywhere.

I immediately undertook to clean the building, improve the condition of the barricades, and fortify our defenses. We spent a whole week there at the end of which the front-line barricades at Martyrs' Square were turned over to the new girls (forty in number) under the leadership of one of the older women fighters and we remained in charge of the Nizamiyyat Building. The coordination between the two groups was superlative, but conditions in our building had become very difficult due to the proximity of the enemy and their use of more volatile weaponry such as the sniper using a rocket instead of a rifle. I remember having spent a sleepless week worried about the new recruits.

Afterwards, I was summoned by the High Command and asked to move to the Kourah region, in the north, to link up with the man responsible for the Diddeh barracks, Samir Geagea, and take over the training of the young girls of the area. A short while later, the Arab Deterrent Forces entered Lebanon and we all went back home to resume our old everyday lives and education for a period of two years.

The Hundred Days' War

I returned to the university, the East Sector Campus in Furn el-Shubbak, and was happy to see my old friends again, wear civilian clothes, and sit in class like everyone else listening to others teach and train me. This was what I had missed during the first year of the war. But the university had changed: It had lost its vigor and the tumult of ideologies and political strife that drove one to work and research in an effort to arrive at the truth. We had all become ideologically identical, for those who differed were afraid to voice their opposing ideologies, and soon all stimulation and incentive were lost. I did not like our new Faculty of Information and liked it better as it used to be, full of diversity and challenge.

I was elected president of our cell in the Faculty of Information and both the Dean and my professors were amazed at my self-control and respect for the rules and regulations set by the faculty. They never knew how anxious I was to lead a quiet, peaceful life.

I was all alone at home with sporadic visits from some of my old comrades. I set up a special niche in my room for the Virgin Mary and took up praying to her nightly from the beginning of May and attended Mass two to three times a week at the St. Anthony Church in Rumayl. I spent most of that quiet year in meditation and remembrance of loved ones who were no longer.

In early 1978, tension started to mount between us and the Syrian army following a series of migratory clashes and a state of alert was declared. The Nizamiyyat came back to our house and we stayed up nights waiting for the unknown. We also went out on patrol duty in the area. One night, Sheikh Bashir Gemayel[1] called me to his office at the general Phalangist headquarters and asked me to form a new unit of five hundred Nizamiyyat of the same caliber as those of the downtown area. I went back home and informed my comrades of his request, but on the next day, fighting broke out again. We heard repeated gunshots near our house, and as I and my two comrades ran out fully armed, around 3:00 P.M., we were targeted and one of my friends was hit. We had to carry her to the hospital, where she underwent emergency surgery.

Unlike previous encounters, the Syrians were now everywhere in Beirut, and it was, therefore, very dangerous to move about the city. The shelling was intense and constant, their caliber beyond anything we were accustomed to. After two days of taking refuge in the hospital, I went out to join the group of commandos in the Karantina area near the Phalangist military headquarters. I used to go there every night to assist in patrol duty and to keep myself fit both physically and psychologically. I also participated in the battle to liberate the employees' cooperative (across the street from our military headquarters) from the Syrians; I joined those providing cover to the assailants.

Afterwards, I moved to the mountains with my wounded comrade, who needed care and safety. From there we moved north to Mayfouk to join the command of Samir Geagea, where we stayed for three months assisting in administrative and organizational work and took part in the fighting at the Batroun front until a cease-fire was instated between us and the Syrians in early 1979, whereupon I returned to the Faculty of Information to complete my last year there.

Metamorphosis and the Foundation of the "Lebanese Forces"

I completed my studies as usual, but the year was not an ordinary one for me, for I increasingly felt the presence of God in my life through events and indicators, starting with the encounter in downtown Beirut. Thus by May 1980, I had become totally immersed in God's glory and started exploring convents and interviewing nuns to find my real self and discover my true calling. I was like that man in the Gospel who discovered a treasure in his field; he sold the field and kept the treasure.

Several months later, I was summoned by Sheikh Bashir Gemayel, and on my way over, I was rehearsing appropriate ways of refusing any request to resume military life, for I was no longer interested in commanding five hundred Nizamiyyat. In fact, I no longer considered the defense of Lebanon so important either. I was, therefore, very pleasantly surprised when Sheikh Bashir asked me, instead, to assume responsibility of the Nizamiyyat in the Lebanese Forces—not to train and fight but to help reinstill the spirit of civic responsibility and morality in the youth. I immediately recognized the potential of this situation and what I could accomplish through such a position, more so than through any convent, and immediately accepted. This was the beginning of a new phase for the Nizamiyyat, the phase of "Lebanon—the Message," that we had had in mind since early 1981.

My appointment was welcomed by the men of the Pierre Gemayel Unit, with whom I had developed a warm friendly relationship. But they were still unaware of my intentions and new outlook. I started work in early September and had to make good use of the last month of summer to gather the Nizamiyyat in a camp and form the core that was to establish the Nizamiyyat corps. I invited all Nizamiyyat from the various regions to a meeting at the Phalangist military headquarters in Beirut, during which we decided on a training camp in Qihmiz. The ten-day training camp was attended by one hundred Nizamiyyat. After the session, we picked the best twenty according to military prowess, intelligence, and commitment. It was the best training camp we ever had. We had intensive daytime military exercises and advanced military training, such as dismantling weapons, use of live ammunition, and all forms of combat fighting, whether as individuals or as groups (artillery and tank units of the Lebanese Forces joined in the exercises as well). At night we held evangelical meetings and discussions.

At the beginning, the Nizamiyyat were surprised by my new attitude: For the first time they heard me discuss religious and spiritual topics and urge them to live as and apply Christian ideals and values in their daily lives to give meaning to our endeavors. I was surprised, in turn, at the enthusiastic acceptance of these principles by my comrades. We ended the camp by holding Mass in which all of us participated, and which gave us great joy and generated a bond of love among all of us.

Only six of the Nizamiyyat who served with me during the two-year war continued to work with me; the rest returned to civilian life. These six formed the nucleus of the central office. We decided to spend the first six months in training the twenty chosen girls militarily and enriching them spiritually. In October 1980, I began my first year of theological studies at the School of Theology of the Holy Spirit University at Kaslik. I chose this field of study to better understand Christian dogma and immerse myself in a religious and spiritual atmosphere to help me serve my comrades all the better.

I asked the central unit to devote every weekend to "the Cause" for a period of six months, and we started on an arduous but beautiful journey of military training and spiritual education as well as combat fighting on all fronts. I insisted on that, because I was aware of the important role military training and combat fighting play in fortifying a girl's self-confidence and sense of accomplishment, not only vis-à-vis herself but vis-à-vis the men as well. Military training emancipates her from fear, for man fears what he does not know, and gives her a sense of strength, and accomplishment, which she needs most of all during times of war and while staying in the same barracks with men. This strength is for herself. As for her relationship with young men, knowledge liberates her from feelings of inferiority and a tendency to withdraw in circumstances where her participation is badly needed. In the beginning, my comrades in the military council watched this integration of religious and military commitment in amazement and disbelief.

The atmosphere of the Lebanese Forces was unfamiliar to me and lacked the feeling of family solidarity we had during the two-year war. The resistance movement had begun to be transformed into an impersonal establishment. Standards had also changed, stress being laid solely on competence. The girls, most of whom we did not know, were scattered over several departments and the central office of the Nizamiyyat had to struggle to bring them together in one body. To that end, we established twenty-day cycles of common training camps, where all the girls would get to know each other, develop a sense of belonging, and become exposed to the proper religious and spiritual teachings without jeopardizing their military duties.

We then established through the central office an office of Nizamiyyat affairs to deal with grievances of the girls, whether relating to their work, interpersonal relations, sexual harassment, or their personal lives. We held monthly meetings to bring the girls up to date with administrative, political, and military developments, and published a monthly newsletter entitled *Rafiqati* (My comrade) in Arabic and French, which included an article on a topic of the hour.

Through the central office, we also provided Front Organization, which dealt with matters pertaining to the First Division (personnel affairs and records) and Fourth Division (logistics and maintenance) and communication, as well as purely military matters when necessary. We also participated in the ʿOuyun al-Siman Front during the famous battle for the city of Zahlé in the Biqaa region, which flared up in April 1981, following the siege of that city by the Syrian army in preparation for invading it.

The city had only one approach left open over the snow-bound mountains of Kissirwan to the Biqaa Valley, and that had to be traveled on foot. I still remember the many heartrending casualties and acts of heroism inspired either by Syrian fire from their strategically imposing tanks or by the severe cold at the top of the mountains. Our task was the organization of the ʿOuyun al-Siman barracks, which was the main station between Zahlé and the "liberated" area. It became the rallying point for fighters from the different regions of the "liberated" area either to go to Zahlé or to be entrenched there. We took it upon ourselves to organize the First and Fourth Divisions and the interior of the barracks, and to participate in the artillery to a limited degree. We held, for the first time, regular Mass before our boys took off for the besieged city, which they did with high spirits and soaring morales. Soon, the barracks of ʿOuyun al-Siman was the most preferred barracks by the combatants, despite the cold and remoteness from any town.

We were so successful that we were asked to do the same for other fronts, like Laqluq, Shuf, the Karob region, and the South. We also convinced our leadership to allow us to recruit twenty priests to provide our young men with spiritual support on the various fronts. By 1985, the number of the Nizamiyyat had reached one thousand.

Day of the Nizamiyyat: May 31, 1984

In 1984, we decided to hold a Day of the Nizamiyyat during May, the month of the Virgin Mary, the month of the New Woman, the Mistress of the Universe, whose image should be emulated by all. We decided on May 31, the day the Virgin Mary visited Elizabeth, who carried Jesus to the other woman. It was our first such festival, the first purely female military parade, and our first address in the Resistance and for the Resistance, titled "As you are today, so your Lebanon will be tomorrow," an address intended as a covenant to this day:

> The Nizamiyyat, following the past ten years' experience, have arrived at the conviction that man is the embodiment of life and all of its values and as such there are no values exclusive of man. Thus, to be in the midst of our country's life, in the words of our leader, is to be in the midst of the life of every citizen, for the life of a nation is dependent upon men who understand the true meaning of life and are committed to its realization.
>
> In the past, many were apprehensive of our experiment, as we were girls swimming against the current and apt to lose sight of our true vocation as women, while, to the contrary, we were maturing, learning to care only for significant matters and to regret, only, the loss of vital projects and issues. We used to give without appreciating the significance of giving. We used to dive into a grand adventure with great love and boundless energy, and the hopeful conviction of assured success. And we arrived at the essential question posed by our Phalangist leader: "What Lebanon do we want?" The answer is in everyone of us: There is no new formula or a comprehensive solution for the whole of Lebanon. We have to try and create the make up of a new citizen to fit any formula to be agreed upon. For experience has taught us that a nation reflects the sum total of its citizens. . . .
>
> To define what sort of a Lebanese we want, we have to look at Lebanese women. The Christian Lebanese woman has to choose what she wants to be and in so doing will influence the makeup of the family and society as a whole. Woman was called Eve because she is the mother of life. The Bible tells us the history of mankind centers on two women: The first Eve, who with the first Adam rebelled against the will of God and thus plunged the whole of humanity into the devastation of sin, pain, and death; and the second Eve, the Virgin Mary, who crushed the snake's head, and gave birth to the second Adam, the Son of God, who reconciled humanity with God and opened the gates of heaven. . . .
>
> The first Eve said "NO" to God because she was narcissistic and could not obey her creator. This reflected on Adam and marked the straying away from freedom, truth, and life. This, in turn, led irrevocably to the dismemberment of the family, and Cain murdered Abel, and mankind deteriorated into confusion and materialism beset by

immorality, hatred, and individualism—from Sodom and Gomorrah to Babylon, from paganism on to our present social structure in the West, East, or Lebanon itself. The dangers threatening our society today, its disintegration and immorality, are nurtured by the venom of the first Eve, whom we find ensconced in our very midst. We see her on the streets, a painted doll devoid of any substance, on the walls, a cheap painted merchandise on poster ads. . . .

Irrespective of the final solution, or the area of the homeland, all will be lost if the citizenry do not agree to unite in the communal life of the nation.

Today, the Nizamiyyah [Woman regular] has decided to address all the young women of Lebanon. She, who has been brought up in the trenches to the music of shelling perfumed by gunpowder and grown prematurely old, learned without being educated and gave without being asked: From the barricade, to the infirmary, on the radio waves providing encouragement to the fighters, and in actual combat beside her male comrades. This Nizamiyyah, today, after all that, refuses to see her society remain as it used to be.

The salvation of our people and country is dependent upon a real woman worthy of being the mother of all life. The Nizamiyyah has chosen to be the second Eve, the true woman: the Virgin of Nazareth, from Bethlehem to Calvary, Mary, who bore our Savior Jesus Christ. Each of us, in turn, must bear a Christian committed to the salvation of Lebanon.

Mary, who altered the fate of humanity by acquiescing to the will of God and overcame evil with truth, purity, and commitment. Mary, who refused to be marginalized and followed her son from Nazareth to the Jordan River, to Galilee, Tyre, and Sidon to hear the Word. Mary, who did not stand idle, when the wine ran out during the wedding at Qana of Galilee. Mary, who dared stand where men dared not at the foot of the Cross, committed to her cause to the bitter end, sharing with her son and her God the redemption of mankind. Mary, who gave up the material pleasures of life to embrace the truth.

Mary must be reborn in the heart of every woman in Lebanon, in every home, brighten it with the light of Truth. She must return to say anew: "Give us this day our daily bread and Thy will be done O Lord." Mary must return to aid in planting new fields of wheat and grapevines, to reap real harvests of freedom, contentment and decency. Mary must return to crush the snake's head anew and destroy all the evils that beset Lebanon.

> The Nizamiyyah now declares that there will be a real change: Lebanon is no longer to be an ordinary homeland but a committed one with a sacred message to all paid for in the blood of 5,000 martyrs headed by their martyred president. . . . The price is too high to be wasted, and must give birth to a new Lebanese committed to the building of a new homeland. Anything less is treasonous and a stab in the back of the truth, history, and martyrdom.
>
> Today we pledge ourselves to carry on the task of those who preceded us on the path of glory, and to carry their blood in our veins, and go forth boldly and faithfully. That is our responsibility, for as we shape ourselves today, so shall we shape the Lebanon of tomorrow.

The Day of the Nizamiyyat on May 31, 1984, was an important landmark for us. It was a declaration of intent, a formalization of a plan of action, a stand. It was the foundation of our new conception of Lebanon as the home of diversity and coexistence. It was our faith that made us accept the Other as a full-fledged partner in the homeland. The joy of gratuitous giving replaced the love of competition and self-assertion. It was thus an affirmation that women can do anything, participate in all endeavors, and contribute on an equal footing with men. It is, therefore, not *what* I can do but *how*. It is, thus, my womanhood, I believe, that prevented me during my stay in downtown Beirut from entering and cleansing a nearby building from the menace of a sniper. For, as two of my comrades and myself were about to enter, we heard the cries of a newly born baby. Knowing that I would have to kill all moving objects if I went in, I decided to withdraw. This incident made me raise two questions that have remained unanswered: Was my sex a determinant of my action? If women were to invade all public spheres with love and compassion would the latter become more humane?

The Lebanese Woman: The Woman of May 31, 1988

The years 1980–85 were spent with the Lebanese Forces in military training, orientation, and actual combat. We supported our comrades, helped them become more effective, and safeguarded their rights and privileges. I can safely declare that the presence of women within the military framework provided actual support of and protection for women in all walks of life, while preserving their relationship with men. It is also my conviction that the establishment of an office or special body concerned with women's issues is essential despite the mixed nature of all military activities.

It provides a point of reference that guards the differences between men and women within the military framework and provides some space through which women can express their own conception of the common cause and in a more humane manner. This will help elevate military action to the level of the cause.

On March 12, 1985, Samir Geagea and Elie Hobeika seized the leadership of the Lebanese Forces. This brought about internal divisions and animosities within the ranks of the heretofore united Lebanese Forces and legitimization of the concept of coups d'état, which led the Nizamiyyat to resign en masse with great regret.

In 1985, I received my master's degree in theology, and, with my old comrades, established a series of cycles teaching the Bible and the history of the Church, while holding bimonthly spiritual retreats.

In 1988, we started making concrete plans to establish a society to house our hopes and experiences for use in the service of our society. And on May 31, 1988, we held a special Mass to celebrate the creation of "The Lebanese Woman—The Woman of May 31"—from the smell of gunpowder to the perfume of incense, a journey of maturity and prayer.

Author's note: Translated from the original Arabic by the editor.

Note

1. He was the son of our leader, Sheikh Pierre Gemayel, and the military commander in the Phalangist Party at the time, who had united all resistance forces under the banner of the "Lebanese Forces" in July 1980. He was martyred on September 14, 1982, after being elected President of the Republic, following years of struggle and strife during which his infant daughter, Maya, was martyred. Bashir was a symbol of the resistance and a charismatic leader of the fighters.

V

Foreign Women

13

Profiles of Foreign Women in Lebanon during the Civil War

Mary Bentley Abu Saba

For centuries Lebanon has drawn foreigners to its shores, some for a short while, others for a lifetime. But with the advent of the civil war (1975–91), foreigners and Lebanese alike fled in large numbers.

Introduction

Among those who stayed behind were many non-Lebanese women. Some remained because they were married to Lebanese or Palestinians and considered Lebanon their home. But others, who had no marital ties, stayed as well. Unlike many of their colleagues, neighbors, and friends, these women were not forced to endure the war; they could have returned to their home countries, but they chose not to.

Whatever their reasons for staying, these foreign women—whose exact number is unknown—suffered the same brutalities and dangers of war as the rest of the population.

During these sixteen years many foreign women contributed invaluable services to Lebanon's welfare. Because of them, institutions remained open and functional, the sick and wounded received help, students continued their education and stories of the war were written and reported to the Western world.

The purpose of this chapter is to present profiles of six foreign women who remained in Lebanon during the war, allowing their story to unfold through their own words. The emotional bonding these women formed with the country and its people was made possible not only by the characteristics of the women themselves, but also by those age-old characteristics of hospitality and generosity of the Lebanese people. Those very characteristics were threatened by a civil war that, in the end, had no apparent purpose other than its own out-of-control destruction. Throughout history, while some people wage war for their own purposes, other people, buffeted by those wars, struggle to keep the civilization intact in the face of untold suffering.

The method of obtaining these profiles has been through taped interviews of the women, a process of oral history that has become extraordinarily significant in recent years in the documenting of women's lives, work, and history. Without this oral history, much of women's influence would not become part of the fabric of general written knowledge. From these tapes, I have quoted large portions of their stories so that the reader can "hear" their own words. As opposed to social scientific and other generalizing models, this method allows readers in the West to come closer to the actual life of Western women who chose to live their lives in a Middle Eastern culture during a brutalizing era. In the West, we heard about the Lebanese civil war, saw its ravages on our television screens, and were enraged about the kidnapping of Americans there. Rarely were we afforded an understanding that helped us bridge the chasm between "us and them."

In keeping with this non-objectifying method of gathering information about participants, scholars have urged writers to "situate themselves" or "bring the researcher inside the investigation."[1] Thus, I believe it will be beneficial to the reader to reveal that, as an American married to a Lebanese who lived in the United States during the war, I was seeking my own understanding of an extraordinarily painful era in our lives as I interviewed these women whose courage seemed to me gigantic.

During the war, I also was viewing it through faraway lenses, but I felt its impact most dramatically when my husband's village of Mia-Mia near Sidon was sacked by the warring factions, his aging mother was murdered, and all the inhabitants were forced into exile for seven years. We sponsored twenty-two members of his family as immigrants to the United States, ten of whom arrived in one weekend, within weeks of the fall of Mia-Mia. In 1994, we accepted an opportunity to live in Lebanon, where I have been teaching counseling psychology at the American University of Beirut. It has been during this period that I have had the privilege of learning more about the courage and endurance not only of the Lebanese but of many of the non-Lebanese who chose to remain all during the war.

I had already finished the writing of these women's profiles when the Israeli bombing invasion and massacre at Qana occurred in April 1996. It seemed that what I had learned from these women buoyed me in my own ability to return to Lebanon from spring break in the United States in the middle of that bombing to be ready to resume classes on time. For three weeks, I lived under the horror of incessant air bombardment from the twentieth century's most technologically sophisticated artillery. I began to recognize the significant utility of carrying out daily activities, like going to classes in spite of the trauma, and to experience the strength of the Lebanese becoming united in a way that they had not been in many years.

The psychological framework in which I view these women is an existential one in which the human is constantly emerging/becoming; searching for meaning, values, and goals in life; and creating identity through meaningful relationships with others.[2] Out of existential philosophy has come a significant body of psychological research that points to the kind of person who thrives under duress, who "rises to the occasion," who indeed appears invigorated by difficult life tasks. Studies of the resilience of this "hardy" personality have been ongoing since the 1970s.[3]

Some types of studies describe the personality as a passive subject of the environment and emphasize negative attributes over which the human being apparently has no control. The hardiness studies, however, take a more positive view by affirming that personality develops as a result of strenuous and active involvement with the environment. Such personalities typically possess three interrelated orientations toward themselves and the world: commitment, control, and challenge.

The committed person is one who seeks active involvement with people and the environment and who finds the events and happenings of daily life meaningful. This person has a sense of commitment that goes beyond the self. The control aspect of the hardy personality connotes a belief that one is influential in confronting life's exigencies. The challenge aspect is the tendency to see life's changes as avenues for growth and development rather than a diminution of opportunity.[4]

The authors of these hardy personality studies have devised a scale called Personal Views Survey to measure this construct. The six women interviewed here completed this scale. I hypothesized that the foreign women who remained in Lebanon during the war would score high in the three areas that constitute the hardy personality: commitment, control, and challenge.

In this hardiness survey, the possible range of scores is from 50 to 150, with hardiness increasing as the scale increases. A low range is from 50 to 83, medium is from 83 to 116, and high is from 116 to 150. The scores of the women interviewed here show a medium-high to high range on the overall scale of hardiness. The lowest score was 100, and the highest was 135. Indeed, my hypothesis was correct.

In the following accounts of these women's experiences in Lebanon, their existential "hardy" characteristics are portrayed dynamically and frequently. The stories that they tell contribute to the growing world literature of the capacities, abilities, and achievements of women.

Rosemary Sayigh (British journalist, anthropologist, author)

Rosemary Sayigh was born in Birmingham, England, in 1927, and lived in the suburbs of London until she went to Oxford University. Upon graduation in 1948, she taught English and literature in Baghdad and Beirut before becoming a journalist for *The Financial Times* and *The Economist.* She received her master's degree in anthropology from the American University of Beirut, in 1975, and her Ph.D. from Hull University in England, in 1994. She is married to Yusef Sayigh, a Palestinian living in Lebanon; they have two sons and a daughter. She is the author of *Palestinians: From Peasants to Revolutionaries* and *Too Many Enemies: The Palestinian Experience in Lebanon.*

"During the bombardments, I kept my thesis, my passport, and my purse right next to the door. The thesis was my most precious possession."

Dr. Sayigh, why did you stay in Lebanon during the war?

"My work was here; I could not have done it anywhere else. I am a social anthropologist. I was writing a thesis through 1975, and then I revised it for a book: *Palestinians: From Peasants to Revolutionaries* (1979). I was using oral history methods from the beginning of my work. I was becoming a professional researcher.

"And family was an important reason to stay. My husband's work was here, and I didn't feel that we should be anywhere else. It was no more dangerous for me as a foreigner than it was for anyone else. And I chose to stay here in Lebanon even when my husband was working in other countries, and even after our children grew up and no longer needed me."

By that time, Sayigh had carved her own space in Lebanon, with regard both to her career and to her family.

Indeed, Sayigh reported that when her son was very young, he could not bear living outside of Lebanon, even though the war had started. She took him to England in 1975 because of physical problems, but he became too homesick to remain there. He missed his friends at school and she felt she had done him a disservice by taking him out of Lebanon. After only six months in England, they returned home. This was the longest period of time she stayed out of Lebanon during the war.

Sayigh continued to write throughout the war: conference papers, book chapters, articles in magazines. She received funding from the Boston-based Arab Research Institute for work with the Palestinian women's movement. It was cut short by the 1982 war. After the 1982 Israeli invasion of Lebanon, she wrote articles for *Afrique-Asie*, the London-based *Middle East International*, and *The Economist*—the publication she wrote for originally. Sayigh was intent on keeping the outside world informed about what was going on in Lebanon.

During this period she used the tape recorder to gather material for her second book: *Too Many Enemies: The Palestinian Experience in Lebanon*.

Were you in contact with other foreign women?

"Oh yes, there were many foreign women here. Many because they were wives of Arabs. But there were other women who were not wives, but they were here in their own capacities. They were a very tenacious group. They stayed until their embassies forced them to leave. For many, it was a trauma to have to leave, which is interesting when you consider how atrocious the war was.

"For instance, Genevieve Maxwell was a journalist writing for *The Daily Star* until she retired in the 1970s. She stayed until she was forced to leave at age eighty. A good-bye party was given for her in 1987 when she left. There was also a journalist named Tabitha Petran, who stayed until she was forced to leave. When the United States made a sudden raid on Libya in 1985, there was retaliation here, and two or three Americans were killed. Almost all remaining Americans were forced to leave. Ms. Petran tried to remain close by, in Cyprus, but then went to Baltimore where she died. Leaving Lebanon was a wrenching event for her.

"Lebanon has been an opening up for me of life choices.

"I guess at an existential level I have a feeling of control over myself. I feel as free here as I do anywhere. Lebanon has been a point of stability for me. I left England as soon as I finished college, went to Italy and Baghdad, and then came to Lebanon, and I've remained very stable here ever since. It's partly being outside one's own culture so that you have always something different to watch. The 'eternal visitor.' It's home, and it isn't home. I am always commuting between knowing it, and not knowing it. I find it a very exciting place. It's dangerous, of course, at times. But it is also full of opportunities. It's a very sociable place.

"Things move rather rapidly: friendships, colleagueships, job possibilities. I've always found Lebanon is a country where one can find something to do, find a role, get interested in something, and put roots down in a niche of it. I feel I need nine lives here to do all the things I'd like to do. There is more here than in a more organized society. I have more opportunities here than, for instance, my mother did in her life. I never feel imprisoned here.

"I've wondered recently about why the war doesn't haunt me more and why I have difficulty recalling it. It's like there is a painkiller in the brain that actually wipes it out."

What were some specific times during the war in Lebanon that were hard for you?

"We were lucky compared with so many others. No close family members were killed or kidnapped. Our home was not destroyed, we were not displaced. We were both able to work throughout the war. Of course, we went through some bad moments. One of those times was when I was bringing my son down from a school in Broumana, in the mountains, on Black Saturday, September 11, 1975. It was hard to know what was happening. I knew that something was happening to drivers of cars. There were these people with masks. I was driving through a Christian-dominated area to get to the 'enemy area.' I wondered if I should stop then and there and ask someone just to protect me. But I continued, and got through safely to the port, where there was a UN convoy. I drove along with them some way, and then got home safely in West Beirut."

It was only later that Dr. Sayigh discovered that the masked men had slaughtered about twenty innocent people in cars, based on what their identity cards noted as their religion.

"Another night our youngest son, a university student, did not come home from a day trip to Sidon, and there was an explosion of a car around Ramlet al-Baida. We were so upset, even my husband, without telling me, started going around to all the morgues to find out if he was there. Much later, we found out he was stuck in a massive traffic jam in Sidon."

How do you think change affects you?

"There has been more change since the war than during it. Many of the pleasant, very touching things about life in Lebanon have disappeared because of the economic pressures. People have become more aggressive, and by necessity perhaps, more greedy. They are more competitive; there is much more cursing.

"If you were out on the streets, and people around you knew there would be violence and conflict, they would warn you. There was a tremendous sense of responsibility for other people. This sense is totally gone since the end of the war. When things were bad, there was a mutual solidarity of the Lebanese people. Anyone here can tell you many stories of people truly helping each other, that offset the stories of terrible violence."

Sayigh was returning home at dusk from visiting a friend when a sudden mobilization took place, like a quick storm. The streets all emptied except for some armed men and she could hear machine-gun fire in the distance. She diverted her route slightly to go to a friend's home, but remembered when she arrived at the closed door that the friend was on holiday. After she banged on the main door of the apartment building, someone opened the door and invited her into an apartment. Here she spent the whole night among strangers while the battle was going on all around them. For Sayigh, the fear and danger were offset by feelings of solidarity with people.

How would you describe your sense of commitment?

"My commitment is not in a direct and political way. I tend to be committed to certain values, rather than certain causes.

"Friendship is important to me, and of course, family. I've been identified with the Palestinian cause most of my adult life, and I've written a great deal about it. I have felt committed to write reports to the world outside Lebanon to explain the various causes that people here may have, but are not able to voice. I feel very committed to the people I have worked with in oral history."

Sayigh was pessimistic that any good would come out of the fighting, but she felt sympathy with, and, interest in, the various causes. "I felt more defensive on the whole, not believing that certain people had to win, but that they had to be protected when they did not win. As a journalist, I felt I had to make known to the world outside the causes for which people were fighting, and these causes are not very well known or understood by people outside.

"There were several periods, in 1982 and 1985–87, when I was involved in relief work. I've always been an active supporter of the Palestinian nongovernmental agencies. I deeply admired the work of so many foreign women. For instance, I was much impressed by foreign medical personnel (mainly women) who set up a clinic in the Palestinian Shatila camp in the aftermath of the massacre, remaining until the 'Battle of the Camps' began in mid-1985. Sometimes I saw myself more as an observer. I think this is something a lot of English people have, this observer stance. In a way, I think this may be a shortcoming."

Throughout her adult life in Lebanon, Sayigh's active involvement—coupled with her observer stance and her calm, pensive look—has directed the path of her poignant writing about others' feelings, values, and causes in the Middle East. Because of this involvement, she has greatly contributed to the education of Westerners about the Middle East. Sayigh is seen frequently in Beirut, striding with her long gait through the streets of Hamra, gazing in the shop windows, halting on the American University of Beirut campus to give long, careful looks at the flora, offering reserved and perspicacious comments at conferences, encouraging students to involve themselves and to observe with her. The commitment of Dr. Sayigh in Lebanon has been widely effective.

Judith Harik (American political science professor)

Judith Harik was born in Staten Island, New York, in 1936. She received her undergraduate degree from Drew University in New Jersey, and her master's degree and Ph. D. from the University of Iowa in political science. She married Antoun Harik, a Lebanese, and they moved to Lebanon in 1978 when their two children were eleven and twelve years old. She is the author of several scholarly articles on the Druze community and Hizballah in Lebanon, as well as on the social services of the Lebanese militias. Dr. Harik has been a professor of political science at the American University of Beirut since 1981.

"When I was a child, I was enamored with adventure stories of the American Old West, the exploits of cowboys, and the love of horses. As a result I entered into horse training and competition, learned Spanish as a foreign language, and pretended with my family for years that we lived on a ranch while, in fact, we lived in the middle of New York City."

Thus began the life of Judith Harik, an American, who came to Lebanon in 1978 and has remained there ever since. During the worst years of the war in Beirut, she continued to live in West Beirut and considered her survival a defiance of the bombs that rained on the city first from the Israelis and then from the various militias within Lebanon.

Harik's study of Spanish led her to seek out the Latin American population in New York and then to major in Spanish and French in college. Her sense of adventure and her interest in foreign cultures helped her to remain undaunted by the prospects of marrying someone from another culture and living with him in another country. Her own commitment to multiculturalism attracted her to her husband who was interested in the social and political progress of the Lebanese.

Deep commitment beyond her own life has always been a strong motivator for Harik. She was not able to imagine just marrying and settling down to a regular job and children.

Ever flexible in her scholarly pursuits, when Harik began teaching at the American University of Beirut in 1982, she realized she had to change her focus from the politics of Latin America to those of the Middle East. As the war continued, increasing numbers of Americans were leaving Lebanon, creating a huge gap in the AUB political science curriculum, a gap Harik adapted herself to fill.

"I never thought I just couldn't stand what was going on. My sense of competitiveness was aroused. I was a national champion in equitation (riding) in 1952 in the United States. I rise to a challenge; it gives me a sense of purpose. I was resisting forces of evil by remaining and staying alive in Lebanon."

Dr. Harik, did you ever think of leaving Lebanon?

"I couldn't think of anywhere to go. My job as a professor of political science was very important to me. Helping to keep the American University of Beirut open and alive was crucial. It could not stay open if all the teachers left. No, I just could not leave. We were all resisting by being here. When the water was cut off, we made do. We rinsed the front of the dishes and not the back. Whoever had water, people would go to that person for a shower.

"There was a factor of heroism here that I was a part of, and emotionally there didn't seem to be any way to leave. My husband and I were involved in the nongovernmental agencies in West Beirut, trying to stock needed commodities like flour, oil, sugar, and so forth. We were not just sitting around waiting for ourselves to be saved. We were doing what we could to help others, as well as ourselves. I could not have gone back to the United States to wait for it to be over, and just watch it all happen from over there."

When she first arrived in Lebanon in 1978, her husband was a professor at the American University of Beirut, and Harik was a faculty wife. They had two small children, and she was working sporadically on her Ph.D. dissertation. In 1981, she went back to the United States and finished her degree. Returning in the fall of 1981, she was hired to teach full-time at AUB.

In November, however, she contracted a serious case of hepatitis which kept her at home until the following spring. She sent tapes of lectures to her classes and read student papers at home. By the time she returned to her classes, the spring semester of 1982 was almost over and the Israelis had invaded. The Harik family's life changed.

They were now living off campus but still in West Beirut, near the lighthouse in the Manara area. Palestinian militia were occupying the bottom floor of their house, and they knew that the Israelis knew they were there.

Israeli gunships began to shoot at their house. Harik was at her dining room table working on a painting when a missile hit the floor above them and shattered the dining room table and chairs. Fortunately no one was on the floor where the missile landed. If the gunner had lowered his sights another millimeter Harik's story would have been different indeed.

Residents in the surrounding buildings immediately took refuge at the lighthouse, a dangerous shelter at best because a rusty old elevator weighing several tons dangled above them. The Israeli gunners followed them there and began to pound the lighthouse. Again, they ran, this time to their cars in order to escape.

The Hariks planned to cross into East Beirut where they had a small apartment at the beach resort of Aquamarina. Their route took them through narrow roads near the museum crossing, the scene of some of the worst bombing. They had rushed the two children, Harik's mother, the maid, and the dog into two cars and sped off. Driving two cars, they could not tell where the bombs were actually hitting, although they heard them all around. Harik knew that at any second their car could be under a bomb and a couple of times she wanted to pull over and just jump out. But they were making a big push to get out of the area, realizing that the Israelis were "softening up" the district before a final onslaught.

When at last they got to East Beirut they were shocked to find people sitting in cafes and restaurants, drinking Pepsi, eating *shawarma* sandwiches, sauntering around, and having a good time. There were large gardens with water splashing. No evidence could be seen of the water and electricity shortages that the West Beirutis were suffering because of the Israeli siege.

"The situation had gotten to the point that if people were not involved directly in the fighting, they would be inured to the fighting. I could be driving through shelling to get to campus, but once there, the campus was serene, beautiful, and calm. A sense of numbness set in.

"We moved on campus for our own safety. We lived on a top floor, and we went through the agony of watching the Israeli planes circle around and then head for the outer reaches of Beirut to the Palestinian camps to bomb there."

Did you ever feel depressed or severely anxious?

"No, I don't think so. I tried to keep in front of me the goals of the struggle. I liked playing a part in overcoming enormous odds. Our living conditions were terrible; but to hang in there was important.

"In general I feel challenged by many different kinds of adversity.

"I was challenged in surviving the war. I had succeeded in doing the difficult chore of finishing my master's degree and Ph.D. while I was working and raising two small children. Then I faced the challenge of changing my whole scholarship focus from Latin American studies to Middle Eastern studies after I began to teach at the American University of Beirut. Then we found out suddenly that the administration was going to start demanding that we do research. We were so busy trying to survive the war, and to teach, it was hard to imagine doing research. But I saw that I must begin doing this, or I would lose my career."

Many of Harik's acquaintances who did not know her competitive background in horse training got a new view of her. Giving research her single-minded attention in a way she could not do during the civil strife, she quickly amassed the scholarly publications that satisfied promotion requirements.

Do you have regrets about your decision to remain in Lebanon?

"The main regret I have about how I dealt with the war was about my children. I seemed to have put upon them my own feelings of being challenged by this war, or even perhaps excited by it, and did not fully consider whether they felt this way. I didn't consider if I were coping with some things as an adult that they did not have the ability to cope with them as children. I think we did not give them the opportunity to express fully, openly and honestly, what they felt.

"We just assumed they were doing all right. If someone asked me again would I knowingly put my children through this again, I would say resoundingly 'NO.' This is one of the big scars of the war."

Wallie Merhege (German medical doctor)

Wallie Merhege was born in Vienna in 1942. Her mother was German, and her father, Austrian. A medical student at the University of Vienna, she came to Lebanon during the last years of her training. She wanted to visit friends she had met through an uncle who, as a ship captain, made regular stops at Beirut port. She finished her medical training in Vienna, but did her residency in Lebanon. Married first to Riyad Nachabe with whom she had three children, she became a widow in 1975. She then married Bishara Merhege, and they have two children. In 1985, she founded the Diagnostic Center for Exceptional Children in Beirut. She also founded First Step Together, an organization of parents and supporters of education and future planning for exceptional children.

"I had very big dreams of doing extraordinary work, humanitarian work. I was thirteen when I wrote on my small wooden table with a nail that I wanted to study medicine. My idol was Albert Schweitzer."

How did you come to Lebanon the first time?

"It's such a familiar story. My roommate in medical school, an Italian woman, was engaged to a Turk. We decided to go there to visit. Once in Turkey, I decided to drive on to Lebanon. 'It's not so far,' I said! I had old family friends there who urged me to come. It was so lovely here in 1967. I was fascinated with Beirut, and I fell in love with the city! My Lebanese friends urged me to stay and I received permission from my university in Vienna to do an assistantship here. They agreed for me to do it in the German hospital. I have been here ever since.

"When I was accepted to study medicine in Vienna, I thought I was living a wonderful dream. Shortly after I arrived, I realized I was an unwelcome foreigner. I was the one from the Reich. It was a big shock to be considered an outsider. I was rootless. But this is what made it so easy for me to go to Lebanon and to find my new roots in another place that accepted foreigners."

Merhege has lived close to war many years of her life. As a child, her family moved to Vienna from Teschen, Czechoslovakia, which was then part of Austria. Her father worked as a lumberjack. He had an impaired leg and only three fingers on one hand. Because he could neither walk well nor carry a rifle, he was spared military duty—a fact that saved his life during the war in Europe.

One day at their home in Vienna, when her father was out working, the family heard shouting. Alarmed, her mother made them all hide in a small storage area under the steps. Soon afterwards, people—to this day she does not know who they were—came through their apartment. Finding no one, the unknown attackers left, but on their way out of the building they shot everyone they found. Merhege and her family had been spared by her mother's quick thinking, but their neighbors had not been so fortunate. She grew up with this memory emblazoned in her mind.

In 1975, Merhege helped set up Nasra Hospital for children of the Tell el-Zaatar Palestinian camp in East Beirut. She helped to establish mother/child centers in the camps, giving information to new mothers about child care. She and her colleagues even sewed the curtains for the rudimentary clinics, bright colors of red, blue, and yellow.

During this period, Merhege also set up a center for disabled children, employing a multidisciplinary team. This was the beginning of her focus on disabled children, an interest that continues today with her establishment of the Diagnostic Center for Exceptional Children.

Dr. Merhege's experience in caring for the sick and the dying did not prepare her for the wrenching effects of her own husband's battle with cancer. Two years after his diagnosis and after many operations, he died on April 9, 1975. Several days later, the civil war started.

"I learned some important life issues from my husband during this time. He found such pleasure in reading short stories during his illness. I was astonished, because I couldn't think of anything else except his disease, and how we could get it cured. I learned that you have to accept what is going to happen, whatever it is. His attitude helped me after his death to accept the idea that life is for the living. This is a very Islamic philosophy. You don't panic. You take things as they are. You don't accuse anybody. This is what my late husband did."

Dr. Merhege decided to remain in Lebanon with her three children, the youngest, one year of age. They had been growing up in close physical and emotional proximity to their father's family. She felt it was healthier for them to stay close to this family in Lebanon, rather than taking them to Germany where family relations might have been less satisfactory. Also, she felt that in Lebanon she could practice medicine on a part-time basis and have more time available to be the only parent for her children.

Thus, Dr. Merhege began her years of widowhood by choosing Lebanon as the country with which she would cast her lot. This was the second time she had made such a decision. On the first occasion she had been married. This time her Lebanese husband had just died and she had three small children to raise. And there would come yet a third crossroads in her life when she would choose to remain in Lebanon.

"Bodies were brought to us in pieces, piled on top of each other. We did the best we could without proper medical equipment to save as many as possible."

It was some forty years after Merhege had hidden under the staircase listening to gunshots as other people in her apartment building were being killed. Now, in 1984, she was working as the director of Ramalla Hospital during what was perhaps the darkest period of her life. She had been in the hospital all morning, trying to save the lives of people who had been injured in a huge explosion at the Lebanese University.

They did not have the sophisticated equipment needed to save lives but the entire staff worked arduously to do what they could.

In the afternoon, she and the other medical workers were recovering from this traumatic morning, when a group of militiamen stormed into the hospital and shot several doctors. This time there was no hiding place, and although Wallie Merhege was spared, her closest colleagues were not so fortunate.

After these horrors, she took her children on an extended trip to Europe, visiting her sister in Hanover, Germany, and relatives in Paris. By then she had five children, the last two from her second marriage. The youngest child was six. Traveling by plane, train, and taxi, the children learned about geography, history, and their European roots. This beautiful trip lasted for three months but the children were eager to get back to Lebanon. Merhege also knew that for all the beauty and peacefulness in Europe, she could not stay. Her children were insisting on returning, and her work commitments were calling her back.

For the third time, then, she decided she must remain in Lebanon. When they returned by car through the border from Syria into Lebanon, the children cheered with joy. It was 1987, and the country was still at war.

"How can you be in your Beirut kitchen baking a cake when they are bombing right outside?"

Merhege has always been a predominantly optimistic person. She had no time to be anxious or depressed during the war years, because just seeing about the basics of life took so much time: getting water, finding food and bread, coping without electricity. Sometimes when there was no bread, she resorted to making cake, not only for the sustenance, but as a treat for the children, and for entertainment!

On those rare occasions when the telephone was working, she would talk to her sister in Germany. But her sister could not imagine the absurdity of Merhege in the kitchen with her children, busy baking cakes in the middle of bombing and shelling in Beirut.

During the war years, Merhage felt almost fearless. She had learned the fatalistic outlook that when her time was up, it was up. In the year 1989, during the fierce artillery duels between General Aoun and the Syrians, she was more afraid because the advanced artillery these forces used was more deadly. She and the children left the house for seven months and stayed in the German embassy shelter in Beirut.

Merhege believes she has a survivor instinct, that the war years in Lebanon represented a time when she was able to penetrate deeply within herself and reach out to help others.

"As a German in Lebanon, I observe important events even while I am completely involved in them. I have a small but significant role in the history of Lebanon, and I intend to continue playing my part to the fullest. Each individual can have an impact on a society."

Gladys Mouro (American director of nursing services)

Gladys Mouro was born in Pawtucket, Rhode Island, in 1953. Her mother is Lebanese and her father American. During her childhood, she and her family traveled frequently to Lebanon to visit her maternal grandparents. She studied nursing at the American University of Beirut, graduating in 1976, and in 1982 obtained her master's degree in nursing from the University of Pennsylvania. She was appointed director of Nursing Services at the American University Hospital in 1983. In 1988, Mouro, as keynote speaker, addressed 10,000 participants of the International Critical Care Nursing Conference in Montreal on "War-related Trauma and Nursing Care." She continues in her position as director of Nursing Services at the American University Hospital.

"After receiving a threat that I would be kidnapped, I was flown by helicopter by the American Embassy in 1989 to Cyprus. Four months later, I flew back via Abu Dhabi to continue my work at the hospital. I belonged here in Lebanon. I had survived all that time during the war. I did not want to give up and let go of the hospital services. It was my baby."

Gladys Mouro must have teethed on tenacity and perseverance, for she shows it in her unrelenting efforts as a nurse at the American University Hospital. As a youngster she used to come with the rest of her American-Lebanese family to Lebanon once a year to see her grandfather, her mother's father. Even though her father was American and she had grown up in Rhode Island, something of the charm of Lebanon of the early 1970s enticed her to apply to the School of Nursing of the American University of Beirut in her freshman year. She completed her degree in 1976, and the war had already started.

"My father had died, and my brother forced me to leave Lebanon. All my family was in the States. I spent one year working at the University of Rhode Island. I kept thinking of Lebanon. I wrote to Sheila Hammon at

AUH, the director of Nursing Services then, and she contacted Dean Asper. He encouraged me to come back. Within the year I was at AUH as a staff nurse. I was happy."

Mouro was promoted rapidly from staff nurse to head nurse, then to supervisor. In 1981, AUB sent her to the University of Pennsylvania to complete her master's degree. The Israeli invasion began in 1982, and she returned to Lebanon as acting director of Nursing Services. Except for the brief exit forced by the American Embassy, Mouro never left Lebanon from 1982 to 1992.

"There was a high employee turnover. We had people leaving left and right, including senior doctors and nurses. We wound up with only 20 percent of our staff. I had such a strong commitment to surviving and keeping the place going. Many nurses accepted positions in other countries, getting offers from New York to work there; it was a prime way of getting immigration papers."

Mouro was a target for assassination and kidnapping threats. She frequently received threatening calls in the middle of the night and was under pressure from the various political parties to hire certain people, to fire, or to promote.

"I never gave in. I insisted that I would stick to my own principles, and not make decisions because I was afraid of someone else."

At the time Terry Waite was kidnapped (the British cleric who came to negotiate the hostages' release), there was an article in a local newspaper alleging that Mouro was in Lebanon as a spy.

"I suppose they just couldn't figure out why I would be here. I wasn't in love with anyone. I didn't have a family here. I wasn't making money to speak of. I didn't belong to a political party. I had so much faith in the American University of Beirut. I had so much commitment to my profession, and to continuing that profession at the American University Hospital."

How do you feel about that commitment now?

"I'm glad I stayed, but there were costs to be paid. Professionally, I probably could have developed more somewhere else. I learned a great deal here, but war is limiting; we were just surviving. I was not progressing financially. I was not going to conferences, giving presentations. Although after the war I did give a conference presentation in the States on how to survive a war. I got a standing ovation! I didn't have time to establish a family. I imagine I'll continue to pay that price, not only now at age forty-one, but as I grow older.

"Lebanon is a beautiful place. The Lebanese are warm and intelligent, and very adaptable. They learn quickly. But I suffered a great deal at first because I didn't know how to deal with the people. I was very young when I was given tremendous responsibility. The war forced me to learn. The years went by so fast, and now I recognize I have spent 365 days a year working for fifteen years. It's difficult to make up now for the things I missed enjoying in young adulthood."

Do you feel you had a sense of control during those war years?

"Most of the time, I'm quite efficient in that kind of sense of control. But there was a time during the war that I really suffered. That was when they started kidnapping lots of people, including Joseph Ciccipio, American University of Beirut assistant comptroller, who was in my same building. I had nightmares , and I became depressed. But I got out of it. I said to myself: This is the challenge. It is difficult, but I must not give in to this fear. I must do my part to make them change."

Mouro kept a journal during those years and wrote frequently about her experiences. Now that the journal is in the hands of a publisher, she says she is weary of reflections about the war.

"The war is over. Forget about it, I tell my people. We can't keep crying about the war. We have been through so much, and now we must move on to keep raising our medical service standards."

How do you experience change in general?

"The changes I had to go through during the war were easier than those now. I have difficulty now dealing with the changes in people's attitudes about work, their sense of loyalty, and their values. They are so concerned about money.

"The poor people are concerned about money, but so are the rich people. No one seems to have enough. Everyone talks about money. It is the prime topic of conversation. During the war we rarely talked about it. Maybe now we just have more time to talk about it. There is not much evidence of respect for work and loyalty to the country. And this kind of change is difficult for me."

Mouro is looking forward to the changes that will occur when foreigners return to Lebanon. She feels that because people in Lebanon are suffering from symptoms of postwar trauma, foreigners will provide a mix that is needed for healing.

"I applied for Lebanese citizenship but I didn't get it. Though my mother is Lebanese, only Lebanese men can petition to have their children become Lebanese citizens."

She has applied twice for Lebanese citizenship but has been turned down both times. Her hurt feelings were obvious when she talked about this. After serving the country for twenty years so arduously, she felt entitled to citizenship. "I'm not going to apply again. I don't want it."

Do you plan on leaving for the States in the next decade?

"Not really. I'd like to go there every year and visit my family. However, right now my commitment is in Lebanon, at the American University of Beirut, at this hospital."

Catherine Bashshur (American educator)

Born in Philadelphia, Pennsylvania, in 1938, Catherine Bashshur obtained her undergraduate degree from the State College of Pennsylvania, and her master's degree in education from the University of Florida. She met her husband, Munir Bashshur, a Lebanese academician, in Chicago, where she was teaching and he was in graduate school. She came to Lebanon in 1964 and began teaching at the American Community School and became principal of the school in 1984. In the midst of extreme war conditions, she and a small staff managed to keep the doors open for the few remaining students. On several occasions the school was bombed while they were inside. Since the end of the war, Bashshur and the Lebanese staff have built the school back up to 1,000 students. She and her husband have two children.

Almost goddess-like with her six-foot stature, white hair, and piercing blue eyes, one can easily project on Catherine Bashshur the archetype Protector. Indeed, she filled exactly this role for students, staff, and parents during the war years in Lebanon when she was teacher, and later, principal at the American Community School.

There was nothing in her life, given her birthplace, that would have predicted this kind of heroic career. But, as a dedicated educator, it fell to her, along with many other educators in Lebanon, to uphold the importance of regular academic efforts in the middle of bombing, kidnapping, and the danger and uncertainty of war waged in the streets of a major world city.

From an original staff of 100, and several hundred students, by the fall of 1975, the staff had shrunk to 25. There were only 100 students in kindergarten through grade 12.

The adults of this school were doing what adults in charge of children throughout Lebanon were doing: protecting their children by insisting that studying was important, that getting to school was worth the risk and the trouble. It was a protective shield they could throw around their children, to keep their minds on their books, to hope and prepare for a better future, to refuse to give in to the despair that nothing was worthwhile in the face of danger.

At night, parents protected their children by taking them to the inside corridors, bathrooms, or the bomb shelters to sleep. By day, they dressed them, and sent them off with their books to school, hiding their own never-ending anxiety: "Will they be all right?" The commitment of the Lebanese to learning runs deep.

And Catherine Bashshur was always standing there, smiling, to receive them at the school door.

"Telephones didn't work, so we didn't know if school had been called off. We arranged to send signals from our verandahs between 7:00 and 7:30 in the morning. A child's red raincoat meant stay at home. A yellow raincoat, go to school."

If Bashshur and her husband disagreed about whether it was safe that day for the children to go to school, he would stay home with their two children and she would go to school to be there for the others.

"By March of 1976, my husband's nerves were raw. We decided to go to Syria to visit his parents. A friend loaned us his armed driver and car and we loaded the car with the two kids, a few toys, our suitcases, and traveled south through Marjayoun, and wound around the mountains arriving in Damascus [an unusually circuitous route].

"We couldn't come back to Lebanon because Syria had closed its borders by late spring. So I went to the States, taking the children with me, planning to live with my mother. We had one suitcase. I did not know until I was on my way that my mother had died."

Bashshur lived in Pennsylvania for a year, working as a reading specialist in a public school, while the children attended local schools. The following summer, her husband came to the States from Lebanon, insisting that everything in Lebanon was back to normal.

Each summer she went to the States, hoping that when she returned, the war would be over. Each time she was disappointed.

"Nineteen eighty-four was a particularly bad year. It started with weird weather: hail, then a landslide, then an earthquake. There was a split in the army, in February 1984, between Moslems and Christians.

"One day, a curfew was clamped on the whole city, and we could not get out of the school. The American University of Beirut had shut its gates. Sixteen students were with me in the school and because of the curfew absolutely no one was allowed to leave. The school building was hit directly at least seven times. Part of the library was destroyed. The United States military was helping to target areas around the school with heavy shelling, so that they could remove the Americans who were about four blocks from the school."

Bashshur and the students could hear the helicopters all night, making trips out to the ships, while the bombs were falling on and around the buildings. The next day they escaped from the building, and by the end of that week, she and both her children were lifted off the beach by a U.S. army helicopter and evacuated to Cyprus.

The following year, she and the children stayed in the United States so the children could go to school.

"I was asked to promise that I would stay in Beirut, if I took over as principal. I promised."

In the fall of 1985, Bashshur was asked to serve as principal of the American Community School. There were four students in the class of 1985, and the same number in the class of 1986. Her son Michael was one of them. In the summer of 1986, Joe Ciccipio, the assistant comptroller at the American University of Beirut and a member of the board of trustees of the school, was kidnapped. Another board member, Zahi Khoury, who had a son the same age as Michael, was kidnapped along with Zahi's brother's wife, their son, and their dog. No one has seen the Khoury family since.

On March 14, 1989, the American Community School lost its first and only student to the war. Sam Abu-Hebba, a Jordanian, was on his way to school when his car was hit at the UNESCO crossroads. Six months from high school graduation, he was an only son, and the youngest of five children.

"Excuse me, but would you please allow me to enter college, even though I didn't finish high school as planned? We were in the middle of a war, my school was bombed, and so they closed and I didn't graduate."

Who could imagine an admissions office of a U.S. college receiving a letter like this?

After Sam's death, no more classes were held that semester. The American Community School was next to a large building where a big gun was emplaced with its sights set toward the east. This building was naturally the target for return fire. It was as if ACS was in a volleyball game, with the shooting going back and forth over their heads.

Yet, there were seniors who needed to graduate from high school so they could begin college in the United States. They had already been accepted. Bashshur arranged with the available teachers to produce a modified correspondence course. The students came to the school, picked up assignments, worked on them, and returned them for correction. Senior papers were written under individual supervision by the teachers. Between shooting sprees, testing times were arranged. Using this piecemeal approach, they successfully graduated four students by July 1989.

Catherine Bashshur and the American Community School survived the winter of 1990; then, in September, the whole war suddenly stopped.

"I don't see anything resolved or settled. People are just burned out. I myself am not willing to go through any more war."

Why did you stay here? You had plenty of family in the States, begging you to come and bring the whole family.

"I saw many people leave, and they were not happier. They got sick. They died. International marriages split up. If you decide you are in this together, it makes a difference. It was impossible to leave, when so many people were here and needed us."

Did you come out of the war with any scars?

"We lost so many years of our life of just what would be normal living. And one bad effect is that having gotten through the war, the sense of community and working together is gone. People now seem to be just out for themselves.

"I feel especially sorry for old people and young people. The enjoyment of old age has been taken away from the old people. There are no memories for the young people of the Lebanon of better years. I don't see that the kids know how to play now. The interaction among children is not normal. I think what the war did was isolate us into little groups. The only interaction was with the immediate family. I think this is why we see so much hyperactivity among children. And I think the war negatively affected our own children.

"In fact, perhaps Munir and I have both forgotten how to play. We got so lost in our work, in coping with the dangers of the war, and then doing our work. We may have become workaholics. We are approaching retirement time now, and we must gear out of this. We need to learn to do other things."

How do you experience change in general?

"I think it is inevitable, and we have to be ready to change. I think I cope with change by expressing my feelings, by getting everything off my chest. I blow up when I need to."

Fortunately for many students learning in an American tradition, Bashshur remained steady, calm, and available for them during a tragic time in their lives.

Anni Kanafani (Danish kindergarten teacher)

Anni Kanafani was born in Copenhagen, Denmark, in 1925. With a degree in early childhood education, she has worked with kindergarten students for the past thirty-five years. She came to Lebanon in 1961 where she met and married Ghassan Kanafani, a Palestinian poet and journalist. When he was assassinated by an Israeli car bomb in 1972, Mrs. Kanafani chose to stay in Lebanon with their two children and establish the Ghassan Kanafani Cultural Foundation. Through this foundation she has established eight kindergartens for Palestinian refugees in Lebanon. She has also founded a training institute for kindergarten teachers in the Mar Elias Palestinian refugee camp in Beirut. In 1989, she spent a year at the Royal Academy of Education in Denmark. She continues as an active teacher and teacher trainer for Palestinians in Lebanon, as well as a dynamic leader of the cultural foundation.

"I actually came to Lebanon in order to learn about the Palestinians. I had met some Palestinian students at a World Organization for Education conference in Denmark. When I knew they were from the Middle East, I said 'I know some Israeli folk dances, so I'd like to know more about you'."

Thus began the inspiring story of Anni Kanafani. A dedicated teacher of children, she has established, and now supervises, kindergartens serving about eight hundred children in Palestinian camps throughout Lebanon. One of these camps is for physically handicapped children; a second one was set up to help those who are mentally handicapped.

In some of the schools, children and staff are on double shifts so the optimum number of pupils can use the facilities. Kanafani also runs a training center for prospective kindergarten teachers at Beirut's Mar Elias camp. Here, she passes on her own philosophy of education—that children need to learn art, music, and drama before they are immersed in the tasks of reading and writing.

"Children need to be allowed to be children. They should not be forced to read and write before they are ready. I believe people in this culture are not reading when they grow up because they were forced to do it too early. It is a burden for them."

Sitting in her living room among the books, art work, and pictures of her late husband, Ghassan Kanafani, Anni Kanafani spoke with passion and wisdom about her love of children, of teaching children, of the necessity of giving them an artistic, playful, early education.

Her husband, a journalist, poet, author, and Palestinian political leader, was assassinated in 1972 by the Israeli Mossad. In 1974, she and friends of her husband, with the help of international organizations, established the Ghassan Kanafani Cultural Foundation. The purpose of the foundation was to publish his prolific writings, and to establish kindergartens in the major Palestinian camps in Lebanon.

"I met Ghassan at his newspaper office where he worked. He asked me what I wanted to do. I said I wanted to know about the Palestinians, I wanted to see some camps. He became upset, and said: 'My people are not animals in a zoo. You need to know more about the Palestinian cause before you go poking around'."

Arriving in Beirut in September of 1961, Kanafani had not intended to stay long. But by November, her relationship with Ghassan had turned into a deep love, and they both knew their lives would be lived together. He was totally honest with her, even in his proposal of marriage: "No country, no future, no money, no passport, and a severe chronic illness (diabetes)."

After her husband's death she was convinced that she must stay in Lebanon. The children needed to grow up there, she thought, to know their father's culture.

"But the decision was also a confrontational one. I wanted to show the Israelis that we would go on, that my husband's message about his people would not be silenced. Somehow it was my way of continuing the struggle. My husband knew he would never go back to Palestine. But he hoped maybe the children would. So I continued his commitment to the children.

"Working on the Foundation was also a kind of psychological treatment, a time to heal from the terrible blow of my husband being killed. For me, it was essential to do this work. Not only for the children. But I think you cannot do work if it is not satisfying to you. This work with children is deeply meaningful to me."

During the war, one of the most difficult times for Kanafani was leaving the district of Achrafieh in East Beirut, where they had lived since 1966. She and Ghassan had established their home there, and had many close friends, both Moslem and Christian. But when the war began in 1975, her neighbors became increasingly worried that the predominantly Christian area would not be safe for her son, because he was Palestinian.

With heavy hearts she and her two children moved first to Kuwait for nine months, and then to Denmark. Feeling that she could no longer stay away from the work of the Foundation, she returned to Lebanon to live in West Beirut in 1977. The children also pressed her to return. The children had done well in the schools in Denmark, and had learned to speak Danish, but they missed their own schools and their friends in Lebanon.

In 1978, however, she decided that her son, Fayyuz, must return to Denmark. There were too many warning signs that as he grew older his life might be endangered in Lebanon. The war was intensifying, and she had foreboding premonitions. "My husband was killed by a car bomb. I couldn't risk anything happening to my son."

Fayyuz now questions if he should have left Lebanon. He feels he missed out on something important by not finishing his schooling there. Kanafani explained, "You never know as a parent if you are doing the right thing. You just have to decide based on the information and feelings you have at the time."

Another extraordinarily difficult time was the Israeli invasion of 1982. "We went on working, because of the children. We had to. People of Bourj Brajneh and Shatila Camps south of Beirut came together because they needed each other, and needed the sense of doing something for their children. We had to rehabilitate the kindergarten building in Sidon because the camp there had been flattened. We reopened by Christmas of 1982. Our kindergarten became a kind of oasis, a place for the women to come together, to bring their children.

"Mothers then were responsible for everything. The men were out. Either they had been killed, or had fled, or were in prison camps. We had about 400 children to whom we could not say 'NO.' We also had to repair the kindergarten in Mar Elias, Beirut, which we opened in 1981. The same in Rashediyeh, Tyre. These places symbolized hope and continuity of life for the people.

"In that period, there was good support from various nongovernmental organizations. Unfortunately, international charitable organizations operate like fashion. They all run to the same place at the same time, stumbling over each other's legs, and then their attention goes somewhere else. Until the end of the 1980s, we had good support. Now it is very difficult to find enough international financial aid."

How did your childhood prepare you for your life in Lebanon?

"My father and, to some degree, my mother were very active in movements for people's rights. My father was active in trade unions, in politics, in international affairs. He was also involved in resistance against the Germans. And even with all this involvement of my family, I was shocked to learn as a young adult that I knew nothing of the story of the Palestinian people.

"When I began to hear more about this, I decided I must come here and see for myself. Denmark suffered under German occupation for five years, and I remember that. There are many similarities with the situation now. I could understand the resistance fight against the Israelis because that is what we did against the Germans when we were occupied.

"What is wrong with the politicians who are waging war is that they have never attended a good kindergarten. Let them come to our kindergarten now; let them play in the sand, sing and dance, maybe they could learn to get along together!"

Several times Kanafani answered questions as if she were focusing through her eyeglasses on imaginary children in the room. On the question of the effect of change, she noted that children have amazing adaptability, and an ability to store memories somewhere until it is safe for them to playact them. They exorcise their frustrations through play, art, and drama.

What do you think is the power of the individual in changing society?

"We need to start with the children. Individuals can effect changes, but to get mass changes in society, we must dwell on the children's needs. They should be given freedom, but they can also learn about responsibility. We must let children learn from an early age about responsibility and about respect for themselves, their friends, the grown-ups."

How do you keep yourself from being discouraged?

"By my working with children; one has to go on. They need us. Most of my life I have been an optimistic person. I usually believe in the good things about people.

"Concerning the wars in the world, I feel pessimistic, because I think they are waged by a few strong males. They start a war here or there, and then they stop it when it suits them. All over the world surplus arms are being shipped from one country to another.

"I still do not believe that this war in Lebanon had anything to do with religion. We have to see the war in terms of whom it profited. I think all wars are fought to make money. Even Sweden and Switzerland are now big armaments-producing countries! We live in a world culture of violence and war."

As we spoke, a cacophony of loud firecrackers went off outside the living room window: children celebrating Ramadan (Muslim feast). This was followed by several window-rattling, ear-splitting explosions. Kanafani, however, never paused in her speech; it was as if nothing were happening. (On my tape recording the sounds were frighteningly like war.)

I asked, "Are those sonic booms?" "Oh yes, they are our neighbors from the South reminding us of their presence."

Our conversation was drawing to an end, and Kanafani spoke again of the closeness of people who live in Lebanon, and how it is different from many other places in the world.

"We must not give up hope here, because we cannot know what will happen, and we must work for changes that will bring a better life to our people."

Conclusion

These are the stories of six non-Lebanese women who remained in Lebanon during the war. We can see some commonalities among them. An obvious one is that they are all deeply involved in their work and have become successful in their careers. Secondly, they have formed their ties with Lebanon and its people through their family bonds, most through marriage, and one through parentage. Two women's husbands died in Lebanon, and yet they still chose to remain and live in Lebanon during the height of its war years.

However, in addition to these family bonds, the women found meaning and commitment in all of their significant relationships. These relationships seemed to be central to their decision to stay in Lebanon. We can see exemplified in these women the words of Jean Baker Miller: "If we study women's experience closely without attempting to force our observations into prior categories, we find that an inner sense of connection to others is a central organizing feature of women's development. I would summarize it briefly this way: women's sense of self and of worth tend to be grounded in the ability to make and maintain relationships."[5]

Another thread running through several women's narratives is their reservations about the negative effects of the war, not on themselves, but on their children. They maintained these reservations in spite of the fact that it was frequently the children who insisted on being nowhere but Lebanon. This may be quite akin to many parents who look back on their child-rearing experiences and question themselves about the benefits of their actions on their children.

Several women expressed their disappointment with Lebanese attitudes after the war. The closeness that citizens felt toward each other as they joined together to combat the trauma of war dissipated when the war was over. Instead of being involved as a community, the war's devastation forced them into individualistic concerns about economic security, and how to rebuild or regain some of what they had lost. A psychological principle about stress is observed here, in which an organism holds up during the stressful events in adequate fashion, only to collapse when the stressful events cease.

A sense of defiance pervaded as the war ground on year after year. In different words, each woman expressed her determination to continue living and working in spite of the madness of the war, and, in fact, as the only way they have to confront this madness.

This brings us to the existential framework presented in the introduction. The reader can see that these women are confronting alienation and meaninglessness in a life full of violence and absurdity by asserting themselves to be connected to others, to be faithful to those ties that bind them in this life, and to work for goals that are worthy of the deepest human yearnings. Not only can we see from their high scores on the "hardiness" inventories, but we can hear in their own words their sense of *commitment* to people and the environment, an involvement that moves far beyond Self.

Each of these hardy women has a wide circle of people in Lebanon whose lives have been touched by their efforts during this period of Lebanese history. We gain a clear perspective from the work and the lives of these six women the paths by which they could *control* their lives. And finally, we can see how they grasped from the jaws of war horror a *challenge* to live as creatively as possible, thus contributing to the eventual demise of the war itself.

The work and the lives of these six women are representative of many non-Lebanese women who remained in Lebanon. Such women stand with their fellow Lebanese who opposed those waging war, and gave hope to those struggling for peace.

Notes

1. Gunn, *A West Bank Memoir*; Stewart, *Toward a Feminist Strategy.*

2. Corey, *Theory and Practice of Counseling and Psychotherapy* (California: Brooks/Cole, 1991), 179.

3. J. R. Averill, "Personal Control over Aversive Stimuli and Its Relationship to Stress," *Psychological Bulletin* 80 (1973):286–303; S. C. Kobasa, S. R. Maddi, and S.

Kahn, "Hardiness and Health: A Prospective Study," *Journal of Personality and Social Psychology* 42, no. 1 (1982):168–77; S. C. Ouellete, L. Goldberger, and S. Breznitz, eds., *Handbook of Stress: Theoretical and Clinical Aspects,* 2nd ed. (New York: Free Press, 1993).

4. Kobasa et al., "Hardiness and Health."

5. Miller, *Toward a New Psychology of Women.*

VI

Psychological Sequelae

14

War Trauma and Women: Predisposition and Vulnerability to Adverse Psychological Health Outcomes

LEILA FARHOOD

The relationships between war stress and psychological impairment have been strongly documented.[1] Over the past decade, research on the epidemiology of disasters has emerged as an area of special interest. Wars and disasters are occurring more frequently around the world, causing damage and impairment on both the psychological and social levels. Disasters cause significant crises in human conditions and interest in studying their effect on health is a growing area. Increasing emphasis is being placed on understanding the impact of disasters. Such understanding is vital to improve the process of preparedness of populations, particularly, vulnerable groups and those at risk, and to minimize the negative effects of disasters. This paper, therefore, will describe the predisposition and vulnerability of women to adverse psychological conditions imposed by war trauma, and, in so doing, identify the salient risk factors.

The term *disaster* has most often been associated with sudden natural happenings, such as floods, earthquakes, hurricanes, storms, and drought caused by natural factors outside human control. The short-term and, to a lesser extent, the long-term health effects of natural disasters have been extensively studied and documented, particularly in terms of the mental health and psychological dimensions. Man-made disasters, such as wars and technological accidents, have generally been less studied. At present, the topic of war is viewed with rising interest by the scientific community. It is believed that war experiences provide material for research about the impact on life events and experiences, and about demographic changes occurring under such war conditions. During war times, exposure to stressful life experiences has been shown to be related to several somatic disorders,[2] as well as a wide range of psychiatric disorders like depression, anxiety, and poor interpersonal relations.[3]

In their review of literature, Logue, Melick, and Hansen (1981) pointed out that it is important to distinguish between natural and man-made disasters because each may be associated with different health problems. Man-made disasters, as such, might threaten the ecologic balance of the community. Also, war-related disasters produce long-term health sequelae. Among the symptoms of human-induced violence are guilt about victims, blame, hostility, and identification with the aggressor. Females are reported to have higher rates of depression and anxiety symptoms than males and an onset rate of psychological disorder approximately twice as high as that seen among men.[4]

Findings, in general, show that, although men and women do not differ greatly in their psychological reactions to war stress and in the number of stressful life events they experience, women are significantly more affected emotionally than men. Aubrey, in a descriptive study with a 2:1 ratio of women to men, found that one-third of all female patients seen complained of "neurotic disorders," whereas one fifth of the men did so.[5] Depression and anxiety were found to be aggravated in those persons who had damage to the home (58 percent) or no domestic shelter (74 percent). The author concluded that neurosis rarely occurs as a war phenomenon except in people who had been neurotic prior to the war. In another section of the same study, it was pointed out that total admissions to psychiatric hospitals were less frequent during wartime, the reduction being slightly greater among men (9 percent) than among women (7 percent). Another finding argued that children's symptoms depended, to a great extent, on their mothers' fears. Although the results were interesting, the study presented crude figures from hospitals and outpatient clinics. Similar results were reported by Hourani, Armenian, Zurayk, and Afifi in a sample of displaced and non-displaced civilians during the 1982 Israeli invasion of Lebanon.[6] Using the Red Cross checklist, individuals were asked to report symptoms of inappropriate or unusual behavior that had occurred only since the beginning of the invasion. Approximately 8.3 percent reported at least one symptom of psychological distress and unusual behavior. Females reported significantly higher symptomatology ($p < 0.05$), with the highest risk score being associated with loss of physical health and the second highest with being repeatedly displaced. The authors' report showed a relatively low incidence of psychological disorders during war. Loss of home and property was positively related to psychological distress. The study does not include male-female ratios or the types of hardship women were exposed to, rendering the findings about women's vulnerability as a whole poorly documented. Lyons reports women's vulnerability to stress in a sample where the ratio of women to men was 3:1.[7] Somatic symptoms, such as abdominal pain, chest oppression, headache, and sweating and trembling associated with feelings of anxiety, were reported. There were no psychotic symptoms or suicidal attempts. Insomnia and situational state anxiety were present in 68.7 percent of patients. There was a significant decrease of depressive illnesses, especially in men. The nature of the design, sampling method, ratio of women to men, and the lack of statistical analysis warn that the reported results should be interpreted with caution.

The psychological effects of adverse circumstances, such as depression and anxiety, were reported to persist over an extended period of time. Murphy concluded that women displayed higher levels of psychological disturbances and were more prone to depression than men. The author explained that the majority of his sample were women and children because men were either fighting or had been killed in action. This poses an important observation that the women of this sample had been overexposed to hassles of daily living, war separations, and excessive household responsibilities in addition to war stress.[8] Saigh points out that in addition to high levels of depression and anxiety, university students reported lower levels of assertiveness but did not develop post-traumatic stress disorder (PTSD) following exposure to war stress.[9] The small sample, restricted to fall semester female students, makes the results not representative of the general female population.

The psychological effects of the adverse reactions to war stress do not only persist over an extended period of time but, as Rosenbeck points out, go on throughout life and into the next generation.[10] The psychological scars of post-traumatic stress disorder were evidenced in the offspring of World War II veterans.

The impact on children's psychological functioning was, to a large extent, dependent on the mothers' psychological health. Bryce points out that depression in mothers was associated with increased morbidity among five-to seven-year-old children. This finding is very important; it focuses attention on the fact that women are not only vulnerable to stressful events but transmit such vulnerability to their children.[11] Older children seem to cope more actively with war stress and have fewer psychological symptoms. Bodman reports that these psychological symptoms occurred twice as often in the five- to seven-year-old group as in the eleven- to fourteen-year-old group.[12] Punamaki also supports the finding that older children showed more active, purposeful, and cognitive coping modes than younger children and girls. In addition, girls expressed more fears than boys.[13]

In another study of Beirut women, Bryce found that the number of environmental problems, levels of crowding, and the number of children under the age of fifteen at home correlated positively with increased levels of depressive symptoms among women. Educational levels and household income were negatively correlated with women's score on the Beck Depression Index (BDI), indicating that women with higher levels of income or education reported fewer depressive symptoms. Women's depression was predicted by emotional coping, life experiences relative to problems in interpersonal relationships, and social coping. Results suggest that events associated with the ongoing war in Lebanon were not strongly linked to depressive symptoms. These findings are similar to what Farhood et al. (1993) reported in a study of a random sample of Beirut families.[14]

Farhood et al. pointed out that anxiety and physical symptoms were reported by both males and females but females tended to have higher levels especially in the twenty-nine to fifty-nine age groups. Reports of lower back pain tended to be higher in the male forty to fifty-nine age groups. The study's findings are noteworthy because both women and men seem to have been aggravated by acts of war and were equally susceptible to depression. However, men tend to report fewer symptoms of depression and more behavioral symptoms of psychosomatic nature.

B.L. Green's study included female gender as one risk factor for developing post-traumatic stress disorder.[15] Also, the community study by Norris showed that women were more vulnerable than men to develop PTSD following exposure to a traumatic event.[16] This study also reported that younger, rather than older, subjects were at higher risk of PTSD.

The most striking characteristic of the review of literature on the impact of war on the psychological functioning of women is that research has not addressed women's issues of psychosocial concerns. The current state of research on war-related disasters does not provide a holistic model with a clear body of knowledge that will guide sound practice for the physical and emotional well-being of women and other war victims. It is important to point out, here, that, in general, and, in nonwar settings, depression and anxiety disorders have been highlighted as key mental health issues for women: Unipolar depression is twice as common in women as in men.[17] Women also develop anxiety disorders at two to three times the rate for men.[18] Symptoms of anxiety and depression motivate women to seek medical and psychiatric care and are a leading cause for the consumption of minor tranquilizers by women.

Despite this fact, little is known about gender-related features and mechanisms.

The reviewed research sheds light on war-related stressors highlighting the vulnerability of women; the findings are not different from other nonwar findings on gender and mental health. The findings indicate a need for further investigation on the impact of war on women, taking into account personal as well as social factors that mediate the outcome of stress. This is especially important in light of the changing role of women during wartime. In a study of seventy-two middle-class families in Beirut, results point out the changing role of women with respect to patterns of decision making, values, and attitudes about sexuality.[19] Over 90 percent of the interviewed sample believed that women's role changed positively by sharing responsibility with the husband or by being solely responsible for the family while the husband was away. Women were left behind to support the family financially by entering the work field.

The following section presents the findings of three studies conducted in Beirut. Although the sample is comprised of both men and women, this paper focuses on the impact of stressful life events on women with its subsequent health outcome. The first study examined a community sample, the second focused on patients seeking psychiatric care, and the third, a traumatized sample with community controls.

Study I

This is a study assessing and predicting health outcome in 1,053 randomly selected subjects (525 mothers, 413 fathers, and 115 adolescents) in Beirut.[20] The following findings were reported.

Prevalence of Physical Symptoms

The sample studied showed considerable prevalence of somatization (table 14.1). Headache was the most frequently reported symptom for both males and females. This was followed by problems in the immunological system, particularly runny nose. Problems in the musculoskeletal system also appear as frequently. For most complaints, more than one-fourth of the individuals reported severe occurrence. It is important to note that, with few exceptions, mothers and adolescent females reported a higher prevalence of complaints than fathers and male adolescents, respectively, with some of these differences reaching statistical significance. For mothers and fathers, the age pattern varies across complaints. However, a significant age pattern was observed only for some complaints reported by mothers.

Table 14.1. Reporting physical symptoms, by gender (in percentages)

	Adolescents					
	M	F	P	Father	Mother	P
Headache	63.5	80.2	—	69.7	80.2	*
Faintness, dizziness	10.4	32.1	*	18.6	33.0	*
Pain in heart or chest	10.4	13.2	—	22.3	20.0	—
Muscle pain	14.8	27.4	*	32.0	41.3	*
Low back or neck pain	25.2	32.1	—	36.3	53.1	*
Constipation	21.7	24.5	—	20.6	24.2	—
Diarrhea	25.2	27.4	—	19.6	16.8	—
Nausea	15.7	38.7	*	10.9	23.6	—
Vomiting	8.7	27.4	*	5.6	13.1	*
Shortness of breath	22.6	39.6	*	27.8	38.5	*
Pharyngitis	28.7	33.0	—	19.9	23.5	*
Running nose	70.4	68.9	—	56.4	52.4	—
Allergic reactions	9.6	25.5	*	16.5	21.3	—
Eye strain	18.3	24.5	—	16.5	25.3	*
Number	115	106		413	525	

*$P = 0.01$.

Prevalence of Mental Health Symptoms

Of the total number of individuals questioned about psychological symptoms (1,159), 115 (9.9 percent) were diagnosed as *clinically depressed* using the criteria of duration and number of symptoms occurring together as specified in the measurement of the concept of *depression*. Detailed results show that adolescent females have a higher rate of depression than adolescent males, as do mothers in comparison to fathers (table 14.2). However, these differences were not significant. Differences in age pattern for mothers and fathers were also not significant. It may be worth noting, nevertheless, that the highest rate of depression, 13.8 percent, was attained by females forty to fifty-nine years of age.

Table 14.2 provides the prevalence rates of *depressive symptoms*. Insomnia, loss of interest and pleasure, and unusual fatigue were the most prevalent reported symptoms for all age and sex groups, reaching close to 50 percent for most groups. Most symptoms showed a higher prevalence among adolescent females than adolescent males, and among mothers as compared to fathers. This was very notable with regard to the symptoms of "poor appetite," "crying easily," "loss of interest and pleasure," and "feeling sad and lonely." Only insomnia showed a significant pattern by age for mothers, with a peak at the forty to fifty-nine age group.

Table 14.2. Reporting depressive symptoms, by gender (in percentages)

	Adolescents					
	M	F	*P*	Father	Mother	*P*
Poor appetite	18.3	39.6	**	23.7	31.4	**
Increased appetite	28.7	19.8	—	10.4	11.2	—
Loss of weight	16.5	27.4	—	19.6	27.6	**
Increased weight	19.1	15.1	—	9.6	11.6	—
Crying easily	8.7	60.4	**	14.5	46.3	**
Loss of interest and pleasure	28.7	51.9	**	45.7	54.1	*
Blaming oneself	20.0	31.1	—	21.5	24.0	—
Feeling sad and lonely	24.3	53.8	**	35.1	49.3	**
Feeling hopeless about future	17.4	20.8	—	23.2	28.6	—
Insomnia	27.8	50.0	**	48.9	53.1	—
Hypersomnia	19.1	19.8	—	11.6	10.9	—
Nightmares	10.4	17.1	—	11.6	17.2	*
Inability to concentrate	26.1	48.1	**	34.1	35.0	—
Inability to make decisions easily	20.0	43.4	**	29.1	33.0	—
Fatigue more than usual	31.3	41.5	—	47.5	59.0	**
Thought about death or suicide	7.0	15.2	*	3.9	5.9	—
Number	115	106		413	525	

*$P = 0.05$.
**$P = 0.01$.

As for *psychological symptoms* other than depression (table 14.3), nervousness was the most prevalent complaint reported by 70 percent or more of all age and sex groups. Moreover, almost 50 percent of the subjects reported this symptom as severe. A majority of mothers and fathers suffered from forgetfulness, as well as a substantial proportion of adolescents. The general pattern, by sex, was maintained with adolescent females reporting higher levels than adolescent males, and mothers, higher than fathers; most of these differences were statistically significant. Age did not exhibit any pattern.

As for war stress and health outcome, multiple regression analysis revealed that social class and social support were found important, especially for women. These important predictors were found to mediate in the impact of stress on depression and in providing strength in marital relationships. Additionally, the effect of nonwar events on health were introduced as control variables. These *nonwar-related life events* impacted all the dimensions of the health outcome for the mother, but only depression and marital relations for the father, and depression and physical symptoms for the adolescent. In addition, the *sex* variable showed a significant effect in adolescents, reflecting the greater vulnerability of females. Age

Table 14.3. Reporting psychological symptoms, by gender (percentages)

	Adolescents					
	M	F	P	Father	Mother	P
Nervousness	69.6	78.3	—	81.4	82.5	—
Trembling	14.8	26.4	*	23.5	34.1	**
Heart pounding	16.5	31.1	**	26.4	36.8	**
Feeling fearful	18.3	40.6	**	21.3	38.5	**
Sudden scare	10.4	28.3	**	12.1	26.5	**
Avoiding activities and places	23.5	37.7	*	20.8	35.0	**
Forgetfulness	39.1	45.3	**	62.0	70.5	**
Number	115	106		413	525	

* $P = 0.05$.
** $P = 0.01$.

was not significantly related to health outcome for adolescents, mothers, and fathers. In terms of differentials, depression was more prevalent in females, reaching its highest level in the forty to fifty-nine age group. The greater vulnerability of females in the face of stress is again demonstrated when looking at the detailed *psychological* or anxiety symptoms as indicators of mental well-being and recognized consequences of stress. High reporting of such symptomatology, particularly among females, is observed. Moreover, a large proportion report severity of complaints for many conditions, particularly nervousness and forgetfulness. These two conditions are the highest reported by males. It may be easier for males in the Lebanese culture to admit to these symptoms than to other symptoms that may seem to reflect weakness.

The high level of psychological symptoms observed is clearly linked to the war conditions in Lebanon. The family's experience with *war-related events* was shown to be significantly associated with psychological symptoms for the mother, father, and the adolescents in the family. Other aspects of the war were also significantly associated with psychological symptoms for the mother and adolescents. For young people, war stress seemed to manifest itself most widely in psychological symptoms.

Study II

In this study, a survey was conducted in Beirut with 364 patients seeking psychiatric help.[21] The survey findings describe patterns of mental illness in clinic attendance. In addition, study results show that there was a significant relationship between gender and diagnosis. A higher proportion of females than males reported that they were depressed (41.7 percent and 28.4 percent, $X^2 = 13, P = 0.011$). The pattern is the same for all age groups (table 14.4). As for anxiety, psychotic disorders, and personality disorders, the difference between males and females was small and not significant (table 14.5).

Results presented in table 14.5 show a rising trend in depression with increase in age for both males and females, especially after the age of thirty. Anxiety reaches a peak at the 30–39 age group and another peak at above age fifty for males. The peak for females is at the twenty to twenty-nine age group. Psychotic disorders show a decrease after age forty for both males and females.

For both sexes, the ever-married had a higher prevalence of depression than the single (table 14.6). Ever-married males showed similar proportions of anxiety to the single males. Single females showed more anxiety than ever-married females. Single males and females showed a higher incidence of psychotic disorders than the married ones, although the difference was not striking for females.

Marriage seems to have a protective role for males but a detrimental effect for females. This may be due to the stressful situations caused by the women's role and responsibilities, especially those related to looking after children and family chores. Being divorced, separated, or widowed is also, as expected, associated with higher rates of psychiatric illnesses in both sexes. There were, in fact, few separated, divorced, and widowed persons in the sample. The relationship of marital status to risk for psychotic diseases has been repeatedly reported in the literature.[22] Single sub-

Table 14.4. Distribution of sample by type of diagnosis and by gender

	Male		Female		Total	
	N	%	*N*	%	*N*	%
Depression	42	(28.4)	88	(41.7)	130	(36.2)
Anxiety	16	(10.8)	26	(12.3)	42	(11.7)
Psychotic disorders	32	(21.6)	49	(23.2)	81	(22.6)
Personality disorders	9	(6.1)	10	(4.7)	19	(5.3)
Substance abuse	12	(8.1)	—	—	12	(3.3)
Mental retardation	10	(6.8)	3	(1.4)	13	(3.6)
Adolescent crisis	2	(1.4)	5	(2.4)	7	(1.9)
Others	7	(4.7)	9	(4.3)	16	(4.5)
Unspecified	18	(12.2)	21	(10.0)	39	(10.9)
Total	148		211		359	

$X^2 = 13; P = 0.011.$

Table 14.5. Distribution of sample by type of diagnosis, gender, and age (in percentages)

		<19	20–29	30–39	40–49	50+	Total
Depression	M	4.5	25.6	32.0	50.0	47.6	30.5
	F	5.6	35.6	47.2	53.1	62.5	43.3
Anxiety	M	4.5	7.0	12.0	5.6	13.0	8.4
	F	—	25.4	9.4	9.4	6.3	12.9
Psychotic disorders	M	18.2	25.6	32.0	11.1	8.7	20.6
	F	27.8	23.7	22.6	18.8	12.5	21.1
Personality disorders	M	9.1	11.6	4.0	—	4.3	6.9
	F	5.6	5.1	5.7	6.3	—	4.6
Other	M	63.3	30.2	20.0	33.3	26.1	33.6
	F	61.1	10.2	15.1	12.5	18.8	18.0
Total	M	22	43	25	18	23	131
	F	18	59	53	32	32	194

Table 14.6. Distribution of sample by diagnosis, gender, and marital status (in percentages)

		Marital status		
		Ever married	Single	Total
Depression	M	46.7	25.4	31.7
	F	48.5	38.5	44.6
Anxiety	M	10.0	9.9	9.9
	F	12.6	15.4	13.7
Psychotic disorders	M	10.0	21.1	17.8
	F	19.4	20.0	19.6
Personality disorders	M	—	9.9	6.9
	F	5.8	6.2	6.0
Other	M	33.3	33.8	33.7
	F	13.6	20.0	16.1
Total	M	30	71	101
	F	103	65	168

jects were at a higher risk for psychoses than married ones. This was explained by the fact that the onset of psychotic illnesses lessens the probability of marriage.

Study III

This study assessed the effects of stressors on post-traumatic stress disorders, depression, and health status in a sample consisting of Lebanese civilians one year after being exposed to a church explosion and of a control group.[23]

Ninety-three subjects (33 victims, 30 family controls, and 30 neighboring controls) were assessed for stressors experienced, PTSD, depression, health status, social support, and other mediating factors. Findings indicate that, in the victims group, 39 percent met PTSD diagnostic criteria, 51 percent were depressed, and 45 percent reported deterioration in their health status. These results were significantly higher than in the control groups. Logistic regression revealed that victims were twelve times and females seven times more at risk of developing PTSD. Females and those with limited social support were three times more at risk for developing depression. Victims were seven times more at risk to develop health status deterioration. No difference in health status was noted between males and females .

Summary

The above studies attest to the negative impact of war and its subsequent stressors on both men and women. Although individuals do not differ greatly in their psychological reaction to war stress and in the number of stressful life events they experience, women are significantly more affected than men. Women seem to live the experience and perceive it more intensely and closer to their proximity. Also, women tend to report their symptoms and express their feelings more freely than men. This is especially true in the Lebanese culture, where men assume the "Male Role," refraining from expressing their emotional pains and fears. The higher risk to females for depression, anxiety, and PTSD is attributed to females' role in assuming responsibility for the household and family chores.

The above findings should draw the attention of clinicians and those working in the public and health sectors to provide strategies for the mental health needs of the Lebanese population, particularly women and those at risk. Support and awareness programs aiming at educating the public, restoring community services, preventing breakdown of individuals, and providing counseling programs are drastically needed.

Notes

1. Logue, Melick, and Hansen, "Research Issues and Directions," 373–93.

2. Farhood, Zurayk, Chaya, Saadeh, Meshefedejian, and Sidani, "The Impact of War," 1555–67; R. Finlay-Jones and G. Brown, "Types of Stressful Life Events and the Onset of Anxiety and Depressive Disorders," *Psychological Medicine* 11 (1981):803–15.

3. Bryce, Walker, Ghorayeb, and Kanj, "Life Experiences," 685–95; H. McCubbin, D. Joy, A. Cauble, J. Comeau, J. Patterson, and R. Needle, "Family Stress, Coping and Social Support: A Decade Review," *Journal of Marriage and the Family* 42 (1980):855–71; D. Mueler, D. Edwards, and C. Patients, "Stressful Life Events and Community Mental Health," *Journal of Nervous and Mental Disorders* 166, no. 1 (1978):16–24; J. Rabkin and E. Streuening, "Life Events, Stress and Illness," *Science* 914 (1976):1013–19.

4. Betrus, Elmore, and Hamilton, "Women and Somatization," 287–97.

5. L. Aubrey, "Incidence of Neurosis in England under War Conditions," *LANCET* 2 (1941):175–83.

6. Hourani, Armenian, Zurayk, and Afifi, "Psychological Distress during War," 269–75.

7. H. A. Lyons, "Civil Violence, the Psychological Aspects," *Journal of Psychosomatic Research* 23 (1979):373–93.

8. J. Murphy, "War Stress and Civilian Vietnamese: A Study of Psychological Effects," *Acta Psychiatrica Scandinavica* 56 (1977):92–108.

9. P. Saigh, "Anxiety, Depression and Assertion across Alternating Intervals of Stress," *Journal of Abnormal Psychology* 97, no. 3 (1988):338–41.

10. R. Rosenbeck, "Impact of Post Traumatic Stress Disorder of World War II on the Next Generation," *The Journal of Nervous and Mental Disorders* 174, no. 6 (1986): 319–27.

11. Aubrey, "Incidence of Neurosis in England," 175–83; Bryce, Walker, Ghorayeb, and Kanj, "Life Experiences," 685–95.

12. Bodman, "War Conditions and Mental Health," 486–88.

13. R. L. Punamaki, "Historical-Political and Individualistic Determinants of Coping Modes and Fears Among Palestinian Children," *International Journal of Psychology* 23 (1988):721–39.

14. Farhood, Zurayk, Chaya, Saadeh, Meshefedejian, and Sidani, "The Impact of War," 1555–67.

15. J. Shore, E. Taturn, and W. Vollmer, "Evaluation of Mental Effect of Disaster," *American Journal of Public Health* 76, suppl. (Mount St. Helens Eruption, 1986): 76–83.

16. F. H. Norris, "Epidemiology of Trauma: Frequency and Impact of Different

Potentially Traumatic Events on Different Demographic Groups," *Journal of Consult. Clinical Psychology* 60 (1922):409–18.

17. J. Hamilton, M. Grant, and M. Jensvold, "Sex Treatment of Depression," in *Psychopharmacology and Women*, ed. M. Jensvold et al. (Washington, D.C.: American Psychiatric Press Inc., 1996).

18. K. Yonkers and J. Ellison, "Anxiety Disorders in Women and Their Pharmacological Treatment," in *Psychopharmacology and Women*, ed. M. Jensvold et al.

19. L. Farhood, "Family Structure."

20. Farhood, Zurayk, Chaya, Saadeh, Meshefedjian, and Sidani, "The Impact of War."

21. L. Farhood, M. Chaya, and J. Madi-Skaff, "Description of Patterns of Mental Illness from Psychiatrists' Caseload as They Relate to a Stressful War Situation," *Arab Journal of Psychiatry 8*, no. 2 (1997):87–98.

22. L. Farhood and S. Noureddine, "PTSD, Depression and Health Status in Lebanese Civilians Exposed to a Church Explosion" (forthcoming).

23. Ibid.

15

Women and the Lebanon Wars: Depression and Post-Traumatic Stress Disorder

Elie G. Karam

It is frequently thought that wars are fought and initiated by men; we do not have a satisfactory explanation for this behavior nor do we know how wars fit into the schema of securing the continuity of the species. On the other hand, and throughout history, women have not, to our knowledge, participated directly and in any significant way in war. Their role, be it symbolic, unconscious, or supportive, has frequently been brought up in battles for the protection of the "mother" land. The role of mothers in "offering" their sons as martyrs has come into the spotlight in recent wars.[1] How much women participate in creating and sustaining the fighter role of males will be an ongoing debate.

Participation in the Military

Military participation of women during the internal phase of the Lebanon wars (1975–90) has not been exhaustively studied, but our field research has yielded a maximum figure of 3.4 percent, which corresponds to the female population of what was called "the green line" areas of Beirut, normally the confrontation lines. Not to be forgotten, however, and, for comparison, 63 percent of the male population of that same area had an active role in the military.[2]

In the three other Lebanese communities we studied over the years, the figures were the following: 0.8 percent of females versus 8.7 percent of males in Bejjeh, ratio of males to females, 10:1; 2.2 percent of females versus 21.0 percent of males in Kornet Shehwan, ratio of males to females, 10:1; 0.2 percent of females versus 37.3 percent of males in Achrafieh, ratio of males to females, 200:1.

Exposure to War

In a large study conducted by our group at St. George Hospital with funds from the U.S. National Institute of Mental Health (NIMH) and the Institute for Development Research and Applied Care (IDRAC), we constructed a questionnaire to evaluate the exposure of the individual Lebanese to war events: These ranged from shrapnel injury without major property destruction to loss of life. We also investigated the effect of the degree of witnessing these war events (destruction of property, kidnapping, physical injuries, and other events). The War Events Questionnaire (WEQ)[3] was passed to 658 subjects randomly selected from four communities: Ain Rimmaneh, Achrafieh, Kornet Shehwan, and Bejjeh. The WEQ has a very good test-retest reliability. These four communities were chosen deliberately to represent differential exposure to war, and all fall within the eastern (Christian) sector of the country.[4]

Each event was given a specific numerical weight that reflected the following: (1) the victim (interviewer or someone close to him/her); (2) the event itself—physical injury and its degree, destruction of property and its degree, kidnapping and its specifics; (3) the witnessing effect, that is, the proximity of the subject to the event when the latter took place.

There was no difference between males and females in the degree of their exposure to war if only civilians who did not participate in the war were compared. However, this was different in 1990, the last year of the internal chapter of the Lebanon wars, with males reporting much more exposure than females.

Depression and War

There are numerous peacetime epidemiological studies across the world, yielding lifetime prevalences of depression (see appendix 15.A) ranging from less than 1 percent to more than 20 percent.[5] If Northern Ireland is a possible, yet remote, comparison to the situation in Lebanon, some studies,[6] but not others,[7] indicate that there might have been a decrease of depressive illness in civilians exposed to "war."

In Phases I and II of our longitudinal study of war and mental health, we used a structured interview: the Arabic Diagnostic Interview Schedule,[8] which was adapted to Arabic from the original English Diagnostic Interview Schedule (DIS).[9] This is one of the most widely used instruments in large epidemiologic studies[10] and can be used to diagnose several mental health disorders, including depression.

Our prospective study of the Lebanese communities has had three phases:

Phase I. Up to 1989: A retrospective study covering the prewar years and the Lebanon wars up to 1989.

Phase II. 1990: This corresponds to the year when the fiercest battles occurred in Lebanon and was the last internal military chapter of the Lebanon wars.

Phase III. 1991–94: This corresponds to the immediate post-"internal" war chapters.

A review of depression in women,[11] drawing on several studies from the United States, Canada, Puerto Rico, Italy, Taiwan, New Zealand, South Korea, France, Germany, and Lebanon, indicates that females were universally more affected than males (table 15.1), with a tendency for the age onset of major depression to be younger for females in some of the sites, including Lebanon (table 15.2).

The instrument used in Phase III is the Arabic Composite International Diagnostic Interview,[12] which our group adapted to Arabic from the original English version[13] (NCSR grant). This instrument allows the researchers, in large epidemiologic studies, to diagnose a large array of mental disorders using two systems of classification: the *Diagnostic Statistical Manual* (3rd ed., revised)(*DSM-III-R*), the American system,[14] and the tenth version of the *International Classification of Diseases* (*ICD-10*), the World Health Organization system.[15]

The lifetime rates we have obtained are quite elevated but what is more striking are the Phase II findings. It is to be remembered that Phase II is a prospective study covering one year only. The rates are quite high: 1990 was a year of constant strife, from January 31 to October 14, with heavy destruction of both the supra- and infrastructures. Both males and females have equally elevated one-year prevalence: This is different from Phase I (lifetime prevalence up to Phase II) and from what is reported internationally (see above). It is possible that this is due to the extreme stress that both males and females were exposed to. Indeed the total war score of just one year (1990) was about half of the preceding fifteen years of war. (See table 15.1.)

Theoretically, this would mean that the whole population of males and females who could ever develop depression had been "recruited." This concept has to be proven, but we believe that it is quite possible that the differential rates of depression in males and females in other studies could be due to the "differentially" lower stressors to which males are

Table 15.1. Gender and war score

	Males	Females
Phase I*	6,369	4,835
Phase II**	4,085	1,475

*$P = 0.9132$.
**$P = 0.000$.

exposed. In other words, if the stressors are both elevated and acutely so, one would not find any sex differences in the prevalence of depression: Males have been pushed to the maximum; females reached it long before (partially due to a higher baseline female to male ratio in depression). This is what we have come to call, in our departmental seminars, extreme situations. These situations made us witness civilians engaging in fierce fighting, sniping, and other wartime activities, although they were quite peaceful citizens only days before fighting had broken out.

A decrease in the rates of depression is observed in Phase III as compared to Phases I and II. The rates in Phase III correspond to the period extending from 1991 to 1994, the year the study was conducted, and, thus, correspond to the immediate post-"internal" wars era.

In an effort to delineate the role of war in the genesis of depression in Phase I, the following factors were analyzed: gender, age, marital status, level of education, involvement in the military, prewar existence of depression, and exposure to war. The following factors were found to be significant: (1) prewar depression; (2) exposure to war; and (3) marriage (for females).

Factors 1 and 3, above, have been described widely in the literature.[16] Factor 2, exposure to war, although suspected theoretically, has been proven beyond doubt in the Lebanon wars study, keeping in mind that the instruments were internationally recognized and that the population was sampled randomly.

Post-Traumatic Stress Disorder

Post-traumatic stress disorder (PTSD) is one of the mental health disorders already recognized to occur after experiencing trauma (including war). In fact, there is no PTSD if there is no identifiable trauma. This disorder can be quite severe and difficult to treat, and, at times, resistant to most forms of intervention.[17] It has been studied in various settings and communities.[18]

Obviously the rates of PTSD vary with the studied populations and with the intensity and nature of the trauma.

We studied PTSD retrospectively until 1989 (Phase I) and prospectively in 1990 (Phase II) (table 15.2).

The risk of developing PTSD was as high in 1990 as it was in the previous fifteen years, again reflecting the intensity of the 1990 chapter of the Lebanon wars (8.9 percent versus 7.5 percent for females). There are no gender differences here, as is true for the risk of depression (6.1 percent and 4.2 percent for males for one year, 1990, and lifetime, respectively). In fact, PTSD is supposed to unveil a different failure in the coping mechanism of an individual. Depression is thought to be linked to loss or entrapment or despair, best illustrated by the loss of a loved one.[19] PTSD is associated with trauma, which is more a threat to one's physical integrity that is so extreme that it reminds us of our inevitable mortality.[20]

As with depression, and, in the studied population (age above eighteen), age was not a determining factor in the occurrence of PTSD: The 18–29, 30–44, and 45–65 age groups yielded comparable levels of PTSD ($p = 0.2827$, in Phase I and $p = 0.3538$ in Phase II). The symptoms of PTSD can be found on pages 278–79.

It is to be noted here that comorbidity of major depression and PTSD is well known, especially if the loss (loved one) occurs in a traumatic setting (the Lebanon wars). We have investigated that issue[21] and found that 40 percent of individuals with bereavement-related depression had PTSD, too, in Phase II.

Consequences of Depression and PTSD on Women's Health

The consequences of the above-studied disorders can be catastrophic. The extreme consequence is suicide. (Thinking of suicide in Phase I and Phase II were 6.7 percent and 3.8 percent, respectively, and attempting suicide in Phase I and Phase II, 2.7 percent and 0.4 percent, respectively.) Other known consequences or comorbidities are substance abuse and severe home environmental and professional disruptions, reflecting a major impact on quality of life. This becomes even more serious when we remember that women hold the primary role of education and care of children in

Table 15.2. Gender and post-traumatic stress disorder (in percentages)

	Males	Females
Phase I* (Lifetime up to 1989)	4.2	7.5
Phase II** (year 1990)	6.1	8.9

*$P = 0.745$
**$P = 0.857$

Lebanese society. Role modeling, cognitive learning,[22] and basic affective and scholastic needs are heavily affected by these two disorders. Marital disharmony is also a direct consequence of these two disorders with the general picture of hopelessness, irritability, decrease in interests and sharing, constricted affect, and loss of energy.

Conclusion

Depression and PTSD invaded the mental health of Lebanese women during the Lebanon wars. The consequences of these disorders are devastating to the individual, the family, and society at large. The recognition of these disorders is of pressing importance with a chance of recovery in most cases of depression and with some hope of relief for PTSD. Women have shared, with their mates, the burden of these man-made disasters and their offspring will undoubtedly pay a heavy price for them.

Appendix 15.A

DSM-IV

American Psychiatric Association, *Diagnostic and Statistical Manual of Mental Disorders*, 4th ed. (Washington, D.C.: American Psychiatric Association, 1994).

I. Depression

A. Presence of a single Major Depressive Episode.

B. The Major Depressive Episode is not better accounted for by Schizoaffective Disorder and is not superimposed on Schizophrenia, Schizophreniform Disorder, Delusional Disorder, or Psychotic Disorder Not Otherwise Specified.

C. There has never been a Manic Episode, a Mixed Episode, or a Hypomanic Episode. Note: This exclusion does not apply if all of the manic-like, mixed-like, or hypomanic-like episodes are substance or treatment induced or are due to the direct physiological effects of a general medical condition.

Appendix 15.B

DSM-IV

American Psychiatric Association, *Diagnostic and Statistical Manual of Mental Disorders*, 4th ed. (Washington, D.C.: American Psychiatric Association, 1994).

Post-Traumatic Stress Disorder

A. The person has been exposed to a traumatic event in which both of the following were present:

(1) The person experienced, witnessed, or was confronted with an event or events that involved actual or threatened death or serious injury, or a threat to the physical integrity of self or others.

(2) The person's response involved intense fear, helplessness, or horror. Note: In children, this may be expressed instead by disorganized or agitated behavior.

B. The traumatic event is persistently reexperienced in one (or more) of the following ways:

(1) Recurrent and intrusive distressing recollections of the event, including images, thoughts, or perceptions. Note: In young children, repetitive play may occur in which themes or aspects of the trauma are expressed.

(2) Recurrent distressing dreams of the event. Note: In children, there may be frightening dreams without recognizable content.

(3) Acting or feeling as if the traumatic event were recurring (includes a sense of reliving the experience, illusions, hallucinations, and dissociative flashback episodes, including those that occur on awakening or when intoxicated). Note: In young children, trauma-specific reenactment may occur.

(4) Intense psychological distress at exposure to internal or external cues that symbolize or resemble an aspect of the traumatic event.

(5) Physiological reactivity on exposure to internal or external cues that symbolize or resemble an aspect of the traumatic event.

C. Persistent avoidance of stimuli associated with the trauma and numbing of general responsiveness (not present before the trauma), as indicated by three (or more) of the following:

(1) Efforts to avoid thoughts, feelings, or conversations associated with the trauma.

(2) Efforts to avoid activities, places, or people that arouse recollections of the trauma.

(3) Inability to recall an important aspect of the trauma.

(4) Markedly diminished interest or participation in significant activities.

(5) Feeling of detachment or estrangement from others.

(6) Restricted range of affect (e.g., unable to have loving feelings).

(7) Sense of a foreshortened future (e.g., does not expect to have a career, marriage, children, or a normal life span).

D. Persistent symptoms of increased arousal (not present before the trauma), as indicated by two (or more) of the following:

(1) Difficulty falling or staying asleep.
(2) Irritability or outbursts of anger.
(3) Difficulty concentrating.
(4) Hypervigilance.
(5) Exaggerated startle response.

E. Duration of the disturbance (symptoms in Criteria B, C, and D) is more than one month.

F. The disturbance causes clinically significant distress or impairment in social, occupational, or other important areas of functioning.

Author's note: This study was supported partially by an NIMH grant (NIMH # R03 MH44978-01 and 1R03MH48887-01), by the Lebanese National Council of Scientific Research (NCSR), and by a grant from the Institute for Development, Research and Applied Care (IDRAC). The author would like to thank Mr. John Jabbour for his help in biostatistical work.

Notes

1. Philip Aractunji, *Le regard des mères* (movie), produced and directed in 1992, Beirut, Lebanon.

2. E. G. Karam, "Dépression et guerres du Liban. Methodologie d'une recherche," *Annales de Pscyhologie et des Sciences de l'Éducation* (Beirut: St. Joseph University, 1992): 99–106 .

3. E. G. Karam, R. Atrash, S. Saliba, N. Melhem, and D. Howard, "The War Events Questionnaire," *Social Psychiatry and Psychiatric Epidemiology* (in press, 1999).

4. E. G. Karam, D. B. Howard, A. N. Karam, A. Ashkar, M. Shaaya, and N. el-Khoury, "Major Depression and External Stressors: The Lebanon Wars," *European Archives of Psychiatry Clinical Neuro-Sciences* 148 (1998):225–30.

5. L. N. Robins, J. E. Helzer, M. M. Weissman, H. Orvaschel, E. Gruenberg, J. D Burke, and D. A. Regier, "Lifetime Prevalence of Specific Psychiatric Disorders in Three Sites," *Archives of General Psychiatry* 41, no. 1 (1984):949–58; J. K. Myers, M. M. Weissman, G. L. Tischler, et al., "The Prevalence of Psychiatric Disorders in Three Communities," *Archives of General Psychiatry* 41, no. 7 (1984):959–67; M. M. Weissman, P. J. Leaf, G. L. Tischler, D. G. Blazer, M. Karno, M. L. Bruce, and L. P. Florio, "Affective Disorders in Five U.S. Communities," *Psychological Medicine* 18 (1988):141–54; K. C. Lee, Y. S. Kovak, and G. Rhee, "The National Epidemiological

Study of Mental Disorders," *Korean Medical Science* 2 (1987):19–34; G. J. Canino, H. R. Bird, P. E. Schrout, et. al., "The Prevalence of Specific Psychiatric Disorders in Puerto Rico," *Archives of General Psychiatry* 44 (August 1987):727–35; M. M. Weissman, J. K. Myers, and P. Harding, "Psychiatric Disorders in a U.S. Urban Community 1975–1976," *American Journal of Psychiatry* 135, pt. 1 (1978):459–62; M. M. Weissman and J. H. Boyd, "The Epidemiology of Affective Disorders, Rates and Risk Factors," in *American Psychiatric Association Annual Review,* ed. L. Grinspoon, American Psychiatric Press, no. 2 (Washington, D.C.: American Psychiatric Press, 1982), 406–28; Bebbington, "The Epidemiology of Depressive Disorders," *Cultural Medical Psychiatry* 2 (1978):297–341; C. Bland Roger, "Depression and Dysthymias in the Americas" (paper presented at the World Psychiatric Association Regional Symposium, Washington, D.C., October 13–16, 1989); Sally W. Vernon and Robert E. Roberts, "Use of the SADC-RDC in a Tri-Ethnic Community Survey," *Archives of General Psychiatry* 39, no. 1 (January 1982):47–52; M. A. Robert Hirschfeld and K. Christine Cross, "Epidemiology of Affective Disorders, Psychosocial Risk Factors," *Archives of General Psychiatry* 39, no. 1 (1982): 35–46; R. C. Bland, H. Orn, and S. C. Newman, "Lifetime Prevalence of Psychiatric Disorders in Edmonton," *Acta Psychiatrica Scandinavica* 77, suppl. 338 (1988):24–32; R. Garcia-Alvarez, "Epidemiology of Depression in Latin America," *Psychopathology* 19, suppl. 2 (1986):22; M. Gastpar, "Epidemiology of Depression (Europe and North America)," *Psychopathology* 19, suppl. 2 (1986):17; T. Helgason, "Epidemiology of Mental Disorders in Iceland. A Psychiatric and Demographic Investigation of 5395 Icelanders," *Acta Psychiatrica Scandinavica* 40, suppl. 173 (1964):73–95.

6. H. A. Lyons, "Depressive Illness and Aggression in Belfast," *British Medical Journal* 1 (1972):342–345.

7. K. Heskin, *Northern Ireland: A Psychological Analysis* (Dublin: Gill and MacMillan, 1980).

8. E. G. Karam, A. N. Karam, M. Barakeh, and N. el-Khoury, "The Arabic Diagnostic Interview Schedule DIS," *Revue Médicale Libanaise* 3, no. 1 (1991):28–30.

9. L. N. Robins, J. E. Helzer, J. Croughan, et al., "National Institute of Mental Health Diagnostic Interview Schedule," *Archives of General Psychiatry* 38 (1981): 381–92.

10. The eight settings are America, Edmonton (Alberta), Puerto Rico, Munich (Germany), Florence (Italy), Paris (France), St. George Hospital, Beirut (Lebanon), Christchurch (New Zealand), and Taiwan. M. Weissman, R. Bland, G. Canino, C. Faravelli, S. Greenwald, H. Hai-Gwo, P. R. Joyce, E. G. Karam, L. Chung-Kyoon, J. Lellouch, J. P. Lepine, S. Newman, M. Rubio-Stipec, E. Wells, P. Wickramaratne, H.-U. Wittchen, and Y. Eng-Dung, "The Changing Rate of Major Depression: Cross-National Comparisons. Cross-National Collaborative Group," *Journal of the American Medical Association* 268, no. 21 (1992):3098–3105.

11. M. Weissman, R. Bland, G. Canino, C. Faravelli, M. Greenwald, H. Hai-Gwo, P. R. Joyce, E.G. Karam, L. Chung-Kyoon, J. Lellouch, J. P. Lepine, S. Newman, S. Rubio-Stipec, E. Wells, P. Wickramaratne, H.-V. Wittchen, and Y. Eng-Dung,

"Facing Depression. Women's Increased Vulnerability to Major Depression: Cross-National Perspectives. Cross-National Collaborative Group," *World Psychiatric Association Press* (WPAP) 4 (1994):1–3.

12. E. G. Karam, P. F. Yabroudi, A. N. Karam, S. Saliba, C. Mansour, and R. Al-Atrash, "The Arabic Composite International Diagnostic Interview CIDI," *Arab Journal of Psychiatry* 6, no. 1 (1995):19–29.

13. J. D. Burke and N. Sartorius, "Development of the Composite International Diagnostic Interview," *Newsletter* (Washington University School of Medicine, St. Louis, Missouri) 5, no. 2 (1988):1.

14. American Psychiatric Association.

15. N. Sartorius, T. B. Ustun, A. Korten, J. E. Cooper, and J. Van Drimmelen, "International Field Trials of the ICD-10 Diagnostic Criteria for Research for Mental and Behavioral Disorders," *American Journal of Psychiatry* 152, no. 10 (October 1995):1427–37.

16. G. W. Brown and T. Harris, *Social Origin of Depression: A Study of Psychiatric Disorders in Women* (New York: Free Press, 1978).

17. Z. Solomon, A. Beich, et al., "The Koach Project for Treatment of Combat-Related PTSD: Rationale, Aims, and Methodology," *Journal of Traumatic Stress* 5, no. 2 (1992):169–93.

18. J. E. Helzer, L. N. Robins, and L. McEvoy, "Post-Traumatic Stress Disorder in the General Population: Findings of the ECA Survey," *New England Journal of Medicine* 317 (1987):1630–34; M. J. Horowitz, *Stress Response Syndrome* (New York: Jason Aronson, 1976); T. Yager, R. Laufer, and M. Gallops, "Some Problems Associated with War Experience in Men of the Vietnam Generation," *Archives of General Psychiatry* 41, no. 1 (1984):327–33; M. Porot, "Les retentissements psychopathologiques des événements d'Algerie," *Presse Medicale* 65 (1957):801–3; P. A. Saigh, "Pre- and Post-Invasion Anxiety in Lebanon," *Behavior Therapy* 15 (1984):185–90; C. F. Shatan, "Stress Disorders among Vietnam Veterans," in *The Emotional Contents of Combat Continues in Stress Disorders among Vietnam Veterans*, ed. C. R. Figley (New York: Brunner/Mazel, 1978); F. S. Sierles, J. J. Chen, R. E. McFarland, and M. A. Taylor, "PTSD and Concurrent Psychiatric Illness, a Preliminary Report," *American Journal of Psychiatry* 140, no. 7 (July 1983):1177–79.

19. E. G. Karam, "The Nosological Status of Bereavement-Related Depressions," *British Journal of Psychiatry* 165 (1994):48–52.

20. "The Future: President's Seminar" (American University of Beirut, Beirut, Lebanon, 1991).

21. E. G. Karam, "Comorbidity of PTSD and Depression in Post-Traumatic Stress Disorder. Acute and Long-Term Responses to Trauma and Disorder," in *American Psychiatric Association Press*, ed. R. Ursano and C. Fullerton (1997).

22. A. N. Karam and E. G. Karam, "La therapie cognitive," *Lebanese Medical Journal* 40, no. 3 (1992):149–55.

16

Substance Use and Abuse: The Lebanese Female and the Lebanon Wars

P. Yabroudi, E. Karam, A. Chami, A. Karam, M. Majdalani, V. Zebouni, N. Melhem, C. Mansour, and S. Saliba

The Lebanon wars, in their major chapters, lasted from 1975 to 1990 and continue to wipe out the lives of Lebanese although, at present, only in the South and West Biqaa. Sixteen years of war! Sixteen years is how long it would have taken a woman to go to college, get her Ph.D., get married, and have two or three children if she was only eighteen at the start of the Lebanon wars. Had she chosen not to go to college, she might have already become a grandmother. Sixteen years are almost a generation. Stress over a whole generation (or a large part of it) would have unimaginable consequences for the mental health of human beings.

Drugs have accompanied the history of mankind. Until the nineteeth century, most drug use was linked to medicinal care or religious practices or restricted to esoteric groups. "Democratization" of drug use started in the second half of the twentieth century. Drugs were widely available in Lebanon during the wars; society was busy planning for fighting or surviving, and practically no control was possible over the circulation or sales of drugs. Thus, the "democratization" process reached chaotic levels and it became possible for any Lebanese to purchase drugs with virtually no risk, especially because drug dealers enjoyed the protection of the military groups running the country. Because the major role of drug use is to induce a feeling of well-being, it became imperative for us to look at the pattern of drug use in Lebanon during the war years.

Drugs made their appearance, on a large scale, in Lebanon in the mid-sixties. It became fashionable among the young, then, to experiment with drugs; it was trendy to smoke a joint because, after all, young people all over the world were doing it. Moreover, "Lebanese red" was acclaimed to be a potent variety of cannabis, in high demand in Europe, the United

States, and North Africa. Large fields in the Biqaa Valley had started producing huge quantities of hashish to be exported all over the world. Opium has been known to Lebanese for many centuries, and engravings of it can be found in the temple of Baalbeck in the Biqaa Valley. Whereas opium was mostly used for several centuries for its medicinal properties, its use for its "mind-altering" effects started on a large scale only in the late nineteenth century. Indeed, for the first half of the twentieth century, Lebanese grandmothers were the users of opium; potions were prepared from *Khashkhash* to soothe the abdominal cramps of their grandchildren and even at times to help them sleep at night. This was, however, limited and occasional.

In contrast to cannabis, grown in Lebanon long before the Lebanon wars, the growth of opium in Lebanese fields took an important turn only during the wars, thanks, apparently, to foreign "experts" who saw in this lawless country a major opportunity for an illegal but lucrative business. The Lebanese soon became important dealers and started smuggling heroin into Europe and the United States.

On another level, a tradition in the "prescription" mores of the Lebanese had persisted during the wars and became established as the normal way to acquire medical products: a person need not have a prescription to buy an antibiotic, a cardiac medication, or a tranquilizer. Frequently, the neighborhood pharmacist would advise patients on what medications to use for their ailments. This was further complicated by the scenery of war.

This chapter is divided into four sections. Section one deals with our research findings on the effects of psychiatric disorders on the emergence of substance abuse and dependence during the Lebanon wars. Section two focuses on a specific age group, college students, and describes their pattern of substance use and abuse. Section three examines in detail the most widely abused substance (other than alcohol), namely, cannabis, among female Lebanese students. Section four describes the pattern of use and abuse of alcohol in both the community and the university.

Dual Diagnosis of Psychiatric Illness and Substance Abuse

Many psychiatric disorders increased during the war. The pain and suffering associated with these illnesses grew more acute as the war progressed while resources to alleviate them became scarce. An obvious outlet was drug use. There are questions then to be addressed. Did women who suffered from psychiatric disorders resort to drugs, and, if so, how did they differ from men? Did drug use itself lead to psychiatric disorders, making them thereby even more intractable? Furthermore, could drug use and psychiatric illness result from a common preexisting predisposition?

The term *dual diagnosis* in mental health has come to designate those patients having both a mental illness and substance abuse disorders. Patients with a dual diagnosis present special difficulties in diagnosis and treatment, recognized as slower, in terms of progress, compared to that of patients who are less symptomatic or have less severe diagnoses.[1]

Since the study of Crowley et al. (1974) on drug and alcohol abuse among psychiatric inpatients, and up to the more recent National Comorbidity Survey (NCS), which looked at 8,098 noninstitutionalized subjects ranging in age between fifteen and fifty-four,[2] studies with this particular interest have sought to increase the understanding of the psychiatric-addictive comorbidity. Most of the existing research varied in terms of whether the issue was addressed in adolescents, as in the studies of Greenbaum et al. (1991), Mckay et al. (1991), and Stowell and Estroff (1992), or in adult patients, as in the studies of Khalsa et al. (1992) and Chen et al. (1992).[3] A third research orientation looked at selective relationships between specific types of substance abuse and categories of mental pathology. The studies by Ardnt et al. (1992), Nace et al. (1993), and Brooner et al. (1993) fall into this last category.[4]

Of particular interest are the studies that looked at gender differences in dually diagnosed patients. A recent example is Fennig et al. (1993), who examined gender differences in first admission psychotic depression. They found no significant demographic differences and no significant differences in symptoms of depression, although more use of alcohol and drugs was found in male patients. Other studies found more affective disorders in females receiving treatment for substance abuse and a greater abuse of benzodiazepines. Males showed a greater prevalence of sociopathy and alcohol abuse.[5]

Brady et al. (1994) studied 50 males and 50 females seeking treatment for substance abuse in a chemical dependency hospital using the Structured Clinical Interview for *DSM-III-R* (SCID) for comorbid psychiatric diagnoses.[6] No significant differences emerged for the variables of race, education, marital status, and age. Alcohol dependence was significantly more likely to be found in males, but cocaine and narcotic dependence was significantly more prevalent among females. A comorbid Axis I disorder was significantly more present in females: Although both genders did not differ in the case of affective disorders, more females were shown to have an anxiety disorder. The onset of substance dependence occurred later in females (twenty-three years and twenty-six years, respectively; $p = 0.08$). For the alcoholic group, females were more likely to have an anxiety disorder ($p < 0.1$), particularly panic disorder. In the case of cocaine abuse, males had a higher prevalence of anxiety disorders compared to females. No significant Axis II gender differences were found.

Halikas et al. (1994) used the Diagnostic Interview Schedule (DIS) to examine psychiatric diagnoses in 207 treatment-seeking adults with reference to cocaine abuse.[7] Most of the patients were males (71 percent), and 45 percent of the sample subjects had never been married. Almost two-thirds met diagnostic criteria for a current comorbid psychiatric condition (most commonly phobic and post-traumatic disorders and major depression), and 73 percent received the diagnosis of at least one lifetime psychiatric disorder; these were, in decreasing order of frequency, antisocial personality disorder, phobic disorder, post-traumatic stress disorder, and major depression. Current and lifetime rates differed significantly by gender: Higher lifetime rates of antisocial personality and higher current and lifetime rates for all other found disorders, with the exception of antisocial personality disorder in females, occurred in men.

Comtois and Ries (1995) examined 338 patients (36 percent females) enrolled in the HRRP (Harborview Recovery and Rehabilitation Program, Harborview Medical Center, Seattle), a dual diagnosis program for severely ill psychiatric patients.[8] No significant gender differences were found for demographics such as age and ethnicity. More females received the diagnosis of affective disorder; more males received the diagnosis of schizophrenia. Men were more often polydrug users and rated more severely in both the frequency and the quantity of substance abuse. In terms of substance use (alcohol, marijuana, cocaine, opiates), no significant gender differences were found. Eighty-two percent of females and 90 percent of males were using alcohol as a single drug of abuse.

The present survey was carried out to help delineate gender differences in substance abuse, comparing Lebanese psychiatric inpatients presenting with psychiatric-addictive comorbidity to those patients with substance abuse disorders but without comorbid other psychiatric illness. All patients admitted from 1980 to 1992 to the St. George Neurosciences Unit in Beirut were the subjects of our study. This unit offers an integrated mental health evaluation (including chemical dependency) and treatment program. In addition to assessing the general prevalence rate of substance abuse dependence in this comprehensive psychiatric inpatient population, we examined gender differences in terms of the clinical characteristics for each of the dually diagnosed and the substance-abusing inpatients with specific focus on psychiatric-addictive relationships, personality disorder, and polydrug abuse. The main implications of this study are twofold: It allows a better understanding of the possible etiological rela–

tionships between substance abuse and other forms of psychiatric morbidity, and once specific combinations of dual diagnosis are defined, then more specific treatment approaches could be adapted toward different groups of substance-abusing patients.

Setting and Data Collection

The Psychiatric Inpatient Unit at St. George Hospital in Beirut is an evaluation and treatment facility that draws patients from the entire country and, to some extent, from neighboring countries. A sample of 222 patients with present and/or past histories of substance abuse were identified by reviewing the available charts of consecutive admissions from January 1980 to September 1992 ($n = 1,643$). Criteria for inclusion in the study were a Lebanese origin and a documented present/past history for substance abuse. The review of the charts for the purpose of assigning diagnostic data included the admission history, mental state examination, physical examination, and toxicology report. Patients with both psychiatric and addictive histories are referred to in this study as comorbids (COM); those with a history of substance abuse in the absence of present and past histories of other psychiatric disorders are referred to as pure substance abusers (PSA).

Results

Demographics

The 222 male and female inpatients with present and/or past histories of substance abuse constituted the study sample and represented 13.5 percent of all reviewed charts ($n = 1,643$). There were 153 males and 69 females (68.9 percent and 31.1 percent, respectively) with a 2:1 male to female ratio. The mean age of the subjects in the sample was 34.5 years (±11.9). No significant difference was found between the mean age of males ($X = 33.9$, $SD = 11.7$) and that of females ($X = 35.8$, $SD = 12.1$) ($p = 0.276$). More than two-thirds of the inpatients (68.9 percent) were found to be comorbids (COM), and 31.1 percent were pure substance abusers. The gender composition of the COM and PSA groups are shown in table 16.1. No statistically significant difference was found in the diagnosis between males and females. The mean age of the COM and PSA groups did not differ significantly, and this nonsignificance also held true when we compared the mean age of the four subgroups (COM males, COM females, PSA males, PSA females).

Marital status was looked at in terms of gender and group-membership (COM versus PSA). In the COM group, almost equal numbers of

Table 16.1. Distribution of the total sample of 222 inpatients by diagnostic group and gender

	Males		Females		Total	
Diagnostic group*	*N*	%	*N*	%	*N*	%
COM	96	62.7	57	82.6	153	68.9
PSA	57	37.3	12	17.4	69	31.1

*Not significant

males and females were married (44.6 percent and 55.1 percent, respectively); however, twice as many males were single (43.2 percent and 22.4 percent, respectively). In the PSA group, almost twice as many females were married (66.7 percent and 37.1 percent, respectively), but males were much more often single (54.2 percent and 33.3 percent, respectively).

Clinical Parameters

The variables first looked at were age at onset of abuse and duration of substance abuse. Males were found to have started their abuse at a significantly earlier age than females (24.6 versus 28.9 years, $p = 0.026$). For the total sample of 222 inpatients, the mean duration of abuse was found to be 8.1 years (±8.5). Males had a longer history of abuse than females (8.9 versus 6.4 years; $p = 0.040$). No significant difference in the length of history of abuse was found comparing COM and PSA groups or between the four subgroups combining gender and group membership.

The types of abused substances could be divided into three major categories: licit substances including tranquilizers, barbiturates, opium/derivatives, stimulants, and codeine; illicit substances including cannabis, cocaine, and heroin; and alcohol. For the total sample of 222 male and female inpatients, alcohol was the most commonly ever abused substance (table 16.2). Illicit substances ranked next (23.4 percent each for cannabis and heroin, and 21.2 percent for cocaine). The abuse of licit substances ranged from 18.9 percent for tranquilizers to 1.8 percent for codeine. Clear gender differences were found for ever abused substances: Female subjects were found to have significantly ever abused more tranquilizers ($p = 0.0018$) and barbiturates ($p = 0.0000$) than males, who, in turn, were found to have significantly ever abused more illicit substances (cannabis, $p = 0.0087$; cocaine, $p = 0.0022$; heroin, $p = 0.0030$) and alcohol ($p = 0.0117$).

The next set of comparisons looked at the history of ever abuse in relation to both gender and group membership (COM versus PSA) for each of the found nine types of abused substances (table 16.3).

Comorbid female inpatients were found to have ever abused more tranquilizers and barbiturates compared to their male counterparts (36.8 percent versus 13.5 percent, $p = 0.0016$, and 31.6 percent versus 3.1 percent, $p = 0.0000$,). Comorbid male inpatients, in turn, were found to have ever abused more alcohol (65.6 percent versus 38.6 percent, $p = 0.0020$), more cannabis (26.8 percent versus 8.8 percent, $p = 0.0168$), and more cocaine (22.9 percent versus 7.0 percent, $p = 0.0209$). For PSA inpatients, females and males differed significantly in the past history of barbiturate abuse only (25.0 percent for females versus 3.5 for males, $p = 0.0000$) (table 16.2). For substances found on admission, and for the total sample, alcohol continued to score as the most abused substance (42.8 percent), followed by heroin, tranquilizers, cocaine, cannabis, and barbiturates (22.5 percent, 17.6 percent, 14.4 percent, 13.1 percent, and 11.7 percent, respectively). All three remaining substances (stimulants, codeine, opium and its derivatives) scored below 10 percent. Female inpatients were significantly more prevalent in licit substances, namely tranquilizers and barbiturates, while male inpatients figured significantly more in all three types of illicit substances and in alcohol. The same trends were found looking at type of substance abuse as a function of group and gender as for ever abuse.

The number of previous detoxifications was another parameter that revealed significant gender differences. One hundred and forty-four in-

Table 16.2. Distribution of the total sample of 222 inpatients by type of substance ever abused and gender

Type of substance	Males		Females		Total	
	N	%	*N*	%	*N*	%
Tranquilizers*	20	13.1	22	31.9	42	18.9
Barbiturates*	5	3.3	21	30.4	26	11.7
Opium derivatives*	12	7.8	6	8.7	18	8.1
Stimulants	4	2.6	6	8.7	10	4.5
Codeine	1	0.7	3	4.3	4	1.8
Cannabis*	44	28.8	8	11.6	52	23.4
Cocaine*	42	27.5	5	7.2	47	21.2
Heroin*	45	29.4	7	10.1	52	23.4
Alcohol*	85	55.6	25	36.2	110	49.5

*Significant

Table 16.3. Gender comparisons: group (COM or PSA) and ever abused substances (*N* = 222)

Type of substance	COM				PSA			
	Males		Females		Males		Females	
	N	%	*N*	%	*N*	%	*N*	%
Tranquilizers*	13	13.5	21	36.8	7	12.3	1	8.3
Barbiturates*	3	3.1	18	31.6	2	3.5	3	25.0
Opium derivatives*	9	9.4	6	10.5	3	5.3	0	0.00
Stimulants	3	3.1	5	8.8	1	1.8	1	8.3
Codeine	0	0.0	2	3.5	1	1.8	1	8.3
Cannabis*	25	26.0	5	8.8	19	33.3	3	25.0
Cocaine*	22	22.9	4	7.0	20	35.1	1	8.3
Heroin*	13	13.5	4	7.0	32	56.1	3	25.0
Alcohol*	63	65.6	22	38.6	22	38.6	3	25.0

*Significant

patients had a history of prior hospital admissions for detoxification (51.4 percent of the sample). Male inpatients had an average of 3.2 detoxifications, compared to 2.3 for females ($p = 0.025$).

Axis I diagnoses of the group of comorbid patients were examined to determine whether major psychiatric disorders are co-occurring with specific substance abuse disorders in the sub-sample of 153 comorbids. Four major psychiatric illnesses were found as the most prevalent disorders on admission: depressive and bipolar disorders, anxiety disorders, and schizophrenia. For both genders, depressive illness figured as the most prevalent diagnosis, followed by bipolar disorders, schizophrenia, and anxiety disorders.

Axis II diagnoses were found in 46.8 percent of the total sample of 222 inpatients. Most personality diagnoses favored the antisocial personality disorder and the obsessive-compulsive personality disorder. Significantly, more males received the diagnosis of antisocial personality disorder (32.7 percent versus 11.8 percent, $p = 0.0039$). Patients with a diagnosis of antisocial personality disorder were found to favor the use of all three types of illicit drugs. No significant gender difference was found in the case of inpatients who received the diagnosis of obsessive-compulsive personality disorder. This diagnosis related significantly to the use of opiates and opiate derivatives ($p = 0.0017$).

A major aim of the present study was to specify various psychiatric-addictive trends of comorbidity, that is, whether specific psychiatric disorders tend to show specific drug preferences. For ever substance abuse, anxiety disorders related significantly to the abuse of tranquilizers in the case of female inpatients only ($p = 0.017$). Depressive illness related, almost significantly, to the abuse of tranquilizers ($p = 0.090$) and alcohol ($p = 0.090$) in females and to cocaine ($p = 0.0010$) and heroin ($p = 0.0118$) in males. Schizophrenia related significantly to the abuse of heroin in males ($p = 0.060$) and to the abuse of cannabis ($p = 0.002$) and heroin ($p = 0.048$) in females. No significant drug association was found for bipolar illnesses. For present abused substances, the only significant associations were found in the case of depression, in males, for heroin ($p = 0.0059$) and nearly so for tranquilizers ($p = 0.067$) and cocaine ($p = 0.063$). Depressive illness figured significantly in schizophrenic males ($p = 0.008$) and almost so for cocaine ($p = 0.069$). Heroin was the only substance that figured significantly in female schizophrenics ($p = 0.048$).

Polydrug abuse was found in 45.4 percent of the sample, equally present in the two subgroups of comorbid and pure substance–abusing patients for male and female inpatients. Males were more likely to be polydrug abusers compared to females (68.8 percent versus 31.2 percent, respectively; $p = 0.0000$). Polydrug abuse figured more frequently in the categories of tranquilizers and all three types of illicit substances and related significantly to the diagnosis of antisocial personality disorder ($p = 0.0008$).

Discussion

When we looked at gender differences in dual diagnosis in the Lebanese during the wars, 222 subjects (153 males and 69 females) formed the final sample, constituting a general prevalence rate of 13.5 percent. There were 153 patients with a dual diagnosis of psychiatric and substance abuse disorders and 69 with a substance abuse disorder diagnosis only.

Gender differences were found for age at onset of abuse and duration of abuse and for types of abused substances. Females were significantly more likely to be abusers of licit substances—tranquilizers and barbiturates—and males figured more in illicit substances and in alcohol, the latter the most frequently abused substance. Males tended to have a significantly greater number of previous detoxifications. For Axis I pathology, males showed a greater preponderance in major depression and bipolar disorders. For Axis II, more males had received the diagnosis of antisocial personality disorder and found to be polydrug abusers. Specific psychiatric-addictive relationships emerged for ever and present substance abuse and for each of the two genders.

The trend toward earlier onset of age of abuse in males is supported by a recent study by Brady et al. (1993) on sex differences in substance abusers (twenty-three years for males and twenty-six years for females, $p = 0.08$) and by other research work examining comorbidity in adolescent substance abusers.[9]

Our results show the overwhelming prevalence of alcohol use, in both adolescent and adult populations. In the studies of Mckay et al. (1991) and Stowell and Estroff (1992), almost 40 percent of their adolescent samples were abusing alcohol. In adult samples, 88 percent of the sample studied by Haugland et al. (1991) were alcohol abusers, and in the study by Brady et al. (1991), alcohol was the most commonly abused substance.

The found psychiatric disorders in the dual diagnosis group of psychiatric inpatients were the same as those reported by Regier et al. (1990), in particular, affective disorder, anxiety disorder, schizophrenia, and antisocial personality disorder. In the present study, and for both genders, depression was the disorder with the widest range of drug associations, including licit and illicit substances and alcohol. The greater prevalence of substance abuse coexisting with depression was also found by Greenbaum et al. (1991). Illicit substances were found to be significantly associated with more "serious" conditions, like schizophrenia, in both genders. Alexander et al. (1994) provide a literature review pointing to similar drug preferences in the more mentally ill patients.[10]

Did the war have any direct bearing on the relation of drug abuse to psychiatric disorders? At first, one might conclude that there is none, as our findings are similar and, at times, identical to those reported by other researchers on populations not subjected to war. Yet we do not know if this relationship would have existed for the Lebanese had they been spared the stressors of war. In addition, the availability of drugs could be a major parameter affecting our present findings.

In chapter 15 (on the effect of war on psychiatric disorders), it was demonstrated that depression did increase during the war and that women were at higher risk. Furthermore, we have found in another study, "The Changing Rate of Major Depression: Cross-National Collaborative Group," that the younger generations will have a huge increase in the prevalence of depression in Lebanon; more than a third of the Lebanese born since 1970 will probably have a depressive episode before they reach age twenty-five.[11] Thus, if depression is increasing and if we know, now, that this disorder increases the risk of a dual diagnosis, it is possible that we will find more women and men dually diagnosed in the years to come in Lebanon. Yet we cannot venture into concluding that the link we found between psychiatric diagnosis and substance abuse will be the same in peacetime Lebanon.

Nevertheless, the study mentioned points out the challenges that will be faced in Lebanon for many years to come by society at large and, more specifically, by legislators and mental health professionals. These are the unavoidable scars that have to be faced and that will follow us in our daily lives. It is true that there are differences between Lebanese women and men, yet it seems that we are, once more, citizens of the same planet and share similar problems. We have a lot to accomplish to solve these difficult problems that should make all of us, men and women, in peacetime and in war, more aware of the immense need for international collaboration in our never ending struggle to alleviate the pain and suffering that plague our lives.

Drug Use and Abuse

The increasing stress, the rise of some psychiatric disorders, the virtual absence of official control, and the easy availability and local production of drugs paved the way, as mentioned, for drug use among the Lebanese. In this section, we shall focus on one aspect of this problem, namely, drug use and abuse by Lebanese female college students during the Lebanon wars.

The issue of substance use among women has not received worldwide attention, probably because substance use has been regarded, for a long time, as a male habit. In fact, most studies on trends of substance use have shown an increase in the use of drugs among females from the 1960s to the 1990s. Sex differentials in drug use and abuse have been highlighted, and these are mainly related to the type of substances used and the amount consumed.[12] Males, in general, show higher rates of illicit drug use, whereas females have higher rates of psychotropic drug use (tranquilizers, barbiturates, and so on); those eighteen to twenty-four years old form the age group in which drug abuse is reported the most for both males and females.[13]

In a study conducted by the National Institute on Drug Abuse (NIDA) on a sample of 1,490 full-time U.S. college students in 1992, males were found to have higher lifetime prevalence rates for most drugs except tranquilizers; 7.1 percent of females reported having ever used tranquilizers compared to 6.7 percent of males (we could not, however, locate the statistical significance of this difference). Cannabis (marijuana) was the most prevalent of all drugs among college students, with males showing higher rates of ever use than females, who, however, had substantial rates (47.6 percent and 41.2 percent, respectively). The lifetime prevalence of use for the various types of drugs found in the NIDA study is shown in table 16.4.[14]

A study in Egypt (1982) involving 5,530 male secondary school students found the highest preference to be for tobacco (18 percent) followed by cannabis (10.5 percent), stimulants (5.7 percent), tranquilizers (5.3 percent), and hypnotics (4.7 percent), but, unfortunately, no corresponding rates were reported for females.[15]

Published studies on substance use are scarce in Lebanon. Nassar et al. conducted a study in 1973, among 436 students of the American University of Beirut (AUB), to determine the prevalence of substance use. Cannabis was found to have been used or tried by 17 percent of their sample. The prevalence rates for LSD and amphetamines were reported to be 2 percent and 8 percent, respectively. More males than females reported using cannabis (18 percent and 14 percent, respectively), but no difference was found for LSD and amphetamines. Tranquilizers were ever used by 17 percent of these students, and 15 percent reported having ever used specifically sleeping pills.[16]

A more recent study was conducted by the Lebanese Family Planning Association to determine the opinions of university students concerning the problem of drug addiction and the way to solve it. This study was conducted among 3,180 students from three universities: the Lebanese University–Beirut, the Lebanese University–Biqaa, and the Lebanese American University (LAU). The methodology of this survey and the tools used to elicit information could not be compared easily to other available international studies, yet the results of this study, published in 1995, have shown cannabis to be the most commonly tried drug (0.9–3.2 percent).[17]

Table 16.4. Lifetime prevalence for various types of drug by gender, 1992: Full-time college students, NIDA study

Type of drug	Males	Females	Total
Any illicit drug	50.8	47.1	48.8
Marijuana	47.6	41.2	44.1
Tranquilizers	6.7	7.1	6.9
Barbiturates	4.2	3.5	3.8
Stimulants	10.6	10.4	10.5
Cocaine	9.5	6.6	7.9
Heroin	0.9	0.2	0.5
Opium derivatives	7.9	6.8	7.3

Methodology

Many sensational reports were circulated in Lebanon over the past decade that gave the impression that Lebanese colleges were literally infested with drugs. Yet the majority of mental health clinicians have the general impression that the use of illicit substances was low despite the fact that cannabis and heroin were grown locally. On another level, the use and abuse of licit substances, especially tranquilizers, are thought by some to have become more prevalent since they have been available in Lebanese professional drugstores without the enforcement of medical prescriptions, thus creating an "open" market.[18] Because speculation abounded about the local use of drugs by Lebanese youth, we started a series of studies to investigate the extent of the use of drugs and other substances among them. The present study was conducted in 1991 among a sample of 1,991 students selected from two major universities (American University of Beirut and St. Joseph University), where class attendance is regularly monitored, thereby avoiding a major selection bias, as substance abusers are commonly known to have a high absenteeism rate. These students were selected randomly and represented 25 percent of the total student population at these universities. Of these students, 1,851 (response rate was 93 percent) completed a self-administered questionnaire based on the Diagnostic Interview Schedule. The questionnaire is highly structured and has been translated by our group into Arabic.[19] It inquires about the use of tobacco, alcohol, and minor substances (tranquilizers, barbiturates, opium derivatives, stimulants, codeine, cannabis, cocaine, and heroin).

Results

The study sample was equally distributed between the two universities. Slightly over half (51.5 percent) of the students were males, and the mean age of the total sample was 20.5 years (± 1.8 years). Drug use was defined as the use of any of the substances without prescription or more than what was prescribed or with a purpose to get "high." Table 16.5 shows the lifetime prevalence of drug ever use (having used them once or more) for males and females.

Females in our study were more likely to have tried tranquilizers and barbiturates than males for (probably) nonmedical reasons, and this difference is found to be highly significant. Overall, the use of these "minor" substances was also reported to be the highest (among all other substances, licit and illicit combined) in the total population studied. Among

Table 16.5. Lifetime prevalence of ever using drugs among Lebanese male and female college students (N = 1,851)

Type of substance	Males		Females		Total	
	N	%	*N*	%	*N*	%
Tranquilizers*	64	7.6	106	13.3	170	10.3
Barbiturates**	52	6.3	81	10.6	133	8.4
Opium derivatives	6	0.7	8	1.1	14	0.9
Stimulants	13	1.6	15	2.1	28	1.8
Codeine	31	3.8	19	2.6	50	3.2
Cannabis	34	3.7	6	0.7	40	2.2
Cocaine	4	0.5	3	0.4	7	0.5
Heroin	5	0.6	1	0.1	6	0.4

*P = 0.0001.
**P = 0.0017; 56 students did not specify their gender.

the illicit drugs, cannabis and codeine were the most frequently tried. For these two drugs, sex differential is also observed, but here the trend is reversed and males are the ones who clearly have tried them more often. "Hard" illicit drugs, like cocaine and heroin, were found to have very low trial rates (0.5 percent and 0.4 percent, respectively); these drugs were tried equally by males and females, but these low rates could be due to the small number of users.

The lifetime prevalence of ever use of drugs more than five times and every day, for at least two weeks, are shown in tables 16.6 and 16.7. As shown, the regular use of any of these drugs is uncommon. The prevalence of use of tranquilizers more than five times was found to be 4.0 percent (3.1 percent for males, 5.0 percent for females; $p = 0.0631$) and that of barbiturates 4.0 percent (2.3 percent for males, 5.8 percent for females; $p = 0.0007$). Ever use of tranquilizers and barbiturates every day for at least a two-week period is found to be low: 1.1 percent and 0.3 percent, respectively. Daily use of tranquilizers for at least two weeks was found not to be different between males and females (both 1.1 percent; $p = 0.9896$). However, ever use of barbiturates every day for two weeks or more was more likely to occur among males than females (0.4 percent and 0.2 percent, respectively; $p = 0.0000$ using Fisher's exact test because of small numbers).

Of the total sample of students, 0.2 percent were found to be abusers of any of the illicit drugs (cannabis, cocaine, heroin, codeine) according to ICD-10 and Feighner criteria, and 0.3 percent were found to be abusers of any of the licit substances about which the students were asked (tranquilizers, barbiturates, opiate derivatives, and stimulants). All abusers of illicit drugs were males. Females, however, were found to abuse licit drugs more than males (0.6 percent and 0.1 percent, respectively; $p = 0.0000$).

To be able to overcome the possibility of underreporting by subjects, especially because use of illicit drugs is illegal, subjects were asked to estimate the prevalence of ever use of substances (that is, drugs, excluding alcohol) in their class and were given the following choices: (1) less than 10 percent; (2) 10 to 25 percent; (3) 25 to 50 percent; (4) more than 50 percent; (5) don't know.

Over two-thirds (67.5 percent) of the students answered that they did not know, and, of those who gave an estimate, 85.7 percent believed that the use of drugs is prevalent among less than 10 percent of their class, a rate that corresponds to the rates we found in our assessment.

Because tranquilizers and barbiturates were most prevalent among our college students, and because females were more likely to have used or tried them, further analysis was conducted to study the determinants of ever use of tranquilizers and/or barbiturates among females once or more, as the number of females ever using them for more than five times and every day for at least two weeks is small.

The lifetime prevalence of ever using of tranquilizers and/or barbiturates for the whole sample is 14.5 percent; it is 18.3 percent for females, and 11.0 percent for males ($p = 0.0000$). The use of tranquilizers/barbiturates among females was found to increase with age, but this trend did not reach statistical significance (table 16.8). Comparing universities, 21.1 percent of USJ females were found to have ever used these substances as

Table 16.6. Lifetime prevalence of ever using drugs five times or more among Lebanese male and female college students ($N = 1,851$)

Type of substance	Males		Females		Total	
	N	%	N	%	N	%
Tranquilizers	23	3.1	34	5.0	57	4.0
Barbiturates	17	2.3	40	5.8	57	4.0
Opium derivatives	4	0.5	1	0.2	5	0.4
Stimulants	2	0.3	6	0.9	8	0.6
Codeine	11	1.5	7	1.1	18	1.3
Cannabis	8	1.1	6	0.9	14	1.0
Cocaine	2	0.3	1	0.2	3	0.2
Heroin	3	0.4	0	0.0	3	0.2

Table 16.7. Lifetime prevalence of ever using drugs every day for at least two weeks among Lebanese male and female college students (*N* = 1,851)

Type of substance	Males		Females		Total	
	N	%	*N*	%	*N*	%
Tranquilizers	8	1.1	7	1.1	15	1.1
Barbiturates	3	0.4	1	0.2	4	0.3
Opium derivatives	3	0.4	0	0.0	3	0.2
Stimulants	3	0.4	3	0.5	6	0.4
Codeine	3	0.4	3	0.5	6	0.4
Cannabis	4	0.6	0	0.0	4	0.3
Cocaine	3	0.4	0	0.0	3	0.2
Heroin	3	0.4	0	0.0	3	0.2

opposed to 14.6 percent of AUB female students. Engineering students seem to have the lowest rate of use of tranquilizers/barbiturates, compared to the arts and sciences students, medical students, and students in other majors (table 16.8).

The effect of religion on susceptibility to substance use is not well documented in the literature. Religion was studied at three levels: the religious affiliation of the student (Christian versus Moslem); belief in God; and the extent to which the student practices religious duties. Of these, only the belief-in-God issue separated, to a significant degree, students who tried or used tranquilizers and/or barbiturates from those who denied ever doing so: Nonbelievers were more likely to use these substances than believers (table 16.9). On the other hand, regular practice of religion appears to be a protective factor against the use of these substances, but the data of this study did not show this fact to be statistically significant, although the numbers seem to indicate a trend.

Family history of drug use was found to be an important risk factor in the use of tranquilizers and/or barbiturates. Twenty-three percent of the female students who identified some of their classmates using drugs were themselves ever users of tranquilizers and/or barbiturates, whereas 16.7 percent of those who did not estimate drug usage among their peers were users of these substances. This difference was statistically significant (table 16.9).

The death of either the father or the mother was not found to be a risk factor for the use of tranquilizers/barbiturates (data not shown here). The age of the students at the death of either parent could be a differentiating variable, because the loss of either of these parental figures at different

Table 16.8. Ever use of tranquilizers/barbiturates among females by demographic characteristics ($N = 871$)

	Female ever users		
	N	%	*P*-value
Age			
16–19	8	11.4	
20–21	112	18.1	0.0931
22+	30	23.8	
University			
AUB	51	14.6	
USJ	99	21.1	0.0167
Class			
Arts and sciences	114	20.3	
Engineering	5	7.8	0.0773
Medicine	16	15.8	
Other	15	16.3	

Table 16.9. Ever use of tranquilizers/barbiturates among females by religion, family use, and classmates' use ($N = 871$)

	Female ever users		
	N	%	*P*-value
Religion			
Christian	100	19.6	
Moslem	40	16.0	0.2235
Belief in God			
Believer	125	17.6	
Nonbeliever	16	27.6	0.0583
Religious practice			
Regular	41	14.9	
Occasional	82	20.2	0.1177
None	14	23.7	
Family use			
Users	50	31.3	
Nonusers	80	13.4	0.0000
Classmate use			
Users	49	23.0	
Nonusers	92	16.7	0.0427

Note: There is a difference in the total number of female ever users in each of the variables studied because of missing information in these variables.

ages could imply a decrease of control at home, the consequences of which would vary depending on the age of the child and the person taking over the authority and responsibility of the lost parental figure. However, unfortunately, this question was misunderstood by some students, who reported the age of their father or mother when he or she died rather than their own age when this event happened, and, thus, this issue cannot be answered by our data.

Of all the variables studied here, university, belief in God, family use, and classmate use were found to be significantly associated with the use of tranquilizers and/or barbiturates by our female college students. These variables were included in a logistic regression to identify the most important predictors of the use of these substances. These variables explained 42 percent of the variability in the use of tranquilizers/barbiturates. Family history of drug use and university were found to be the most important predictive variables of this use. Females with parents having a history of drug use were 3.3 times more likely to use these substances than females with no such family history ($R^2 = 29$ percent, $P = 0.0000$). Controlling for all other variables, USJ female students were 1.8 times more likely than their counterparts at AUB to use these substances ($R^2 = 7.6$ percent, $P = 0.0059$). The effect of belief in God and classmate use disappeared in the presence of family use and university.

Discussion

The above findings are, in a way, quite startling: Lebanese college students, and more specifically females, had not become addicted to drugs in the huge numbers that many "experts" and nonexperts had believed or predicted.

In spite of the wide availability of drugs, the enormous stressors the Lebanese were subjected to, and, the virtual loss of hope by the young adolescents and adults in our colleges, drug use had not come close to what the alarmists had been claiming in the Lebanese mass media.

Young Lebanese women and men were faced with the atrocities of war daily along with severe educational and economic hardship and an ever growing list of personal losses: friends, neighbors, and family members were decimated by the wars. In addition, Lebanon had become a notorious center for drug trafficking, and, yet all of these factors combined do not seem to have pushed the young college students into the abyss of drug addiction or abuse. Only 0.2 percent were found to have abused any illicit drug and 0.3 percent to have abused licit substances.

There still remains, in spite of our low prevalences, an opportunity for us to compare the differential rates of males and females, and to compare these rates, in turn, to the international literature. The results of the study are consistent, on this specific issue, with the findings of other international studies.[20] Differences in drug preference between males and females could be attributed to the fact that women tend to use drugs that are more socially acceptable. In this study, females were significantly more likely than males to ever use tranquilizers and barbiturates and to use them five times or more.

Our rates of use of all drugs are much lower than those found by the NIDA study in the United States except for tranquilizers and barbiturates, in which cases we obtained higher rates of use. It is possible that our definition of use for nonmedical reasons was too narrow where use of drugs was defined in the questionnaire as use to get "high." It is possible that feeling "high" might have been misunderstood by some students and was thought just to mean "relaxed," or that, indeed, our students have tried tranquilizers/barbiturates more often than their U.S. counterparts because these drugs are more readily available in homes or through the pharmacy (where they are easily accessible without prescription). But the Lebanese may not necessarily have abused them, as the rates of ever use of these substances, more than five times, and every day for two weeks or more have shown. Unfortunately, rates of abuse of these drugs are not presented in the NIDA study so we are unable to compare the use of tranquilizers and barbiturates by our university students to use of those drugs among students in the United States.

The rate of ever use of heroin and cocaine among our college students seems to be comparable to that found among the U.S. students (0.4 percent and 0.5 percent, respectively). In the NIDA study, however, males were more likely to use heroin than females, whereas no difference in the use of heroin by sex was observed in our sample. The same sex differential is true for cocaine, except that U.S. college students have higher rates of use.

Our rates are also lower than those reported by Nassar et al. (1973). This difference in rates could reflect a decreasing trend of substance use among this population, or it could be due to differences in methodology and definition of use. We believe that the time frame when the Nassar study was conducted (1960s or early 1970s) was clearly a time of well-known major social upheaval, when Lebanese youth were part of the large international wave, when drug use was equivalent to "peace" and "freedom" of individuals, a period exceptional in this century and ranging from the mid-sixties to the mid-seventies. This does not mean that substance use will not climb again when the worries of wars are behind us and it is "time again" to indulge in drug use. This is our personal interpretation, and we are not at all sure that it will hold true. Indirect evidence does not support our view if one refers to the experience of U.S. Vietnam veterans in the use of heroin: Most of the young U.S. soldiers who abused heroin in Vietnam spontaneously stopped using it when they went home to the United States. So are we really free to say that peace could be a risk factor for drug use? There is no evidence to suggest it, but the reason we think it might be true in Lebanon is that drug use might draw a lot on the complex issue of "modeling." Indeed, we know that the Lebanon wars have kept the Lebanese youth away from the lifestyle (of drug abuse) of their peers in other countries of the world; we know, too, that the close coexistence of the young and the adult members of the family for long periods of time (shelter time) might have been a source of strong parental control. This inevitably loosened up when war was over and young men and women were free again to spend their days and nights away from home, even traveling abroad, more often trying substances that cannot be condemned by the adults: A father or mother would accept, more or less readily, that a daughter takes Lexotanil[R] or Ativan[R] but would find it difficult to tolerate seeing her smoke a joint. Now that the wars are over, and parents are not around all the time anymore, the daughter would be free to engage in the use of illicit drugs.

The fact that USJ female students use more tranquilizers and/or barbiturates than AUB females could be attributed to any of the following:

(1) The wider openness in the traditionally more Westernized USJ "catchment" area to take tranquilizers and/or barbiturates if needed. Because the number of females using these substances five times or more is too small for analysis and comparison of USJ and AUB, abuse cannot be studied further from this sample.

(2) The availability of more pharmacies around USJ females that could be "advising" the use of these substances.

(3) Religion: USJ female students are more likely to be Christians (rather than Moslems) than AUB females. Controlling for religion, USJ females were still more likely to have ever tried these substances than AUB females.

(4) Belief in God, though this was not found to differ between the two universities.

(5) Religious practice: USJ females were more likely to practice their religious duties regularly, whereas AUB females were more likely not to practice these duties at all ($p = 0.0002$). How-

ever, this difference is attributable to the difference in religion in the two universities where Moslems were found less likely than Christians to practice religious duties, probably because of the more rigid obligations imposed by Islam for a Moslem to be considered as practicing regularly.

(6) It is possible, too, that the French version of the DIS could have misled USJ students when compared to AUB students, to whom the original English version was administered: "Feeling high" was translated into *plaisir* in French, perhaps giving the impression that what we looked for in our interview was use of substances for "fun"; to feel high is a qualification obviously used more frequently in illegal "fun"; thus, the prevalence of substance use among USJ students could have been overestimated.

Reporting that members of one's family have ever used drugs predicted the use of drugs among female university students and draws our attention to the possible risk factors of availability, role modeling, lack of control, genetic predisposition, and other factors. The other finding, namely, that fellow classmates' use predicts one's own use could be explained through either "alertness" to who is using drugs in class and, thus, ending up reporting more use by the users (than those who never tried), or it might be an overreading of what happens around users in an effort to "excuse" themselves. Ever users of tranquilizers and/or barbiturates estimated the prevalence of use of drugs among their classmates to be in the range of 10 to 50 percent, which gives support to the second hypothesis.

Belief in God rather than religion per se (Christian or Moslem) was found to be the important factor in the use of these two substances. This is unlike what most people assume, namely, that substance use is more prevalent among Christians with more "lax" and "Western" mores.

The use of tranquilizers and/or barbiturates by our female college students, as found in this study, is determined by the history of family use of drugs (and possibly the university they attend), by classmates' use (as a theoretically possible proxy for peer pressure), and by belief in God (rather than religious affiliation or practice). Generalizing these results to the total female student population in Lebanon should be dealt with cautiously. Not all universities were included in our sample (to date, there are four large universities in Lebanon), so the rates of use of drugs in general, and of tranquilizers and barbiturates in particular, and the determinants of their use could differ between universities in different regions because of the varying backgrounds of the pool of student population that each university attracts. Nevertheless, drug use is not an epidemic among Lebanese women and is probably still at the endemic level.

It remains a challenge to exploit the findings of this study. It is indeed a relief to see that Lebanese women have not been plagued by drug abuse in spite of all that they have endured during the ferocious Lebanon wars.

Use of Cannabis

Lebanon has been growing cannabis since even before the Lebanon wars erupted. This substance was trendy among the more educated and "open" baby boomers in the early sixties and was considered "soft" by Lebanese youth. It was more often used in groups, which is not the case with heroin and tranquilizers, and Lebanese youth look for groups more readily than their Western counterparts.

Hashish is not an expensive drug to buy and is thus affordable for almost anyone. Hashish users do not have to resort to prostitution or stealing to support their habit. In most countries in the world, cannabis use is still considered illegal; in Lebanon, the law goes further: It does not differentiate between the use of cannabis and the use of cocaine or heroin. Furthermore, most parents view the use of cannabis as being as serious as the use of cocaine or heroin. In fact, drug users in Lebanon are commonly referred to as *hashashine*, the literal translation of which is *use of hashish*; thus, any user of any drug would be labeled as a hashish taker.

There is a growing awareness in educated circles that cannabis is in a class apart and that the recreational use of hashish is, indeed, different from that of heroin. The baby boomers of the sixties have become the parents of the nineties, and many of them do make a distinction between hashish and heroin, but this has not led to a relaxation of their attitude toward the possible use of cannabis by their own children.

Worldwide, the second half of the twentieth century has witnessed an explosion of drug use among adolescents and adults.[21] A major public concern in both educational and health fields focused on cannabis use, as this substance was found to be the most common illicit drug used by adolescents and adults.[22]

In the United States, a national survey on drug use among high school seniors, carried out in 1993 and reported by P. O'Malley et al. (1995), showed that cannabis (ever use) ranked first, followed by inhalants (17.4 percent), amphetamines (15.1 percent), LSD (10.3 percent), tranquilizers (6.4 percent), cocaine (6.1 percent), steroids (2 percent), and heroin (1.1 percent).[23] Almost the same ranking was reported for Brazilian college students (in the State of São Paulo): inhalants (28 percent), cannabis

(26 percent), over-the-counter tranquilizers and stimulants (17 percent), and cocaine (10 percent).[24]

Most studies are consistent in their findings: Cannabis use is significantly more prevalent than other drugs among males in high school and college student populations.[25]

In 1992, the U.S. National Institute on Drug Abuse found that the lifetime prevalences of cannabis ever use among college students were 47.6 percent and 41.2 percent for males and females, respectively.[26] In that same year (1992), lifetime prevalences of cannabis ever use reported in Switzerland among adolescent students aged fifteen to twenty years revealed 39.3 percent for males and 24.1 percent for females.[27]

In 1984, a study conducted among high school students in Greece showed that males were twice as likely as females to have ever used illicit drugs (including cannabis).[28] In Egypt, the National Research on Addiction in 1996 provided figures from a study conducted by Soueif in 1990 on cannabis use among university students showing a much higher prevalence among males (8.79 percent) compared to females (0.09 percent).[29]

Gender differences have also been looked at when evaluating other risk factors related to cannabis use, such as tobacco. In a 1988 study in Nigeria, contemporaneous use of cigarettes and cannabis occurred significantly more among male students.[30]

Alcohol use also seems to be a risk factor compounded by gender: A study of Norwegian students showed that male users of cannabis drank 2.8 times more alcohol than their female counterparts, whereas the corresponding male-to-female ratio in the cannabis nonusers was 1.5.[31]

A 1973 study by Nassar et al. of university students at the American University of Beirut (Lebanon) showed that the most widely used drug was cannabis (17 percent), followed by amphetamines (8 percent) and LSD (2 percent).[32] Males used cannabis more than females (18 percent and 14 percent, respectively), but the difference was not statistically significant.

Our group (IDRAC) carried out a study in 1991 to examine gender differences in cannabis use and the association between cannabis use and use of tobacco, alcohol, and other drugs in a university setting in Lebanon.

Methodology

Data collection was carried out in spring 1991.

Sample Selection

Two major universities (St. Joseph University and the American University of Beirut) were chosen. Class attendance in these two institutions is regularly monitored and reinforced. This precaution was necessary because of the known rate of absenteeism among substance abusers.

A sample of 1,991 students was selected randomly, representing 25 percent of the total university population; 1,851 students completed the questionnaires, a 93 percent response rate, with no refusals.

Instrument and Data Collection

The questionnaire was based on the Diagnostic Interview Schedule (DIS), translated into Arabic by our group. This instrument covers the use of alcohol, tobacco, and drugs. It was passed to the students during or at the end of a class or laboratory session. Questions were designed to cover most of *DSM-III-R*, Feighner, and Research Diagnostic criteria for substance abuse.[33]

Results

Of the total sample of 1,851 students, 2.2 percent reported having ever used cannabis in their life.

Compared to the other tried illicit drugs studied in our sample, cannabis was the most commonly used (2.2 percent), followed by morphine (0.75 percent), cocaine (0.38 percent), and heroin (0.32 percent).

The prevalence rate of having used cannabis more than five times was 0.8 percent, that of having used it for at least two weeks was 0.3 percent, and that of satisfying the criteria of abuse was 0.16 percent.

Males were much more likely than females to have ever tried cannabis in their lifetime (3.7 percent and 0.7 percent, respectively, $p = 0.000$). The rate of cannabis ever use increased with age for males, but the reverse is true for females (table 16.10).

Tobacco

Some other possible correlates of cannabis use, such as tobacco, alcohol, and other drugs, were investigated (table 16.11). Among nicotine smokers, significantly more males than females have tried cannabis once or more (10.3 percent and 3.4 percent, $p = 0.042$) but this was true too in the nonsmoking population (1.8 percent for males and 0.3 percent for females, $p = 0.007$). On the other hand, significantly more smokers than nonsmokers have tried cannabis at least once: for males, 10.3 percent of smokers and 1.8 percent of nonsmokers ($p = 0.000$); for females, 3.4 percent and 0.3 percent, respectively ($p = 0.0015$). It looks as if nicotine use is a greater risk for females, as the risk is fivefold for males and tenfold for females, but we need much larger prevalence rates of cannabis use to substantiate this finding statistically.

Alcohol

Among alcohol drinkers, again significantly more males than females were cannabis ever users (6.1 percent and 1.7 percent, respectively, $p = 0.0026$). All females who ever tried cannabis at least once (N = 6) were found to have ever tried alcohol, too. Among nondrinkers, only one male student was found to have ever tried cannabis.

Other Drugs

When overall drug use (licit and illicit), including cannabis, was examined for gender differences, males were more likely than females to have ever tried illicit drugs, 4.3 percent of males and 1.4 percent of

Table 16.10. Distribution of college students ever trying cannabis by age and gender

Age	Males	Females
16–18	1.6% (1)	2.7% (2)
19–21	2.5% (15)	0.6% (4)
22–27	6.8% (18)	0.0% (0)
Total	3.7% (34)	0.7% (6)
Significance	$p = 0.0057$	$p = 0.0718$

Table 16.11. Distribution of college students ever trying cannabis by gender controlling for use of other substances (tobacco, alcohol)

	Males	Females	Significance
Tobacco			
Smokers	10.3% (21)	3.4% (4)	0.042
Nonsmokers	1.8% (13)	0.3% (2)	0.007
Alcohol			
Drinkers	6.1% (33)	1.7% (6)	0.0026
Nondrinkers	0.3% (1)	0.0% (0)	0.8831

females (p = 0.00019), and females were more likely than males to have tried licit drugs, 19.4 percent of females and 11 percent of males (p = 0.0000) (table 16.12).

Discussion

Many predicted we would find high prevalence rates of cannabis use among Lebanese college students. Looking at comparable studies,[34] the prevalence of trying cannabis (and of abuse) in college students in Lebanon is, on the contrary, quite low; however, in line with previous research,[35] the prevalence of cannabis in college students shows that cannabis remains the most commonly tried illicit drug (2.2 percent and 0.75 percent for morphine derivatives, 0.38 percent for cocaine, and 0.32 percent for heroin).

More males than females have tried cannabis (3.7 percent and 0.7 percent, respectively, p = 0.0000). This sex differential is in concordance with the international literature;[36] these gender differences were found to be smaller in younger adolescents in some[37] but not all studies.[38] Our findings suggest that the trial of cannabis in the younger age groups (sixteen to eighteen years) was more frequent in females, but this did not reach statistical significance (2.7 percent and 1.6 percent, p = 1.000). In the age bracket nineteen to twenty-one years, equal percentages (2.2 percent) were noted; in the age bracket twenty-two to twenty-seven, males outnumbered females (2.7 percent and 1.4 percent) but, again, without any statistical significance (p = 1.000). Nonetheless, females could, in fact, outnumber males in the youngest age groups and males outnumber females in the oldest, but this situation cannot be assessed statistically because of the overall low prevalence. It could be argued, as O'Malley did, that this is due to the fact that younger females tend to associate with older males.[39]

In addition, we found that trials of cannabis increased with age in males (p = 0.0057) and probably decreased with age in females (p = 0.0718), who tended to try more licit drugs (such as tranquilizers), a finding shared by other investigators.[40]

Table 16.12. Distribution of college students ever trying any drugs, by gender

	Males	Females	Significance
Licit drugs	11% (102)	19.4% (169)	0.0000
Illicit drugs	4.3% (40)	1.4% (12)	0.00019

Cannabis has been frequently thought of (rightly or wrongly) as the gateway between licit (alcohol, tobacco) and illicit drugs. The association between these substances has been investigated by many authors, and our results are no exception: both male and female college students who are users of alcohol and/or tobacco have tried cannabis more than the alcohol abstainers and the nonsmokers. The results of this study are not surprising in a "conservative" society like Lebanon, where drug use is less acceptable for women than men. Cannabis is the most commonly tried illicit substance; its prevalence in our study is low compared to other international studies (44.1 percent).[41] The effects of gender and age seem to be consonant with Western countries. Moreover, the specific increased risk for tobacco and alcohol users may indicate a common pathway to substance abuse. The question is whether cannabis use increased after the Lebanon wars were over. Did parental control contribute to the low prevalence of this "social" illicit drug? We know that young women ventured away from home infrequently during the Lebanon wars; they stayed in, or close to, the safer environment of their community and were, most of the time, at home or in the shelter their parents had prepared. Because it is unthinkable to imagine young Lebanese women smoking a joint in the presence of their parents, it is obvious that the opportunities to use cannabis during the wars were almost nil. In a separate analysis, we tried to look at the possible effects of living away from home in university dormitories on the use of cannabis. Unfortunately, we are still unable to report our results, as the analysis is not yet complete.

Yet, we think that cannabis is not a necessary exception to the general issue of drug use in Lebanon; drug use and abuse remain low despite sixteen years of war. We hope that this study has contributed to the larger understanding of the factors that induce young men and women to try or use illicit substances in spite of the possible negative consequences in their professional and family lives. On the other hand, cannabis may be decriminalized one day, which may explain why cannabis is the "most commonly" tried "illicit" substance.

Use and Abuse of Alcohol

Alcohol has been used by humans for several millennia. The mere presence of enzymes directed at the metabolism of alcohol speaks in favor of the exposure of primates and their predecessors to alcohol in one way or another. It is suggested by some that the earliest exposure to alcohol might have been through the accidental exposure of animals to fruits fermenting on the ground. It is plausible that humans, having discovered the euphoriant effect of these naturally fermenting fruits, turned this discovery into the alcohol industry that has since become a major undertaking in most countries.

Today alcohol is present in many of our social rituals and is considered by many an essential constituent of our way of life. The "happiness," "relaxation," "conviviality" that alcohol induces are sought by most. However, the dark side of alcohol is also as real, and different cultures at different times have tried to limit its use or ban it all together. Even where alcohol use is accepted and encouraged, alcohol intoxication is shunned (except for "special" occasions) and has become a major public concern; it is beyond the scope of this paper to give an exhaustive review of the "bad" effects of alcohol but the link of alcohol to car accidents and violence is well known. Yet, alcohol accompanies our daily lives and the fine line between recreational and dangerous use is, unfortunately, crossed by many. In Lebanon alcohol is sold openly, and its use is not forbidden by law (except for minors).

From 1975 to 1990, during the Lebanon wars, the Lebanese spent countless days and nights hiding in shelters. They often found themselves trapped, with their friends and neighbors in basements of buildings for several days in a row, frightened and terrorized by the endless sounds of shrieking missiles and mortars, especially when bombardments lasted for several weeks at a time. Alcohol, which was readily available, assumed a new role in the lives of the Lebanese: to bring a welcome soothing to the pain and suffering that occurred during this never ending tragedy.

Our group tried to look at the extent of use and abuse of alcohol among the Lebanese, hoping to evaluate the extent of the problems (if any) that alcohol induced during the Lebanon wars. More specifically, we looked at the differences between women and men in the use and abuse of alcohol during the Lebanon wars.

For many years, research on alcohol abuse and dependence concentrated on men, and much less attention has been paid to female alcohol consumption, probably because of the widespread idea that alcohol consumption is a male characteristic or because women tend to consume alcohol at home and thus their alcohol problems are less public and less visible than those of men.[42] It is only recently that female alcoholism has begun to receive attention. This attention has been largely due to the important gender differences recently highlighted in the patterns of alcohol drinking, in the response to alcohol, and in the biological consequences of alcohol use.[43]

Almost all studies on alcohol have been consistent in the finding that males drink more than females,[44] but the ratio of male to female alcoholics varies with the population being studied. Descriptive epidemiological data for *DSM-III-R* alcohol abuse and dependence, from general population samples, were compared in five countries in North America and Asia: the United States (St. Louis, Missouri), Canada (Edmonton, Alberta), Taiwan, Korea, and Puerto Rico. All were surveyed with the same instrument, the diagnostic interview schedule (DIS). Rates of alcohol abuse, dependence, or both in men were found to be substantially above those for women at all sites. The lifetime prevalence of alcohol abuse ranged from 6.6 percent to 23.6 percent for men, whereas women had a range of 0.3 percent to 2.9 percent in the five locales included in the study. The lifetime prevalence of alcohol dependence ranged from 2.9 percent to 20.4 percent for men and from 0.1 percent to 3.9 percent for women. The sex differential was found to be correlated with the prevalence rate of alcohol abuse and dependence in the population—that is, as the population prevalence increases, the male-female prevalence ratio of alcoholism falls. Women represent an increasing proportion of the alcoholic population as the prevalence rises. This trend provides evidence that alcoholism in women in a certain community is probably a function of the general acceptance of alcohol in that community.[45]

Women also differ from men in their age at the onset of alcoholism; women lag behind men, but the lag is not very great. The mean age at the onset of alcoholism for both men and women is found to be in the twenties. Also, the mean number of alcoholism symptoms among alcoholics varies by sex and ranges from 5 to 5.9 for men and from 4 to 5.1 for women.[46]

Biological research has highlighted important gender differences in response to alcohol. Female alcoholics are found to experience a greater number of medical problems than male alcoholics, particularly liver disease, even though female alcoholics report less alcohol consumption. Also, mortality rates among female alcoholics have been reported to be significantly higher than those for male alcoholics. Women, then, have an increased susceptibility to the deleterious effects of alcohol. This could be due in part to the fact that women have a smaller amount of the alcohol-destroying enzyme (alcohol dehydrogenase), a higher percentage of body fat, a smaller percentage of body water, and a smaller volume of distribution. As a result, toxic effects occur with smaller amounts of alcohol.[47]

Alcoholism in women has also been associated with gynecological dysfunction, where 67 percent of premenopausal women link drinking episodes to premenstrual tension and with sexual dysfunction.[48]

Other risk factors in alcohol consumption that seem to have different impacts on men and women are education and income. Many studies have reported increased use of alcohol among men and women to cope with the stress of economic hardship; still others believe that alcohol abuse and dependence could contribute to economic difficulties (absenteeism, sickness, and so on). In a study conducted by Prescott et al. (1994)[49] to investigate the patterns, correlates, and underlying mechanisms of alcohol abuse and alcohol-related problems among older adults, males with a history of alcohol-related problems tended to have lower levels of current family income and lower educational attainment. Neither of these characteristics was associated with lifetime drinking problems for women, perhaps because regular drinking among women tends not to begin until their mid-twenties, by which time their education would be complete. In addition, for many of the women, family income is likely to depend on a husband's employment and would thus be less affected by a wife's disability from alcohol problems.

Prescott et al. found that the severity of lifetime alcohol problems was associated with a positive family history: greater abuse severity was related to a higher probability of having an affected father, mother, or both, and this association was stronger for females. Also, greater abuse severity was associated with shorter intervals between the onset of drinking problems and three milestones: first drink, first intoxication, and the onset of regular drinking. Although gender differences were not significant for the three measures, females tended to have shorter intervals than males.[50]

Findings in the Community Setting

It is variously reported that because of the Lebanon wars, Lebanese, especially females, have increased their consumption of drugs, including alcohol. To look at this issue more specifically, we conducted a community survey in 1995 as part of a prospective longitudinal study started in 1989 in four Lebanese regions.

Methodology

The present study was conducted in two of the original four areas (Achrafieh and Ain El-Rimmaneh). A total of 208 subjects collaborated (out of 296), and the others were either dead or not found or refused to participate. Keeping in mind that substance abusers are difficult to track down, five contacts were undertaken before the subjects could be classified by the research team as "not found." The sample consisted of 89 males (42.8 percent) and 119 females (57.2 percent); the mean age was 43.1 years. The instrument used in this study is the Composite International Diagnostic Interview (CIDI), the Arabic version of which had been developed by the IDRAC team at the Department of Psychiatry and Psychology of St. George hospital.[51] Interviews were conducted by two trained interviewers at the homes of subjects outside the presence of any other family member. This is consistent with the preset conditions that surround the administration of the CIDI.

Results

The lifetime prevalence of alcohol ever drinking was 65.4 percent. "Ever drinking" is defined as the consumption of at least twelve drinks in any one-year period of one's life. The prevalence of alcohol abuse and alcohol dependence for men and women in the total sample was found to be 5.3 percent and 2.9 percent, respectively (table 16.13). Males were more likely to drink alcohol than females (74.1 percent of the males and 44.5 percent of the females) and more likely to be abusers and/or dependents (18 percent for males and 0.9 percent for females). This result was statistically significant with $P = 00000$. The mean age at the onset of drinking was 15.3 years for males, whereas females lagged behind by about two years (mean age 17.5 years). Males were found to have, on the average, 3.3 drinks/day on the days of drinking; this number was 1.6 drinks/day for females ($P = 0.0006$).

The lifetime prevalence of intoxication in the sample was 33.1 percent. The occurrence of intoxication was found to vary by sex: 42.7 percent of males have ever gotten intoxicated compared to 18.5 percent of females ($P = 0.0034$).

Findings in the University Setting

All of the above numbers correspond to the findings of the community study. In an attempt to investigate the prevalence of alcohol and alcohol-

Table 16.13. Characteristics of drinking behavior in Lebanese males and females: community study

	Males	Females
Alcohol ever drinking (%)*	74.1	44.5
Alcohol abuse/dependence (%)*	18.0	0.9
Mean age at onset of drinking (years)*	15.3	17.5
Average no. of drinks per day (d/day)	3.3	1.6
Prevalence of intoxication (%) (once or more)*	42.7	18.5

*Significant.

related problems among university students in 1991, a randomly selected sample of 1,851 students from two universities (AUB and USJ) completed the structured questionnaire of the Diagnostic Interview Schedule.

Of the students included in our sample, 49.4 percent were found to have drunk alcohol at least once in their lives, 2.1 percent were found to be abusers, and 2.4 percent were dependents. Females were less likely to drink alcohol than males and were less likely to be abusers and dependents (table 16.14). Male drinkers were found to consume more alcohol than their female counterparts. In the excessive alcohol consumption section, the amount of drinking was divided into three categories: one bottle of liquor in one day, ± seven drinks per day for two weeks, and seven drinks per day once a week for two months or more (table 16.14). In each of these categories, males were more prevalent than females. In addition, the lifetime prevalence of intoxication among drinkers in this sample was found to be 35 percent (ever gotten intoxicated at least once in their life). As expected, males were more likely to have ever had a history of intoxication than females (44.1 percent and 21.0 percent, respectively).

Discussion

All of the above findings of the community and the university studies are in line with the literature presented at the beginning of this chapter. However, it is important to keep in mind that the results of the community study cannot be generalized to the whole Lebanese population because the sample was derived from Achrafieh and Ain El-Rimmaneh, areas primarily populated by Christians. Also, the results of the university study are to be dealt with cautiously, as our sample was taken from only two

Table 16.14. Characteristics of drinking behavior in Lebanese males and females: university study

	Males	Females
Alcohol ever drinking*	58.3	40.3
Alcohol abuse/dependence*	13.7	2.2
Amount of drinking*		
1 bottle of liquor in 1 day	13.0	2.0
± 7 drinks/day for 2 weeks	7.3	0.9
7 drinks/day once a week for 2 months or more	15.5	4.0
Prevalence of intoxication (once or more)*	44.1	21.0

*Significant.

major universities, and it is possible that the other universities in Lebanon could have different patterns of use.

A comparison of the rates of alcohol abuse/dependence in males and females found in the community study to those of the five countries of North America and Asia listed[52] shows clearly that our rates are within the "broad" range reported in these countries. It is to be noted that males in our study are closer to the upper range whereas females are closer to the lower limit. In the national household survey on drug abuse conducted by the National Institute on Drug Abuse (NIDA) in the United States, the lifetime prevalence of alcohol use was reported to be 88.1 percent in males and 78.7 percent in females,[53] whereas in our study these rates were 74.1 percent and 44.5 percent, respectively. The rates of alcohol use and abuse/dependence in males in the Lebanese community are closer to those found in the Western countries, whereas those for females are still lagging behind. Another study conducted by NIDA but among college students showed a lifetime prevalence of alcohol use of 91.8 percent (92.4 percent in males and 91.2 percent in females), much higher than what we found among our students (for males and females). Because rates of abuse and dependence are not presented in the NIDA study, comparison of our rates to those of U.S. college students is not possible.

The finding that females have lower rates of use, abuse, and dependence and lighter patterns of alcohol drinking is a common and a solid one: It was true in the community and among the young generation represented by the university population. It is not clear at present whether the trends of alcohol drinking observed in these studies will hold in the future or whether Lebanese females will increase their drinking in the next generation, producing major upward shifts in the rates of alcohol abuse/dependence. In conclusion, Lebanon has a specific and unique sociodemographic structure of a mixture of religions with different attitudes toward alcohol: Islam considers it as one of the *muharramat* (forbidden acts), while the Christian community tolerates it. Yet it is possible that the "conservative" attitude of women in all religious groups in Lebanon might play a role in any theoretical delay that females might have in matching the rates of alcohol abuse and dependence in males.

This word of caution becomes more important when we know that women start "looking" more like men with increasing education, participation in the labor force, and upward social mobility. This reality is already unfolding, and its consequences on the differential rates of alcohol use and abuse in women will need to be assessed in the near future. Nevertheless, it is essential to note, based on the findings above, the importance of the protective shielding of gender, namely, being a woman, has had on the abuse of alcohol in our society even in the worst circumstances—war. This becomes even more important when we see that even in a higher educational setting (when compared to the community findings)—the university—only 2.2 percent of females had problems with alcohol use. To be kept in mind, here, is that Christians, for whom alcohol use is not religiously forbidden, constitute the majority of the surveyed university student population. On the other hand, Lebanese men, as outlined above, seem to have alcohol-related problems similar to those found in more developed countries. The obvious question is whether Lebanese males would have had these rates if the Lebanon wars had not occurred. Did war help reveal a hitherto dormant potential?

What will the effect of this major public health problem (in males) be on females in the years to come? We know that alcohol-related behavior in women cannot remain immune to what happens to their fathers, brothers, and sons. It is possible that women, living increasingly in an atmosphere in which alcohol abuse occurs, become themselves future abusers of alcohol.

Additionally, one must not forget the effect of alcohol abuse and dependence on the daily lives of mothers, wives, and daughters. Tragedies keep unfolding with the known consequences of marital disharmony, separation, divorce, and physical and sexual abuse, to name a few.

It has become imperative for public health officials and government bodies alike to study the findings of this research and to do their best to address this social hazard.

Authors' note: The authors wish to thank the Research Unit staff of the Department of Psychiatry and Psychology for their assistance and John Jabbour for his help in biostatistical work and Tania Gebara for reviewing parts of this chapter. This study was supported partially by a grant from the National Council of Scientific Research (NCSR) and a grant from the Institute for Development Research and Applied Care (IDRAC).

Notes

1. K. L. Sloan and T. Rowe, "Substance Abuse and Psychiatric Illness," *American Journal of Addiction* 4 (1995): 60–69.

2. T. Crowley, D. Chesluk, S. Dilts, R. Hart, "Drug and Alchol Abuse among Psychiatric Admissions: A Multi-Drug Clinical Toxicologic Study," *Archives of General Psychiatry* 30 (1974): 13–20; R. C. Kessler, K. A. McGonagle, S. Zhao, et al., "Lifetime and 12-Month Prevalence of DSM-III-R Psychiatric Disorders in the United States: Results from the National Comorbidity Survey," *Archives of General Psychiatry* 51, no. 1 (1994): 18–19.

3. C. Chen, M. Balagh, J. Bathija, et al., "Substance Abuse among Psychiatric Inpatients," *Comprehensive Psychiatry* 33, no. 1 (1992): 60–64; P. E. Greenbaum, M. E. Prange, R. M. Friedman, et al., "Substance Abuse Prevalence and Comorbidity with Other Psychiatric Disorders among Adolescents with Severe Emotional Disturbances," *Journal of the American Academy of Child and Adolescent Psychiatry* 30, no. 4 (1991): 575–83; H. K. Khalsa, A. Shaner, M. D. Anglin, et al., "Prevalence of Substance Abuse in a Psychiatric Evaluation Unit," *Drug Alcohol Dependence* 28, no. 3 (1991): 215–23; J. R. Mckay, R. T. Murphy, T. R. Rivinus, et al., "Family Dysfunction and Alcohol and Drug Use in Adolescent Psychiatric Inpatients," *Journal of the American Academy of Child and Adolescent Psychiatry* 30, no. 6 (1991): 967–72; and R. J. Stowell and T. W. Estroff, "Psychiatric Disorders in Substance-Abusing Adolescent Inpatients: A Pilot Study," *Journal of the American Academy of Child and Adolescent Psychiatry* 31, no. 6 (1992): 1036–40.

4. I. O. Arndt, G. Tyrrel, M. Falum, et al., "Comorbidity of Substance Abuse and Schizophrenia: The Role of Premorbid Adjustment," *Psychological Medicine* 22 (1992): 379–88; R. K. Brooner, J. H. Herbsdt, C. W. Schmidt, et al., "Antisocial Personality Disorder Among Drug Abusers: Relations to Other Personality Diagnoses and the Five-Factor Model of Personality," *Journal of Nervous and Mental Diseases* 181 (1993): 313–19; and E. P. Nace, C. W. Davis, and J. P. Gaspari, "Axis II Comorbidity in Substance Abusers," *American Journal of Psychiatry* 148, no. 1 (1991): 118–20.

5. S. Fenning, E. Bromet, and L. Jandorf, "Gender Differences in Clinical Characteristics of First-Admission Psychotic Depression," *American Journal of Psychiatry* 150 (1993): 1734–36; J. A. Wilcox and W. R. Yates, "Gender and Psychiatric Comor-bidity in Substance-Abusing Individuals," *American Journal of Addiction* 2 (1993): 3.

6. K. T. Brady, D. E. Grice, L. Dustain, et al., "Gender Differences in Substance Use Disorders," *American Journal of Psychiatry* 150, no. 2 (1993): 1707–11.

7. J. A. Halikas, R. D. Crosby, V. C. Pearson, et al., "Psychiatric Comorbidity in Treatment-Seeking Cocaine Abusers," *American Journal of Addiction* 3 (1994): 25–35.

8. K. A. Comtois and R. K. Ries, "Sex Differences in Dually Diagnosed Severely Mentally Ill Clients in Dual Diagnosis Outpatient Treatment," *American Journal of Addiction* 4 (1995): 245–53.

9. Greenbaum, Prange, Friedman, et al., "Substance Abuse Prevalence and Comorbidity with Other Psychiatric Disorders among Adolescents with Severe Emotional Disturbances"; Stowell and Estroff, "Psychiatric Disorders in Substance-Abusing Adolescent Inpatients: A Pilot Study."

10. M. J. Alexander, T. J. Graig, J. MacDonald, et al., "Dual Diagnosis in a State Psychiatric Facility: Risk Factors, Correlates, and Phenomenology of Use," *American Journal of Addiction* 3 (1994): 314–24.

11. M. Weissman, R. Bland, G. Canino, C. Faravelli, S. Greenwald, H. Hai-Gwo, P. R. Joyce, E. G. Karam, L. Chung-Kyoon, J. Lellouch, J. P. Lepine, S. Newman, M. Rubio-Stipec, E. Wells, P. Wickramaratne, H.-U. Wittchen, and Y. Eng-Dung. "The Changing Rate of Major Depression: Cross-National Comparisons. Cross-Na-

tional Collaborative Group," *Journal of the American Medical Association* 268, no. 21 (1992): 3098–3105.

12. World Health Organization, Programme on Substance Abuse, *Women and Substance Abuse, Interim Report* (Geneva, 1992).

13. J. M. Russell, S. C. Newman, and R. C. Bland, "Drug Abuse and Dependence," *Acta Psychiatrica Scandinavica Supplement* 89, no. 376–81 (1994): 54–66.

14. L. Johnston, P. O'Malley, and J. Bachman, *National Survey Results on Drug Use from the Monitoring the Future Study, 1975–1992* (National Institute of Drug Abuse, U.S. Department of Health and Human Services, 1993).

15. M. I. Soueif, "The Extent of Non-Medical Use of Psychoactive Substances Among Secondary School Students in Greater Cairo," *Drug-Alcohol-Dependence* 9 (1982): 15–41.

16. N. Nassar, L. Melikian, and A. Der-Karabetian, "Studies in the Non-Medical Use of Drugs in Lebanon: The Non-Medical Use of Marijuana, LSD, and Amphetamines by Students at the American University of Beirut," *Lebanese Medical Journal* 26, no. 3 (1973): 215–32.

17. Lebanese Family Planning Association in Lebanon, *Against Addiction* (Beirut, 1995).

18. E. G. Karam, *Substance Abuse in Lebanon: Women—AIDS* (WHO, Geneva, August 2–4, 1993).

19. L. Robins, J. Helzer, L. Cottler, and E. Goldring, *Diagnostic Interview Schedule Version III*, 3d rev. (St. Louis: Washington University, 1989); E. Karam, M. Barakeh, A. Karam, and N. El-Khoury, "The Arabic Diagnostic Interview Schedule (C)," *Revue Médicale Libanaise* 3, no. 1 (1991): 28–30.

20. Johnston, O'Malley, and Bachman, *National Survey Results on Drug Use;* Russell, Newman, and Bland, "Drug Abuse and Dependence"; World Health Organization, Programme on Substance Abuse, *Women and Substance Abuse.*

21. M. E. Alfaro, "Drug Abuse in Costa Rica: A Review of Several Studies," *Bulletin of the Pan American Health Organization* 24, no. 1 (1990): 30–34; R. H. Fonseca, J. B. Garcia, and E. H. Rodriguez, "Drug Use among Adolescents in Asturias, Spain," *Bulletin of Narcotics* 37, nos. 2 and 3 (1985): 43–48; D. B. Kandel and M. Davies, "High School Students Who Use Crack and Other Drugs," *Archives of General Psychiatry* 53, no. 1 (1996): 71–80; A. Kokkevi and C. Stefanis, "The Epidemiology of Licit and Illicit Substance Use among High School Students in Greece," *American Journal of Public Health* 81, no. 1 (1991): 48–52; D. Munodawafa, P. J. Marty, and C. Gwede, "Drug Use and Anticipated Parental Reaction Among Rural School Pupils in Zimbabwe," *Journal of School Health* 62, no. 10 (1992): 471–74; A. Okasha, "Young People and the Struggle against Drug Abuse in the Arab Countries," *Bulletin of Narcotics* 37, nos. 2–3 (1985): 67–73; and J. D. Wright and L. Pearl, "Knowledge and Experience of Young People Regarding Drug Misuse, 1969–94," *British Medical Journal* 310 (1995): 20–24.

22. Alfaro, "Drug Abuse in Costa Rica"; P. M. O'Malley, L. D. Johnston, and J. G. Bachman, "Adolescent Substance Use: Epidemiology and Implications for Public Policy," *Pediatric Clinics of North America* 42, no. 2 (1995): 241–60.

23. O'Malley, Johnston, and Bachman, "Adolescent Substance Use," 241–60.

24. M. T. Silva, R. S. Barros, and M. P. de Magalhaes, "Use of Marijuana and Other Drugs by College Students of Sao Paulo, Brazil," *International Journal of Addiction* 29, no. 8 (1994): 1045–56.

25. O. A. Abiodun, M. L. Adelekan, O. O. Ogunremi, G. A. Oni, and A. O. Obayan, "Psychosocial Correlates of Alcohol, Tobacco and Cannabis Use among Secondary School Students in Illorin, Nigeria," *West African Journal of Medicine* 13, no. 4 (1994): 213–17; Alfaro, "Drug Abuse in Costa Rica"; Kokkevi and Stefanis, "The Epidemiology of Licit and Illicit Substance Use," 48–52; P. A. Michaud, F. Narring, A. F. Dubois, and F. Paccaud, "Health Survey of 15–20-Year-Old Adolescents in French Speaking Switzerland," *Schweizerische Medizinische Wochenschrift. Journal Suisse de Medecin* 123, no. 40 (1993): 1883–95; O'Malley, Johnston, and Bachman, "Adolescent Substance Use"; and R. G. Smart and E. M. Adlaf, "Drug Use in Ontario, Canada," *Bulletin of the Pan American Health Organization* 24, no. 1 (1990): 22–29.

26. Johnston, O'Malley, and Bachman, *National Survey*, vol. 2, *College Students and Young Adults*.

27. Michaud, Narring, Dubois, and Paccaud, "Health Survey of 15–20-Year-Old Adolescents," 1883–95.

28. Kokkevi and Stefanis, "The Epidemiology of Licit and Illicit Substance Use," 48–52.

29. *National Research on Addiction in Egypt (Use, Abuse, Dependency and Addiction), Preliminary Report* (Arab Republic of Egypt: Ministry of Health, March 12, 1996).

30. O. A. Abiodun et al., "Pattern of Substance Use amongst Secondary School Students in Illorin, Northern Nigeria," *West African Journal of Medicine* 13, no. 2 (1994): 91–97.

31. H. Pape, T. Hammer, and P. Vaglum, "Are Traditional Sex Differences Less Conspicuous in Young Cannabis Users than in Other Young People?" *Journal of Psychoactive Drugs* 26, no. 3 (1994): 257–63.

32. Nassar, Melikian, and Der-Karabetian, "Studies in the Non-Medical Use of Drugs in Lebanon."

33. American Psychiatric Association, *Diagnostic and Statistical Manual of Mental Disorders*, 3rd ed., rev. (*DSM-III-R*) (Washington, D.C., 1987); J. P. Feighner, E. Robins, S. B. Guze, R. A. Woodruff, G. Winokur, and R. Munoz, "Diagnostic Criteria for Use in Psychiatric Research," *Archives of General Psychiatry* 26, no. 1 (1972): 57–63; R. L. Spitzer, J. Endicott, and E. Robins, *Research Diagnostic Criteria*, 3rd ed. (New York State: Psychiatric Institute Biometrics Research Division, 1978).

34. Johnston, O'Malley, and Bachman, *National Survey Results*; Nassar, Melikian, and Der-Karabetian, "Non-Medical Use of Drugs in Lebanon," 215–32; O'Malley, Johnston, and Bachman, "Adolescent Substance Use," 241–60.

35. Alfaro, "Drug Abuse in Costa Rica," 30–34; O'Malley, Johnston, and Bachman, "Adolescent Substance Use," 241–60; Silva, Barros, and de Magalhaes, "Use of Marijuana and Other Drugs," 1045–56.

36. Alfaro, "Drug Abuse in Costa Rica"; Johnston, O'Malley, and Bachman, *National Survey Results*; Kokkevi and Stefanis, "The Epidemiology of Licit and Illicit Substance Use," 48–52; Nassar, Melikian, and Der-Karabetian, "Non-Medical Use of Drugs in Lebanon," 215–32; O'Malley, Johnston, and Bachman, "Adolescent Substance Use," 241–60; Smart and Adlaf, "Drug Use in Ontario, Canada," 22–29.

37. O'Malley, Johnston, and Bachman, "Adolescent Substance Use," 241–60.

38. I. Allister and T. Makkai, "Whatever Happened to Marijuana? Patterns of Marijuana Use in Australia, 1985–1988," *International Journal of Addiction* 26, no. 5 (1991): 491–504.

39. O'Malley, Johnston, and Bachman, "Adolescent Substance Use," 241–60.

40. Kokkevi and Stefani, "The Epidemiology of Licit and Illicit Substance Use," 48–52.

41. Abiodun et al., "Pattern of Substance Use," 91–97; Munodawafa, Marty, and Gwede, "Drug Use and Anticipated Parental Reaction among Rural School Pupils in Zimbabwe," 471–74; Pape, Hammer, and Vaglum, "Traditional Sex Differences," 257–63; World Health Organization, *The Health of Youth, Facts for Action, Youth and Drugs* (Geneva, 1989); Johnston, O'Malley, and Bachman, *National Survey Results*.

42. World Health Organization, Programme on Substance Abuse, *Women and Substance Abuse, Interim Report* (Geneva, 1992).

43. J. L. York and J. W. Welte, "Gender Comparisons of Alcohol Consumption in Alcoholic and Nonalcoholic Populations," *Journal of Studies on Alcoholism* 55 (1994): 743–50; J. Gearhart, D. Beebe, H. Milhorn, and R. Meeks, "Alcoholism in Women," *American Family Physician* 44, no. 3 (1991): 907–13.

44. J. E. Helzer, G. J. Canino, E. K. Yeh, R. C. Bland, C. K. Lee, H. G. Hwu, and S. Newman, "Alcoholism—North America and Asia," *Archives of General Psychiatry* 47, no. 1 (1990): 313–19; R. C. Kessler, K. A. McGonagle, S. Zhao, C. B. Nelson, M. Hughes, S. Eshleman, H. S. Wittchen, and K. S. Kendler, "Lifetime and 12-month Prevalence of *DSM-III-R* Psychiatric Disorders in the United States," *Archives of General Psychiatry* 51, no. 1 (1994): 8–19; L. N. Robins, J. E. Helzer, M. M. Weissman, H. Orvaschel, E. Gruenberg, J. D. Burke, and D. A. Regier, "Lifetime Prevalence of Specific Psychiatric Disorders in Three Sites," *Archives of General Psychiatry* 41, no. 7 (1984): 949–58.

45. Helzer, Canino, Yeh, Bland, Lee, Hwu, and Newman, "Alcoholism—North America and Asia," 313–319.

46. Ibid.

47. York and Welte, "Gender Comparisons of Alcohol Consumption."

48. Gearhart, Beebe, Milhorn, and Meeks, "Alcoholism in Women," 907–13.

49. C. A. Prescott, J. K. Hewitt, K. R. Truett, A. C. Heath, M. C. Neale, and L. J. Eaves, "Genetic and Environmental Influences on Lifetime Alcohol-Related Problems in a Volunteer Sample of Older Twins," *Journal of Studies on Alcoholism* 55 (March 1994): 184–201.

50. Ibid.

51. L. Cottler, "Difficulties to Recruit Respondents and Their Effect on Prevalence Estimates in an Epidemiologic Survey," *American Journal of Epidemiology* 125, no. 2 (1987): 329–39; World Health Organization, *Composite International Diagnostic Interview (CIDI)*, Core Version 1.1 (Geneva: WHO, 1993); E. G. Karam, P. F. Yabroudi, A. N. Karam, C. Mansour, R. al-Atrash, "The Arabic Composite International Diagnostic Interview CIDI," *Arab Journal of Psychiatry* 61, no. 1 (1995): 19–29.

52. Helzer, Canino, Yeh, Bland, Lee, Hwu, and Newman, "Alcoholism—North America and Asia," 313–19.

53. National Institute on Drug Abuse, *National Household Survey on Drug Abuse, Main Findings, 1990* (North Carolina: National Institute on Drug Abuse 1990).

VII

Conclusion

Conclusion

"A War of Survival"

I went out, peace seemed imminent. I hurried back home, pursued by peace. It has suddenly struck me that there might be a future, that a foreign land was going to emerge out of this chaos where no one would wait any more . . . . Every one's impatient because peace is so slow in coming . . . . The whole world is waiting.

Marguerite Duras, *War*

Lebanon is one of the few countries that hosts two cultures: the East and the West. Geographically located in the Middle East and once comprising one of the territories of the Ottoman Empire as well as home of a large Muslim population, it certainly espouses Middle Eastern culture and customs. It has also been a fertile land for Western missionaries, as it was once subject to the French Mandate as well as home for a sizable Christian population since the days of the Roman Empire. It consequently adopted and was affected by Western culture and customs, and became the natural crossroad between East and West, as well as the arena of intercommunal and intraregional conflicts. In 1975, Lebanon evolved from being the playground of its neighbors to their battleground. Etel Adnan described the situation in her *Sitt Marie Rose* when she said, "All the quarrels of the Arab World have their representatives here. . . . The wretched and the downtrodden are terrorized."[1] After the Israeli invasion, in 1982, the Lebanese mosaic became even more complex, as each group sought to impose its own ideology. Lebanese society disintegrated into autonomous fragments that found it difficult to communicate. This led to a total transformation at the cultural, social, and economic levels. Many of the inhabitants had to flee their homes either as refugees in their own country or as exiles abroad. The great majority of Lebanese, however, tried, heroically, to adapt to the ever shifting situation characterized by violence, war, and terror with intermittent periods of relative calm. Work had to be attended to, the home and family had to be kept together, and the children helped through an increasingly irregular education. Survivors seemed to need oblivion to the numbness of war and concentration on individual needs and preoccupations. When property was damaged, the Lebanese tirelessly reconstructed. Reconstruction developed into one of the routine everyday chores imposed by the war. No one complained as it became one more chore to carry out. The militia was simultaneously the perpetrator and protector, the police and criminal. This became more acute as the government and governmental institutions disintegrated. As Leila Osseiran succinctly said, "We lived knowing that there was no plan and no protection other than our fierce clinging to life and our resistance."[2] Every now and then the nightmare seemed to recede into the crevices of the city, creating with its withdrawal an illusion of normalcy when men and women would go on with their daily routines, no matter how precariously or feebly. The unpredictability of the situation made long- and short-term planning inconceivable, for anything could happen without warning. The capriciousness of the fighters made any undertaking, such as going to the supermarket, a high risk enterprise. The concept of time, and its hallmarks, changed its meaning and the Lebanese improvised new measures for it. This instability jeopardized continuity and efficiency whether at school or in the marketplace, and led to apathy, loss of interest in productivity, and frustration. Slowly, however, unpredictability became the norm. Food had to be provided, electricity made available, water fetched, schools attended and, most important, wages earned. Munir Chamoun, a Lebanese psychoanalyst, called this situation the "double-bind," in which people adjusting to prevalent conditions in order to survive contribute indirectly to the status quo.[3] The daily life of the Lebanese revolved more and more around news bulletins of the militias and their radio stations, waiting for announcements of a cease-fire, waiting for Godot. Bubbly, prosperous Beirut was suddenly transformed into Albert Camus's Oran in *The Plague*. Just as tightly as Oran, Beirut was placed in quarantine to minimize the spread of the disease. The surrealism that pervaded the city can best be described by a mound of garbage, which had become commonplace during the war, near the Cité Sportif at the southern entrance of Beirut, symbolizing death and destruction. From the garbage sprang a poster from years past, having miraculously escaped destruction. The poster read, "Keep your city clean"!

Quite paradoxically, along with the laws of destruction, emerged new "life-affirming" laws that helped the Lebanese transcend their obsession with survival and elevate themselves to the realm of production. Thus, Miriam Cooke says in her book, *War's Other Voices*, "This was not a war of suicide, but a war of survival. There is no doubt that had individuals given in to the anger and senseless carnage, Beirut would now be lying in ruins. It is not. Its people will not let it die. They will not let themselves die."[4] Thomas Friedman wrote in 1982, "It may not always be true that the violent clash of men and ideas must be a prerequisite for artistic creation, but that seems to be the case in post-civil-war Lebanon . . . whether it is despite the brutality of daily life or because of it, Lebanese artists seem to draw a nervous energy and inspiration from the madness swirling around them."[5] Those who responded with alacrity to the challenge were women.

The preceding chapters have shown how war, entering the homes, politicized the daily lives of women and forced them out into the public arena to meet new situations, armed only with antiquated traditional skills and patterns that they skillfully used to help their families remain afloat. The roles of mother and housewife acquired a new political dimension, whether on the individual or the collective levels: Individual women had to provide for their children, and sometimes parents as well, in the absence of their husbands due to death, kidnapping, fighting, traveling, or simply hiding from local militias; collectively, women extended their maternal role to provide food and welfare for the community. Mothers of martyrs, who may never have been politically active, found their maternal sacrifice hailed as a political act. The war, thus, raised the social awareness of women and made them conscious of the importance of their role in developing a dynamic civic society for the purpose of advancement and development. This led not only to an increase in governmental organizations but an increase in the rate of women's participation in such organizations. Many of the tasks traditionally undertaken by women served to link the private with the public domain, as society came to realize the necessity of their skills and values for continued survival.

The most evident and numerous victims of the war were the displaced. In addition to losing their property, they had to relocate and start from scratch. Displaced women faced many obstacles in the way of their security and that of their families. In fleeing from their neighborhoods, many were subjected to physical and mental violations. Others managed to make it safely to other regions but faced problems of unemployment, cultural differences, dialect barriers, and sometimes hostility of the local population. Many, as a result, suffered psychologically from what is known as post-traumatic stress disorder and had to be treated. One such woman, who had to flee her home at a moment's notice, was so overcome by frustration and feelings of impotence at having to leave all her belongings behind her that she unconsciously carried the telephone in the entrance hall with her, deluding herself into saving something from her fully stocked home.

These conditions, however, did not prevent women from plunging in. In the words of Harriet Stanton Blatch describing American women during World War I, war "make[s] the blood course through the veins" as it forces women into the labor market sending them "over the top . . . up the scaling-ladder and out into 'All Man's Land'."[6] The war in Lebanon introduced new variables that had distinct effects on the labor market, women's work, and the economy in general. Thus we have seen from the preceding chapters the active role women played in the labor market and the media: The few available studies on the Lebanese labor force in 1970 indicate that women made up 17.5 percent of the economically active population and were employed in traditional occupations of the service sector, such as elementary schoolteachers, nurses, secretaries, and housemaids.

But, although economic need seems to be the primary incentive for women's participation in the labor force, a survey conducted by ESCWA showed that 31.5 percent of the women working in the informal sector did so because they enjoyed working, and 71 percent of the women questioned in the Nabatiyyeh region of southern Lebanon wanted to continue working because it enabled them "to secure a place (for themselves) in society."

The surveys in the preceding chapters have shown that the labor force grew considerably during the war years. Whereas the economically active population in 1970–75 included 17.5 percent of the female population, female participation increased steadily during the war until it reached 27.8 percent in 1990 and continues to rise steadily in postwar Lebanon, despite the ready availability of men. The survey showed advancement not only in the labor force but in education and the professions. Female enrollment in universities increased from 25.2 percent in 1973 to 48.2 percent in 1993. What is also of interest is that the ratio of the highly educated of both sexes dropped from 4.6 percent in favor of men in 1970 to 1.3 percent in 1990. The evolution that has taken place in the social and economic conditions of women in Lebanon is further evidenced by the disproportionality observed between the rate of growth of the female population of 1.2 percent per year (1975–90) and the rate of growth of female participation in the economically active population of 2.3 percent per year. The correlation between higher education and economic activity becomes even more evident in the increase of the percentage of highly educated women in the economically active female population from 17.4 percent in 1975 to 50.7 percent in 1990.

Women, during the war, showed expertise and stamina in the world of the media as well. The proportion of women reporters in the five most highly distributed papers was 32 percent, of women in the audiovisual media between 25 and 50 percent. This onslaught by women on the media is further illustrated by the number of women students registered in the

Faculty of Information and Documentation of the Lebanese University, where women make up 75 percent of the total number of students in the faculty.

Lebanese women, during the war, showed what they can do, making it, therefore, very difficult to confine them to their homes or to certain stereotypical occupations. Admittedly, it is still too early to determine whether women will retire to their homes once the shadow of the war is completely lifted. But the immense economic and social contributions of women are being recognized, and women, through their forced emancipation, are gaining confidence and self-esteem, are, naturally, increasing their control over their lives, and are acquiring greater strength and power through the workforce and their exodus out of the private and into the public sphere. Women have, thus, managed to link the private sphere of the home with the public sphere of production, causing what seems to be a structural change in the economy, the media, and education, and a fundamental change of social relations.

While it is still impossible to see the final outcome, and the struggle is far from over, I believe that the momentum built so far by women's awareness and their accomplishments is difficult to reverse. The cumulative effect of changes brought on by the war should continue to open new opportunities at all stages of career development. This effect is enhanced by the growing global participation of women in the labor market. With the reconstruction of Lebanon, there is an urgent need for trained personnel. Educated women are ready to fill this need.

However, despite women's infiltration of all fields, it would seem that their sex status is still pivotal in determining the course of their life, possibly due to rigid cultural definitions that limit the range of their horizon. In war, as well as in peace, there were sharp differences in the activities and status of men and women. Although war may have forced women out of the domestic sphere, fortified with better education, capabilities and experience, and at times even joining men in the battlefield, women were unable to break through the hierarchy of power. Although today women are found in large numbers in all domains, they are virtually nonexistent in decision-making positions, which are still monopolized by men. It was not until 1992 that three women were elected to Parliament, which comprises 128 members: Nayla Moʿawwad, widow of assassinated president, René Moʿawwad, Maha Khoury al-Asaad, sister of a deceased political figure, who won uncontested, and Bahiyya al-Hariri, sister of tycoon Rafiq al-Hariri (who is the present prime minister). All three have won seats in Parliament for and through traditional parameters. None was known for any political or feminist activism. In 1996, Nayla

Moʿawwad, Bahiyya al-Hariri, and Nuhad Seʿayd were elected to Parliament. The marginalization of women during elections was not limited to candidacy for Parliament but included ignoring women as an important voting body.[7]

The role of women during the war was not limited to the labor market in the public sphere. The war left its imprint on the Lebanese psyche as well. All Lebanese, men and women, carry within them part of the war, which has affected not only their vision of reality but has left an indelible mark of emptiness and endless waiting. In an effort to fill that void and make sense out of the madness that prevailed, women, in an attempt at catharsis, resorted mainly to writing poetry, short stories, and novels, as well as to painting.

Although Lebanon, with a plethora of writers and publishing houses, had been the literary center of the Arab world before the war, few women made their appearance on the literary scene. But by 1976 the situation had changed radically as the war spawned extensive female literary activity. Miriam Cooke quotes Etel Adnan, who describes women's attachment to language by considering "words like little atoms, like particles emanating from our organism, like audible emanations of our mental and emotional make-up, like creations closest to our beings. These little 'energies' are similar to atoms in the sense that they contain tremendous power." The role and importance of words, like atoms, are expressed by their participation "in the energies of Life, and they still have the power to create Paradise or Hell." According to Cooke, language and literature in such a context lose their role as descriptions of an external situation and become "interventions in a political situation."

Some wrote in English, others, in French, and still others, in Arabic. Some wrote self-consciously about the war, like Samira Aghacy, Jean Makdisi and Nadia Tuéni, but others wrote, according to Miriam Cooke, of a war in which women were the only rational actors, and still others, like Emily Nasrallah, completely ignored the war and its brutality and concentrated on life in the village with its traditional values as it had been in prewar times. But whatever the subject matter, women wrote in unprecedented abundance in an attempt either to say or do something in a situation that was not of their doing and in the face of which they felt impotent, or to hold onto a traditional way of life, which was being swept away by the war, or simply to describe a surrealistic reality like Hanan el-Shaykh in *The Story of Zahra* and Ghada al-Samman in *Kawabis bayrut* (Nightmares of Beirut). Ghada al-Samman says, "I saw the potion of insanity . . . fire burning in water. . . . I saw man while stopping to drink from the fountain, his fingers would metamorphose into the claws of a beast . . .

bringing about the overflow of the spring of madness to give the people of the city to drink. . . . Some drank and I did not know whether I slept or not . . . whether I drank or not." Or, finally, some wrote to stand in judgment of man's irrationality, like Huda Barakat in *Hajar al-dahik* (The laughing stone). These women became the mouthpiece of those who were left speechless by the violence they witnessed during the war. Thus, women's voices in poetry and fiction managed to transform the cold statistics and events of the war into heartrending stories of humanity's capacity for degradation, compassion, and renaissance. To create untraditional images of women or, rather, images that do not fit the stereotypical woman in a certain culture is difficult for all writers. Yet, we see this challenge being inadvertently taken up by women writers who offered images that may give a negative representation of women at first glance (Hanan el-Shaykh) or even appear to support existing stereotypes, but, on closer inspection, can be seen to be subversions of those stereotypes.[8]

The same activity could be seen on the artistic scene. Again, although Lebanon, where art galleries and art exhibitions for Arab and Western artists flourished everywhere, was the center of artistic activity in the Arab world, women artists, though present on the scene, were not numerous. Yet, as soon as the war became a fixture of the Lebanese scene, innumerable women artists made their appearance in an attempt to express emotions they were not allowed to voice or simply to escape an unbearable situation where violence and carnage prevailed. Art became their only weapon for, or means of, survival.

But not all Lebanese women resorted to sublimation as a means of escaping the absurdity of war. Some, as mentioned earlier, joined the labor market, while others felt the best way to confront the war was to become politically active either through education, ideological dissemination, helping the bereaved and displaced, paramedical support, provision of food and supplies to the combatants, support in administrative affairs—such as secretarial work, telephone operation, communications, news media, and so forth—or simply by joining the fighting themselves and carrying guns, hoping to bring the war to an end in a shorter period of time. Joining the fighting helped many control their fear and anxiety and thus they were better able to cope with the ravages of war. It gave them a sense of control over their lives instead of remaining potential victims, never knowing when they or their relatives would be hit. Military training and actual combat fortified their self-confidence and esteem and drove away their fears, as fear is, normally, that of the unkown. This involvement further swept away their feelings of inferiority to men, encouraging women to actively participate in areas in which they previously had dared not tread.

That women should man barricades, carry guns, and kill was unprecedented in Lebanese tradition and recent history, but those women combatants were soon accepted by their communities. Thus, while women's "peaceable" nature may be acclaimed universally, women's attitudes toward war and active participation in it vary substantially from one period to another and from one culture to another. There are moments when women's behavior challenges facile assumptions regarding women's nature and their involvement in politics. The Lebanese experience has shown that, just as both men and women are victims of war and violence, so are they both responsible for military activities. It is true that women did not participate in the decision to wage war, but they contributed to the building and maintaining of war machinery. There were those who actively participated in the fighting, but they were no more patriotic or involved than those who raised their sons and who encouraged and drove their husbands and sons to go to battle. Women, thus, as combatants, military personnel, protesters, demonstrators, civic organizers, mourners, paramedics, and political sympathizers fully demonstrate the extent of their roles and participation in war and society, thereby putting an end to categoric views regarding the peaceful, nurturant nature of women in general.

Besides direct casualties brought on by the war and exposure to harmful physical conditions that enhanced the spread of disease, war produced a variety of stressful life experiences, which have been shown to result in several somatic disorders, as well as a wide range of psychiatric disorders, such as depression, anxiety, and poor interpersonal relations. The question to ask is whether the war had a different psychological effect on women than men.

Field research has shown that the incidences of post-traumatic stress disorder, varied psychiatric illnesses, and substance use and abuse have significantly increased during the war years. Women tended to succumb to psychiatric illnesses more than men, probably because of the higher number of stressor elements they were exposed to. Thus, the findings of Farhood demonstrated that, although marriage seemed to have a protective role for males, it had a detrimental effect on women. Women, as mentioned earlier, were in charge of keeping the family together and ensuring the smooth running of the usual routines of the home—water, electricity, provision of food, cooking, cleaning, taking children to school, teaching them after school, and relieving them and the father from any imposed stressful situation. Moreover, the divorced, separated or widowed, in addition to all the above, had to replace their absent(ed) husbands in the public sphere. Furthermore, I believe that most depressed women were confined to the home in their traditional wifely and motherly roles and, seldom if at all, did women working in the public sphere ever develop any form of depression. Thus, the observation of the prevalence of women suffering from depression does not reflect gender differences but rather the differences in the different roles played by men and women during the war. However, in the area of substance use and abuse, men superseded women in incidence rates and tended to indulge more in illicit substances and drugs; women tended to gravitate more towards the use of licit drugs, like tranquilizers and barbiturates. This could be attributable to the more conservative attitudes of most Lebanese women of all religious affiliations.

Of interest, however, is the finding that substance use and abuse was much less prevalent in Lebanese college students of both sexes but was more pronounced in males than in females. This is all the more interesting in view of the ready availability of drugs and the plethora of stressor factors. In this context, it looks as if the war has kept Lebanese youth away from drug abuse, possibly due to their close coexistence with their families for security purposes, thereby strengthening the element of parental control. If so, the incidence of such abuse should rise in this population in the postwar period due to the relaxation of such controls.

The war thus subverted conventional space: Men and women were no longer definable by the space they occupied and the roles they played. The war front and the home front became indistinguishable as women were drawn away from the role of political observers and plunged into the arena of action. For better or worse, women gave up their traditional passive role in society and joined men in action at all levels—except the decision-making arena.

Wars have been described as periods of rapid political and social change that act as the precondition for the liberation of women. A body of evidence has been compiled, some of which affirms this assertion and some of which denies it.[9] The first group of findings affirms that wars provide "a springboard from which they (women) leaped beyond the circumscribed women's sphere into arenas heretofore reserved to men."[10] These studies drew mainly on the experience of women who either participated actively in combat or were propelled into the workforce to replace men—mainly the experience of British women, who managed to obtain certain political rights after the war. Furthermore, writers such as Simone de Beauvoir maintained that through their struggle in wars of liberation, women liberated themselves as well as their oppressors.[11] The second set of findings, although, like the first set of findings, agreeing that during wars women are liberated to enter the public sphere at all levels, finds that there is still the attempt of patriarchal society to call women back to the domestic sphere once the war is over and their help is no longer needed. Margaret R. and Patrice Higonnet call this phenomenon the "double helix," whereby women's liberation during or through wars is tied to the control of men. Thus wartime changes are bound to be short-term and are bound to be followed afterwards by a complete reversal, rendering women's liberation a mere illusion, until of course, the cycle is complete and they are needed once again.[12]

Still others, like Jean O'Barr, question this theory of wars as "watersheds" for the advancement of women. She maintains that although, in times of conflict, women learn new skills, gain political awareness, and assume new roles in the public arena, there is little evidence that they ever participate in decision-making processes or even have a say in developing policies that deal with women's lives. The political conflict, according to O'Barr, has enlisted women's energies but failed to produce collective action for the promotion of women's interests.[13] Still others propound the theory that women are by nature pacifists and, as such, never partook actively in wartime activities.

Thus, some historians insist that war has brought changes that improve women's status in the long run, while others see the gains accrued during the war as only temporary and "for the duration," with no permanent impact on women's sociopolitical standing. The sexual division of labor, this second group maintains, continued even after women proved their capabilities and skills.[14] Thus, although there is substantial agreement that war effects change for women, there is disagreement on the nature of and duration of this change.

Based on the Lebanese experience as described in the preceding chapters, women have, indeed, been liberated in many respects. They have managed to quickly take on roles that were previously assigned only to men. Thus, the ranks of women lawyers, judges, engineers, physicians, and businesswomen have swollen significantly. We now even have a number of female taxi-drivers, mechanics, parking lot attendants, and, more significiantly, a female jumbo jet pilot. More women have been elected to Parliament and, for the first time, one woman has been appointed to chair a parliamentary committee and another, director-general of the Ministry of Social Affairs. The war altered the meaning of female dependence, improved the lives of working women, and granted economic independence and self worth to others. The war has indeed functioned in so many different ways to liberate women—revolution in economic expectations, release of passionate energies, aesthetic creativity. Niʿmat Kanaan, director-general of the Ministry of Social Affairs, said, in an interview that the primary gain for the Lebanese woman from the war is that she has found her place alongside men in the work place. Samira Aghacy, the poet and literary critic, and Houry Chekerdjian, the artist, both asserted their emancipation from patriarchal society through the war. Historically, wars have always been the quintessential domain of men, where violence, aggressiveness, and ruthlessness reigned supreme; women, on the whole, remained in the background, protected by men at the front. In Lebanon, the war invaded the inner sanctum of every home; the war front and the home front became identical and women had to participate in this war at all levels in order to survive and protect their families, who suddenly became their responsibilities rather than the men's. Thus, despite the massive tragedy that the war represented to the whole population, it also signaled the removal of social strictures and constraints on women, which brought about the first rupture in a socio-economic history that had so far denied most women access to the public arena.

The war has probably changed some traditional attitudes towards women's role in society. Women, six years after the end of the war, are still in the public arena, fighting for more equal rights with men. Thus, several discriminatory laws have been repealed: In 1983, the penal law against contraception was repealed; in 1987, the age of retirement for women was made the same as that of men; in 1993 and 1994, women were granted the right to testify in real estate matters, and married women the right to start businesses of their own without the approval of their husbands, respectively; the law prohibiting women of the diplomatic corps, stationed abroad, from marrying, was abrogated in 1995; and finally, the UN Convention for the Elimination of All Forms of Discrimination against Women was signed (with reservations) in 1996. Furthermore, although the Lebanese Council of Women may have failed to act as a pressure group for the advancement and development of women, Amane Kabbara Chaarani, then-president of the council, clearly targeted universal women's issues while preparing for the Fourth World Conference on Women. Not only did she actively involve the council in women's issues, but she also formed the Nongovernmental Committee for the Preparation of the Fourth World Conference on Women, held in Beijing in 1995. Then, in October 1995, the Nongovernmental Committee Pursuant to Women's Issues (after Beijing) was established under her leadership. Unfortunately, none of these three bodies has succeeded in forming a pressure group either for the advancement of women's rights or as an effective electoral body. However, it is still too early and, therefore, premature to judge the impact of the war in the long run. One must certainly wonder whether this new mood is far-reaching or long-lasting. Some of the changes may have been only temporary, governed by the circumstances that produced them. Can a society with deeply ingrained attitudes regarding the sexual division of labor permanently and smoothly embrace the concept of the autonomous, emancipated woman?

It is certainly of the utmost importance that women partake in the decision-making process, from which they are still excluded, and play a more active role in the peaceful resolution of conflicts, so that a new era may dawn, an era free from insecurities and fear. It is only when men and women equally and freely share the fruits of this planet that hope for peaceful resolution of conflicts can be envisaged.

Notes

1. Etel Adnan, *Sitt Marie Rose* (California: Post Apollo Press, 1982).
2. Cooke, *War's Other Voices,* 126.
3. Kassab, "Paramount Reality," 68.
4. Cooke, *War's Other Voices,* 123.
5. *New York Times,* May 13, 1982.
6. Gilbert, "Soldier's Heart," 429.
7. For further information, see table 3.2.
8. For a full discussion, see Goodman, "Supply and Demand," 79–93.
9. Cf. Scott, "Women and War," 2–6; Theweleit, "The Bomb's Womb and the Gender War," 283–315; Elshtain, *Women and War,* 185–86.
10. Ibid., 186.
11. Maksoud, "The Case of Lebanon," 91.
12. Theweleit, "The Bomb's Womb and the Gender War," 296–97.
13. Callaway, "Survival and Support," 227–228.
14. Scott, "Women and War," 2; Higonnet and Higonnet, "The Double Helix," 31.

SELECTED BIBLIOGRAPHY

Books

Abu Nasr, Julinda, Nabil F. Khoury, and Henry T. Azzam, eds. *Women, Employment, and Development in the Arab World.* Berlin: Mouton, 1985.

Accad, Evelyne. *Sexuality and War.* New York: New York University Press, 1990.

Actes du colloque. *La femme libanaise témoin de la guerre.* Mission de la ligues des états arabes à Paris, October 1987.

Addis, Elisabetta, and Valeria Russo, eds. *Women Soldiers: Images and Realities.* New York: St. Martin's Press, 1994.

Afkhami, Mahnaz, ed. *Faith and Freedom: Women's Human Rights in the Muslim World.* London: I. B. Tauris, 1995.

Ahmed, Leila. *Women and Gender in Islam: Historical Roots of a Modern Debate.* New Haven: Yale University Press, 1992.

Ajami, Fouad. *The Vanished Imam: Musa al-Sadr and the Shi'a of Lebanon.* London: I. B. Tauris, 1986.

al-Amine, Adnan. *al-Ta'lim fi lubnan* (Education in Lebanon). Beirut: Dar al-Jadid, 1993.

al-Amir, Daisy. *Fi duwwamat al-hubb wa al-karahiyah* (In the vortex of love and hatred). Beirut: Dar al-Nidal, 1979

Anderson, Benedict. *Imagined Communities.* London: Verso, 1983.

Ball, George W. *Error and Betrayal in Lebanon.* Washington, D.C.: Foundation for Middle East Peace, 1984.

Beneria, Lourdes, and Shelly Feldman, eds. *Unequal Burden: Economic Crises, Persistent Poverty, and Women's Work.* Boulder, Col.: Westview Press, 1992.

Berch, Bettina. *The Endless Day: The Political Economy of Women and Work.* San Diego: Harcourt Brace Jovanovich, 1982.

Berger, Milton M., ed. *Women Beyond Freud: New Concepts of Feminine Psychology.* New York: Brunner/Mazel, 1994.

Bonner, Frances, L. Goodman, R. Allen, L. Janes, and C. King, eds. *Imagining Women: Cultural Representations and Gender.* London: Polity Press in association with the Open University, 1992. Reprint, 1995.

Braybon, Gail, and Penny Summerfield. *Out of the Cage: Women's Experiences in Two World Wars.* London: Pandora Press, 1987.

Bulloch, John. *Final Conflict.* London: Century, 1983.

Bullock, Susan. *Women and Work.* London: Zed Books, 1994.

Cashman, G. *What Causes War?: An Introduction to Theories of International Conflict.* New York: Lexington Books, 1993.

Chadwick, Whitney. *Women, Art, and Society.* London: Thames and Hudson, 1990.

Chamie, J. *Religion and Population Dynamics in Lebanon.* Population Studies Center. Ann Arbor: University of Michigan Press, 1977.

Cobban, Helena. *The Making of Modern Lebanon.* Boulder, Col.: Westview Press, 1985.

______. *The Shiʿa Community and the Future of Lebanon.* The Muslim World Today, Occasional Paper 2. Washington, D.C.: American Institute for Islamic Affairs, 1985.

Cock, Jacklyn. *Women and War in South Africa.* Cleveland, Ohio: Pilgrim Press, 1993.

Cooke, Miriam. *War's Other Voices. Women Writers on the Lebanese Civil War.* London: Cambridge University Press, 1988.

______. *Women and the War Story.* Berkeley: University of California Press, 1996.

______. *Women Write War.* Papers on Lebanon, no. 6. Oxford: Centre for Lebanese Studies, 1987.

Cooke, Miriam, and Angela Woollacott, eds. *Gendering War Talk.* Princeton, N.J.: Princeton University Press, 1993.

Cooper, Helen M., A. A. Munichs, and S. M. Squier, eds. *Arms and the Woman.* Chapel Hill: University of North Carolina Press, 1989.

Crompton, Rosemary, and Kay Sanderson. *Gendered Jobs and Social Change.* London: Unwin Hyman, 1990.

Dajani, Nabil. *Disoriented Media in a Fragmented Society: The Lebanese Experience.* Beirut: American University of Beirut, 1992.

Davies, Miranda, ed. *Third World—Second Sex.* 4th ed. London: Zed Books, 1987.

Deeb, Marius. *The Lebanese Civil War.* New York: Praeger, 1980.

Elshtain, Jean Bethke. *Women and War.* New York: Basic Books, 1987.

Elshtain, Jean Bethke, and Sheila Tobias, eds. *Women, Militarism, and War.* Savage, Md.: Rowman and Littlefield, 1990.

Enloe, Cynthia. *Does Khaki Become You? The Militarisation of Women's Lives.* London: Pluto Press, 1983.

Epstein, Cynthia Fuchs. *Woman's Place: Options and Limits in Professional Careers.* Berkeley: University of California Press, 1970.

ESCWA. *The Role of Women in the Informal Sector.* Series of Studies on Arab Women in Development, no. 16. Baghdad: United Nations, 1989.

Fernea, Elizabeth Warnock, ed. *Women and the Family in the Middle East: New Voices of Change.* Austin: University of Texas Press, 1985.

Fine, Ben. *Women's Employment and the Capitalist Family.* London: Routledge, 1992.

Foster, Carrie A. *The Woman and the Warriors.* Syracuse, N.Y.: Syracuse University Press, 1995.

Freeman, Jo, ed. *Women: A Feminist Perspective.* 4th ed. Mountainview, Cal.: Mayfield, 1989.

Gadant, Monique. *Women of the Mediterranean.* London: Zed Books, 1986.

Gilmour, David. *Lebanon: The Fractured Country.* New York: St. Martin's Press, 1983.

Gluck, Sherna Berger. *Rosie the Riveter Revisited: Women, the War, and Social Change.* Boston: G. K. Hall, 1987.

Gordon, David C. *Lebanon: The Fragmented Nation.* Stanford, Cal.: Hoover Institute Press, 1980.

Griffin, Susan. *A Chorus of Stones: The Private Life of War.* New York: Doubleday, 1992.

Gunn, J. V. *A West Bank Memoir: Second Life.* Minneapolis: University of Minnesota Press, 1995.

Haddad, Wadi D. *Lebanon: The Politics of Revolving Doors.* Washington Papers, no. 114. New York: Praeger, 1985.

Halawi, Majed. *A Lebanon Defied: Musa al-Sadr and the Shi'a Community.* Boulder, Col.: Westview Press, 1992.

Haley, P. E., and L. W. Snider, eds. *Lebanon in Crisis.* Syracuse, N.Y.: Syracuse University Press, 1979.

Hanf, T. *Coexistence in Wartime Lebanon.* London: Centre for Lebanese Studies in association with I. B. Tauris, 1993.

Hansson, P. *Mamma Karasjok.* Oslo: Gyldenal Norsk Forlag, 1970.

Harik, I. *Anatomy of Conflict.* Hanover, N.H.: American Universities Fieldstaff, 1981.

———. *Politics and Change in a Traditional Society, Lebanon, 1711–1845.* Princeton, N.J.: Princeton University Press, 1968.

Higonnet, M. R., J. Jenson, S. Michel, and M. C. Weitz, eds. *Behind the Lines: Gender and the Two World Wars.* New Haven, Conn.: Yale University Press, 1987.

Hoss, S. *Lebanon: Agony and Peace.* Beirut: Islamic Center for Information and Development, 1984.

Hourani, A. *Political Society in Lebanon: A Historical Introduction.* London: Centre for Lebanese Studies, n.d.

______. *Syria and Lebanon.* Oxford: Oxford University Press, 1954.

Ibrahim, Emily Fares. *Kalimat wa mawaqif* (Words and opinions). Beirut: Dar Maktabat al-Turath al-Adabi, 1992.

Institute for Women's Studies in the Arab World. *Women and Economic Development in the Arab World.* A regional conference. Beirut: Beirut University College, 1988.

———. *Women and Work in Lebanon.* Monograph Series, no. 1. Beirut: Beirut University College, Arab Institute for Research and Publishing, 1980.

International Bechtel Inc., and Dar al-Handasah Consultants (Sha'ir and Partners). *Recovery Planning for the Reconstruction and Development of Lebanon.* Working Paper 8, Labour Supply, Council for Development and Planning, Government of Lebanon, September 1991.

Iskandar, Marwan, and E. Baroudi. *The Lebanese Economy in 1981–82.* Beirut: Middle East Economic Consultants, 1982.

Jabbra, Joseph G. and N. W. Jabbra, eds. *Women and Development in the Middle East and North Africa.* Leiden: E. J. Brill, 1992.

Jessup, Henry. *The Women of the Arabs.* New York: Dodd and Mead, 1873.

Junblat, Kamal. *This Is My Will.* Paris: Mu'assassat al-Watan al-Arabi, 1978.

Khal, Helen. *The Woman Artist in Lebanon.* Institute for Women's Studies in the Arab World. Beirut: Beirut University College, 1987.

al-Khatib, Haneefa. *Tarikh tatawwur al-harakah al-nisa'iyyah fi lubnan 1800–1975* (History of the development of the women's movement in Lebanon). Beirut: Dar al-Hadathah, 1984.

Khoury, Nabil, and Valentine E. Moghadam, eds. *Gender and Development in the Arab World.* London: Zed Books; Tokyo: United Nations University Press, 1995.

Kiwan, Fadia. *'Amal al nisa' fi al-hay'at al-ahliyyah* (Role of women in nongovernmental organizations). Beirut: Friedrich Ebert Institute, 1994.

Kliot, N. *The Territorial Disintegration of a State: The Case of Lebanon.* Occasional Papers Series, no. 30. England: Centre for Middle Eastern and Islamic Studies, University of Durham, 1986.

Lamb, Franklin P., ed. *Israel's War in Lebanon.* Boston: South End Press, 1984.

Lauter, Estella. *Women as Mythmakers: Poetry and Visual Art by Twentieth-Century Women.* Bloomington: Indiana University Press, 1984.

The Lebanese National Committee for the Preparation for the Fourth World Conference on Women. *The National Report.* Beirut, 1995.

The Lebanon Report. Beirut: Lebanese Center for Policy Studies, March 1993.

Lewis, Jane. *Women in Britain since 1945: Women, Family, Work, and the State in the Post-War Years.* Oxford: Blackwell, 1992.

Longrigg, S. H. *Syria and Lebanon under French Mandate.* New York: Octagon Books, 1972.

Macdonald, Sharon, Pat Holden, and Shirley Ardener, eds. *Images of Women in Peace and War.* Madison: University of Wisconsin Press, 1988.

MacKinnon, Catherine A. *Sexual Harassment of Working Women.* New Haven, Conn.: Yale University Press, 1979.

Makdisi, Jean Said. *Beirut Fragments: A War Memoir.* New York: Persea Books, 1990.

Maksoud, Marie. "Les adolescents libanais et la guerre: Attitudes et réactions des jeunes de classe terminale à Beyrouth et en banlieue." Ph.D. diss., Université de Paris, 1980.

Malraux, André. *The Voices of Silence.* Translated by Stuart Gilbert. Garden City, N.Y.: Doubleday and Company, 1953.

McDowall, David. *Lebanon: A Conflict of Minorities.* N.p., n.d.

McDowell, Linda, and Rosemary Pringle, eds. *Defining Women: Social Institutions and Gender Divisions.* United Kingdom: Polity Press in association with the Open University, 1992. Reprint, 1994.

Mernissi, Fatima. *The Forgotten Queens of Islam,* translated by Mary Jo Lakeland. Cambridge: Polity Press, 1993.

Mies, Maria, Veronka Bennholdt-Thomsen, and Claudia von Werlhof. *Women: The Last Company.* London: Zed Books, 1988.

Miller, Jean Baker. *Toward a New Psychology of Women.* Boston: Beacon Press, 1976.

Moghadam, Valentine M. *Modernizing Women: Gender and Social Change in the Middle East.* Boulder, Col.: Lynne Rienner, 1993.

______, ed. *Gender and National Identity.* London and New Jersey: Zed Books, 1994.

Momen, Moojan. *An Introduction to Shi'i Islam: The History and Doctrines of Twelver Shiism.* New Haven, Conn.: Yale University Press, 1985.

Mutahhari, Murtada. *The Rights of Women in Islam.* Tehran: World Organization for Islamic Services, 1981.

Nashashibi, Salwa Mikdadi. *Forces of Change: Artists of the Arab World.* Lafayette, Cal.: International Council for Women in the Arts and the National Museum of Women in the Arts, 1994.

Nochlin, Linda. *Women, Art, and Power.* 2nd ed. London: Thames and Hudson, 1994.

Norton, Augustus Richard. *Amal and the Shi'a: Struggle for the Soul of Lebanon.* Austin: University of Texas Press, 1987.

Odeh, B. J. *Lebanon: Dynamics of Conflict.* London: Zed Books, 1985.

Page Andrews, Mathew. *The Women of the South in War Times.* Baltimore, Md.: Dixie Books of Days, 1924.

Parker, Rozsika, and Griselda Pollock. *Old Mistresses: Women, Art, and Ideology.* London and Henley: Routledge and Kegan Paul, 1981.

Patton, Paul, and Ross Poole, eds. *War/Masculinity.* Sydney: Intervention, 1985.

Peteet, Julia M. *Gender in Crisis: Women and the Palestinian Resistance Movement.* New York: Columbia University Press, 1991.

Petran, T. *The Struggle over Lebanon.* New York: Monthly Review Press, 1987.

Phares, W. *Lebanese Christian Nationalism.* Boulder, Col.: Lynne Rienner, 1995.

Piland, Sherry. *Women Artists: An Historical, Contemporary, and Feminist Bibliography.* 2nd ed. London: Scarecrow Press, 1994.

Porter, Cathy. *Women in Revolutionary Russia.* Cambridge: Cambridge University Press, 1987.

Qubaysi, Bushra. *al-Mar'ah fi al-tarikh wal-mujtama'* (Women in history and society). Beirut: Amwaj lil-Nashr wal Tawzi', 1995.

Rabinovich, I. *The War for Lebanon, 1970–1985.* Rev. ed. Ithaca, N.Y.: Cornell University Press, 1984.

Reardon, Betty. *Sexism and the War System.* New York: Teachers College Press, 1985.

Redclift, Nanneke, and M. Thea Sinclair, eds. *Working Women: International Perspectives on Labour and Gender Ideology.* London: Routledge, 1991.

Reeves, Minou. *Female Warriors of Allah.* New York: E. P. Dutton, 1989.

Ridd, Rosemary, and Helen Callaway, eds. *Women and Political Conflict.* New York: New York University Press, 1987.

Rowbotham, Sheila. *A History of Women and Revolution in the Modern World.*

Women, Resistance, and Revolution. New York: Vintage, 1972. Reprint, 1974.
______. *Women in Movement*. New York: Routledge, 1992.
Sabbagh, Suha, ed. *Arab Women—Between Defiance and Restraint*. New York: Olive Branch Press, 1996.
Salem, Elie. *Modernization without Revolution: Lebanon's Experience*. Bloomington: Indiana University Press, 1973.
______. *Prospects for a New Lebanon*. Washington, D.C.: American Enterprise Institute for Public Policy Research, 1982.
Salibi, K. *The Modern History of Lebanon*. London: Weidenfeld and Nicolson, 1965.
______. *Cross Roads to Civil War*. Delmar, N.Y.: Caravan, 1976.
Shaaban, Bouthaina. *Both Right and Left Handed: Arab Women Talk about Their Lives*. London: Women's Press, 1988.
Smart, Carol, ed. *Regulating Womanhood: Historical Essays on Marriage, Motherhood, and Sexuality*. London and New York: Routledge, 1992.
Stewart, A. J. *Toward a Feminist Strategy for Studying Women's Lives: Women Creating Lives*. San Francisco: Westview Press, 1994.
Stichter, Sharon, and Jane L. Parpart, eds. *Women, Employment, and the Family in the International Division of Labour*. London: Macmillan, 1990.
United Nations, Special Economic and Disaster Relief Assistance, Special Programme of Economic Assistance for the Reconstruction and Development of Lebanon. *Report of the Secretary General, Addendum*. November 1991.
United Nations. *World Demographic Estimates and Projections, 1950–2025*. New York: United Nations, 1988.
Vickers, Jeanne. *Women and War*. London: Zed Books, 1993.
Walther, Wiebke. *Women in Islam: From Medieval to Modern Times*. Princeton, N.J.: Marcus Wiener, 1981.
Waring, Marilyn. *Women, Politics and Power*. Wellington: Unwin, 1985.
Warren, Karen J., and Duane L. Cady, eds. *Feminism and Peace*. *Hypatia* 9, no. 2 (1994) (special issue).
Winston, Kenneth, and Mary Jo Bane, eds. *Gender and Public Policy: Cases and Comments*. Boulder, Col.: Westview Press, 1993.
Wright, R. *Sacred Rage: The Wrath of Militant Islam*. 2nd ed. New York: Simon and Schuster, 1986.
Young, Kate, Carol Wolkowitz, and Roslyn McCullough, eds. *Of Marriage and the Market: Women's Subordination Internationally and Its Lessons*. 1981. Reprint, London: Routledge, 1991.
Zamir, M. *The Formation of Modern Lebanon*. Ithaca, N.Y.: Cornell University Press, 1985.

Articles

Abu Nasr, Julinda. "The Effects of War on Women in Lebanon." In *Arab Women—Between Defiance and Restraint*, edited by Suha Sabbagh. New York: Olive Branch Press, 1996.

Accad, Evelyne. "Feminist Perspective on the War in Lebanon." *Women's Studies International Forum* 12, no. 1 (1989): 91–95.

______. "Gender and Violence in Lebanon and Yugoslavia." *Al-Raida,* 11, no. 65 (1995): 38–45.

Addis, Elisabetta. "Women and the Economic Consequences of Being a Soldier." In *Women Soldiers: Images and Realities,* edited by Elisabetta Addis and Valeria Russo. New York: St. Martin's Press, 1994.

al-Amine, Naziha. "al-Tahjir wa atharuhu ʿala dawr al-marʾah fi al-awsat al-shaʿabiyyah" (The impact of displacement on women in popular circles). In *La femme libanaise témoin de la guerre.* Actes du colloque, mission de la ligue des états arabes à Paris, October 1987.

Amyuni, Mona Takieddine. "And Life Went on . . . in War-Torn Beirut," *Arab Studies Quarterly* 15, no. 2 (spring 1993): 1–14 (special issue, *The Impact of War and Revolution in the Arab World*).

Assaf, Hind Al-Soufi. "Historical Overview." *Al-Raida* 13, no. 73 (1996): 12–15.

Azzam, J., J. Abu Nasr, and I. Lorfing. "An Overview of Arab Women in Population Employment and Economic Development." In *Women, Employment, and Development in the Arab World,* edited by Julinda Abu Nasr, Nabil F. Khoury, and Henry Azzam. Berlin: Mouton, 1985.

Badawi, Marie Thérèse Khair. "Le manqué destructurant spécificités psychosociologiques du libanais et apprentissage de la vie civile." In *La génération de la relève: Une pédagogie nouvelle pour la jeunesse libanaise de notre temps,* edited by Louis Marie Chidiac, Abdo Kahi, and Antoine N. Messara. Vol. 2. Beirut: Publication du Bureau Pédagogique des Saints Coeurs, 1992.

Balbo, Laura. "Crazy Quilts: Re-thinking the Welfare State Debate from a Woman's Point of View." In *Women and the State,* edited by Ann Showstack Sassoon. London and New York: Routledge, 1987. Reprint, 1992.

Barakat, Halim. "The Social Context." In *Lebanon in Crisis,* edited by P. E. Haley and L. W. Snider. Syracuse, N.Y.: Syracuse University Press, 1979.

Bennholdt-Thomsen, Veronka. "Why Do Housewives Continue to Be Created in the Third World Too?" In *Women: The Last Company,* edited by Maria Mies, Veronka Bennholdt-Thomsen, and Claudia von Werlhof. London: Zed Books, 1988.

Berkman, Joyce. "Feminism, War, and Peace Politics: The Case of World War I." In *Women, Militarism, and War,* edited by Jean Bethke Elshtain and Sheila Tobias. Savage, Md.: Rowman and Littlefield Publishers, 1990.

Betrus, P., S. Elmore, and P. Hamilton. "Women and Somatization: Unrecognized." *Health Care for Women International* 16, no. 4 (July/August 1995): 287–97.

Binder, Leonard. Foreword to *Amal and the Shiʿa: Struggle for the Soul of Lebanon,* by Augustus Richard Norton. Austin: University of Texas Press, 1987.

Bizri, Dalal. "al-Marʾah al-lubnaniyyah wal sahwah al islamiyyah" (Lebanese women and Islamic revival). In *La femme libanaise témoin de la guerre.* Actes du colloque, mission de la ligue des états arabes à Paris, October 1987.

Blau, Francine, and A. Ferber. "Women's Work, Women's Lives: A Comparative Economic Perspective." In *Women's Work and Women's Lives: The Continuing Struggle Worldwide,* edited by Hilda Kahne and Janet Z. Giele. Boulder, Col.: Westview Press, 1992.

Bodman, F. "War Conditions and the Mental Health of the Child." *British Medical Journal* 2 (1941): 486–88.

Borchorst, Anette, and Birte Sim. "Women and the Advanced Welfare State—A New Kind of Patriarchal Power." In *Women and the State,* edited by Ann Showstack Sassoon. London: Routledge, 1987. Reprint, 1992.

Boustani, Samih, and Nada Mufarrij. "Female Higher Education and Participation in the Labour Force in Lebanon." In *Gender and Development in the Arab World,* edited by Nabil Khoury and Valentine E. Moghadam. London: Zed Books; Tokyo: United Nations University Press, 1995.

Bryce, J., N. Walker, F. Ghorayeb, and M. Kanj. "Life Experiences, Response Styles and Mental Health among Mothers and Children in Beirut, Lebanon." *Social Science and Medicine* 18, no. 1 (1989): 685–95.

Bryce, J., N. Walker, and C. Peterson. "Predicting Symptoms of Depression among Women in Beirut: The Importance of Daily Life." *International Journal of Mental Health* 18, no. 1 (1989): 57–70.

Cainkar, Louise. "The Gulf War, Sanctions and the Lives of Iraqi Women." *Arab Studies Quarterly* 15, no. 2 (spring 1993): 15–51.

Callaway, Helen. "Survival and Support: Women's Forms of Political Action." In *Women and Political Conflict,* edited by Rosemary Ridd and Helen Callaway. New York: New York University Press, 1987.

Campbell, D'Ann. "The Regimented Women of World War II." In *Women, Militarism, and War,* edited by Jean Bethke Elshtain and Sheila Tobias. Savage, Md.: Rowman and Littlefield, 1990.

Carroll, Berenice. "'Women Take Action'! Women's Direct Action and Social Change." *Women's Studies International Forum* 12, no. 1 (1989): 3–24.

Chafetz, Janet Saltzman. "Marital Intimacy and Conflict: The Irony of Spousal Equality." In *Women: A Feminist Perspective,* edited by Jo Freeman. 4th ed. Mountainview, Cal.: Mayfield, 1989.

Chamie, M. "Labour Force Participation of Lebanese Women." In *Women, Employment, and Development in the Arab World,* edited by Julinda Abu Nasr, Nabil F. Khoury, and Henry T. Azzam. Berlin: Mouton, 1985.

Charafeddin, Fahmiyyeh. "Athar al-harb ʿala al-marʾah fi lubnan" (Impact of war on women in Lebanon). In *Proceedings of Symposia Held in Preparation for the Beijing Conference.* Prepared by the Lebanese Non-Governmental Committee for the Preparation for the Beijing Conference. Beirut: Friedrich Ebert Institute, 1995.

Chikhani-Nacouz,Leila. "Maternité et travail au Liban" (Maternity and work in Lebanon). In *Women and Economic Development in the Arab World.* A regional conference sponsored by the Institute for Women's Studies in the Arab World. Beirut: Beirut University College, 1988.

Cooke, Miriam. "The Globalization of Arab Women Writers." *Bahithat* 2 (1995): 175–98.

______. "Woman, Retelling the War Myth." In *Gendering War Talk,* edited by Miriam Cooke and Angela Woollacott. Princeton, N.J.: Princeton University Press, 1993.

Cooley, J. K. "The Palestinians." In *Lebanon in Crisis,* edited by P. E. Haley and L. W. Snider. Syracuse, N.Y.: Syracuse University Press, 1979.

Corm, Georges. "Myths and Realities of the Lebanese Conflict." In *Lebanon: A History of Conflict and Consensus,* edited by Nadim Shehadi and Dana Haffar Mills. London: Centre for Lebanese Studies in association with I. B. Tauris, 1988.

Dajani, Nabil. "Wasa'il al-iʿlam wal waʿi al-ijtimaʿi fi lubnan" (The media and social awareness in Lebanon). Forthcoming.

Delphy, Christine. "A Theory of Marriage." In *Defining Women: Social Institutions and Gender Divisions,* edited by Linda McDowell and Rosemary Pringle. United Kingdom: Polity Press in association with the Open University, 1992.

Ehrenreich, Barbara. "Life without Father: Reconsidering Socialist-Feminist Theory." In *Defining Women: Social Institutions and Gender Divisions,* edited by Linda McDowell and Rosemary Pringle. United Kingdom: Polity Press in association with the Open University, 1992.

Elshtain, Jean Bethke. "Women as Mirror and Other: Toward a Theory of Women, War, and Feminism." *Humanities in Society* 5, nos. 1–2 (1982): 29–44.

Farhood, L. "Family Structure and Socio-cultural Change in Lebanon: Its Effects on Mental Health." In *Proceedings of the Eighth International Congress of Cross Cultural Psychology,* Istanbul, Turkey, July 6–10, 1986.

Farhood, L., H. Zurayk, M. Chaya, F. Saadeh, G. Meshefedejian, and T. Sidani. "The Impact of War on the Physical and Mental Health of the Family: The Lebanese Experience." *Social Science and Medicine* 36, no. 12 (1993): 1555–67.

Fishman, Sarah. "Waiting for the Captive Sons of France: Prisoner of War Wives, 1940–1945." In *Behind the Lines: Gender and the Two World Wars,* edited by Margaret R. Higonnet, J. Jenson, S. Michel, and M. C. Weitz. New Haven, Conn.: Yale University Press, 1987.

Flint, Julie. "Crushed Hopes and Shattered Senses." *Guardian,* July 31, 1993.

Fox, Mary Frank. "Women and Higher Education: Gender Differences in the Status of Students and Scholars." In *Women: A Feminist Perspective,* edited by Jo Freeman. 4th ed. Mountainview, Cal.: Mayfield, 1989.

Ghorayib, Rose. "Lebanon: The Harem Window." In *Sisterhood Is Global,* edited by Robin Morgan. Garden City, N.Y.: Anchor Press, 1984.

Gibai, Yousif. "Dawr al-naqabat fi tanshit al-musharakah al-siyasiyyah lil-marʾah al-lubnaniyyah" (The role of unions in activating Lebanese women's political participation). Unpublished.

______. "al-Marʾah fi al-ʿamal wa furas al-taʾhil wal tadrib" (Women in the labor force and opportunities for rehabilitation and training). In *Proceedings of Symposia Held in Preparation for the Beijing Conference.* Prepared by the Lebanese

Non-Governmental Committee for the Preparation for the Beijing Conference. Beirut: Friedrich Ebert Institute, 1995.

Giele, Janet Z. "Promise and Disappointment of the Modern Era: Equality for Women." In *Women's Work and Women's Lives: The Continuing Struggle Worldwide,* edited by Hilda Kahne and Janet Z. Giele. Boulder, Col.: Westview Press, 1992.

Gilbert, Sandra. "Soldier's Heart: Literary Men, Literary Women, and the Great War." *Signs: Journal of Women in Culture and Society* 8, no. 3 (1983): 422–50.

Goodman, Lizabeth. "Supply and Demand: Women's Short Stories." In *Imagining Women: Cultural Representations and Gender,* edited by Frances Bonner, L. Goodman, R. Allen, L. Janes, and C. King. London: Polity Press in association with the Open University, 1992. Reprint, 1995.

Graeff-Wassink, Maria. "The Militarization of Woman and 'Feminism' in Libya." In *Women Soldiers: Images and Realities,* edited by Elisabetta Addis and Valeria Russo. New York: St. Martin's Press, 1994.

Green, B.L. "Psychological Research in Traumatic Stress: An Update." *Journal of Traumatic Stress,* (1994): 341–62.

Halabi, Dominique. "Dawr al-tarbiyah fi nahdat al-mar'ah al-lubnaniyyah" (The role of education in the renaissance of Lebanese women). In *Symposium on the Role of Women in Lebanon Today.* Beirut: Fondation René Moʿawwad and Friedrich Naumann Stiftung, 1994.

Hamzeh, A. Nizar. "Lebanon's Hizbullah: From Islamic Revolution to Parliamentary Accommodation." *Third World Quarterly* 14, no. 2 (1993): 321–36.

Harik, I. "The Iqtaʿ System in Lebanon." *Middle East Journal* 4, no. 19 (1965): 405–21.

Haugland, G., C. Siegel, M.J. Alexander, and M. Galanter. "A Survey of Hospitals in New York State Treating Psychiatric Patients with Chemical Abuse Disorders." *Hospital Community Psychiatry* 42, no. 12 (1991): 1215–20.

Hause, Steven C. "More Minerva Than Mars: The French Women's Rights Campaign and the First World War." In *Behind the Lines: Gender and the Two World Wars,* edited by Margaret R. Higonnet, J. Jenson, S. Michel, and M. C. Weitz. New Haven, Conn.: Yale University Press, 1987.

Hazzaz, May. "Le défi à la guerre: Témoignage de femmes issues de milieux défavorisés" (Defiance of war: Testimony of modest women). In *La femme libanaise témoin de la guerre.* Actes du colloque, mission de la ligue des états arabes à Paris, October 1987.

Hernes, Helga Maria. "Women and the Welfare State: The Transition from Private to Public Dependence." In *Women and the State,* edited by Ann Showstack Sassoon. London: Routledge, 1987. Reprint, 1992.

Higonnet, Margaret R. "Civil Wars and Sexual Territories." In *Arms and the Woman,* edited by Helen M. Cooper, A. A. Munichs, and S. M. Squier. Chapel Hill: University of North Carolina Press, 1989.

______. "Not So Quiet in No-Woman's Land." In *Gendering War Talk,* edited by Miriam Cooke and Angela Woollacott. Princeton, N.J.: Princeton University Press, 1993.

Higonnet, Margaret R., and Patrice L.-R. Higonnet. "The Double Helix." In *Behind the Lines: Gender and the Two World Wars,* edited by Margaret R. Higonnet, J. Jenson, S. Michel, and M. C. Weitz. New Haven, Conn.: Yale University Press, 1987.

Hourani, L.L., H. Armenian, H. Zurayk, and L. Afifi. "A Population-based Survey of Loss and Psychological Distress during War." *Social Science and Medicine* 23 (1986): 269–75.

Ismail, Ghena. "Young Women in Post-War Lebanon." *Al-Raida* 12, nos. 70–71 (1995): 57.

Joseph, Suad. "Gender and Citizenship in Middle Eastern States." *Middle East Report* 26, no. 1 (1996): 4–10.

______. "Gender, Culture and Human Rights." *Al-Raida* 12, no. 65 (1994): 8–9.

Kahne, Hilda. "Progress or Stalemate? A Cross-National Comparison of Women's Status and Roles." In *Women's Work and Women's Lives: The Continuing Struggle Worldwide,* edited by Hilda Kahne and Janet Z. Giele. Boulder, Col.: Westview Press, 1992.

Kaplan, Laura D. "Woman as Caretaker: An Archetype that Supports Patriarchal Militarism." In *Feminism and Peace,* edited by Karen J. Warren and Duane L. Cady. *Hypatia* 9, no. 2 (1994) (special issue).

Karam, Elie G., Sabah Saliba, and Rima al-Atrash. "Vulnerability of Women in the Lebanese Wars." *Al-Raida* 10, no. 62 (1993): 14–15.

Karamé, Kari H. "L'Expérience des jeunes militantes. Étude de cas et conséquences éducationelles." In *La génération de la relève: Une pédagogie nouvelle pour la jeunesse libanaise de notre temps,* edited by Louis Marie Chidiac, Abdo Kahi, and Antoine N. Messara. Beirut: Publications du Bureau Pédagogique des Saints Coeurs, 1989.

______. "Girls' Participation in Combat: A Case Study from Lebanon." In *Children in the Muslim Middle East,* edited by Elizabeth Warnock Fernea. Austin: University of Texas Press, 1995.

______. "Milicien farouche et fils plein d'égards" (Fierce militiamen and respectful son). Unpublished.

Kassab, E. Suzanne. "The Paramount Reality of the Beirutis: War Literature and the Lebanese Conflict." *Beirut Review* no. 4 (fall 1992): 63–83.

Kawar, Amal. "National Mobilization, War Conditions, and Gender Consciousness." *Arab Studies Quarterly* 15, no. 2 (1993): 53–67 (special issue, *The Impact of War and Revolution in the Arab World*).

Kerber, Linda. "May All Our Citizens Be Soldiers and All Our Soldiers Citizens: The Ambiguities of Female Citizenship in the New Nation." In *Women, Militarism, and War,* edited by Jean Bethke Elshtain and Sheila Tobias. Savage, Md.: Rowman and Littlefield, 1990.

Khalaf, Mona. "Assessing the Economic Contribution of Women: A Study of Two Lebanese Villages." In *Women and Economic Development in the Arab World.* A regional conference sponsored by the Institute for Women's Studies in the Arab World. Beirut: Beirut University College, 1988.

______. "The Lebanese Woman and the Labor Market." *Al-Raida* 10, no. 61 (1993): 14–17.

______. "Women and Education in Lebanon." *Al-Raida* 11, no. 68 (1995): 12–15.

Khalaf, Samir, and Guilain Denoeux. "Urban Networks and Political Conflict in Lebanon." In *Lebanon: A History of Conflict and Consensus,* edited by Nadim Shehadi and Dana Haffar Mills. London: Centre for Lebanese Studies in association with I. B. Tauris, 1988.

el-Khalil, Ali. "The Role of the South in Lebanese Politics." In *Lebanon: A History of Conflict and Consensus,* edited by Nadim Shehadi and Dana Haffar Mills. London: Centre for Lebanese Studies in association with I. B. Tauris, 1988.

Khuri, F. "The Arab-Israeli Conflict." In *Lebanon in Crisis,* edited by P. E. Haley and L. W. Snider. Syracuse, N.Y.: Syracuse University Press, 1979.

King-Irani, Laurie. "Arab Women in the Fine Arts." *Al-Raida* 13, no. 73 (1996): 11.

______. "Recovering Women's Voices in Post-War Lebanon." *Al-Raida* 12, nos. 70–71 (1995): 12–13.

______. "Subjectivity vs. Subjection: The Role of Women's Art in Contemporary Arab Society." *Al-Raida* 13, no. 73 (1996): 2.

Kiwan, Fadia. "al-Waqiʿ wal murtaja fi wadʿ al-marʾah al-siyasi fi lubnan" (Present and future of women's political role in Lebanon). In *Proceedings of Conference on Enhancement of Women's Role in Public Policy.* Friedrich Ebert Institute in association with the Lebanese Council of Women. Beirut: Gibrayil Feghali Press, 1992.

Kiwan, Fadia, and Fahmiyyeh Charafeddin. "Tatawwur wadʿ al-marʾah fi al-sultah wa ittikhadh al-qarar fi lubnan 1980–1994" (The development of women's position in power and decision making in Lebanon, 1980–1994). Unpublished.

Lipps, Hilary M. "Gender-Role Socialization: Lessons in Femininity." In *Women: A Feminist Perspective,* edited by Jo Freeman. 4th ed. Mountainview, Cal.: Mayfield, 1989.

Logue, J. N., M. E. Melick, and H. Hansen. "Research Issues and Directions in the Epidemiology of Health Effects of Disaster." *Epidemiologic Reviews* 3 (1981): 140–62.

Lorfing, I. Introduction to *Women and Work in Lebanon,* edited by the Institute for Women's Studies in the Arab World. Monograph Series, no. 1. Beirut: Beirut University College, Arab Institute for Research and Publishing, 1980.

______. "Le travail des femmes au Liban 1970–1985—Realités et perspectives" (Work of women in Lebanon, 1970–1985—Reality and perspective). In *La femme libanaise témoin de la guerre.* Actes du colloque, mission de la ligue des états arabes à Paris, October 1987.

Lorfing, I. and J. Abu Nasr. "Sex-Role Orientation of Arab University Students." In *Women, Employment, and Development in the Arab World,* edited by Julinda Abu Nasr, Nabil F. Khoury, and Henry T. Azzam. Berlin: Mouton, 1985.

Macdonald, Sharon. "Growing the Lines—Gender, Peace and War: An Introduction." In *Images of Women in Peace and War,* edited by Sharon Macdonald, Pat Holden, and Shirley Ardener. Madison: University of Wisconsin Press, 1988.

MacKechnie, Rosemary. "Living with Images of a Fighting Elite: Women and the Foreign Legion." In *Images of Women in Peace and War,* edited by Sharon Macdonald, Pat Holden, and Shirley Ardener. London: Macmillan Education, 1987.

Mackintosh, Maureen. "Gender and Economics: The Sexual Division of Labour and the Subordination of Women." In *Of Marriage and the Market: Women's Subordination Internationally and Its Lessons,* edited by Kate Young, Carol Wolkowitz, and Roslyn McCullough. 1981. Reprint; London: Routledge, 1991.

Makdisi, Jean Said. "Speaking Up: Why I Wrote." *Bahithat* 2 (1995): 127–38.

Maksoud, Hala. "The Case of Lebanon." In *Arab Women—Between Defiance and Restraint,* edited by Suha Sabbagh. New York: Olive Branch Press, 1996.

Moghadam, Valentine M. "Women, Employment and Social Change in the Middle East and North Africa." In *Women's Work and Women's Lives: The Continuing Struggle Worldwide,* edited by Hilda Kahne and Janet Z. Giele. Boulder, Col.: Westview Press, 1992.

Moghaizel, Laure. "Musharakat al-marʾah fi al-sultah wa mawaqiʿ ittikhad al-qarar" (Women's participation in power and decision-making positions). In *Proceedings of Symposia Held in Preparation for the Beijing Conference.* Prepared by the Lebanese Nongovernmental Committee for the Preparation for the Beijing Conference. Beirut: Friedrich Ebert Institute, 1995.

______. "Participation politique des femmes pendant la guerre." In *La femme libanaise témoin de la guerre.* Actes du colloque, mission de la ligue des états arabes à Paris, October 1987.

Moulali, Amal. "Afifeh Karam." *al-majal,* no. 275 (March 1994): 30.

Nicholson, Linda J. "Feminist Theory: The Private and the Public." In *Defining Women: Social Institutions and Gender Divisions,* edited by Linda McDowell and Rosemary Pringle. United Kingdom: Polity Press in association with the Open University, 1992.

Osseiran, Hania. "An Interview with Maitre Laure Moghaizel." *Al-Raida* 12, nos. 70–71 (1995): 15.

Peach, Lucinda J. "An Alternative to Pacifism? Feminism and Just-War Theory." *Hypatia* 9, no. 2 (1994) (special issue, *Feminism and Peace,* edited by Karen J. Warner and Duane L. Cady).

Pierson, Ruth Roach. "'Did Your Mother Wear Army Boots?' Feminist Theory and Women's Relation to War, Peace and Revolution." In *Images of Women in Peace and War,* edited by Sharon Macdonald, Pat Holden, and Shirley Ardener. Madison: University of Wisconsin Press, 1988.

Pohl, Ray E. "Work and Employment." In *Defining Women: Social Institutions and Gender Divisions,* edited by Linda McDowell and Rosemary Pringle. United Kingdom: Polity Press in association with the Open University, 1992.

Rabinovich, Itamar. "The Limits of Military Power: Syria's Role." In *Lebanon in*

Crisis, edited by P. E. Haley and L. W. Snider. Syracuse, N.Y.: Syracuse University Press, 1979.

Regier, D.A., M.E. Farmer, D.S. Rae, B.Z. Locke, S.J. Keith, L.L. Judd, and F.K. Goodwin. "Comorbidity of Mental Disorders with Alcohol and Other Drug Abuse Results from the Epidemiologic Catchment (EAC) Study." *Journal of the American Medical Association* 264, no. 19 (1990): 2511–18.

Richards, Evelyn. "The Employment Status of Women in Lebanon." In *Women and Work in Lebanon,* edited by the Institute for Women's Studies in the Arab World. Monograph Series, no. 1. Beirut: Beirut University College, Arab Institute for Research and Publishing, 1980.

Ridd, Rosemary. "Powers of the Powerless." In *Women and Political Conflict,* edited by Rosemary Ridd and Helen Callaway. New York: New York University Press, 1987.

Ruddick, Sara. "The Rationality of Care." In *Women, Militarism, and War,* edited by Jean Bethke Elshtain and Sheila Tobias. Savage, Md.: Rowman and Littlefield, 1990.

Russo, Valeria E. "The Constitution of a Gendered Enemy." In *Women Soldiers: Images and Realities,* edited by Elisabetta Addis and Valeria Russo. New York: St. Martin's Press, 1994.

Salman, Nur. "Dawr al-ʾiʿlam fi musharakat al-marʾah fi al-ʾinmaʾ" (The role of the media in women's participation in development). In *Proceedings of Symposia held in Preparation for the Beijing Conference.* Prepared by the Lebanese Non-Governmental Committee for the Preparation for the Beijing Conference. Beirut: Friedrich Ebert Institute, 1995.

Saraceno, Chiara. "Division of Family Labor and Gender Identity." In *Women and the State,* edited by Anne Showstack Sassoon. London: Routledge, 1987. Reprint, 1992.

Sassoon, Anne Showstack. "Women's New Social Role: Contradictions of the Welfare State." In *Women and the State,* edited by Ann Showstack Sassoon. London: Routledge, 1987. Reprint, 1992.

al-Sayyid, Afifeh. "al-Munazzamat al-nisaʾiyyah wa ibraz dawr al-marʾah" (The role of women's organizations in crystalizing women's role). In *Symposium on The Role of Women in Lebanon Today.* Beirut: René Moʿawwad Institute and Friedrich Naumann Stiftung, May 1994.

Schulze, Kirsten E. "Communal Violence, Civil War, and Foreign Occupation: Women in Lebanon." Forthcoming.

______. "Isreali and Maronite Nationalisms: Is a Minority Alliance 'Natural'?" In *Nationalism—Minorities and Diasporas: Identities and Rights in the Middle East,* edited by Kirsten E. Schulze, Martin Stokes, and Colm Campbell. London: Tauris Academic Studies, I. B. Tauris, 1996.

Schwartz, Paula. "Redefining Resistance: Women's Activism in Wartime France." In *Behind the Lines: Gender and the Two World Wars,* Margaret R. Higonnet, J. Jenson, S. Michel, and M. C. Weitz. New Haven, Conn.: Yale University Press, 1987.

Scott, Joan W. "Women and War: A Focus for Rewriting History." *Women's Studies Quarterly* 12, no. 2 (1984): 2–6.

Sebesta, Lorenza. "Women and the Legitimation of the Use of Force: The Case of Female Military Service." In *Women Soldiers: Images and Realities,* edited by Elisabetta Addis and Valeria Russo. New York: St. Martin's Press, 1994.

Shapira, Shimon. "The Imam Musa al-Sadr: Father of the Shiʿite Resurgence in Lebanon." *Jerusalem Quarterly* 44 (fall 1987): 128.

Sharara, Yolla Polity. "Women and Politics in Lebanon." In *Third World—Second Sex,* edited by Miranda Davies. 4th ed. London: Zed Books, 1987.

Shehadeh, Lamia Rustum. "The Legal Status of Married Women in Lebanon." *International Journal of Middle East Studies* 30, no. 4 (1998): 501–19.

Shils, E. "The Prospect for Lebanese Civility." In *Politics in Lebanon,* edited by L. Binder. New York: John Wiley and Sons, 1966.

Sinclair, M. Thea. "Women, Work and Skill: Economic Theories and Feminist Perspectives." In *Working Women: International Perspectives on Labour and Gender Ideology,* edited by Nanneke Redclift and M. Thea Sinclair, eds. London: Routledge, 1991.

Snider, L. W. "Inter-Arab Relations." In *Lebanon in Crisis,* edited by P. E. Haley and L. W. Snider. Syracuse, N.Y.: Syracuse University Press, 1979.

Snider, L. W., P. E. Haley, A. R. Wagner, and N. J. Cohen. "Israel." In *Lebanon in Crisis,* edited by P. E. Haley and L. W. Snider. Syracuse, N.Y.: Syracuse University Press, 1979.

Sobh, Alawiyyeh. "al-Intaj al-thaqafi al-nisaʾiy fi al-harb" (Women's cultural production during the war). In *La femme libanaise témoin de la guerre.* Actes du colloque, mission de la ligue des états arabes à Paris, October 1987.

Sunderman, Paula. "Between Two Worlds: An Interview with Hanan al-Shaykh." *Literary Review,* in press.

Tarnowski, Stephan. "Interview with Claire Gebeyli." *Al-Raida* 12, nos. 70–71 (1995): 40.

Theberge, Nancy. "Women's Athletics and the Myth of Female Frailty." In *Women: A Feminist Perspective,* edited by Jo Freeman. 4th ed. Mountainview, Cal.: Mayfield, 1989.

Theweleit, Klaus. "The Bomb's Womb and the Genders of War." In *Gendering War Talk,* edited by Miriam Cooke and Angela Woollacott. Princeton, N.J.: Princeton University Press, 1993.

Unterhalter, Elaine. "Women Soldiers and White Unity in Apartheid South Africa." In *Images of Women in Peace and War,* edited by Sharon Macdonald, Pat Holden, and Shirley Ardener. Madison: University of Wisconsin Press, 1988.

Warren, Karen J., and Duane L. Cady. "Feminism and Peace: Seeing Connections." In *Feminism and Peace,* edited by Karen J. Warren and Duane L. Cady. *Hypatia* 9, no. 2 (1994) (special issue).

Werholf, Claudia von. "Women's Work: The Blind Spot in the Critique of Political Economy." In *Women: The Last Company,* edited by Maria Mies, Veronka Bennholdt-Thomsen, and Claudia von Werlhof. London: Zed Books, 1988.

Whetten, Lawrence L. "The Military Dimension." In *Lebanon in Crisis,* edited by P. E. Haley and L. W. Snider. Syracuse, N.Y.: Syracuse University Press, 1979.

Wilcox, J. A. "Gender and Psychiatric Comorbidity in Substance-Abusing Individuals." *American Journal of Addiction* 2 (1993): 202–6.

Yoder, Janice. "Women at West Point: Lessons for Token Women in Male-Dominated Occupations." In *Women: A Feminist Perspective,* edited by Jo Freeman. 4th ed. Mountainview, Cal.: Mayfield, 1989.

Yonkers, K., and J. Ellison. "Anxiety Disorders in Women and their Pharmacological Treatment." In *Psychopharmacology and Women,* edited by M. Jensvold et al. Washington, D.C.: American Psychiatric Press, 1996.

Zurayk, Huda, and Fadia Saadeh. "Women as Mobilizers of Human Resources in Arab Countries." In *Gender and Development in the Arab World,* edited by Nabil Khoury and Valentine Moghadam. London: Zed Books; Tokyo: United Nations University Press, 1995.

CONTRIBUTORS

Mary Bentley Abu Saba is assistant professor of educational psychology at the American University of Beirut.

Mona Takieddine Amyuni is associate professor of cultural studies at the American University of Beirut.

Miriam Cooke is professor of Arabic at Duke University.

Leila Farhood is professor of nursing/psychiatry at the American University of Beirut.

Maria Holt is information officer at the Council for the Advancement of Arab-British Understanding.

Elie Karam, M.D., is clinical lecturer of psychiatry at the American University of Beirut and director of the program of psychiatry and psychology at St. George Hospital in Beirut.

Kari Karamé is researcher at the Norwegian Institute of International Affairs, Oslo.

Jocelyn Khweiri is researcher, editor, and publisher of the quarterly *Yawmiyyat* in Lebanon.

Elise Salem Manganaro is associate professor of literature at Fairleigh Dickinson University.

Lamia Rustum Shehadeh is associate professor of cultural studies at the American University of Beirut.

Philippe Yabroudi is consultant clinical psychologist at St. George Hospital in Beirut.

INDEX

Lamia Rustum Shehadeh is associate professor of cultural studies at the American University of Beirut. She is the editor of several collections of writings of the Arab historian Asad J. Rustum and has published articles in *International Journal of Middle Eastern Studies* and *Feminist Issues*.